# THE MINOR LEAGUE BASEBALL BOOK ™

# THE MINOR LEAGUE BASEBALL BOOK ™

by Bruce Adelson, Rod Beaton, Bill Koenig and Lisa Winston

A Balliett & Fitzgerald Book

Macmillan • USA

# A Disclaimer

Readers are advised that prices fluctuate in the course of time and travel information changes under the impact of the varied and volatile factors that affect the travel industry. Neither the author nor the publisher can be held responsible for the experiences of readers while traveling. Readers are invited to write to the publisher with ideas, comments, and suggestions for future editions.

### USA TODAY
Managing Editor, Sports: Gene Policinski
### GANNETT NEW MEDIA
Associate Director: Susan Bokern
Manager, Product Development: Silvia Molina Neves
Account Manager: Michelle Mattox
Researcher: David Brown
Special thanks to Professional Baseball and the Minor Leagues, especially to Misann Ellmaker and Lori Whitson for all of their help.

### BALLIETT & FITZGERALD, INC.
Project Editor: Tom Dyja
Managing Editor: Duncan Bock
Copyeditor: John Shostrom
Proofreader: Theresa Braine
Editorial Assistants: Herb Ackerman, Milly Hui, and Edward Foley.
Special thanks to Larry Peterson, John Jordan, and, of course, Mike Spring.

Book Design by Lynne Arany

Photo Credits
Pages 13, 29, 45, 59, 115, 143, 161, 18, 201 and 213—Bruce Adelson
Page 73—Chattanooga Lookouts
Page 87—El Paso Diablos
Page 101—Stockton Ports
Page 127—Daytona Cubs
Page 227—Dave Endress

Macmillan Travel
A Simon & Schuster/Macmillan Company
15 Columbus Circle
New York, New York 10023

ISBN 0-02-860474-1
Library of Congress Catalog Card No.: 95-76110

Manufactured in the United States

10 9 8 7 6 5 4 3 2 1

First Edition

# INTRODUCTION

Across the USA and Canada, millions of baseball fans are learning that the game doesn't end with the big-leagues. In places like Hickory, North Carolina, Rockford, Illinois and Visalia, California, the excitement, intimacy and small-town color of minor-league baseball<sub>TM</sub> is alive and well, presenting teams with histories and traditions as rich as any in the majors. In 1994, 33, 355, 199 fans paid to see games in more than 150 communities; the most since 1949, when more than 400 teams drew 39,800,000 fans in the days before televised baseball.

The appeal is obvious. Minor league ball, played largely in small and mid-sized cities and towns, retains a purity of spirit which the majors no longer possess. There are no mega-salaries, no enormous stadia. It is baseball in its simplest form—just balls, bats, gloves and lifelong dreams. The parks are generally small, the players hard-working young men whom local fans are likely to run into the next day at the mall or maybe the corner bar. A family of four can see a game, eat dinner— maybe even pick up a souvenir or two—with-

out having to consider a second mortgage. No lockouts, no holdouts, no five-dollar beers, and the umpire is the only one who can call a strike. Just the national pasttime, played like the game it is.

Of course, for every big city fan looking for his field of dreams in the mountains of West Virginia or the Texas plains, there are two more fans who've been watching minor-league ball for decades. For over a century, genera-tions of big-leaguers from Babe Ruth to Frank Thomas have learned the professional game on these ballfields, far away from name sports-writers and big-city pressures. As you'll read in the Local and Team History sections, base-ball has been played in some of these towns since before the Civil War. A few once hosted big-league organizations in the early days of the game; after their teams pulled out of the majors, the game just went on. The minors have seen a pitcher strike out 27 men in one game, a hitter knock in 254 runs in one sea-son and a 33-inning marathon. Fans in Toledo wear their Mud Hen caps as proudly as any Cub or Yankee fan wears hers.

## MINOR LEAGUE FACTS

The minor leagues are governed by the National Association of Professional Baseball Leagues (**NAPBL**). The relationship between the NAPBL and the major leagues is controlled by the Professional Baseball Agreement (**PBA**). For the most part, major league baseball teams sup-ply the players to the NAPBL teams with which they are affiliated, though there are some inde-pendent NAPBL franchises. Big-league teams have a Player Development contract (**PDC**) with each of their minor league affiliates. Once these contracts, which usually last at least two years, expire, the affiliates and their parent teams are free to negotiate a new PDC and either maintain their relationships or search for other affilia-

tions. Affiliations can change for many reasons, such as dissatisfaction with the quality of play-ers sent to the minor league teams or the desire of the big league organization to have a particu-lar farm team located closer to the major league city.

The minors are divided into eighteen con-stituent leagues and four classifications: **AAA**<sub>TM</sub>, **AA**<sub>TM</sub>, **A**<sub>TM</sub> and **Rookie**<sub>TM</sub>, with each designation relating to the skills of the players at each level. Each major league team has at least a AAA, a AA and full season A team. All have **Short-sea-son**<sub>TM</sub> affiliates, in Class A, Rookie or both. Decisions about which level to operate teams in can be based on financial or geographic considerations, or an organization's philosophy about how to develop their young players.

**AAA**, the highest level, is said to be just "a phone call away" from the majors since this is the first place big league teams generally look for replacements and where they send selected upcoming players for a final tune-up. This is where you will find the minors' biggest cities, largest ballparks, and many players with names familiar from stints in the big leagues.

**AA** is considered by many in baseball to be the minors' most competitive level. After players advance from Class A, this is the place to prove whether they have big league caliber talent. Two steps away from the big leagues, players who perform well in AA are thought to have a legitimate shot at playing in the majors.

**Class A** has more leagues—seven—and more teams—82—than any other level. This is where the big league organizations look for early flashes of talent from players. Since there are only three AA leagues, there are not enough teams for all A players to advance to the next level, making Class A the level where major league teams begin winnowing players from their orga-

nizations. There are two Class A leagues which play a **short season**, beginning in mid-June. Most of the players here are just out of college, having been recently drafted to play professional ball.

**Rookie** is baseball's entry level. This is where you will generally find the game's youngest players and smallest communities. The players here are mainly recent draftees right out of high school. Rookie teams play a short season which starts in mid-June. The Arizona and Gulf Coast leagues, also at the Rookie level, play their seasons in spring training complexes. You will not find many fans here, compared to the Pioneer and Appalachian leagues.

At various points in the book's historical sections, you will find references to such classifications as B, C and D. These levels, which had existed for several decades, were eliminated in 1962 when minor league baseball was streamlined and the current classification system was adopted. Another frequently mentioned term, "organized baseball," refers to the founding of the NAPBL in 1901 and the beginning of an organized minor league baseball system in 1902.

## ABOUT THIS BOOK

THE MINOR LEAGUE BASEBALL BOOK is a travel and reference guide to all 156 minor league ballparks, from the high minors in Pawtucket, Rhode Island all the way down to the Rookie League in Lethbridge, Alberta. Each league has its own chapter, starting with a brief introduction to the league itself. The teams then run alphabetically by city or town name.

The team entries have a number of features. First, there's **a description of each ballpark**, ranging from ultra-modern facilities. to the quaint, older parks, full of memories. Unlike the huge major-league stadiums, the parks of the minors are set within their communities. You won't find many minor-league parks surrounded by a sea of parking lots, but you will find them nestled under mountains, abutting forests, and beside the local high school.

Next, there's a section called "**Local and Team History.**" Here you'll read about the history of baseball in the town, the many leagues and teams that have played here, (including the Negro leagues where appropriate), the history of this franchise and any memorable baseball moments that may have taken place here. The exploits of famous alumni are also here, along with a separate diamond that lists others not mentioned in the text. This is where you'll learn about Stockton, Calif., the real Mudville, and the man on whom Casey in "Casey At The Bat" is based. You'll read about three different towns that all claim to be the site of the longest home run in baseball history. (The reason why there's a controversy has something to do with the fact that railroad tracks run next to each of the three parks.) And you'll learn about the early careers of everyone from Cy Young to Cecil Fielder.

"Ballpark Extras" is next, featuring recommendations on concessions, information about team promotions and other useful facts about the park itself.

This is followed by sections on **local dining, lodging and nearby attractions**, with one or two recommendations for each, along with addresses, phone numbers and an approximate driving time from the ballpark. When possible, we've tried to find restaurants that will either please a sports fan, or spots that serve up regional specialties and local flavor, and attractions that either give you a feeling for the place, or will help divert a Blazer full of children.

After that, you'll find **driving directions** to the park, a "stadium ticket" with the address, relevant telephone number, capacity and dimensions of each and, finally, a section with **tentative game times, schedules and ticket prices**. The addresses provided are largely mailing addresses, rather than those of the ballparks. Team offices are not always at the ballpark.

At the end of many chapters, you'll see "Minor League Memories," which are comments of former and current minor league players recalling their experiences in the minors. Some are funny; some are touching; but they all give a taste of what it's like to play there.

Three more sections follow the 15 league chapters. First, there's a section on the **Independent leagues**, which have recently begun operations, mostly in response to the growing popularity of minor league baseball. These leagues are unaffiliated with the NAPBL and contain teams with no connection to Major League Baseball. The four independent leagues included in this book were chosen because they have a track record of success or have otherwise demonstrated their viability. Future editions of THE MINOR LEAGUE BASEBALL BOOK may include expanded treatment.

Second, there's a section on the **Instructional leagues**, which play in Arizona and Florida.

Geared mainly to baseball scouts and professionals, fans are still allowed to watch future players make their first forays into pro ball. For both the Independent and Instructional sections, we give you addresses and phone numbers for each team, allowing you to contact the teams directly for more information.

Finally, there's **a complete wrap-up of all 28 major-league farm systems**, arranged alphabetically by major league city. These include the final 1994 records of each team at each level, and short pieces on the top five prospects in each system.

To help you find exactly what you want, there are **two tables of contents** directly following this introduction. The first breaks the book down by league, and second breaks it down by major league organization. If you're a Carolina League fan you can head right to what you want, and if you're a Chicago Cubs fan you can easily check out each team in the Cubs organization.

All ticket prices, game times, affiliations and other such information included in this book were accurate at press time. However, since this material can change, you should contact the teams of your choice before making any plans. We have also made every effort to ensure the accuracy of the statistics and records contained in this book, but since records of minor league baseball are sometime spotty, particulary those from the 19th and first half of the 20th centuries, there may be discrepancies between the material here and that provided in other sources. Also, in mid-February 1995, the Seattle Mariners selected Wilmington, N.C. as their AA affiliate in the Southern League and named them the Port City Roosters. This resolved a lengthy dispute which began when Seattle objected to the League's original decision to locate its tenth team in Bayamon, Puerto Rico. The late resolution of this franchise location issue prevented the inclusion of Port City in this book's Southern League section.

—*Bruce Adelson*

# CONTENTS

## TEAMS BY MAJOR LEAGUE AFFILIATION

### ATLANTA BRAVES

| | |
|---|---|
| AAA/Richmond Braves | 37 |
| AA/Greenville Braves | 78 |
| A/Durham Bulls | 116 |
| A/Macon Braves | 176 |
| Short-Season A/Eugene Emeralds | 204 |
| Rookie/Danville Braves | 217 |

### BALTIMORE ORIOLES

| | |
|---|---|
| AAA/Rochester Red Wings | 38 |
| AA/Bowie BaySox | 61 |
| A/Frederick Keys | 117 |
| A/High Desert Mavericks | 103 |
| Rookie/Bluefield Orioles | 214 |

### BOSTON RED SOX

| | |
|---|---|
| AAA/Pawtucket Red Sox | 35 |
| AA/Trenton Thunder | 71 |
| A/Sarasota Red Sox | 136 |
| A/Battle Creek Golden Kazoos | 144 |
| Short-Season A/Utica Blue Sox | 195 |

### CALIFORNIA ANGELS

| | |
|---|---|
| AAA/Vancouver Canadians | 57 |
| AA/Midland Angels | 91 |
| A/Lake Elsinore Storm | 104 |
| A/Cedar Rapids Kernels | 147 |
| Short-Season A/Boise Hawks | 203 |

### CHICAGO CUBS

| | |
|---|---|
| AAA/Iowa Cubs | 19 |
| AA/Orlando Cubs | 85 |
| A/Daytona Cubs | 131 |
| A/Rockford Cubbies | 155 |
| A/Williamsport Cubs | 199 |

### CHICAGO WHITE SOX

| | |
|---|---|
| AAA/Nashville Sounds | 22 |
| AA/Birmingham Barons | 74 |
| A/Prince William Cannons | 121 |
| A/South Bend Silver Hawks | 156 |
| A/Hickory Crawdads | 175 |
| Rookie/Bristol White Sox | 215 |

### CINCINNATI REDS

| | |
|---|---|
| AAA/Indianapolis Indians | 18 |
| AA/Chattanooga Lookouts | 77 |
| A/Winston-Salem Warthogs | 125 |
| A/Charleston (W.Va.) Alley Cats | 167 |
| Rookie/Billings Mustangs | 228 |
| Rookie/Princeton Reds | 224 |

### CLEVELAND INDIANS

| | |
|---|---|
| AAA/Buffalo Bisons | 16 |
| AA/Canton/Akron Indians | 62 |
| A/Kinston Indians | 119 |
| A/Columbus Redstixx | 170 |
| Short-Season A/Watertown Indians | 198 |
| Rookie/Burlington Indians | 216 |

### COLORADO ROCKIES

| | |
|---|---|
| AAA/Colorado Springs Sky Sox | 48 |
| AA/New Haven Ravens | 66 |
| A/Asheville Tourists | 163 |
| A/Salem Avalanche | 122 |
| A/Portland Rockies | 206 |

### DETROIT TIGERS

| | |
|---|---|
| AAA/Toledo Mud Hens | 42 |
| AA/Jacksonville Suns | 81 |
| A/Lakeland Tigers | 135 |
| A/Fayetteville Generals | 171 |
| Short-Season A/Jamestown Jammers | 190 |

### FLORIDA MARLINS

| | |
|---|---|
| AAA/Charlotte Knights | 30 |
| AA/Portland Sea Dogs | 68 |
| A/Brevard County Manatees | 128 |
| A/Kane County Cougars | 151 |
| A/Elmira Pioneers | 186 |

### HOUSTON ASTROS

| | |
|---|---|
| AAA/Tucson Toros | 55 |
| AA/Jackson Generals | 90 |
| A/Kissimmee Cobras | 134 |
| A/Quad City River Bandits | 153 |
| Short-Season A/Auburn Astros | 184 |

### KANSAS CITY ROYALS

| | |
|---|---|
| AAA/Omaha Royals | 27 |
| AA/Wichita Wranglers | 96 |
| A/Wilmington Blue Rocks | 123 |
| A/Sultans of Springfield | 157 |
| Short-Season A/Spokane Indians | 209 |

### LOS ANGELES DODGERS

| | |
|---|---|
| AAA/Albuquerque Dukes | 46 |
| AA/San Antonio Missions | 92 |
| A/Vero Beach Dodgers | 140 |
| A/San Bernardino Spirit | 108 |
| Short-Season A/Yakima Bears | 210 |
| Rookie/Great Falls Dodgers | 230 |

### MILWAUKEE BREWERS

| | |
|---|---|
| AAA/New Orleans Zephyrs | 24 |
| AA/El Paso Diablos | 89 |
| A/Stockton Ports | 111 |
| A/Beloit Snappers | 145 |
| Rookie/Helena Brewers | 231 |

### MINNESOTA TWINS

| | |
|---|---|
| AAA/Salt Lake Buzz | 53 |
| AA/Hardware City Rock Cats | 63 |
| A/Fort Myers Miracle | 133 |

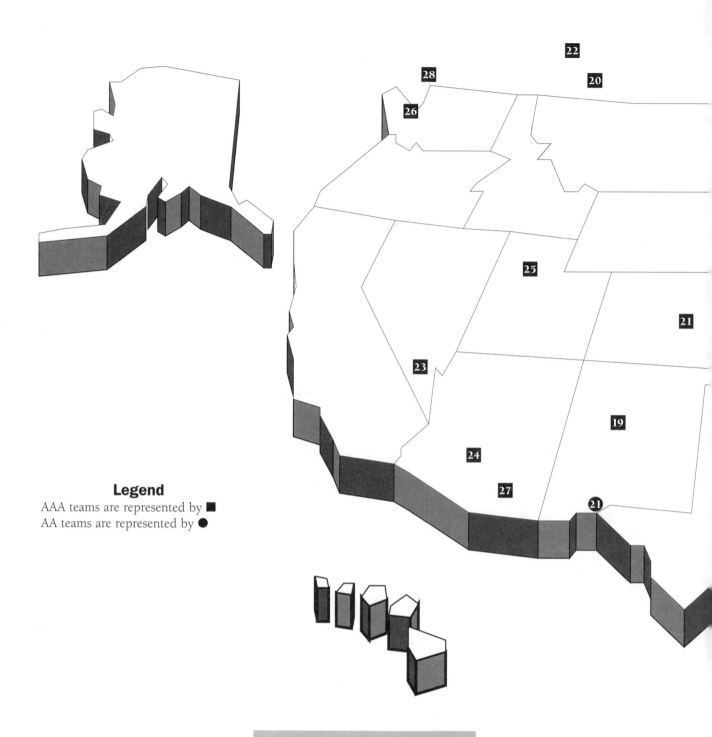

## Legend

AAA teams are represented by ▪
AA teams are represented by ●

## AAA

### AMERICAN ASSOCIATION

1. Buffalo Bisons/Buffalo, N.Y.
2. Indianapolis Indians/Indianapolis, Ind.
3. Iowa Cubs/Des Moines, Iowa
4. Louisville Redbirds/Louisville, Ky.
5. Nashville Sounds/Nashville, Tenn.
6. New Orleans Zephyrs/New Orleans, La.
7. Oklahoma City 89ers/
   Oklahoma City, Okla.
8. Omaha Royals/Omaha, Neb.

### INTERNATIONAL LEAGUE

9. Charlotte Knights/Fort Mill, S.C.
10. Columbus Clippers/Columbus, Ohio
11. Norfolk Tides/Norfolk, Va.
12. Ottawa Lynx/Ottawa, Ont.
13. Pawtucket Red Sox/Pawtucket, R.I.
14. Richmond Braves/Richmond, Va.
15. Rochester Red Wings/Rochester, N.Y.
16. Scranton/Wilkes-Barre Red Barons/
    Moosic, Penn.
17. Syracuse Chiefs/Syracuse, N.Y.
18. Toledo Mud Hens/Toledo, Ohio

### PACIFIC COAST LEAGUE

19. Albuquerque Dukes/Albuquerque, N.M.
20. Calgary Cannons/Calgary, Alta.
21. Colorado Springs SkySox/
    Colorado Springs, Colo.
22. Edmonton Trappers/Edmonton, Alta.
23. Las Vegas Stars/Las Vegas, Nev.
24. Phoenix Firebirds/Scottsdale, Ariz.
25. Salt Lake Buzz/Salt Lake City, Utah
26. Tacoma Rainiers/Tacoma, Wash.
27. Tucson Toros/Tucson, Ariz.
28. Vancouver Canadians/Vancouver, B.C.

## AA

### EASTERN LEAGUE

1. Binghamton Mets/Binghamton, N.Y.
2. Bowie Baysox/Bowie, Md.
3. Canton/Akron Indians/Canton, Ohio
4. Hardware City Rock Cats/
   New Britain, Conn.
5. Harrisburg Senators/Harrisburg, Penn.
6. New Haven Ravens/New Haven, Conn.
7. Norwich Navigators/Yantic, Conn.
8. Portland Sea Dogs/Portland, Maine
9. Reading Phillies/Reading, Penn.
10. Trenton Thunder/Trenton, N.J.

### SOUTHERN LEAGUE

11. Birmingham Barons/Birmingham, Ala.
12. Carolina Mudcats/Zebulon, N.C.
13. Chattanooga Lookouts/
    Chattanooga, Tenn.
14. Greenville Braves/Greenville, S.C.
15. Huntsville Stars/Huntsville, Ala.
16. Jacksonville Suns/Jacksonville, Fla.
17. Knoxville Smokies/Knoxville, Tenn.
18. Memphis Chicks/Memphis, Tenn.
19. Orlando Cubs/Orlando, Fla.
28. Port City Roosters/Wilmington, N.C.

### TEXAS LEAGUE

20. Arkansas Travelers/Little Rock, Ark.
21. El Paso Diablos/El Paso, Texas
22. Jackson Generals/Jackson, Miss.
23. Midland Angels/Midland, Texas
24. San Antonio Missions/
    San Antonio, Texas
25. Shreveport Captains/Shreveport, La.
26. Tulsa Drillers/Tulsa, Okla.
27. Wichita Wranglers/Wichita/Kan.

# AMERICAN ASSOCIATION

A fter the National League forced the collapse of its rival major league, the American Association, following the 1891 season, the current, minor-league version of the American Association opened for business in 1903 as a Class A circuit. It acquired an AA designation five years later and held it through 1945. The Association operated as a Class AAA league from 1946 to 1962 and then again from 1969 to date. Today, there are eight teams in the American Association, located in eight mostly Midwestern states—Indiana, Kentucky, Iowa, Nebraska, Oklahoma, Louisiana, Tennessee and New York. Each team plays 144 games, with the 1995 regular season beginning April 7 and ending September 5. In 1994, for the seventh consecutive season, the American Association had the minors' attendance leader, the Buffalo Bisons, who drew 982,493 fans to Pilot Field.

• • •

*The Nashville Sounds have the most distinctive scoreboard in the American Association, if not all the minor leagues.*

# BUFFALO BISONS

## CLEVELAND INDIANS

**B**uffalo is simply the jewel in the crown when it comes to minor-league venues. This city has it all — a great ballpark with good food and plenty of atmosphere plus an interesting baseball past. If you can get to only one AAA city in your travels, make it Buffalo. You won't be disappointed.

Pilot Field was built in 1988 and was the first venture by the architects who would eventually become famous for creating Baltimore's Camden Yards. Located downtown, with Buffalo's skyline behind the uncovered grandstand and Lake Erie several blocks away, Buffalo's home field is now the envy of other minor-league teams. Behind the center-field scoreboard, you will find the tent where the Bisons hold their famous fridaynightbash!, a weekly party featuring a local band, Knuckleball Nick and the Sliders, plus lots of food, beer and postgame fireworks. There are similar celebrations earlier in the week—Molson's Monday Madness and Labatt's Blue Tuesday. There is much to enjoy at Pilot Field, so find your seat, grab a hot dog and relax at the minors' premier ballpark.

### ◆ LOCAL AND TEAM HISTORY

Pro baseball began its history here in 1877 when a local team toured the USA playing other squads, including the Chicago White Stockings. One of the players on Buffalo's first team was future Hall of Famer John Montgomery Ward. The next year, Buffalo joined the International Association, baseball's first minor league, and won the pennant behind the pitching of future Hall of Famer James "Pud" Galvin, who posted a record of 28-10 for the champions. That Buffalo team also won 10 of 17 exhibition games against teams from the National League, a record which may have convinced the NL to admit them to the National League in 1879, beginning Buffalo's seven-year stint as a big-league team. Buffalo dropped to the Eastern League (the predecessor to the International League, which debuted in 1912) in 1886. With the exception of the years 1890 and 1899-1900, this city played continuously in the EL/IL for more than 80 years, 1886-1970. Although Buffalo did not belong to the Eastern League in 1890, baseball was still played here. Buffalo fielded a team in the Players League, a third major league formed to compete with the NL and the American Association. The league folded after only

one season, in which Buffalo finished last with an abysmal record of 36-96. The team's pitching shouldered a big share of the responsibility for the team's failure. The Bison's team ERA was an astronomical 6.11, almost two full points higher than Cleveland's next-to-worst 4.23. The next season, Buffalo returned to the International League, remaining there for eight seasons. In 1899-1900, Buffalo played in the Western League.

Buffalo also had a two-year (1914-15) stint with the Federal League, another renegade major league. In 1979, Buffalo began a six-year association with yet another Eastern League, which was by then a AA circuit. Finally, Buffalo joined the American Association in '85. In '95 Buffalo has its first year of affiliation with the Cleveland Indians, following a six-year relationship with the Pittsburgh Pirates.

Connie Mack hit .269 as the starting catcher for Buffalo's Players League team in 1890. Mack went on to win 3,731 games in 53 years as a major-league manager, the most in big-league history. Dan Brouthers never batted under .300 in his five seasons (1881-1885) with Buffalo. He was the National League's leading hitter in '82 (.368) and '83 (.374). Hoss Radbourn made it to the Hall of Fame as a pitcher on the strength of 308 career wins, including a phenomenal 60 victories in 679 innings for Providence in 1884. But in 1880, Radbourn, who had not yet found his niche on the mound, batted only .143 in six games for Buffalo.

Lou Boudreau played his first year in the majors with Cleveland in 1939, but he started that season in Buffalo, where his success (.331 average, 17 home runs and 57 runs batted in) prompted the Tribe to promote him. In 1962, Ferguson Jenkins finished up the year here after spending most of the season with Miami of the Florida State League. Jenkins appeared in only three games and finished with a 1-1 record and 5.54 ERA. Five seasons later, Johnny Bench batted .259 for Buffalo with 23 homers and 68 runs batted in. He was promoted to Cincinnati at the end of the year. One season earlier, Lee May, Bench's future teammate with the Reds, was the Bisons' main offensive weapon, leading the team in batting average (.310), runs batted in (78) and triples (five).

During 1961-70 and 1979-87, the Bisons played at War Memorial Stadium, a football facility built as a WPA project in 1937. Known as the Rockpile, it was used as the home field of the celluloid New York

**OTHER FAMOUS ALUMNI** Bucky Harris, Joe McCarthy, Ray Schalk, Gabby Hartnett, Bill Dickey, Herb Pennock, Jimmy Collins, Jim Bunning, Bud Harrelson, Cleon Jones, Ivan Calderon, Al Martin, Otis Nixon, Carlos Garcia, and Ron Swoboda all played here.

Knights in the 1983 film *The Natural*. Don Mincher, who is today the general manager of the AA Huntsville Stars, hit a home run at the Rockpile that is still remembered by many in Buffalo. It eventually traveled more than 500 feet after hitting the stadium's football press box and then bouncing over the roof and into the street. Hard times eventually fell on War Memorial as the surrounding neighborhood deteriorated, and in Buffalo in 1967 resulted in a citywide curfew, forcing the Bisons to play night games in Niagara Falls for the next two seasons.

When Rick Lancellotti went to play baseball in Italy in 1992, he left home as the active minor-league home-run leader, with 276 four-baggers. His '79 season with Buffalo was the best of his career when he belted 41 homers (most among minor leaguers that year), drove in 107 runs (first in the league) and batted .287. In his brief big league career, Lancellotti batted just .169 in 36 games and hit only two home runs. Four years later, Steve Farr posted a 13-1 record and 1.61 ERA (best in the Eastern League) for Buffalo. In 1989, Jay Bell's .285 average and 10 home runs helped Buffalo finish second in the American Association's Eastern Division, five games behind Indianapolis, the eventual league champions.

On the minors' all-time single-season attendance list, Buffalo occupies the top six slots, drawing at least 1 million fans each year from 1988 to '93. In 1991, the Bisons drew 1,240,951 fans to the ballpark, the most in minor-league history. Each year since the Bisons moved into Pilot Field in 1988, Buffalo has achieved single-season attendance totals better than those of two big-league teams.

### ◆ BALLPARK EXTRAS

Outside the main gates, you will find a pregame carnival with jugglers, mimes and clowns performing. The Food Court behind home plate on the Main Level has some of the best food in the minors. Check out the kosher hot dogs, grilled chicken sandwiches, Italian sausage and gourmet coffee. On the Mezzanine Level behind home plate, there is Luke 'n Ollie's, where you can get chicken wings, fried bologna, Cajun fries, steak hoagies, French-bread pizzas and calzones. In the Club Level Cafe, you can choose from among a variety of subs. Down the right-field line, you will find Pettibone's Grill, which is a full-service restaurant, and the Power Alley Pub.

While the food choices at Pilot Field are very alluring, the main attraction as far as concessions are concerned can be found in the grandstand, where the Bisons' vendors put on a great show. The Earl of Bud, Zorro, Conehead and the Foz stroll through the stands entertaining the crowd with their costumes and antics while hawking their wares. Buffalo's mascot, Buster, dressed predictably like a buffalo, and his sidekick, Chip, are part of the entertainment as well. The team also schedules several Kids' Days in which children can take part in the Shoe Race and the Diaper Derby or audition for a shot at singing the national anthem.

### ◆ ATTRACTIONS

The Albright-Knox Art gallery features paintings by Matisse and Picasso. Admission is $4, $3 for senior citizens over 61. Children under 13 are free. For further information, call (716) 882-8700.

The Buffalo Museum of Science has a dinosaur exhibit and hands-on displays designed for kids. Admission is $3, $2 for senior citizens over 61, $1.50 for children 3 to 12. For further information, call (716) 896-5200.

For additional information about Buffalo, call the Visitors' Bureau, (716) 852-0511/(800) BUFFALO.

### ◆ DINING

The Spaghetti Warehouse, less than 10 minutes from the ballpark, offers a variety of Italian dishes, such as lasagna, manicotti and ravioli in a casual, entertaining atmosphere. 141 Elm Street, Buffalo, (716) 856-1350.

### ◆ LODGING

Best Western Downtown is on Delaware Avenue, about 10 minutes from the ballpark. (716) 886-8333/(800) 528-1234.

Holiday Inn Buffalo Gateway is at exit 53 off I-90, about 20 minutes from the ballpark. (716) 896-2900/(800) HOLIDAY.

### ◆ DIRECTIONS

From I-190, take the Elm Street exit. Turn left on Swan Street and follow signs to the ballpark. Parking for $3 or $4 is available at numerous private lots in the area.

> **PILOT FIELD**
> P.O. Box 450
> Buffalo, NY 14205
> (716) 846-2000
>
> ---
>
> Capacity: 20,900
> LF 325, CF 410, RF 325

### ◆ TICKET AND SCHEDULE INFORMATION

Most games are played at night, starting at 7:05 P.M. Most Sunday games begin at 2:05 P.M. Selected weekday games start at 1:05 P.M.

The Bisons' home opener is usually in early April, and the season ends in the first week of September. Purchasing tickets on the day of the game may be difficult because of the popularity of baseball here. The team also operates a Bisons' Hotline (716-852-4700), which provides information on ticket availability.

Ticket prices: $7.75 club level; $7.75 special reserved; $6.25 reserved; $3.75 bleachers; $3.25 for seniors and children 12 and under; and $3.75 standing room.

# INDIANAPOLIS INDIANS

## CINCINNATI REDS

**T**his year is your last chance to see one of the most venerable old-time ballparks in the USA. Owen Bush Stadium, built in 1931 and named for a former big leaguer and team president, will close down following the season as the Indians move into a state-of-the-art downtown facility. But before time passes this place by, Bush is definitely worth a visit. As you enter the stadium, there are several photographs to the right commemorating Indianapolis' American Association championship teams of the late 1980s. A bit farther up, there are several life-size portraits of former Indianapolis stalwarts who have been inducted into the Indians' Wall of Fame. Beyond the grandstand, Bush Stadium has its own ivy-covered brick outfield wall, à la Wrigley Field. The old left-field scoreboard is manually operated. In center field, a metal, ivy-covered fence stands in front of a tepee, home of a previous team mascot, and the center-field flagpole, nearly 500 feet from home plate. As testament to the many historic qualities of this ballpark, Bush Stadium was used as the setting for the film *Eight Men Out*.

### ◆ LOCAL AND TEAM HISTORY
Baseball has a long, distinguished history in this city. Professional baseball has been played continuously here since 1895, one of the longest stretches among minor-league teams today. According to newspaper accounts, a doubleheader was played in Indianapolis on July 19, 1867. In the first game, the Indianapolis Actives defeated Lafayette 54-31 while the Western Club of Indianapolis was crushed by the Washington Nationals 106-21 in the nightcap. In 1877, the Indianapolis Blues joined the International League. This city subsequently had five years (1878, 1887-90) in the big leagues as a member of the National League. After the turn of the century, in 1902, Indianapolis joined the American Association as a charter member. Except for three brief interruptions (1913-14, Federal League; 1963, International League; 1964-68, Pacific Coast League), Indianapolis has remained in the Association ever since. Indianapolis had a remarkable run from 1986 through '89 when the Indians captured four straight league championships. The Indians began their affiliation with the Reds in 1993.

Over the past century, an impressive array of Hall of Famers has played in Indianapolis, including Henry Aaron, as a member of the Indianapolis Clowns of the Negro American League; Three Finger Brown; Joe McCarthy; "Deacon" Bill McKechnie; and Edd Roush. Napoleon Lajoie capped off a 22-year pro career in 1918 by batting .282 in 78 games as the Indians' player-manager. Al Lopez batted .268 and led the team to 100 victories and a pennant in '48, his first of three seasons as manager. Rube Marquard led the Association in games (47), innings pitched (367), wins (28) and strikeouts (250) in 1908 before being sold to the New York Giants for $11,000 that September, and Amos Rusie began his pro career (in which he won 254 games) with 13 victories for Indianapolis in 1889. Luke Appling (1962) and Ray Schalk (1938-39) managed teams in Indianapolis. Appling's team captured the league pennant with 89 wins but lost in the first round of the playoffs to Louisville.

*OTHER FAMOUS ALUMNI* Ken Griffey Sr., George Foster, Dave Concepcion, Don Buford, Felipe Alou, Delino DeShields, Moises Alou, Wil Cordero, John Franco, Randy Johnson, Marquis Grissom, Mel Rojas, Willie Greene, Larry Walker, and Ray "Razor" Shines all played here.

Harmon Killebrew struggled with American Association pitching in his 38-game tenure with Indianapolis, batting .215 with two homers and 10 runs batted in. Rocky Colavito belted 68 four-baggers here in 1954 and '55, leading the Association with 38 in 1954. That same year, he also hit three home runs in a game (the last Indian to do so) in Minneapolis. Three decades after Colavito left town, Andres Galarraga played for Indianapolis and hit 25 homers while amassing 87 runs batted in and scoring a league-high 75 runs.

In 1965, Dave DeBusschere was both a pitcher for the Indians and player-coach of the NBA's Detroit Pistons. He won 15 games for the Indians while also posting a 3.65 ERA. At the end of the season, he retired from baseball, deciding to devote himself completely to basketball.

### ◆ BALLPARK EXTRAS
Bush Stadium features several kinds of sausages, such as Italian and knackwurst. Check out the Polish-sausage sandwich and the Firedog, a spicy hot dog. There is also sausage and pepperoni pizza.

### ◆ ATTRACTIONS
The legendary Indianapolis Motor Speedway is just down the street from the ballpark on 16th Street. In addition to the racetrack, there is a Hall of Fame Muse-

um with a variety of racing memorabilia. Admission to the museum is $2. Children are free. For further information, call (317) 248-6747.

The Eiteljorg Museum of American Indian and Western Art has an excellent collection of Native American art and artifacts. Admission is $3, $2.50 for senior citizens over 65, $1.50 for children 5 to 17. For further information, call (317) 636-WEST.

For additional information about this area, call This is Indianapolis, (800) 323-INDY.

### ◆ DINING

Union Station, near the RCA Dome in downtown Indianapolis and about 15 minutes from the ballpark, is a restored railroad depot with several good restaurants. Norman's (317-269-2545) features a variety of seafood dishes, including king salmon and yellow-fin tuna. Avanti's (317-632-6600) serves Italian food.

### ◆ LODGING

Ramada Inn South is at exit 52 from I-465, about 20 minutes from the ballpark. (317) 787-3344/ (800) 2-RAMADA.

Holiday Inn Union Station is downtown in Union Station, about 15 minutes from the ballpark. (317) 631-2221/(800) HOLIDAY.

### ◆ DIRECTIONS

From I-65, take the Martin Luther King Jr. exit and go south to 10th Street. Turn right on 10th and then right on Stadium Drive. Stay on Stadium until you reach 16th Street. Turn left and the ballpark will be on your left about ½ mile away. From I-465, take the Crawfordsville Road exit. Crawfordsville turns into 16th at the Indianapolis Motor Speedway. Stay on 16th until you reach the ballpark, which will be on your right. Parking is plentiful and free.

---

**OWEN J. BUSH STADIUM**
**1501 W. 16th Street**
**Indianapolis, IN 46202**
**(317) 269-3545**

**Capacity: 12,934**
**LF 335, CF 395, RF 335**

---

### ◆ TICKET AND SCHEDULE INFORMATION

Most games are played at night, starting at 7:15 P.M. Sunday games begin at 2 P.M. between April and June, and at 6 P.M. for the rest of the season. Verify all game times with the Indians.

The Indians' season opener is usually in early April, and the season ends in the first week of September. Purchasing tickets in advance should be no problem, with the possible exception of major promotional events and commemorations in honor of the stadium's final season.

Ticket prices: $7 box seats; $6 reserved grandstand, $5 for children 14 and under; $4 general admission, $3 for children 14 and under.

---

# IOWA CUBS

**CHICAGO CUBS**

This comfortable ballpark opened in 1947 on a peninsula at the confluence of the Des Moines and Raccoon rivers, providing Sec Taylor with a uniquely scenic location. The Raccoon flows past the ballpark's first-base side while the Des Moines spans the entire outfield. During the Great Flood of 1993, two-thirds of Sec Taylor's outfield was covered by two feet of water. So many home runs to right have carried over the 16-foot-high wooden outfield wall and bounced into the Des Moines River, more than 500 feet from home plate, that the Cubs have become almost blasé about this achievement. The left field wall in fair territory next to the foul line has its own trademark—it doubles as the Cub Club, a members-only restaurant with windows facing the field. Over the years, several club windows have been broken by an assortment of fly balls and line drives. Any balls that strike the club are in play since they must carry over the building to be homers. Fans in the partially covered grandstand are also afforded a perfect view of the state capitol over the left-center-field wall. The building, with one large dome covered in 22-karat gold and four smaller ones, is hard to miss.

### ◆ LOCAL AND TEAM HISTORY

On April 15, 1887, Des Moines made its professional debut in the Western League, beating Kansas City 5-3. After the turn of the century, Des Moines began a 46-year (1902-37, 1947-58) relationship with the Class A Western League. After that circuit disbanded, this city joined the Class B Three-I League (1959-61). In 1961, after 53 years of baseball, that league also went out of business. After a seven-year hiatus, organized baseball returned in 1969 when Des Moines joined the American Association. In 1993, this franchise won its first Association championship. Iowa began its current affiliation with the Chicago Cubs in 1981.

The first game to be played under fixed stadium lights took place on May 2, 1930, in Des Moines' Holcumb Avenue Park. Nearly 12,000 fans came to watch the Demons take on the Wichita Aeros. Perhaps inspired by the crowd, the lights and the presence of Commissioner Kenesaw Mountain Landis, Des Moines scored 11 runs in the first and beat Wichita 13-6. Four days earlier, the Independence Producers of the Class C Western Association tried to upstage Des Moines by rigging temporary lights, loaned to the team by the owner of the Negro National League's Kansas City Monarchs, for their game against the Muskogee Chiefs. The Producers took their lights down after the ballgame. Hall of Famer Urban "Red" Faber pitched two seasons for Des Moines, 1912-13. In 1913, he was the workhorse of the Western League, topping all pitchers in innings pitched (373) and strikeouts (265). He also won 20 games. In 1932, Iowa native Mace Brown, who while with the Pittsburgh Pirates became the first relief pitcher named to an All-Star Game (1938) and the first to be tagged with the nickname Fireman, struggled with Des Moines, going 8-10.

**OTHER FAMOUS ALUMNI   OTHER FAMOUS ALUMNI**

Harold Baines, Jay Howell, Rick Wilkins and Bob Tewksbury also played here.

Some of the greatest players in minor-league history have played in Des Moines, including the minors' two most prolific base-stealers. George "Hoggy" Hogriever is No.1 on the all-time list, with 948 stolen bases. During his three seasons with Des Moines (1905-07), he swiped 140 bases. One of his teammates on the 1906 team was Ed Cicotte, banned from baseball in 1920 for his role in the Black Sox scandal. Kid Mohler is right behind Hogriever in career steals, with 776. While playing for Des Moines in 1897, he led the Western Association with 75 stolen bases. In Stan Keyes' 17-year minor-league career, he banged out 2,641 hits, including 343 home runs. In 1930 and '31, he was the Western League's leading hitter. He amassed 63 homers and 300 runs batted in to top the circuit over those seasons. His league-leading .369 average, 203 hits and 144 runs scored in '31 helped Des Moines win the pennant.

Ray French's 3,254 career hits place him seventh all-time among minor leaguers. In his 28-year (1914-41) pro career (including three seasons in the big leagues, where he hit .193), he also came to bat more times, 12,174, than any other minor leaguer. As a 25-year-old shortstop for Des Moines in 1921, he batted .267, the same as his career average would be when he retired 20 years later.

Vida Blue led the American Association with an .800

winning percentage and 165 strikeouts in 1970. Three years later, Goose Gossage won five games and posted one save for Iowa. One of his teammates was Bucky Dent, who would later team with Gossage on the White Sox and the Yankees.

Joe Carter led the Association in at-bats (522) in 1983. He also hit .307 with 22 homers and 83 runs batted in. Greg Maddux (10-1, two shutouts, 3.02 ERA), Rafael Palmeiro (.299, 11 home runs) and Mark Grace (.254) played for Iowa in '86, '87, and '88, respectively. Three big-league managers, Tony La Russa, Rene Lachemann and Marcel Lachemann, were teammates from 1969 to 1971.

### ◆ BALLPARK EXTRAS

The Cubs serve several good concession items. Try the grilled ribs with spuds, grilled bratwurst and boneless rib sandwich. Deli sandwiches and corn dogs are also popular. There is a picnic area down the left-field line. The I-Cubs are a popular local attraction. In 1994, 485,734 fan came to Sec Taylor, the eighth-highest total in the minors.

### ◆ ATTRACTIONS

Living History Farms is located at exit 125 from I-35. This is an open-air agricultural museum with exhibits describing the history of farming. Admission is $7, $6 for senior citizens over 60, $4 for children 4 to 16. For further information, call (515) 278-2400.

The Des Moines Art Center, featuring modern and 19th-century art, has a wing designed by I.M. Pei. Admission is $2, $1 for senior citizens. For further information, call (515) 242-2934.

For additional information about Des Moines, call the Visitors' Bureau, (800) 451-2625.

### ◆ DINING

At the Iowa Beef Steak House, about 15 minutes from the ballpark, you can grab a beer and cook your own steak in one of the restaurant's two open pits. If you prefer, the chef can do it for you. 1201 E. Euclid, (515) 262-1138.

### ◆ LODGING

Best Western Starlite Village is near the 3rd Street exit from I-235, about 10 minutes from the ballpark. (515) 282-5251/(800) 528-1234.

Savery Hotel and Spa is near the 2nd Street exit from I-235, about 10 minutes from the ballpark. (515) 244-2151.

### ◆ DIRECTIONS

From I-235, take the 3rd Street exit. Head south on 3rd through downtown and go left on Court. Turn right on 2nd Street. Turn right into the ballpark. Parking costs $3. Parking is also available about four blocks away in downtown lots.

### ◆ TICKET AND SCHEDULE INFORMATION

Most games are played at night, starting at 7:15 P.M. Sunday games begin at 2:05 P.M. in April and May, and at 6 P.M. the rest of the season.

The Cubs' home opener is usually in early April, and the season ends in the first week of September.

Ticket prices: $8 club box, closest to the field; $6.50 field box, past the dugouts down each line; $6.50 reserved box, behind the club seats in the grandstand, $4.50 for children 13 and under; $4.50 general admission; $3 for children.

# LOUISVILLE REDBIRDS

## ST. LOUIS CARDINALS

Upon entering Cardinal Stadium, built in 1959, you will immediately notice that this is one big ballpark. It has the largest seating capacity in the minors, due in part to its added role as home of the University of Louisville Cardinals football team. This explains the presence of artificial turf and outfield bleachers here. The bleachers allow the stadium to accommodate more than 40,000 fans for football games. In the right-field bleachers, there is a large concave wooden barrier which extends above and behind the standard fence. This barrier is designed to make it harder to hit a home run to right, which at only 312 feet from home is AAA's shortest right-field porch. When a ball thuds against this wood structure, it is still in play. The expansive grandstand, with an array of blue, green, yellow and red seats, is completely covered. Behind home plate you can find the stadium's organist, who performs on a small platform right in the middle of the crowd.

### ◆ LOCAL AND TEAM HISTORY

Louisville has one of baseball's most distinguished histories. The game made its debut here on April 19, 1865, when the amateur Louisville Club defeated the Nashville Cumberlands 22-5. Eleven years later, pro ball came to town when Louisville became one of the charter members of the new National League, which was formed in the back room of a downtown Louisville saloon. After a two-year stint in the NL, Louisville joined that circuit's major league rival, the American Association, in 1882. The city remained in the Association through its final season of 1892. In 1903, Louisville joined a re-formed American Association, which was by then a minor league. Louisville remained in the Association for 59 years. After a five-year absence, organized baseball returned here in 1968 when the Louisville Colonels began a five-year membership in the International League. In 1982, following another baseball drought, this one lasting nine seasons, Louisville had a team again when the Redbirds' franchise moved here from Springfield, Illinois. and began its current affiliation with St. Louis. The following season, the Redbirds became the first minor-league team to attract a million fans (1,052,438) to the ballpark, breaking their own record of 868,418, which was set in '82.

In one sense, many subsequent ballplayers have Pete "The Gladiator" Browning to thank for their livelihoods. Browning, who played nine full seasons (1882-89, '93) and part of another (1892) for Louisville, was the recipient of the first Louisville Slugger bat. In 1884, after breaking his favorite stick in a ballgame, Browning went to the Louisville woodworking shop of J.F. Hillerich. After a long night of work, they produced a bat that drew much attention throughout the American Association. Shortly thereafter, this small business became the world-renowned Hillerich & Bradsby, makers of Louisville Sluggers.

**OTHER FAMOUS ALUMNI OTHER FAMOUS ALUMNI**

Phil Niekro, Ted Simmons, Carlton Fisk, Todd Worrell, Keith Hernandez, Willie McGee, Jim Fregosi, Lance Johnson, Todd Zeile, Bob Tewksbury, Bernard Gilkey, Ray Lankford, Andy Van Slyke, Tom Pagnozzi and Terry Pendleton also played here.

Several other greats followed Browning to Louisville. Dan Brouthers stopped here briefly in 1895 after being sold to Louisville by Baltimore for $700. In Honus Wagner's three seasons in Louisville (1897-99), his lowest batting average was .299. On September 1, 1905, Hillerich & Bradsby signed Wagner ( by then a Pittsburgh Pirate) to the company's first autograph-series bat contract. Earle Combs, who batted .325 for the New York Yankees over 12 seasons, started his pro career here with a bang, leading the American Association with 18 triples in his rookie season of 1922 and 214 hits the next year. Combs' manager while with the Yankees was Joe McCarthy who played for and then managed

Louisville (1916-25) before being named the Chicago Cubs' skipper in 1926. Pee Wee Reese was a scrawny 120-pound 19-year-old when he signed his first pro contract with Louisville in 1938 for $150 per month. The next year, he batted .279 and led the league in putouts (307) and triples (18).

Louisville's Hall of Fame list also includes Hughie Jennings, Billy Herman, and Jimmy Collins. Burleigh Grimes and Max Carey managed here following the end of their playing careers.

### ◆ BALLPARK EXTRAS

Cardinal Stadium features a wide concourse, painted red and white and ringed by hundreds of small white lights, giving the area the festive look of a carnival midway. Along the concourse, you will find an impressive series of plaques and pictures that detail Louisville's professional baseball past, as well as a small display about the Hillerich & Bradsby Company. The highlight of this exhibit is sample bats of such famous ballplayers as Hank Aaron, Babe Ruth, Joe DiMaggio and George Brett, whose model T-85 was first used by "Marvelous" Marv Throneberry of the 1962 New York Mets. These displays were put together in 1987 by Walter Barney, whose wife Mary is the Redbirds' director of baseball operations. Several good concession items are available. Grilled chicken and barbecue platters, which include a sandwich, coleslaw, chips and a pickle, are relative bargains. Bratwurst, metts (spicy sausage), banana splits and milkshakes are also good choices. Don't forget to check out the Stadium Club Lounge, which is open to all ticket holders. The entrance is lined with replica Louisville Slugger bats of Honus Wagner, Pee Wee Reese and Carlton Fisk; inside, it's a comfortable gathering place furnished with an array of sports memorabilia.

### ◆ ATTRACTIONS

Churchill Downs is the world-famous site of the Kentucky Derby. While here, you can take a tour of the track (502-636-4400) and visit the Kentucky Derby Museum. Admission to the museum is $3.50, $2.50 for adults over 55, $1.50 for children 5 to 12. For further information, call (502) 637-1111.

Slugger Park is the home of Hillerich & Bradsby Co. in nearby Jeffersonville, Indiana. Admission is free. For information about a tour of the Louisville Slugger factory or the museum, call (502) 585-5226.

For further information about this area, call the Visitors' Bureau, (502) 584-2121.

### ◆ DINING

Paul Clark's Bar-B-Q, about five minutes from the ballpark, serves excellent ribs plus pork, chicken, beef and mutton barbeque. Save room for homemade country custard pie for dessert. This place closes at 5 P.M. but it is well worth coming out early for. 2912 Crittenden Drive, just across from the Kentucky State Fairgrounds, (502) 637-9532.

### ◆ LODGING

Executive Inn is at the Fairgrounds exit from I-264, about five minutes from the ballpark. 978 Philips Lane, (502) 367-6161.

Executive West is just across the street from the Inn. 830 Phillips Lane, (502) 367-2251.

### ◆ DIRECTIONS

From I-65, take the Crittenden Drive/Fairgrounds exit. Make your first left and enter the fairgrounds through Gate 4. Make a quick right and then a left, and the ballpark will be in front of you. From I-264, take the Airport/Fairgrounds exit, which leads you right up to the main gate. Parking costs $1 and is very plentiful.

```
CARDINAL STADIUM
P.O. Box 36407
Louisville, KY 40233
(502) 367-9121
─────────────────
Capacity: 33,500
LF 360, CF 405, RF 312
```

### ◆ TICKET AND SCHEDULE INFORMATION

The Redbirds' home opener is usually in early April, and the season ends in the first week of September. Given the size of Cardinal Stadium, purchasing tickets on the day of the game should be no problem. Most games are played at night, starting at 7:15 P.M.

Ticket prices: $7 box seats, Friday and Saturday; $5 box seats, Sunday through Thursday; $4 box seats for children 12 and under, Friday and Saturday; $3.50 general admission; $3 box seats and general admission for seniors 60 and over; $2 children's box seats, Sunday through Thursday; $1 children's general admission.

# NASHVILLE SOUNDS

## CHICAGO WHITE SOX

Once you enter Herschel Greer Stadium, which opened in 1978, you will see proof positive that Nashville is indeed Music City USA. The left-field scoreboard is shaped like an enormous guitar. Installed in 1993, painted royal blue and also containing a temperature gauge, it is 60 feet long and 53 feet high. The inning-by-inning score is kept on the guitar's neck. You may also notice two features located right outside the fence: Railroad tracks run behind the left-field wall, and Fort Negley, a prominent part of Nashville's defensive fortifications during the Civil War, lies behind the ballpark. Herschel Greer Stadium was actually built within the confines of the park that includes this fort. The grandstand here is largely uncovered.

### ◆ LOCAL AND TEAM HISTORY

According to a local tale, baseball was first played here in 1862 when occupying Union troops showed off the sport to Nashville residents. The first documented game here occurred in 1876. Various teams played pro ball in this city during the 1880s and 1890s. In 1902, Nashville began a 59-year membership in the Southern Association. During that time, the Nashville Vols played in Sulphur Dell Field, one of the most distinctive ballparks in the history of the minor leagues, where baseball had been played since the late 19th century. Renowned as a hitter's paradise, it had a slope in right field that started behind first base and rose to a height of about 25 feet, plus a right-field fence only 262 feet from homeplate, pitchers nicknamed this ballpark Suffer Hell. Outfielders here were likened to mountain goats because they played most of the ballgame climbing up and down the hill. Following a one-year absence, organized baseball returned here in 1963 when Nashville fielded a team in the South Atlantic League. After the '63 season, Sulphur Dell was torn down so they could put up a parking lot on this historic site. In 1978, baseball was back and Nashville was associated with the Southern League. Seven years later, Nashville joined the American Association. Nashville's current affiliation with the Chicago White Sox began in 1993. Nashville has also hosted the Elite Giants and the Black Vols, of the Negro National League (1929, '30, '33-34) and the Negro Southern League (1926, '32, '45), respectively.

In 1910, Nashville and Chattanooga played one of the shortest games in history, lasting a mere 42 minutes.

Hall of Famers Kiki Cuyler (1923) and Waite Hoyt (1918) played for the Nashville Vols. Cuyler batted .340

**OTHER FAMOUS ALUMNI** Tom Browning, Jim Deshaies, Jay Howell, Willie McGee, Chris Sabo, Jerry Reuss, Jose Rijo, Rod Bolton, and Jason Bere all played here.

while also hitting nine homers and driving in 108 runs. Fellow Hall of Famer Satchel Paige pitched briefly for the Nashville Elite Giants in the early 1930s. Over the years, while several players took advantage of Sulphur Dell's favorable hitting dimensions, three stand out as having been particularly successful. In 1930, Jim Poole blasted 50 home runs to lead the Southern Association. Poole hit only 13 homers in his three big-league seasons. Chuck Workman captured the Southern Association home run title twice, in '42 (29) and '48 (52). He hit 231 four-baggers in his minor-league career and 50 over four seasons with the National League's Boston Braves and Pittsburgh Pirates. In 1954, Bob Lennon won the Triple Crown with a .345 batting average, 64 homers (42 of them over Sulphur Dell's short right-field fence) and 161 runs batted in. That season, he twice hit three home runs in a single game. His 64 four-baggers were bested by Joe Bauman, who set an organized-baseball record in '54 by hitting 72 homers for Roswell of the Class C Longhorn League. Lennon was unable to duplicate his batting prowess in the majors. He played in only 38 big-league games in 1954 and '56-57, hitting just .165 with no homers.

More recently, in 1980, Steve "Bye Bye" Balboni topped the Southern League with 34 homers, 122 runs batted in, 288 total bases, and 17 intentional walks. The next season, Don Mattingly batted .316 while leading the league with 35 doubles, a Nashville Sounds record. In '82, manager Johnny Oates led Nashville to a Southern League pennant. Buck Showalter played parts of four seasons for Nashville, leading the Southern League in hits twice, in 1980 and '82. He ranks among the top 10 in most of this franchise's batting categories. Bob Tewksbury won a total of 16 games here in 1983 and '84. One of his teammates in '84 was Doug Drabek.

Last season marked the end of a two-year experiment in which the Sounds shared their ballpark with the Nashville Xpress, then the AA affiliate of the Minnesota Twins.

### ◆ BALLPARK EXTRAS

The Stadium Club restaurant offers a selection of burgers and sandwiches and is open to all ticketholders once the game begins. Otherwise, standard concession items are sold here, including smoked sausage, chicken sandwiches and pizza. While in Nashville, check out the Sounds' logo, a ballplayer taking his cuts with a guitar for a bat.

### ◆ ATTRACTIONS

The Country Music Hall of Fame and Museum has several displays and exhibits relating to the history and personalities of country music, including Elvis Presley's solid-gold Cadillac. You can also visit Studio B on Music Row, where many country music stars have cut records over the years. Admission is $7.50, $2 for children 5 to 11. For further information, call (615) 255-5333.

Belle Mead Plantation is a well-preserved antebellum mansion. Admission is $5.50, $5 for senior citizens, $3.50 for children 13 to 18, $2 for those 6 to 12. For further information, call (615) 356-0501.

For additional information about Nashville, call the Chamber of Commerce, (615) 259-4700.

### ◆ DINING

South Street, about 15 minutes from the ballpark, serves a variety of imaginative dishes in a funky roadhouse atmosphere. Distinctive items include smoked chicken with barbecue sauce, crayfish and shrimp enchilada, and bread pudding. 907 20th Avenue South, (615) 320-5555.

### ◆ LODGING

Quality Inn Hall of Fame Hotel is at exit 209B from I-40, about 15 minutes from the ballpark. (615) 242-1631/(800) QUALITY.

Days Inn Downtown Convention Center is at exit 84B from I-65, about 15 minutes from the ballpark. (615) 242-4311/(800) 627-3297.

### ◆ DIRECTIONS

From I-65, take the Wedgewood Road exit. Stay on Wedgewood and go north on 8th Street. Turn right on Chestnut, and the ballpark will be visible on your left. Parking costs $2 and is plentiful.

---

**HERSCHEL GREER STADIUM**
P.O. Box 23290
Nashville, TN 37202
(615) 242-4371

Capacity: 17,000
LF 327, CF 400, RF 327

---

### ◆ TICKET AND SCHEDULE INFORMATION

Most games are played at night, starting at 7:35 P.M. Verify all game times with the Sounds.

The Sounds' home opener is usually in early April, and the season ends in the first week of September. Purchasing tickets on the day of the game may be a problem if the White Sox send Michael Jordan here in 1995. If that happens, you should call ahead to get your tickets. To purchase tickets in advance or for additional information, call the Sounds' offices.

Ticket prices: $7 box seats; $5 reserved grandstand; $4 left field corner seats; $3 general admission. Children 12 and under receive $1 off the price of all tickets. If Jordan does play here, these prices could change and more seats could become reserved.

# NEW ORLEANS ZEPHYRS

### MILWAUKEE BREWERS

**P**rivateer Park proves that the American Association is a league of extremes. At once it has Louisville, with the largest ballpark in the minors, and New Orleans, where the Zephyrs play in the smallest ballpark in AAA. Located near Lake Ponchartrain and the University of New Orleans' new Lakefront Arena, this park is also the home field for the collegiate Privateers' baseball squad. This is apparent to all fans here—the scoreboard lists the home team as UNO, not the Zephyrs. You can also see the connection between the two teams before the game while the field is being prepared. Some members of the grounds crew are University of New Orleans baseball coaches, and if you come out early, you can catch them practicing their golf games in the large unpaved field that doubles as driving range and parking lot.

The two-tiered outfield wall here is unusual. The bottom half is a chain-link fence with another wall above and behind it. A ball must clear both fences to be a home run—those that fall in between the walls are ground rule doubles. The grandstand is uncovered. 1995 will be the Zephyrs' final season in Privateer Park as a new stadium, being built in nearby Jefferson Parish, should be ready by '96.

### ◆ LOCAL AND TEAM HISTORY

The New Orleans Pelicans joined the Southern League in 1887 and won the pennant in their first season. Before the turn of the century, this team captured two more championships. New Orleans' 57-year association with the Southern Association began in 1902. After a 17-year absence (1960-76), minor-league baseball returned to the Crescent City in 1977 when the Pelicans played one season in the Super Dome while affiliated with the American Association. Baseball left town again following that season and did not return until 1993, when the Zephyrs franchise, newly arrived from Denver, moved into New Orleans. In 1886, 1920, '41, '45, and '51, the city also hosted five different Negro leagues teams.

Shoeless Joe Jackson had a memorable season here in 1910, leading the Class A Southern Association in batting (.354), runs scored (82) and hits (165). Later that season, he was traded to the Cleveland Indians, for whom he made his big-league debut. In four of Roy

Walker's seasons with New Orleans, he led the Southern Association in strikeouts, and he whiffed a total of 841 batters in nine years here. Ike Boone, the minor leagues' all-time leading hitter with a .370 career average, is also the holder of the organized-baseball record for total bases (553) in one season. While playing for New Orleans in 1921, he topped the Southern Association in batting average (.389), doubles (46) and triples (27). Hall of Famer Buddy Myer, who compiled a .303 lifetime average in 17 big-league seasons, batted .336 for New Orleans in 1925. Five years earlier, two Hall of Famers played for the Pelicans. Joe Sewell was the shortstop while Dazzy Vance was one of the team's leading pitchers, winning a total of 16 games that season. That season, the Cleveland Indians bought Sewell and brought him up to replace Ray Chapman, who had died after being hit by a pitch.

**FAMOUS ALUMNI**

Danny Murtaugh, Earl Weaver, Tony La Russa and Jim Riggleman either played or managed here.

### ◆ BALLPARK EXTRAS

Privateer Park's concession facilities were somewhat limited even before the June 1994 accident that burned the roof off the main concession stand during renovations to the ballpark. Although the Zephyrs were forced to use makeshift replacements for the rest of that season, they will have a rebuilt concession area in 1995. The best and most memorable dining choice here is a Muffaletta. Devised by Italian immigrants to this area in the early part of the 20th century and now a local delicacy, it is a large sandwich on Italian bread stuffed with salami, other meats, cheese, dressing and olive spread.

### ◆ ATTRACTIONS

There is plenty to see in New Orleans' French Quarter, including the St. Louis Cathedral. For further information, call (504) 861-9521.

Preservation Hall is famous for its jazz music. Admission is $3. For further information, call (504) 522-2841.

For additional information about this area, call the New Orleans Tourist and Convention Commission, (504) 566-5031.

### ◆ DINING

New Orleans is one of the culinary capitals of the USA. There are many good places to eat here, particularly in the French Quarter. For Cajun cooking, check out Ralph & Kacco's (519 Toulouse Street, 504-522-5226,

about 25 minutes from the ballpark) and Michael's Live Cajun Music Restaurant (701 Magazine Street, 504-522-5517, about 25 minutes from the ballpark).

### ◆ LODGING

Holiday Inn-East Rise is at the intersection of I-10 and U.S. 90, about 15 minutes from the ballpark. (504) 241-2900/(800) HOLIDAY.

Comfort Inn East is at the intersection of I-10 and U.S. 90, about 15 minutes from the ballpark. (504) 241-5650/(800) 4-CHOICE.

### ◆ DIRECTIONS

Take I-10 to I-610. Exit at Franklin Street. Follow the signs to Lakefront Arena. Turn right on Leon C. Simon. After about 1/2 mile, turn left on Press Drive. The ballpark, which is adjacent to the arena, will be in front of you and to the left. Parking costs $2 and is plentiful.

**PRIVATEER PARK**
P.O Box 24672
New Orleans, LA 70184
(504) 282-6777

Capacity: 4,700
LF 330, CF 400, RF 330

### ◆ TICKET AND SCHEDULE INFORMATION

Most games are played at night, starting at 7:05 P.M.

The Zephyrs' home opener is usually in early April, and the season ends in the first week of September.

Ticket prices: $7 reserved seats; $5 general admission, $2 for seniors 62 and over, children 12 and under and military personnel with identification.

# OKLAHOMA CITY 89ERS

**TEXAS RANGERS**

All Sports Stadium, located on the Oklahoma State Fairgrounds, opened in 1962. This is a relatively basic ballpark, with a three-tier uncovered grandstand that makes it one of the minors' most expansive. In 1984, All Sports Stadium became one of the first minor-league ballparks to feature luxury boxes. In addition to being the 89ers home, the ballpark is also host to collegiate baseball. The University of Oklahoma and Oklahoma State University play an annual series here, and the Big Eight baseball tournament is held at the stadium as well. As part of a major downtown development, a new ballpark for the 89ers, slated to open in 1996 or '97, is being built in the Bricktown entertainment district.

### ◆ LOCAL AND TEAM HISTORY

When white settlers arrived here in the 1889 land rush, they quickly built two ballparks with temporary seating made of wooden planks and beer kegs, and baseball was played there until the end of the century. Years later, these pioneering men and women who settled Oklahoma would be the inspiration for a local schoolteacher who, in 1961, suggested the name 89ers be used for this city's new team.

After the turn of the century, the Oklahoma City Mets spent the 1904 season in the Class D Southwestern League. The next year marked the first of nine (1905-08, '14-17) for this city in the Class C and D Western Association. Over the following decades, Oklahoma City fielded teams in five other minor leagues, including the Texas League (1909-11, '33-57, Oklahoma State League (1912), the Western League (1918-32), the Pacific Coast League (1963-68) and the American Association (1962, '69 to date). The 89ers began their current affiliation with the Texas Rangers in 1983.

**OTHER FAMOUS ALUMNI** Steve Buechele, Ruben Sierra, Cesar Cedeno, Lonnie Smith, Jerry Grote, Willie Hernandez, Rick Lancellotti, John Mayberry, and Sammy Sosa all played here.

In the 1920's, Oklahoma City fans at Western League Park had a tradition of laying out guest towels for visiting ballplayers. But hometown fans had an unexpected surprise one season for two unpopular visitors, Omaha's Pug Griffin and Tulsa's Karl Black. The pugnacious natures of both players incurred the wrath of many in this community, and Griffin and Black let little stand in their way when it came to razzing Oklahoma City players or the local fans. Griffin was even known to scale the screen behind home plate to keep up a running argument with fans seated nearby. So when Griffin and Black visited this time, they found broken razor blades tucked between the folds of their towels.

Hall of Famer Carl "The Meal Ticket" Hubbell pitched for the Oklahoma City Indians in 1924 and '25,

winning 18 games over those two seasons. A teammate of Hubbell's was shortstop Eddie Hock, one of the most prolific hitters in minor-league history. Hock enjoyed a 23-year pro career, including 19 games in the majors when he collected just one hit in 10 at-bats for the Cardinals and the Reds. But he amassed 2,944 singles in the minors, more than any other player, and his 3,474 career hits rank him third on the minors' all-time list. Of Hock's five seasons (1923-26, '35) in Oklahoma City, 1926 was his best. He played in 166 games and collected 230 hits for a .322 batting average, but the Indians finished the season in second place, only ½ game out of first. Jack Brillheart's 309 career wins in the minors place him 16th all-time. From 1935 to '38, 71 of those victories were tallied for Oklahoma City. The Indians won two Texas League pennants in Brillheart's four seasons here. In 1940, Hall of Famer Rogers Hornsby was hired as Oklahoma City's manager. "Rajah" stayed here through the middle of the '41 season when he resigned after the team could no longer pay his salary due to financial problems.

In 1964, Rusty "Le Grand Orange" Staub batted .314 with 20 homers in only 226 at-bats for the 89ers. Staub played 23 years in the majors and batted .279 with 2,716 hits. J.R. Richard led the American Association with a 2.45 ERA and 202 strikeouts in 1971. He won 10 more games the next year before being promoted to Houston. Ryne Sandberg (.293, nine homers, 62 runs batted in) and Julio Franco (.300, 21 homers, 66 runs batted in) played here in successive seasons, '81 and '82, when the 89ers were a Phillies farm team.

From 1990 to '92, the 89ers featured three of the American Association's most prodigious sluggers. In '90, Juan Gonzalez led the league with 252 total bases, 29 home runs and 101 runs batted in. The following year, Dean Palmer stepped in and topped the Association with 22 homers in only 234 at-bats. From '91 to '93, Steve Balboni belted 86 four-baggers for the 89ers. In 1992, his 30 homers and 104 runs batted in paced the league and helped Oklahoma City win the American Association championship. In 1993, Balboni's last season in organized baseball, his 36 four-baggers again led the league. He retired from the game with 239 homers and six home-run titles (tied for third best all-time) in nine minor-league seasons.

Two famous broadcasters, Curt Gowdy (1947-48) and Bob Murphy (1949-53) began their careers here as the voices of the Oklahoma City Indians.

### ◆ BALLPARK EXTRAS

You can find good grilled chicken and burgers at All Sports Stadium. Barbecue sandwiches are also available. The 89ers do a good job of keeping the fans entertained with a variety of between-innings promotions, with one of the most notable being country-and-western dancing in the grandstand.

## ◆ ATTRACTIONS

The National Cowboy Hall of Fame has several displays and exhibits on famous cowboys and western life. For further information, call (405) 478-2250.

While in the area, check out the rodeo at the Lazy E Arena in Guthrie. For further information, call (405) 282-3004.

For additional information about Oklahoma City, call the Chamber of Commerce, (405) 297-8900.

## ◆ DINING

Cocina De Mino, about 15 minutes from the ballpark, is a local chain featuring well-prepared, tasty Mexican food. Try the chicken or beef fajitas and tamales. The pork with homemade salsa verde is particularly noteworthy. 3830 N. McArthur, Oklahoma City, (405) 495-6789.

## ◆ LODGING

Holiday Inn Northwest is on N.W. 39th Street just off I-44, about 10 minutes from the ballpark. (405) 947-2351/(800) HOLIDAY.

Marriott is on the N.W. Expressway, about 15 minutes from the ballpark. (405) 842-6633/(800)228-9290.

## ◆ DIRECTIONS

From I-44, take the N.W. 10th Street exit. Go east on 10th until you reach the ballpark, which is also visible from I-44. There is plenty of parking for $2 per car.

---

**ALL SPORTS STADIUM**
P.O. Box 75089
Oklahoma City, OK 73147
(405) 946-8989

Capacity: 15,000
LF 340, CF 415, RF 340

---

## ◆ TICKET AND SCHEDULE INFORMATION

Most games are played at night, starting at 7:05 P.M. Doubleheaders begin at 6:05 P.M. Sunday games in April and May start at either 7:05 P.M. or 1:35 P.M. and at 7:05 P.M. the rest of the season.

The 89ers' home opener is usually in early April, and the season ends in the first week of September.

Ticket prices: $6.50 box seats; $5.50 reserved seats; $4.50 general admission.

# OMAHA ROYALS

**KANSAS CITY ROYALS**

**R**osenblatt Stadium, which opened in 1948, is currently in the midst of a sizable renovation. New outfield bleachers have been added, and permanent seating down the right-field line was installed for the 1995 season. As you enter this symmetrical ballpark, you will walk right into Rosenblatt's picnic area, which is surrounded by several trees. On weekends, a Dixieland Band plays here, creating a festive, lively atmosphere. Down the right-field line, you will see a large, three-tier members-only club called Stadium View. The name is perfect since the wall facing the field is made almost entirely of glass, affording fans a clear view of the ballgame. Besides hosting the Royals since 1969, "the Blatt" has also been the home of the NCAA College World Series for more than 40 years. The metal grandstand here is largely covered between the corner bases.

## ◆ LOCAL AND TEAM HISTORY

Like other teams in the American Association, Omaha has its own distinctive baseball past. Pro ball was first played here in 1879 when Omaha was a charter member of the fledgling Northwest League, the first professional baseball circuit established someplace other than on the East Coast. In 1885, Omaha joined the Western League, an association that would continue with only one interruption (1937-46) until 1954. Omaha in that time won championships in 1889, 1904, '07, '16, '24 and '50-51. In 1955, the city jumped from the Class A league up to AAA by joining the American Association, where it has been most of the time (1955-59, '61-62, '69 to date) since. Omaha began its current affiliation with the Kansas City Royals in 1969.

Hall of Famer Kid Nichols posted a 36-12 record here

*OTHER FAMOUS ALUMNI* Charlie Leibrandt, Paul Splittorff, Don Slaught, Steve Farr, Willie Wilson, Danny Jackson, David Cone, Bob Hamelin and Babe Herman all played here *OTHER FAMOUS ALUMNI* in 1889. According to Nichols' personal memoirs, he was sold to St. Joseph at the start of the '89 season. But after a contract dispute in which that team wanted to pay Nichols less than he had been receiving, he became one of baseball's early free agents and signed with Omaha. In his one season here, he led his new team to the Western League pennant. From 1889 to 1898, Nichols won at least 30 games per season except 1890, when he won 27 for Boston of the National League. In 1902, Three Finger Brown competed against Nichols, his fellow future Hall of Famer, for top pitching honors in the Western League. Brown led the league in games, 43, and tied Kansas City's Nichols for most wins, 27. The battle of the great pitchers ended effectively in a draw as Omaha and K.C. finished the season tied for first place. In 1922, 20 years later, Hall of Famer Heinie Manush batted .376 for Omaha, with 20 homers, the most in his 19-year pro career, and a league-best 20 triples.

Fred "Snake" Henry's 3,384 career hits place him fifth on the minors' all-time list. In 1926, he led the Western League with 247 hits while batting .369. Two years later, Henry collected 212 hits and batted .347, but Omaha finished sixth. Henry got only a cup of coffee in the majors, batting .187 in 29 games in 1922-23. Nick Cullop, a renowned power hitter, holds the record for the most career runs batted in, 1,857, of any minor leaguer. In his two seasons with Omaha, 1923-24, he drove in 236 runs, including 155 in '24, when he hit 40 homers. His 420 career home runs place him fourth on the all-time list. Cullop played in 173 big-league games, hitting just 11 homers and batting .249, compared to his loftier minor-league average of .312. Three future big-league managers received early managerial training in Omaha: Johnny Keane from 1955-56; Danny Ozark in 1962; and Gene Lamont from 1984-85.

More recently, Omaha provided the nucleus of the successful Kansas City Royals teams of the late 1970s and early '80s. George Brett played parts of two seasons in Omaha, '73 and '74, batting a combined .281 with 10 homers and 78 runs batted in. Frank White began his career here in '73, and Dennis Leonard holds the Omaha Royals' record for most innings pitched in a single season, 223 in '74.

### ◆ BALLPARK EXTRAS

The Royals have several good concession items, including pizza made fresh at the ballpark. Garlic cheese bread is also available. Check out the six different grilled sausages.

### ◆ ATTRACTIONS

The Omaha Henry Doorly Zoo, adjacent to the stadium, has a large number of animals and interesting displays, including a tropical rain forest, an underwater polar-bear exhibit and an aquarium. Admission is $6.25, $4.50 for seniors, $3.50 for children 5 to 11. For further information, call (402) 733-8401.

The Western Heritage Museum, housed in an old railroad station, features exhibits on the history of Omaha. Admission is $3, $2.50 for seniors over 61, $2 for children 5 to 12. For further information, call (402) 444-5072.

For additional information about Omaha, call the Omaha Information Center, (800) 332-1819.

### ◆ DINING

Ross' Steak House, about 20 minutes from the ballpark, has been a popular Omaha restaurant for almost 40 years. Not surprisingly here in beef country, Ross' specialty is steak. 909 S. 72nd Street, (402) 393-2030.

### ◆ LODGING

Best Western Crossroads of the Bluffs is across the Missouri River along I-80 in Council Bluffs, Iowa, about 10 minutes from the ballpark. (712) 322-3150/(800) 528-1234.

Holiday Inn Express is at exit 2B off I-480 in Omaha, about 15 minutes from the ballpark. (402) 345-2222/(800) HOLIDAY.

### ◆ DIRECTIONS

From I-80, take the 13th Street exit and go south one block to the ballpark, which is surrounded by plenty of free parking. Rosenblatt also shares a lot with the Henry Doorly Zoo, which is next door.

**JOHNNY ROSENBLATT STADIUM**
**P.O. BOX 3665**
**Omaha, NE 68103**
**(402) 734-2550**

Capacity: 22,000
LF 332, CF 408, RF 332

### ◆ TICKET AND SCHEDULE INFORMATION

Most games are played at night, starting at 7:05 P.M. Sunday games begin at 2:05 P.M.

The Royals' season opener is usually in early April, and the season ends in the first week of September.

Ticket prices: $6.50 field box; $5.50 view box; $3.50 general admission. Seniors plus students 18 and under receive a $1.50 discount off the prices of each ticket. Children under 5 are free.

# INTERNATIONAL LEAGUE

The International League was founded in 1884, making it the oldest AAA circuit in baseball. The IL was given its AAA designation in 1946. It was in '46, on April 18, that Jackie Robinson of the International League's Montreal Royals became organized baseball's first African-American ballplayer of the 20th century. Robinson had a smashing debut in the Royals' 14-1 victory over Jersey City. After grounding out in his first at-bat, he recorded four straight hits, including a home run, scored four runs and stole two bases.

Today, the International League consists of 10 teams in fairly large cities spread over a wide area that includes Ohio, North Carolina, Pennsylvania, Rhode Island, New York, Virginia and, in keeping with the league's name, Ontario. Each team plays 142 games, with the regular season beginning April 7 and ending September 3. In recent seasons, the IL has experienced a dramatic upsurge in attendance. The league drew more than 9 million fans in 1993 and '94, more than any other minor-league circuit.

• • •

*A view from atop Rochester's Silver Stadium as the hometown Red Wings threaten to score a run.*

# CHARLOTTE KNIGHTS

**FLORIDA MARLINS**

Despite the Charlotte moniker, this $15 million stadium just south of the state line is actually in Fort Mill, South Carolina. Built in 1990, Knight's Castle features a state-of-the-art scoreboard and sound system. The ownership group, led by George Shinn and Spencer Stolpen, also owns the NBA Charlotte Hornets, so the team shares not only the distinctive purple-and-teal color scheme of the basketball squad, but also a deluxe training center and entertainment complex. It's hard to miss Knight's Castle as you are driving by. Right next door, clearly visible from the interstate highway adjacent to the ballpark, there is an enormous baseball atop a tall pole, reminiscent of the giant Louisville Slugger bat outside Yankee Stadium.

What "the Castle" lacks in old-fashioned ambience, it more than makes up for in family fun. The complex has a miniature golf course and supervised play area for young fans—including swings, slides and a merry-go-round; it's a huge relief to parents worn out by the fifth inning from chasing their toddlers up and down the stands.

The stadium was also built to major-league specifications, and should Charlotte ever receive a major-league expansion franchise, it could be renovated to seat 45,000.

### ◆ LOCAL AND TEAM HISTORY

George Shinn purchased the Charlotte team in 1988. The club had been a AA affiliate of the Baltimore Orioles since 1976, but became the Cubs' Southern League entry from 1989 until 1993, when it moved up to AAA.

Charlotte has had pro ball off and on since the beginning of the National Association, back in 1902, and has been in nine leagues other than the International League. That '02 club was 39-8 and posted a 25-game winning streak. Ironically, one of the earliest Charlotte baseball teams was known as the Hornets. From 1940 to '85, the local pro teams played at Calvin Griffith Park, later renamed Crockett Park. That stadium was destroyed by a fire in March 1985 (arson was suspected) and the team played in a temporary facility until the Castle was built.

Hall of Famer Early Wynn spent two (1938-39) seasons with the Piedmont League's Charlotte Hornets,

winning a total of 25 games with an ERA of 4.52. The Washington Senators sent Harmon Killebrew to Charlotte in 1956 after he had spent nearly two seasons in the big leagues. Killebrew responded to the demotion by batting .325 and hitting 15 home runs in only 70 games. Graig Nettles led the Southern League with 19 four-baggers in '67. In 1980, Cal Ripken Jr. batted .276, belted 25 homers and was an All-Star for the Charlotte Hornets, Southern League champions that season.

A member of the Southern League for 17 years, Charlotte was promoted to AAA in 1993 when the major league expansion in 1992 created a need for two more teams at that level.

### ◆ BALLPARK EXTRAS

Don't worry about the weather getting too hot at Knight's Castle—among the popular offerings are Lemon Quench, a soft frozen lemonade, and Tropical Sno, a shaved-ice dessert. The Knights will kick off a new promotion in 1995—postgame concerts every Friday night. The team mascot is Homer the Dragon, who zips around on his mini-motorcycle. Promotions have ranged from an Elvis look-alike contest to lawn-mower races.

**OTHER FAMOUS ALUMNI**

Eddie Murray, Sandy Alomar Jr., Tony Oliva, Pete Harnisch and Steve Finley have played here.

### ◆ ATTRACTIONS

Carowinds, a Paramount theme park, features such rides as the Vortex stand-up roller coaster and has recently added a Wayne's World section. It's located on I-77 just south of the North-South Carolina border. 15423 Carowinds Boulevard, (800) 888-4FUN.

Auto-racing fans from all over the country flock to Charlotte and you can find out what the excitement is about with a visit to the Charlotte Motor Speedway, America's premier NASCAR facility, which hosts such events as the Coca-Cola 600 and Champion Spark Plug 300 each May. It's in nearby Concord, North Carolina, For more information, call (704) 455-3200. If you feel adventuresome, check out the Richard Petty Driving Experience, a race-car driving school at the speedway. For further information, call (704) 784-8310.

For more information about the Charlotte area, call the Chamber of Commerce, (704) 378-1300.

### ◆ DINING

Gratzi Bar & Grille, 15 to 20 minutes away, offers a prime-rib buffet on Friday and Saturday evenings. Kids under 6 eat free. Charlotte Marriott Executive Park, 5700 W. Park Drive, Charlotte, (704) 527-9650.

Voted Charlotte's top sports restaurant for six years running, the Scoreboard, about a half hour drive away, offers four six-by-eight-foot screens and the popular NTN Trivia Network as well as an opportunity for outdoor dining during the pleasant weather. East Independence Boulevard at Crown Point, (704) 84-SPORT.

### ◆ LODGING

Charlotte Marriott Executive is about 15 to 20 minutes away. 5700 W. Park Drive, Charlotte, (704) 527-9650/(800) 228-9290.

Howard Johnson's is about 10 to 15 minutes away. 2825 Cherry Road, Rock Hill, South Carolina, (803) 329-3121/(800) 223-1900.

### ◆ DIRECTIONS

I-77 to exit 88. The stadium is ½ mile off the highway from either direction and can be seen from the highway. Parking is plentiful and free.

---

**KNIGHT'S CASTLE**
**2280 Deerfield Drive**
**Fort Mill, SC 29716**
**(803) 548-8050**

**Capacity: 10,000**
**LF 325, CF 400, RF 338**

---

### ◆ TICKET AND SCHEDULE INFORMATION

Most Knights home games begin at 7:05 P.M. with early-season Sunday afternoon games at 2:05 P.M. and later-season Sunday evening games at 6:05 P.M. There are occasional Wednesday day games at 12:30 P.M.

The Knights' home opener is in early April, and the season ends in the first week of September.

Ticket prices: $7 field and club level; $6 reserved seats; $5 general admission; $3.50 youth and seniors.

# COLUMBUS CLIPPERS

## NEW YORK YANKEES

Those who enter this ballpark quickly learn about some of the players who have passed through here on their way to the big leagues. Along the concourse of Harold Cooper Stadium, which was built in 1932 and remodeled in the late 1970s, there are several cartoon-style drawings of prominent former Clippers who made their mark in this team's record book. And Dysart Memorial Park, behind the outfield wall, not only gives visitors a bird's-eye view of batting practice through the transparent Plexiglas outfield wall, but has plaques honoring some of the greatest players in Columbus baseball history from the years prior to the Clippers' arrival in 1977. Dysart Park closes 15 minutes before the start of each game.

The covered grandstand here is large. Its metal seats provide fans with both a good view of the action on the artificial-turf field and at the downtown Columbus skyline. The ballpark is named for the man who went from being team clubhouse boy in 1935 to president of the International League decades later.

**OTHER FAMOUS ALUMNI**

Al Oliver, Bernie Williams, Bob Tewksbury, Jose Rijo, Deion Sanders, Doug Drabek and Jay Buhner all played here.

### ◆ LOCAL AND TEAM HISTORY

This city's storied pro baseball past goes back to 1876, when the Buckeyes were the toast of Columbus. The following year, they joined the International Association, regarded today as the first so-called minor league. Columbus later had a three-year fling (1889-91) in the majors as a member of the American Association, which was then in competition with the rival National League. Following the '91 season, Columbus belonged to several different minor leagues before rejoining the new American Association as a charter member in 1902. A 52-year affiliation with the Association ended in 1954. The next season, Columbus joined the International League, which this city has belonged to since, except for six years (1971-76) when there was no organized-baseball team here. Since affiliating with the Yankees in 1979, Columbus has won eight league titles, including three straight twice ('79-81 and '90-92).

Columbus' Hall of Famers include Willie Stargell, Rick Ferrell, Enos Slaughter and Dazzy Vance. Sammy Baugh, a star NFL quarterback from 1937 to '52 and a charter member of the Pro Football Hall of Fame, spent 1938 as both a quarterback and pro baseball shortstop. He batted .220 for Columbus in 16 games. Paul "Daffy" Dean, Dizzy's younger brother, won 22 games for Columbus in 1933. Three years later, "Long Tom" Winsett slammed 21 home runs in a month and finished the season with a league-leading 50 four-baggers. Enos Slaughter was the American Association's hitting sensation in 1937, topping the league in batting average (.382), runs scored (147) and hits (245). In contrast to his minor-league productivity, Kirke recorded just 346 lifetime hits in his seven-year big-league career (1910-15, '18).

Harvey Haddix, who pitched a perfect game for 12 innings, the longest such effort in major league history, recorded 18 wins and 160 strikeouts for the Columbus Redbirds in 1950. Two years earlier, Joe Garagiola hit .356 while with the Redbirds. More recently, Don Mattingly batted .315 for the Clippers in 1982 before getting his first shot at the big leagues later that season with the Yankees. Dave Righetti pitched parts of four seasons here (1979, 1980-82), winning 15 games. Steve "Bye Bye" Balboni hit 92 home runs over his Columbus career, making him No.1 on the Clippers all-time list.

### ◆ BALLPARK EXTRAS

Although the Clippers' fans can be somewhat reserved, they come to life to take part in two Columbus traditions. They bring their own mini-cowbells to the park and when prompted by the public address system, they ring them as accompaniment to the line, "Columbus Clippers, ring your bell." You can buy your own cowbell at the Clippers' souvenir stands. They also join in and sing their team's theme song, Columbus Clippers—Hometown Heroes. Although the concession items are standard, the Clippers do have good meatball-and-pepperoni pizza subs, served on French bread.

### ◆ ATTRACTIONS

Ohio's Center of Science and Industry in downtown Columbus is a hands-on science museum with many exhibits for children. Admission is $5, $3 for seniors over 55 and children 3 to 18. For further information, call (614) 228-2674.

German Village, located just off I-70, is a collection of restaurants, beer gardens, shops and old homes. For further information, call (614) 221-8888.

The Santa Maria is a recreation of one of the ships

Columbus used to sail to the New World. Admission is $3.50, $3 for seniors over 60, $1.50 for children 5 to 17. For further information, call (614) 645-8760.

For additional information about the Columbus area, call the Convention and Visitors' Bureau, (614) 221-6623/(800) 345-4FUN.

### ◆ DINING

There are several restaurants in the Brewery District and German Village, which are both about 10 minutes from the ballpark. Check out Hoster Brewing Company, a microbrewery with Southwestern-style fare. 550 S. High Street, (614) 228-6066. Carolyn's serves imaginative cuisine, including numerous vegetarian dishes. 489 Park Avenue, (614) 221-8100.

### ◆ LODGING

Holiday Inn City Center is located downtown near U.S. 23, about 10 minutes from the ballpark. (614) 221-3281/(800) HOLIDAY.

Best Western Executive Inn is located off I-71 in Grove City, just south of Columbus, about 15 minutes from the ballpark. (614) 875-7770/(800) 528-1234.

### ◆ DIRECTIONS

From I-70 west, take exit 98B/Mound Street. Turn left at the traffic light, and the ballpark will be almost immediately on your right. From I-70 east, take exit 97/Broad Street. Turn left and stay on Broad for about 1 mile. Turn right on Glenwood. You will see the ballpark in less than a mile. Parking is plentiful and costs $1.50 per car.

**HAROLD COOPER STADIUM**
**1155 W. Mound Street**
**Columbus, OH 43223**
**(614) 462-5250**

**Capacity: 15,000**
**LF 355, CF 400, RF 330**

### ◆ TICKET AND SCHEDULE INFORMATION

Most games are played at night, starting at 7:05 P.M. Sunday games begin at 7:05 P.M. from April to late June and 2:05 P.M. from late June through the end of the season.

The Clippers' home opener is usually in early April, and the season ends in the first week of September.

Ticket prices: $6 box seats; $4.50 reserved seats; $3.50 general admission, $1 seniors and children 12 and under.

# NORFOLK TIDES

**NEW YORK METS**

Harbor Park is one of the most attractive of the minors' next generation of ballparks. Built in 1993 and designed by the architects who are responsible for Baltimore's Camden Yards and Cleveland's Jacobs Field, the Tides' home affects a nautical image, befitting the large ports and shipbuilding facilities that abound in Virginia's Tidewater area. Behind the outfield wall is a small harbor complete with ships and dry docks. Harbor Park is also ringed by an array of flags and its light towers are vaguely reminiscent of shipyard cargo cranes. The entire lower grandstand concourse area of this downtown ballpark is open. After leaving your seat, you can keep track of the game while getting something to eat or taking a seventh-inning stretch, giving the whole park a comfortable feeling of accessibility.

### ◆ LOCAL AND TEAM HISTORY

Pro baseball in Norfolk dates to the 1880s. After the turn of the century, several organized-baseball teams were based in this coastal city. From 1906 to '28, Norfolk was associated with the Class C Virginia League, and three years later, with the Class A Eastern League (1931-32). In 1955, the Norfolk Tars ended their 21-year association with the Class B Piedmont League. For two years, 1961-62, Portsmouth and Norfolk jointly operated a team in the South Atlantic League. Norfolk did not have its own team again until 1969 when the Tidewater Tides joined the International League. The Tides dropped the Tidewater portion of their name following the 1992 season. Organized-baseball teams also played in nearby Portsmouth intermittently for nearly 40 years, until the last squad left following the 1968 season.

Three Hall of Famers, Bucky Harris, Christy Mathewson and Yogi Berra, played here in the first half of the century. Mathewson won 20 games and lost only two for Norfolk in 1900. The next season, he was playing full-time for the National League's New York Giants. Harris hit just .120 in 15 games for Norfolk in 1917 before the Virginia League disbanded, only to reform the following year. Berra was an 18-year-old rookie in his first season of professional baseball when he played for the Piedmont League's Norfolk Tars in 1943. That season, Berra batted .253 and hit seven home runs while leading the

league's catchers with 480 putouts. One season before Berra played here, Norfolk's first baseman was Chuck Connors who would eventually star in TV's *The Rifleman*. He batted .264 with five homers and 45 runs batted in. After three years of military service, he led the Piedmont League in 1946 with 17 home runs for nearby Newport News. Connors' big-league career consisted of 67 games in which he hit only two homers. In 1951, Moose Skowron, who played 14 years in the majors, led the Norfolk Tars to a pennant by finishing first in the Piedmont League with a .334 batting average, while also belting 18 home runs. Mayo Smith, Norfolk's manager in '51, led the Detroit Tigers to a World Series title 17 years later.

*OTHER FAMOUS ALUMNI*

*OTHER FAMOUS ALUMNI*

Rick Aguilera, Kevin Mitchell, Ed Kranepool, Darryl Strawberry, Sid Fernandez, Mookie Wilson, Kevin Tapani, Gregg Jefferies and Ryan Thompson all played here.

### ◆ BALLPARK EXTRAS

Harbor Park has proven to be a very popular place to watch baseball. The Tides have drawn over 1 million fans in the park's first two seasons combined. In '94, Norfolk's attendance of 546,858 ranked fifth in the minor leagues. Perhaps one reason for Harbor Park's popularity is the degree to which the Tides maintain their ballpark. The stadium is kept quite clean and there are several good concession items. Try the grilled chicken and the polish sausage, or for something different, check out the cheddar-smoked sausage, which has a tangy cheese flavor. You can also sample some Virginia bagged peanuts. While walking on the concourse, listen to the Tides' strolling brass band. A picnic area is located in left field underneath the scoreboard. Down the right field line, there is an enclosed restaurant with menu items ranging from burgers to grilled tuna and a Sunday brunch. The mascot here, a furry blue creature with red hair and a baseball nose, was kicked out of a ballgame in 1993 when the umpires took offense at some of his antics.

### ◆ ATTRACTIONS

Nauticus/National Maritime Center in downtown Norfolk features a variety of hands-on exhibits concerning marine life and oceanography. Admission is $8.25; $7 for seniors 62 and over, and children 12 to 18; $5.50 for children 4 to 11. For further information, call (804) 623-9084.

*The Spirit of Norfolk*, berthed at the downtown Waterside Market Place, is available for cruises of the Hampton Roads area. Weekday fares for adults are approximately $20, $10 for children under 12. For further information, call (804) 627-7771.

For additional information about the Norfolk area, contact the Visitors' Bureau, (804) 441-5266/(800) 368-3097.

### ◆ DINING

Waterside Market Place, about five minutes from the ballpark, has several restaurants. Phillip's (804-627-6600) offers a variety of well-prepared seafood items, including raw-bar selections. The All-Star Bar and Grill (804-625-5483) features such varied dishes as the Incredible Hulk Hoagie and Steamed Shrimp Ella Fitzgerald.

### ◆ LODGING

Norfolk Waterside Marriott is downtown off I-264 at the corner of Main and Atlantic, about five minutes from the ballpark. (804) 627-4200/(800) 228-9290.

Omni International Hotel is adjacent to the Waterside Market Place, about five minutes from the ballpark. (804) 662-6664/(800) THE-OMNI.

### ◆ DIRECTIONS

From I-264 west, take exit 9. At the first traffic light, turn left at Water Street. The ballpark will be visible in front of you as you pass under the I-264 overpass. Parking is plentiful at $2 per car.

---

**HARBOR PARK**
**150 Park Avenue**
**Norfolk, VA 23510**
**(804) 622-2222**

**Capacity: 12,057**
**LF 333, CF 410, RF 338**

---

### ◆ TICKET AND SCHEDULE INFORMATION

Most games are played at night, starting at 7:15 P.M. Sunday games begin at 1:15 P.M. from April through June and 6:15 P.M. from July through September. Several weekday afternoon games are also scheduled.

The Tides' home opener is usually in early April, and the season ends in the first week of September.

Ticket prices: $6.50 box seats; $5 reserved seats, $4 for seniors, children, and military with identification.

# OTTAWA LYNX

## MONTREAL EXPOS

Ottawa Stadium opened in 1993 and features most of the state-of-the-art amenities major-league fans expect now, such as 32 luxury sky boxes (they're all sold through the 1998 season). Located just minutes from downtown Ottawa, it is owned by the city. Hoping for a more creative name for the stadium, as well as some cash, the city of Ottawa is offering a unique deal: For just C$1.5 million, you can name the stadium, based on acceptance from the city.

If you aren't a cold-weather fan, you might want to plan your trip to Ottawa a little later than Opening Day—the big event in 1994 was canceled due to more than six inches of snow.

A night at the ballpark here is also a good way to learn basic French—since the city is bilingual, all announcements are made in both languages.

### ◆ LOCAL AND TEAM HISTORY

Ottawa hosted various teams in different leagues off and on between 1912 and '54, including the last four in the International League. But that so-called International League had not been truly so since 1971, when Winnipeg, Manitoba, had a franchise in the league. Ottawa, located conveniently between Montreal and Toronto, was awarded one of the two new AAA franchises when major-league baseball expanded, and the team began play in 1993.

FAMOUS ALUMNI

Cliff Floyd, Rondell White, Ken Hill, Kirk Rueter and Urban Shocker all played here.

FAMOUS ALUMNI

But instead of getting one of the new expansion franchises as a parent club, Ottawa was the big winner in the National Association's annual team shuffle—the city received the fan favorite Expos as a parent club. How quickly did the good people of Ottawa take to having pro baseball in their midst? In 1993, the team's inaugural year, the Lynx drew 620,726 to set an International League record, breaking a mark set in Baltimore in 1946.

The team nickname was chosen through a fan contest which drew more than 35,000 entries—and in a bilingual society, it has the advantage of having the same meaning and spelling in both French and English.

### ◆ BALLPARK EXTRAS

With the Canadian weather remaining a bit chilly in April, one popular spot is Tufts' Restaurant, located on the upper level of the stadium, where fans can watch the game and dine in warmth inside. It has a full bar and remains open until 1 A.M. after weeknight games. Players frequently come by to chat with fans and sign autographs. For C$18 apiece, fans can purchase a seat which also includes a C$10 food credit. Among the most popular concessions at Ottawa Stadium are Beaver Tails, sweetened dough covered with cinnamon and shaped like . . . a beaver's tail. There is also open-flame barbecue available.

The Lynx have offered many unusual promotions. Among the most popular in 1994 were Caribbean Night, in which calypso dancers performed between innings on the dugouts and Jamaican beef patties were on the concession menu; the Corn Roast, which included an on-field corn-eating contest; and Christmas in July, which featured Santa in Hawaiian cruise wear, with proceeds going to the Ottawa Food Bank.

### ◆ ATTRACTIONS

Located in the middle of the city, the Central Experimental Farm Arboretum offers more than 2,000 varieties of trees and shrubs that date back to the region's first plantings. There are many winding walking trails, where you can look out over Dow's Lake and the city of Ottawa. From May on, you can take a Tally Ho wagon ride pulled by a pair of Clydesdales. Call (800) 538-9110 for more information.

Valleyview Little Animal Farm is located just outside of Ottawa and would be a treat for the kids, from the farm, with its variety of animals and birds to the Little Animal Barn where the smaller animals and babies reside. There is a mini-train to carry visitors around and seasonal activities are offered. 4750 Fallowfield Road, Nepean, (613) 591-1126.

For more information about the Ottawa area, call the Ottawa Board of Trade, (613) 236-3631.

### ◆ DINING

R.B. Barn, about 10 minutes away, offers casual gourmet dining such as ribs, chicken, steak and seafood. Its specialty is Sunday brunch, featuring more than 70 items from which to choose. 1630 Woodward Drive, (613) 225-9746.

Rockin' Johnny's Diner, about 10 minutes away, is a blast from the past that features classic diner food served by bobby-soxed waitresses to the tunes of an antique jukebox. 1309 Carling Avenue, (613) 761-7405.

### ◆ LODGING

The Chimo Hotel is about 15 minutes from the ballpark. 1199 Joseph Cyr Street, Ottawa. (613) 744-1060.

Embassy West Motor Hotel is about 10 minutes away. 1400 Carling Avenue, Ottawa. (613) 729-4331.

### ◆ DIRECTIONS

417 Queensway to Venier Parkway exit. Head north, then turn right onto Coventry Road. Parking is ample and costs C$5.50.

> **OTTAWA STADIUM**
> **300 Coventry Road**
> **Ottawa, Ontario K1K 4P5**
> **(613) 747-5969**
>
> **Capacity: 10,332**
> **LF 325, CF 404, RF 325**

### ◆ TICKET AND SCHEDULE INFORMATION

Weeknight games are at 7:05 P.M. with most Saturday and Sunday games beginning at 2:05 P.M. There are two Saturday-night games on the slate, June 17 and July 29.

The Lynx open their 1995 home schedule early in April, and the season ends the first week of September.

Ticket prices: C$8.45 box seats; C$6.35 lower reserved; C$4.25 for upper level.

# PAWTUCKET RED SOX

## BOSTON RED SOX

You want to talk about fan-friendly? How about the fact that the "PawSox" have raised ticket prices a grand total of three times in the last 18 years. McCoy Stadium is cozy, yet it manages to keep the fans coming out in record numbers, having broken its own attendance record for eight years running.

McCoy Stadium has all sorts of interesting features befitting its status as one of the oldest ballparks in the league. Built in 1942, the PawSox' home has become known as a hitters' ballpark. Balls carry well to the 360-foot power alleys, and center field is only 380 feet from home, the shortest in AAA. At the main entrance, next to the ticket windows, you will see a veritable shrine to McCoy's biggest claim to fame: the longest ballgame in organized-baseball history, a 33-inning marathon in 1981 that featured future Hall of Famers Wade Boggs and Cal Ripken Jr. There are display cases with a variety of memorabilia from that game, including tickets, a program autographed by the players and the somewhat faded uniform of Dave Koza, the Pawtucket player who drove in the Longest Game's winning run.

Not everything stays the same here, though. In a long-standing tradition of frequent off-season improvements, the PawSox have installed a new playing surface at McCoy for 1995, the third time in seven years they've done so. The 1994 renovations included adding more than 600 bleacher seats.

### ◆ LOCAL AND TEAM HISTORY

A member of the International League since 1973, Pawtucket first hosted pro ball as a member of the Atlantic Association in 1908. After playing for a season in the Colonial League in 1914, Pawtucket was without a club until 1946, when it joined the New England League for a few years. The club also played in the Eastern League for several seasons in the late '60s and early '70s.

And then there's the longest game in pro baseball history—33 innings against Rochester, in 1981. The two teams were tied 2-2 at 4 A.M. on April 18 when the game was suspended in the 32nd inning. It reconvened a few months later, and the PawSox won in the 33rd, 3-2. A total of 156 baseballs were used in the game. One item from the Longest Game is not commonly known. Dave Huppert spent 31 innings as Rochester's catcher. No catcher in baseball history has caught more innings in a single ballgame than he did on that cold April night in 1981. In those 31 innings, he went one for 11, with one run batted in, 26 putouts and no stolen bases allowed.

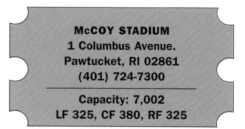

OTHER FAMOUS ALUMNI OTHER FAMOUS ALUMNI

Roger Clemens, Oil Can Boyd, Phil Plantier, Bob Ojeda, Mark Fidrych, Fred Lynn, Bruce Hurst, Brady Anderson, Rick Burleson, Mo Vaughn, Mike Greenwell, Ellis Burks, Jim Rice, Cecil Cooper and Carlton Fisk all played here.

### ◆ BALLPARK EXTRAS

Do not expect to find any glitz here. There is no fancy scoreboard, no mascot, no cavalcade of musical hits over the PA system, just baseball, which seems to suit the locals in this working-class community fine. Since Boston is so close, fans here are fervently loyal fans of both the Red Sox and the PawSox.

The Italian sweet sausage, with onions and peppers on a torpedo roll, is one of the best food items here, and make sure to try out the fried doughboys—even if it means not eating again for days!

### ◆ ATTRACTIONS

Pawtucket is an easy trip to the beautiful and historic city of Boston, as well as the beaches of Cape Cod and Martha's Vineyard island.

For more information about the Pawtucket area, call the Providence Area Visitors Bureau, (401) 274-1636/(800) 233-1636.

### ◆ DINING

My Brother's Pub Ltd. specializes in pregame and postgame gatherings and family-style banquets. About five minutes from the park, it has very good fish and chips. In the Pub Room, try to get the PawSox table, which is surrounded by various team pictures and a box score from the Longest Game. 176 Columbus Avenue. Wright's Farm Restaurant, about 20 minutes away, offers family-style chicken dinners and has been a local favorite for more than 40 years. It's off Route 102, at 84 Inman Road, Harrisville, (401) 769-2856.

### ◆ LODGING

The Comfort Inn is five minutes away. 2 George Street, Pawtucket, (401) 723-6700.

Holiday Inn Downtown is at exit 21 off I-95 in Providence, about 20 minutes from the ballpark. (401) 831-3900/(800) HOLIDAY.

### ◆ DIRECTIONS

From I-95 north, exit 28 for School Street From I-95 south, exit 2A for Newport Avenue.

**McCOY STADIUM**
**1 Columbus Avenue.**
**Pawtucket, RI 02861**
**(401) 724-7300**

**Capacity: 7,002**
**LF 325, CF 380, RF 325**

### ◆ TICKET AND SCHEDULE INFORMATION

Weeknight games begin at 6 P.M. through May 6, moving to 7 P.M. on May 17. Most Saturday games begin at 7 P.M., with day games April 9 and 23 and May 7 beginning at 1 P.M. Sunday games start at 1 P.M. except July 3, a 5:30 P.M. start to allow for postgame fireworks. There are also a few midweek businessmen's specials starting at noon throughout the season.

The PawSox open their 1995 season in early April and close out the first week of September.

Tickets: $5.50 box seats, $4.50 children and seniors; $4 general admission, $3 children and seniors.

# RICHMOND BRAVES

## ATLANTA BRAVES

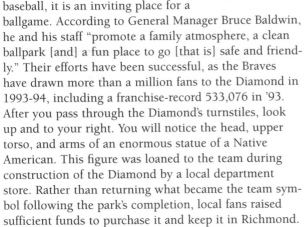

The Braves make a serious effort to create an enjoyable atmosphere for their fans, and it begins with the team's ballpark, the Diamond, built in 1985. One of the best-maintained facilities in pro baseball, it is an inviting place for a ballgame. According to General Manager Bruce Baldwin, he and his staff "promote a family atmosphere, a clean ballpark [and] a fun place to go [that is] safe and friendly." Their efforts have been successful, as the Braves have drawn more than a million fans to the Diamond in 1993-94, including a franchise-record 533,076 in '93. After you pass through the Diamond's turnstiles, look up and to your right. You will notice the head, upper torso, and arms of an enormous statue of a Native American. This figure was loaned to the team during construction of the Diamond by a local department store. Rather than returning what became the team symbol following the park's completion, local fans raised sufficient funds to purchase it and keep it in Richmond.

### ◆ LOCAL AND TEAM HISTORY

This city's involvement with professional baseball goes back more than 100 years. Richmond's first pro team, which began play in the 1870s, was operated by a local shoemaker named Harry "Daddy" Boschen. In addition to owning the team and the ballpark, Boschen Field, where games were played, Boschen was also a pitcher who is credited with being one of the first to throw the spitball.

Less than 20 years after Boschen brought pro ball to the Confederacy's former capital, Richmond had a brief flirtation with the big leagues. In August 1884, the Washington Nationals dropped out of the American Association, then one of three recognized major leagues. For the rest of the '84 season, the Richmond Virginians, a charter member of the fledgling International League, joined the Association as Washington's replacement. But the Virginians struggled against their big-league competitors, winning only 12 of 42 games and finishing 10th in the 13-team league. The following year, the Virginians returned to the minors.

Eighty-two years later, the current Richmond franchise was established. When the Milwaukee Braves moved south to Atlanta in 1966, the team shifted its AAA team, the Atlanta Crackers, to Richmond. Since then, the Braves have won four International League titles (the Governors' Cup), with the most recent championship in 1994.

**FAMOUS ALUMNI** Luke Appling, Eddie Lopat, Bobby Cox, David Justice, Dale Murphy, Jeff Blauser, Darrel Evans, Phil and Joe Niekro, Steve Avery, Tom Glavine, John Smoltz, Ryan Klesko, Ron Gant, and Tommie Aaron, Henry's younger brother, all either played or managed here.

### ◆ BALLPARK EXTRAS

The Braves sell good grilled Italian sausages with onions and peppers on the main concourse. Local favorites such as corn dogs and plastic mini-baseball helmets filled with ice cream are also available. Be advised that during the summer, the ice-cream line can be very long. Behind Sections 101-104 on the main concourse there's the Diamond Room, a full-service restaurant open to all ticketholders. The Diamond is also one of the cleanest ballparks in professional baseball, minor or major league. GM Baldwin and his staff actually seek out and encourage complaints and comments from their customers, so don't be shy about voicing your opinions.

### ◆ ATTRACTIONS

As the former capital of the Confederate States of America, many of Richmond's attractions are Civil War-oriented. The following two are especially noteworthy:

The Museum of the Confederacy features Civil War exhibits and relics, with a largely Confederate point of view. The White House of the Confederacy, home of President Jefferson Davis and his family throughout most of the war, is adjacent to the museum. Admission to both is $8, $7 for seniors, $3.50 for children 7 to 12. For further information, call (804) 649-1861.

The Richmond National Battlefield Park includes sites from several Civil War battles relating to attempts by the Union to capture Richmond. Admission is free. For further information, call (804) 226-1981.

For more information about Richmond, call the Chamber of Commerce, (804) 648-1234.

### ◆ DINING

Bill's Virginia Barbecue is across the street from the Diamond. This fast-food establishment serves primarily pork barbecue. The barbecue is unremarkable, but the strawberry pie is another matter. (804) 358-8634.

### ◆ LODGING

Holiday Inn–Central is a block away from the park, off I-95 at exit 14 and I-64 at exit 78. 3207 N. Boulevard, Richmond, (804) 359-9441/(800) HOLIDAY.

Days Inn is a long fly ball away, off I-95 at exit 14 and I-64 at exit 78. 1600 Robin Hood Road, Richmond, (804) 353-1287/(800) 325-2525.

### ◆ DIRECTIONS

Take exit 14 (the Boulevard) from I-95. Head west on the Boulevard, and you will see the ballpark on your left in less than a mile. The Diamond is located across from the bus station. There is ample parking available at the ballpark for $2. You may also find parking across the street, on East Boulevard next to the bus station.

---

**THE DIAMOND**
3001 N. Boulevard
Richmond, VA 23230
(804) 359-4444

---

Capacity: 12,134
LF 330, CF 402, RF 330

---

### ◆ TICKET INFORMATION

Games are at 7 P.M.; 6 P.M. for doubleheaders; 2 P.M. on Sundays.

The Braves' home opener is usually in early April, and the season ends in the first week of September. To purchase tickets, learn about group discounts or find out additional information, call the Braves' offices.

Ticket prices: $6 box seats; $5 reserved seats; $4 general admission, $2 children (12 and under) and seniors (60 and older).

# ROCHESTER RED WINGS

**BALTIMORE ORIOLES**

**S**ilver Stadium opened in 1929 to a crowd of 14,855 fans and it is the grande dame of the league. Still, this is expected to be its final season

as the city has signed an agreement to build a new stadium downtown for the 1996 season.

Originally known as Red Wing Stadium, the park was renamed in 1968 in honor of Morrie Silver, who led the effort to keep pro ball in Rochester in the '50s and '60s by selling more than 8,000 shares of stock to the community. His family still runs the team, and his daughter Naomi is not only the club's chief operating officer, but also the 1994 Rawlings Woman Baseball Executive of the Year in the National Association. Her cousin, Elise, is married to White Sox slugger and two-time defending AL MVP Frank Thomas.

### ◆ LOCAL AND TEAM HISTORY

The Red Wings have been playing as a National Association member nonstop in Rochester since 1902 and have been a member of the International League since its inception in 1912. They are the only original International League club to still be affiliated with the league.

On August 18, 1902, versus New Jersey, first baseman Harry O'Hagen executed the first authenticated unassisted triple play in the history of pro ball. In that same game, third baseman "Herky Jerky" Horton made five errors.

The 1929 team set an all-time pro baseball record that still stands, turning 225 double plays (the major-league mark is 217). In 1933, the stadium became one of the first in the minors to install lights.

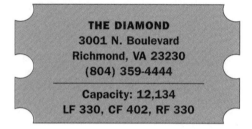

OTHER FAMOUS ALUMNI OTHER FAMOUS ALUMNI

Wally Pipp, Boog Powell, Don Baylor, Jim Palmer, Jocko Conlan, Red Schoendienst, Dennis Martinez, Fernando Valenzuela, Mike Mussina, Ben McDonald, Cal Ripken Jr., Eddie Murray, Davey Johnson and Luke Easter all played here.

Rochester also made it into the record books in 1981 when the team participated in the longest game in minor-league history, losing to the Red Sox at Pawtucket in 33 innings, 3-2.

The team has been affiliated with the Baltimore Orioles since 1961, the longest such relationship in AAA. Before that they had been an affiliate of the St. Louis Cardinals since 1927.

The Red Wings' 27-year string of former managers going on to lead the Orioles ends in 1995 when Phil Regan takes over the helm of the Baltimore club. Since Earl Weaver took over the O's in 1968, other Red Wing managers who went on to the major-league job included Joe Altobelli, Cal Ripken Sr., Frank Robinson and Johnny Oates.

### ◆ BALLPARK EXTRAS

While the longtime popular concessions at Silver Stadium include the Baseline Bar-B-Que, a pizza stand and a deluxe ice-cream stand, there are also more unusual offerings available at the Chez Stadium Specialty Stand and the Hardball Cafe. At the former you can get chicken noodle soup, chili and bottled spring water, while the latter offers the popular, locally brewed Red Wing Red Ale as well as wine coolers and margaritas.

### ◆ ATTRACTIONS

The George Eastman House is a photographic and film museum named for the founder of Eastman-Kodak film and offers lectures, exhibits and other activities. 900 East Avenue, (716) 271-3361.

The Rochester Museum and Science Center explores upstate New York's natural and cultural history. There is a permanent exhibit on Seneca Iroquois Indian life as well as a planetarium. 667 East Avenue, (716) 271-1880.

Gaslight Village, just 45 minutes from Rochester in Wyoming, New York, features more than 70 buildings on the National Historic Register and offers something for the entire family. There are quaint cafes and pubs, a beautiful Christmas Shoppe open year-round and many stores with unique items for sale. It's 16 miles south of exit 47 off the New York Thruway.

For more information about the Rochester area, call the Chamber of Commerce, (716) 454-2220.

### ◆ DINING

Romeo's, about five minutes from the ballpark, specializes in American and Italian cuisine in a family atmosphere. Homemade soups, ravioli, and pasta and meatballs are among the specialties, while patrons can watch games on one of the seven TVs or the largest big screen in the Irondequoit Valley. 2256 Hudson Avenue, (716) 342-9340.

Winfield Grill, about five minutes away, is a Rochester landmark and offers all varieties of food in casual elegance. A Sunday champagne breakfast is one specialty, as are the fish fries on Wednesday and Friday and prime rib and New York strip steaks on Saturday. 647 N. Winton Road, (716) 654-8990.

### ◆ LODGING

Holiday Inn–Genesee Plaza is about 10 minutes from the park. 120 Main Street E, Rochester, (716) 546-6400/(800) HOLIDAY.

Radisson Hotel is about 20 minutes away. 70 State Street, Rochester, (716) 546-3450/(800) 333-3333.

### ◆ DIRECTIONS

I-490 to N.Y. Route 104 exit. Follow Seneca or Clinton Street. Stadium is 2 blocks south of Route 104, between Seneca and Clinton. Parking is $3 and limited on-street parking in the area is also available.

---

**SILVER STADIUM**
**500 Norton Street**
**Rochester, NY 14621**
**(716) 467-3000**

**Capacity: 11,469**
**LF 315, CF 415, RF 320**

### ◆ TICKET AND SCHEDULE INFORMATION

Weeknight games are at 7:05 P.M., although the Red Wings offer a few weekday games in April. Saturday games in April are at 2:05 P.M. and at 7:05 P.M. thereafter, with Sunday games at 2:05 P.M. except August 20, when it will be at 6:05 P.M.

The Red Wings open their last season at Silver Stadium in early April and they are slated to play their last game in the historic stadium on August 31, when they face Charlotte.

Ticket prices: $8 field boxes; $7 upper box seats; $6 reserved seats; $4 general admission. Children and seniors get 50 cents off all tickets.

---

# SCRANTON/ WILKES-BARRE RED BARONS

### PHILADELPHIA PHILLIES

Lackawanna County Stadium, which opened in 1989, is located in Moosic between the two cities of the team's name. In a valley, literally cut out of a mountain, it boasts gorgeous views of the surrounding cliffs  and is among the most beautiful in baseball. The irony is that it is modeled after one of the game's least attractive stadiums. Phillies prospects one step away from the majors play in a park designed to be identical to Veterans Stadium, right down to the AstroTurf, outfield dimensions and height of the outfield wall.

The great fishing, beautiful countryside and wildlife really set Lackawanna apart, though, from its parent team. Sometimes that wildlife can get up-close and personal, as former Scranton/Wilkes-Barre reliever Chuck Malone found out when a small black bear cub found its way into the bullpen one afternoon. Legend has it that

Malone responded by giving the cub a peanut butter and jelly sandwich.

If you want to see players of a caliber that rivals the quality of the setting, plan ahead to come to town for the 1995 AAA All-Star Game, which is slated for July 12, the day after the major-league classic, if the strike ends.

### ◆ LOCAL AND TEAM HISTORY

The area has a long baseball tradition going back to 1865, when the Susquehanna Baseball Club was based in the hardscrabble coal-mining town of Wilkes-Barre. The team became notorious for its rowdy fans. At one point, the journal *Sporting Life* even recommended that the Wilkes-Barre team hire off-duty policemen to eject the most offensive fans from the often highly charged bleachers. Through many of the 19th century's remaining seasons, Wilkes-Barre and Scranton were archrivals in the Eastern and International Leagues. From 1904 to '53, these cities continued their baseball battles when they fielded teams in the New York State, New York–Penn and Eastern leagues.

OTHER FAMOUS ALUMNI · OTHER FAMOUS ALUMNI

Tommy Greene, Dave Hollins, Allie Reynolds, Bob Lemon, Jimmy Piersall, Heinie Manush, "Big Ed" Walsh, Charlie Hayes and Marvin Freeman all played here.

The Wilkes-Barre Barons folded in 1951, and the Scranton team lasted until 1953, after which the stadium was dismantled and moved to Richmond, Virginia. One row of seats was preserved from that stadium and is now a sitting area at Lackawanna County Stadium.

The formation of the Scranton/Wilkes-Barre Red Barons in 1989 marked the marriage of these two long-time rivals, and the name honors both of those squads—the Scranton Red Sox and the Wilkes-Barre Barons.

Babe Ruth was a fairly regular sight in and around Scranton back in the '20s when he came here to use his cabin as a base for hunting and fishing. Ruth's first visit to Scranton was on October 17, 1919, when he played for the Keyser Valley All-Stars in a charity benefit game. Although Ruth's team lost that day, he did hit two long doubles into the overflow crowd of fans who were allowed to stand in the outfield to watch.

Hall of Famer Jesse "The Crab" Burkett was 18 when he began his pro career in Scranton in 1888 by batting .226. In 1943, Chet Covington was the Minor League Player of the Year after leading the Eastern League in ERA (1.51), wins (21), and strikeouts (187). He also pitched the first perfect game in Eastern League history on May 23, 1943, when he bested the Springfield Rifles. Covington's career ERA of 2.57 is one of the lowest in minor-league history.

In 1906, when the two clubs played in the New York State League, a Scranton player won the league's batting title by hitting .336. He was Archibald "Moonlight" Graham, who went on to play one game in the major leagues and who was featured in the film *Field of Dreams*.

### ◆ BALLPARK EXTRAS

Among the more unusual offerings at the concession stands are pirogi and Texas wieners. Hungry fans can eat at the full-service restaurant behind the right-field bleachers and never miss a play, watching the action from their tables. And though he's not the Phillie Phanatic, the Red Barons have their own mascot in the Grump, whose big red smile belies his nickname. Among the more offbeat events at the ballpark in 1994 was a celebrity softball game featuring the teams of pop star Michael Bolton and morning TV star Regis Philbin.

### ◆ ATTRACTIONS

Steamtown National Historic Site, located in an old railyard in Scranton, houses several vintage locomotives and exhibits relating to the history of rail travel. Admission is free. For further information, call (717) 961-2035.

The Pennsylvania Anthracite Heritage Museum has various displays on the mineral which was once the lifeblood of this region. Admission is $3, $2 for seniors over 60, $1 for children 6 to 17. For further information, call (717) 963-4804.

The Performing Arts Center at the Montage Mountain Resort offers big-name artists in concert—1994 acts included Aerosmith, Bonnie Raitt, Jackson Browne and Meatloaf. Located right near the stadium at exit 51 off I-81 in Scranton. For information, call (717) 969-7669.

For more information about the Scranton/Wilkes Barre area, call the Chamber of Commerce, (717) 342-7711.

### ◆ DINING

Patte's Sportsbar and Restaurant has been around for 30 years serving family-style food. It's about a 20- to 30-minute drive. 65 W. Hollenbeck Avenue, Wilkes-Barre, (717) 824-8015.

The Lobster Trap features an outdoor deck for dining and offers fresh seafood nightly. During the 1994 season they offered a special where you could bring your ticket stub the day of a game and receive 10% off any dinner entree. It's about 15 minutes away, on Route 315, Wilkes-Barre. (717) 825-6909.

### ◆ LODGING

Days Inn–Montage is at exit 51 off I-81, less than 10

minutes from the ballpark. 4130 Birney Avenue, Moosic, (717) 457-6713/(800) 325-2525.

Hampton Inn is at exit 51 off I-81, less than five minutes from the ballpark. Davis Street and Montage Mountain road, Scranton, (717) 342-7012/(800) 426-7866.

### ◆ DIRECTIONS

From I-81, take exit 51/Montage Mountain Road. At the end of the exit ramp, turn right and then take another quick right down the hill. The ballpark will be on your left after about 1 mile. Plentiful parking is available for $1 per car.

```
LACKAWANNA COUNTY STADIUM
235 Montage Mountain Road
Moosic, PA 18505
(717) 963-6556
─────────────────────────
Capacity: 10,832
LF 330, CF 408, RF 330
```

### ◆ TICKET AND SCHEDULE INFORMATION

Most weeknight games are at 7 P.M. in April and May and at 7:30 P.M. for the rest of the season, while weekend times vary among day and night games. There are also several weekday games in April and May.

The Red Barons open their 1995 home schedule in early April and close out at home in late August. The season ends the first week of September.

Tickets: $6.50 box seats, $4.50 upper reserved; $3.50 bleachers.

# SYRACUSE CHIEFS

**TORONTO BLUE JAYS**

Construction has already begun on a new 12,000-seat park to replace MacArthur Stadium for the 1996 season, so players will have just one more year to try to get on the elite list of folks who have homered over center-field wall, 434 feet from home plate. (When the stadium was originally built in 1934, it had a 464-foot center field!) In 1994 Syracuse slugger Carlos Delgado became the eighth player to achieve that feat since the most recent renovations in 1971 put the wall at that distance. The

others on that list: Richie Zisk and Danny Walton ('71), Jack Baker and Jim Fuller ('76), Mike Young ('82), Willie Mays Aikens ('85) and Domingo Martinez ('92). Three of those players—Walton, Aikens and Martinez— were playing for the Chiefs.

That deep center-field wall also helps explain why so many players who were power hitters at the Blue Jays' AA Knoxville club in recent years have looked like they were having off-years upon their promotions.

If you're coming out to the stadium in 1995, be aware that the new stadium is being built in the current facility's main parking lot; you might want to consider public transportation. Otherwise, assistant GM John Simone assures that "we'll find somewhere for people to park." The farmer's market behind the stadium will be sharing its spaces and the Carousel Mall nearby has 10,000 parking spaces. The Chiefs will provide a shuttle bus. The new stadium, by the way, will measure just 408 feet to center.

### ◆ LOCAL AND TEAM HISTORY

Pro baseball in this upstate New York city goes back more than a century, to at least the 1840s. In 1876, the Star Baseball Club became Syracuse's first pro team. Through the remaining seasons of the 19th century, the Stars played intermittently in the New York State and International leagues. In 1890, Syracuse spent one season in the American Association, then a major league, finishing seventh with a record of 55-72, 30½ games out of first. The next season, Syracuse was back in the minors, with the International League. Since 1902, organized baseball has been played here with the exception of only seven seasons (1919, '30-33, '58-60). Syracuse's association with the International League goes back more than a century, to 1885.

Moses "Fleet" Walker, who became the first African-American big-league player in 1884 with Toledo, ended his pro career here five years later, batting .216 in 70 games. The season before, in 1888, Syracuse, with Walker as catcher, won the International League title. Hall of Famer Grover Cleveland Alexander led the New York State League with 29 wins and 12 shutouts in 1910, the same year he started and won both games of a doubleheader for the Stars against the Wilkes-Barre Barons. Fellow Hall of Famer "Sunny Jim" Bottomley batted .348 with 94 runs batted in for Syracuse in 1922.

**OTHER FAMOUS ALUMNI**

Ron Guidry, Jimmy Key, Tony Fernandez, Mark Whiten, Willie Horton, Ed Kranepool and Mike Cuellar all played here.

The 1940s were especially good years for the Chiefs, who have gone by that nickname since baseball returned to the city in 1934. They finished in the top three of the league five times in that decade and won the league title three times. Since 1963, the Chiefs have had an American League East flavor. They were affiliated with the Detroit Tigers from '63-66, the Yankees from '67-77 and the newly born Toronto Blue Jays from 1978 to the present.

MacArthur Stadium was heavily damaged by fire in May 1969, as 3,500 seats, the offices, press box, concession stands and the center of the stadium were destroyed. The Chiefs played some games at Falcon Park in Oneonta until MacArthur was made playable nearly a month later.

Hank Sauer still tops the all-time Syracuse leaders list with his 141 runs batted in and 50 homers in 1947. Future home-run kings Cecil Fielder and Fred McGriff were teammates here in 1986, when they combined to hit 37 homers.

### ◆ BALLPARK EXTRAS
Bratwurst is among the most popular concession offerings, but the club also features an all-you-can-eat pregame buffet in the picnic area if you want to concentrate solely on the game after the first pitch; the area is booked on a first-come, first-serve basis.

### ◆ ATTRACTIONS
The Salt Museum in Onondanga Lake Park features a re-created boiling block where salt was made in the 19th century. There are also displays on how salt is made. Syracuse is sometimes called "The Salt City," since salt was made here until the 1920s. Call (315) 453-6715 for more information.

For more information about this area, call the Chamber of Commerce at (315) 470-1800.

### ◆ DINING
Twin Trees Too is a family restaurant about 10 minutes from the park that specializes in pizza. 1029 Milton Avenue, (315) 488-6066.

Ling Ling on the Square, about 15 minutes away, offers Chinese food in an elegant atmosphere. In 1994, the restaurant offered patrons 15% off their bill with a Syracuse Chiefs ticket stub. 218 W. Genesee Street, (315) 422-2800.

### ◆ LODGING
Ramada Inn is about 10 minutes from the ballpark. 1305 Buckley Road, Syracuse, (315) 457-8670.

Sheraton Inn Syracuse is about five minutes away. Electronics Parkway, Liverpool, (315) 457-1122/(800) 325-3535.

### ◆ DIRECTIONS
From I-81 take exit 22/Hiawatha Boulevard. Follow 60 north for about three minutes. The ballpark will be on the left. Parking is $2 and should be ample, although construction for the new ballpark will reduce availability somewhat.

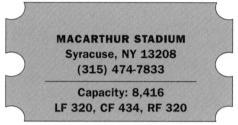

**MACARTHUR STADIUM**
Syracuse, NY 13208
(315) 474-7833

Capacity: 8,416
LF 320, CF 434, RF 320

### ◆ TICKET AND SCHEDULE INFORMATION
Weeknight game times are generally at 7 P.M. with a few early-season games at 6 P.M. Saturday and Sunday day games are at 2 P.M. Saturday night games are at 7 P.M., and Sunday night games begin at 6 P.M. The first two games of the season, on a Thursday and a Friday, will also be at 2 P.M.

The Chiefs' home schedule begins in early April and closes the first week of September.

Ticket prices: $6.50 box seats, $5.50 children; $5.50 reserved seats, $4.50 children; $3.50 general admission, $1.75 children.

# TOLEDO MUD HENS

### DETROIT TIGERS

Ned Skeldon Stadium, named for a former local politician, opened for baseball in 1965. Before then, the facility had several previous sports-related incarnations, according to Mud Hens General Manager Gene Cook. "This was formerly a thoroughbred racetrack," he recalls. "It was called Maumee Downs. As late as the '50s and all the way up to the early '60s, they still ran race meets here. We had a minor-league professional football team called the Toledo Tornadoes. They played here for two years. They went out of business in 1964."

When Toledo was awarded its current AAA franchise in '65, the former racetrack and football stadium was converted into a ballpark and given its current name. Today, the stadium is part of a county-owned athletic complex that also contains softball fields, a swimming pool and running track, but it can't escape its past: some of the seats are still angled in a way that seems better for watching a horse race than a ballgame.

### ◆ LOCAL AND TEAM HISTORY

Toledo has known pro baseball for more than 100 years. In 1883, the Toledo Blue Stockings, this city's first pro team, won the Northwestern League pennant. The following year, Toledo was awarded a franchise in the American Association, a rival major-league circuit to the more senior National League and made baseball history even though the team finished eighth in the standings. Moses "Fleet" Walker and, later, his brother Welday played for Toledo in '84, becoming the first African-American ballplayers in major-league history, preceding Jackie Robinson by more than 60 years. Unfortunately, when Toledo dropped out of the League in 1885, the Walker brothers' major-league careers ended as well.

In 1896, the Toledo team played in a park near some marshland, which was home to mud hens, birds with short wings and long legs, hence the team's name. In the 20th century, Toledo teams have been associated with the American Association (1902-13, '16-55), Southern Michigan League ('14) and International League ('65-to date). In 1987, the Mud Hens began their current affiliation with the Detroit Tigers.

**OTHER FAMOUS ALUMNI**
Hack Wilson and Bill Terry, and Kirby Puckett, Frank Viola, Travis Fryman and Kirk Gibson played here.

Hall of Fame Yankee manager, Joe McCarthy, played here in 1908 through 1911, and fellow Hall of Famer Addie Joss made his pro debut for Toledo in 1900, posting a 19-16 record. He won 25 games here the next year.

Another tidbit of Toledo baseball history happened in 1927. Long before he became a household name by winning championships with the Yankees, a young Casey Stengel served as Toledo's player-manager, learning how to run a professional baseball team. He certainly seems to have been a fast learner since the Stengel-led Mud Hens of '27 captured the Junior World Series title, beating Buffalo five games to one.

Today, the Mud Hens are enjoying record-setting popularity. By drawing 293,124 fans to Ned Skeldon Stadium in 1994, Toledo set an all-time club attendance record.

### ◆ BALLPARK EXTRAS

The Mud Hens feature tasty pizza, which is made fresh at the ballpark. The pepperoni is a good choice.

### ◆ ATTRACTIONS

The Ohio Baseball Hall of Fame features various displays and memorabilia items associated with several famous figures in Ohio's baseball past, including Cy Young, Thurman Munson, Walter Alston, Johnny Bench, Bob Feller and Satchel Paige. Admission is $2, $1.50 for seniors, $1 for children. For further information, call (419) 893-9481.

The Toledo Museum of Art is a hidden treasure, featuring a respectable ancient art collection and works by Van Gogh, Rubens and Rembrandt. Admission is free, but a donation is requested. For further information, call (419) 255-8000.

For additional information about Toledo, call the Chamber of Commerce, (419) 243-8191.

### ◆ DINING

Tony Packo's has been a Toledo institution for decades, even before Jamie Farr made it famous in M*A*S*H. The food, Hungarian hot dogs, stuffed cabbage and chili, is stick-to-your ribs excellent. Tony Packo's walls are studded with laminated hot-dog buns signed by various celebrities, including the cast of M*A*S*H. There are two locations: 1902 Front Street, (419) 691-6054, about 20 minutes from the park, and 5827 Monroe Street, (419) 691-6054, about 15 minutes from the park.

### ◆ LODGING

Comfort Inn West is on U.S. 20, south of the Ohio Turnpike, about 15 minutes from the ballpark. (419) 893-2800/(800) 4-CHOICE.

Cross Country Inn is at exit 4 off I-475, about 10 minutes from the park. (419) 891-0880/(800) 621-1429.

### ◆ DIRECTIONS

From I-475, take exit 4. Proceed on U.S. 24 east, about two miles to Maumee. Turn left on Key Street. The ballpark will be on your right in less than a mile. Parking is plentiful and free.

**NED SKELDON STADIUM**
P.O. Box 6212
Toledo, OH 43614
(419) 893-9483
—
Capacity: 10,025
LF 325, CF 410, RF 325

### ◆ TICKET AND SCHEDULE INFORMATION

Most games are played at night, starting at 7 P.M. Sunday games begin at 2 P.M.

The Mud Hens' home opener is usually in early April, and the season ends in the first week of September.

Ticket prices: $5 box seats; $4 reserved seats; $3 general admission. Seniors and children receive a $1 discount.

# MINOR LEAGUE MEMORIES

### JERSEY CITY

*Dick Bouknight became part of history on April 19, 1946, when his Jersey City Giants faced the Montreal Royals and Jackie Robinson in his organized-baseball debut. Bouknight was the Giants catcher that day.*

"We had 30,000 people in the ballpark in Jersey City. Just about everybody in Jersey City had to buy a ticket, even the mayor. A lot of black people came up from Philadelphia, Baltimore and Washington, D.C., for that game. They were pretty excited. But after [Montreal] blew the game open, it sort of calmed down. Very few of the players said anything about [Jackie]. I'm from North Carolina. I played with black ballplayers all the time growing up, so it was no big deal to me. He was just another guy trying to make a living. [At the plate], he was very quiet. He didn't say anything. He just did his job."

### PAWTUCKET

*New York Yankees third baseman Wade Boggs remembers when he played for the Pawtucket Red Sox in baseball's longest game.*

"It was very cold and windy that night. It wasn't easy to keep warm. We had to get some bats and build a fire in one of the trash cans. I remember it got over about 5 o'clock in the morning. They couldn't find the league president. The umpires didn't want to make a decision [to stop the game] until they got in touch with the league president. . . . When the game resumed [on June 23], the strike was going on in the big leagues, so we had 800 media people there from all over the world. . . . It was kind of anticlimactic because it only went one inning. I guess they thought we'd play longer."

### BUFFALO

*In 1966, Gus Gil was the top-fielding baseman in the International League.*

"When I played with Buffalo [1966], we had an excellent year in the infield with double plays. [Our] shortstop, Frank Obregon, and I played together here in the United States for 3 years and down in winter ball for about 10 years. We know each other real well. Every time we play Rochester, for some reason, we made four or five double plays. One day, we got to the ballpark, we went in the clubhouse and we couldn't find our gloves. We started asking around and nobody [else's] glove is missing. We borrowed some gloves for the game and it just happened that we made six double plays in that game. After the game, we were sitting in the clubhouse. The clubhouse door opened and here comes [Rochester manager] Earl Weaver. He has the two gloves with him. He said, 'Here, you s.o.b.s. I give up."

### EDMONTON

*Bowie Baysox manager Bobby Miscik played nine years in the minor leagues, the last two (1987-88) in Edmonton. It was in this Canadian city that he witnessed one of the more unusual situations he ever saw in the minors.*

"John Ducey Stadium is an older stadium. I can remember a game there in 1987 where the light bank in left field went out. One whole row went out. It was fairly dark in left field. It's fairly dark [even] with the lights on. They didn't want to cancel the game, so we played with a whole row of lights out. I was playing shortstop. Our left fielder was a veteran guy [Ricky Adams] who really didn't care about what people thought about what he was doing. As a joke, he tied a flashlight onto the top of his head with sanitary [hose]. It stabilized it up there so when he ran, it was still up there. It wasn't falling off. You turn around and you'd see him out in left field with this beam of light like a coal miner's helmet."

### OKLAHOMA CITY

*Razor Shines remembers a memorable game in 1987 between his Indianapolis Indians and the Oklahoma City 89ers:*

"In Oklahoma City, they gave away free pizzas if the home team scored in double digits and won. In one game, they were leading 12-1 and the announcer was talking to the fans about turning in your tickets for pizza. We were down until they started razzing us. That motivated us, and we got going. We started chipping away. We started talking to the fans about maybe they should get their pizzas now. Alonzo Powell hit a two-run homer in the top of the ninth. He was running around the bases, yelling, 'There goes your pizza!' We won the game 13-12."

# PACIFIC COAST LEAGUE

The Pacific Coast League has been in operation since 1903 and has owned so lofty a reputation that at times it has not really been considered a minor league. Some have even called it "the third major league."

The PCL has a colorful history. It began in 1903 with teams in Los Angeles, Oakland, Portland, Sacramento, San Francisco and Seattle. The late Fatty Arbuckle served in 1919 as president of the Vernon Tigers, and, according to *Baseball's Hometown Teams* by Bruce Chadwick, Barbara Stanwyck, Gary Cooper, Bing Crosby and many other celebrities once owned pieces of the Hollywood Stars. Two of the greatest players ever—Ted Williams and Joe DiMaggio—had healthy stays in the PCL, and *Baseball America* has said the finest team in the history of the minors was Spokane of 1970. The Albuquerque Dukes won the PCL championship in 1994.

The PCL season was once nearly year-round, leading to some dazzling numbers. Future Hall of Famer Tony Lazzeri holds season records with 60 home runs, 222 runs batted in and 202 runs scored. Doc Newton and Rube Vickers won 39 games in 1904 and '06, respectively.

● ● ●

*The Asheville Tourists limber up at picturesque McCormick Field.*

# ALBUQUERQUE DUKES

## LOS ANGELES DODGERS

When you get to Albuquerque Sports Stadium, you might think this is a drive-in movie theater. It is the only place in organized baseball where you can park in an elevated area about 40 feet above and behind the outfield fence and watch the game from your car. There is room for about 175 vehicles here, and people pull in their campers, set up barbecues, spread blankets and make themselves right at home. But no alcohol is allowed. Over the years, several home run balls have struck or flown over several vehicles in the Dukes' interior parking lot. Check out the slope that leads up to this area. It is made of lava rock from now dormant volcanoes. This stadium opened in 1969 and was built in a bowl, several feet below ground level. Seats in the stadium offer dazzling mountain views of Sandia Peak and the other Sandia Mountains.

### ◆ LOCAL AND TEAM HISTORY

The Albuquerque Dukes of the Class D Rio Grande Association finished third in 1915, the first year of organized baseball here. That year, Frank Huelsman, one of the early minor-league home-run kings, led the league with 10 four-baggers. He finished his career with 133 minor-league round-trippers and six home run titles, tied for the third best all-time. In 1932, one of the highest scoring games in baseball history took place at Albuquerque's new Tingley Field when the home team pounded El Paso 43-15. There were 46 hits, including 13 triples, 10 doubles but only one home run in the highlight of the '32 season for the Arizona-Texas League, which folded during the summer. Stan Wasiak, the winningest minor-league manager in history with 2,530 victories over 37 seasons, guided the

*OTHER FAMOUS ALUMNI*

Mike Piazza, Eric Karros, Raul Mondesi, Rick Sutcliffe, Fernando Valenzuela, Ron Cey, Pedro Guerrero, Bob Welch, John Wetteland, Mike Marshall, Joe Ferguson, John Franco, Sid Fernandez, Mike Scioscia, Sid Bream, Candy Maldonado, Ramon Martinez, Steve Yeager, Bill Buckner, Tom Lasorda, Charlie Hough, Don Sutton and Steve Garvey all played or managed here.

Dukes for four years (1973-76), posting 275 wins and capturing the Eastern Division title in '74 before being swept in the championship series by Spokane, three games to none. The Dukes began their current affiliation with L.A. in 1972.

The first game held at Albuquerque Sports Stadium was a San Francisco–Cleveland exhibition on March 31, 1969. Albuquerque was a Class AA Texas League team from 1969 to '71, but in 1972 it became home to the Class AAA Pacific Coast League Dukes. In the first 11 years of Albuquerque Sports Stadium, the resident team won five league championships, and Albuquerque won the PCL championship again last season.

### ◆ BALLPARK EXTRAS

The drive-in is a unique seating area in much demand. It can accommodate more than 100 cars. You can watch the game seated behind lava rocks, barbecue in the drive-in area and watch prairie dogs in action too.

### ◆ ATTRACTIONS

Old Town is an historic area that includes an Indian market, shops and restaurants. This was the original city proper and plaza.

Sandia Peak has the Sandia Peak Tramway, which is one of the longest single-span aerial trams in the world. The Peak is a 10- to 15-mile trip from downtown. For further information, call (505) 856-7325.

For more information about the Albuquerque area, call the Chamber of Commerce, (505) 764-3700.

### ◆ DINING

Fans tend to wait until they get to the ballpark to eat, with the drive-in area a favorite. If you want to eat out, though, Mexican food is big in Albuquerque, and Sanitary Tortilla Factory is regarded as the best. It's 7 minutes from the ballpark. 403 2nd Street SW, (505) 242-4890.

### ◆ LODGING

The Plaza Inn Albuquerque, about 10 minutes away, is popular and is used by visiting teams and some players from the Dukes. 900 Medical Arts NE, Albuquerque, (505) 243-5693.

### ◆ DIRECTIONS

Take I-25 South to the Stadium Boulevard exit. Go east two blocks to the ballpark. Parking is $1 and plentiful.

---

**ALBUQUERQUE SPORTS STADIUM**
**1601 Stadium Boulevard SE**
**Albuquerque, NM 87106**
**(505) 243-1791**

**Capacity: 10,510**
**LF 360, CF 410, RF 340**

---

## TICKET AND SCHEDULE INFORMATION

Games are at 7 P.M. on Sundays and 1 P.M. all other days.

The Dukes' season usually opens during the first week of April and closes out in early September.

Ticket prices: $5 box seats; $4 general admission; $3.50 for seniors 62 and over and students 13 through college age; $2 for children 6 to 12. Children under 5 are free.

# CALGARY CANNONS

### PITTSBURGH PIRATES

Foothills Stadium was built in 1967. It had a major renovation in 1985 and then another one before 1995. The Cannons did $2.5 million in work during the most recent campaign, including the addition of a second deck in right field that fully encloses the stadium. The change still allows the Rocky Mountains to be seen from some outfield seats, but while the view is the same, the new deck will not please long-ball hitters. Calgary has long been one of the power parks in the minors; in fact, the Cannons hit three grand slams in one game May 16, 1991 (Dave Cochrane, Chuck Jackson and Alonzo Powell hit them). Now, with less wind blowing out, hitters will have to work harder for their home runs. In addition, new clubhouses were built, new seats replaced older wooden ones, a new scoreboard was erected and a beer garden was added. Out of all these changes, the new beer garden is probably the most popular.

## LOCAL AND TEAM HISTORY

Calgary has had minor-league teams off and on since 1907. There was a Pioneer League entry in 1977, but Calgary sports business-people aimed higher.

The Calgary Broncos spent 9 years (1907, 1909-14, '20-21) in the Western Canada League. Calgary also fielded teams in the Class B and Class A Western International League (1922, '53-54), the Rookie Pioneer League ('77-84) and the PCL ('85-to date). In 1984, Russ Parker bought the Salt Lake City franchise and moved it to Calgary, in the foothills of the Canadian Rockies. The Cannons have reached the PCL championship final twice, in '87 and '91, but lost each time. The Cannons switched their major-league affiliation after last season from Seattle to Pittsburgh.

Danny Tartabull terrorized the PCL in 1985 when he led the league with 43 homers and 109 runs batted in. Future big-league manager Steve Boros ('83-84, '86) was the skipper of the Calgary Expos when they finished the '80 Pioneer League season with a 23-46 record.

**OTHER FAMOUS ALUMNI**

Billy Swift, Jay Buhner, Edgar Martinez, Harold Reynolds and Bret Boone all played here.

## BALLPARK EXTRAS

The Foothills Frank might be the best hot dog in the PCL. The secret is the toasted bun, modeled on that used in the legendary Montreal Forum dog.

## ATTRACTIONS

Just 1½ hours to the West is Banff National Park, perhaps the most beautiful in North America, site of most of the Alpine events of the 1988 Olympic Games.

Scenic Lake Louise is ½ hour west of that.

The Calgary Stampede, an immensely popular rodeo, runs July 7-16 this year.

For more information about Calgary, call the Visitor's Bureau at (403) 262-2766.

## DINING

Earl's is right by the ballpark. It's a family dining spot that draws turnaway crowds for stir fries and other simple meals. Calgary has a modest Chinatown for Chinese food aficionados.

## LODGING

Some Cannons stay at the Village Park Inn, five minutes away. 1804 Crowchild Trail W, Calgary, (403) 289-0241.

Visiting teams stay at the Sandman Hotel right in downtown Calgary, 10 to 15 minutes away. 888 7th Avenue SW, Calgary, (403) 237-8626.

## DIRECTIONS

Take Highway 1 (Trans-Canada Highway) to Crowchild Trail West. Head North ½ mile. Parking is plentiful and costs C$1.50.

**BURNS STADIUM**
**2255 Crowchild Trail NW**
**Calgary, Alberta T2M 4M4**
**(403) 284-1111**

Capacity: 7,500
LF 345, CF 405, RF 345

◆ **TICKET AND SCHEDULE INFORMATION**

Day games are at 1:30 P.M. Night games start at 7:05 P.M.

The Cannons' season begins in early April and goes through the start of September.

Tickets prices: C$9 lower box; C$7.70 upper box; C$6.50 reserved general admission; C$6 rush (first come, first served). Seniors over 60 and children 5 to 12 receive a C$2 discount. Children under 4 are free.

# COLORADO SPRINGS SKY SOX

## COLORADO ROCKIES

Y ou don't just have a hot time at the ballpark here. You can have a hot *tub* at the ballpark.

Sky Sox Stadium has become quite well known for its hot tub, which has been sold out for the last two years. Those interested buy tickets in an eight-person package, get a bottle of champagne in the deal, and then watch the game from the tub. No sex and no nudity, please.

Despite the fact that some of your fellow fans will be watching in their bathing suits, you should bring a jacket. Early and late in the season, night games are almost always chilly. As a bonus, most ballpark seats have a view of the Rockies, including famous Pikes Peak.

The ballpark is 6,400 feet above sea level, 1,000 feet higher than Mile High Stadium or Coors Field, the past and present homes of the Colorado Rockies. The elevation means the ball really carries.

◆ **LOCAL AND TEAM HISTORY**

Colorado Springs first had pro baseball in 1901, and it was played by a bunch of Millionaires. Actually, they were the Colorado Springs Millionaires of the Western League.

Owner David Elmore brought the Sky Sox over to "The Springs" and Spurgeon Stadium in 1988. The name Sky Sox came from a Class D team that played in Colorado Springs from 1950-57. The Sky Sox didn't need socks in their previous home. They were the Hawaii Islanders, a team that played in a stadium said to be rotting from termites. The franchise was the Sacra-

mento Solons from 1918 to '60 and the Hawaii Islanders from '61 to '87.

In the 1988 season, there were 13 home runs hit in one Colorado Springs game, on May 7 against Phoenix. It wasn't a record, though. There were 14 hit once in Sacramento when the left-field fence was 250 feet away. Ed Lynch had just joined Phoenix; he gave up five of those home runs, then retired to move on to another tough post; he is the new general manager of the Chicago Cubs.

Albert Belle, Carlos Baerga and Sandy Alomar Jr. played here.

OTHER FAMOUS ALUMNI

None of the three Sky Sox players whose jersey have been retired—Sam Hairston, Luis Medina and Chuck Manuel—became famous major-league players. The Sky Sox won the PCL championship in 1992, their last year affiliated with Cleveland.

◆ **BALLPARK EXTRAS**

There's the hot tub, of course, but there's more. The Sky Sox handle their own concessions and pay attention to quality. They have a Mexican stand that is popular. There is also Fry-Babies, which serves fried food. Fried dough is a hot item and there is a beer cart offering beers of the world.

◆ **ATTRACTIONS**

Pikes Peak is one-half hour west of the ballpark, a delight for hikers, joggers and sightseers.

The Olympic Training Center facilities are a few minutes' drive. For information, call (719) 578-4500.

The Air Force Academy is a can't-miss destination for tourists. It's a 20-minute drive north. For further information, call (505) 472-1818.

For more information about the Colorado Springs area, call the Chamber of Commerce, (719) 635-1551.

◆ **DINING**

The best bet is Old Chicago restaurant. About 30 minutes from the park, they serve pizza, pasta and the like. 7115 Commerce Center Drive, (719) 593-7678.

◆ **LODGING**

The Broadmoor hotel and resort is one of the finest and most revered hotels in the nation. It's about 25 minutes away and is expensive. 1 Lake Avenue, Colorado Springs, (719) 634-7711.

Visiting teams stay at the LeBaron Hotel downtown,

about 15 minutes away. 314 Bijou Street, Colorado Springs, (719) 471-8680.

## ◆ DIRECTIONS
From I-25, take the Woodman Road exit. Turn left and go through several traffic lights until you reach Powers Boulevard. Turn right on Powers. To reach the ballpark, which will be visible on your left, turn left on Barns Road. Parking is limited in the main lot and costs $3. An unpaved overflow parking area is also available.

> **SKY SOX STADIUM**
> **4385 Tutt Boulevard**
> **Colorado Springs, CO 80922**
> **(719) 597-1449**
> _____
> **Capacity: 9,000**
> **LF 330, CF 410, RF 330**

## ◆ TICKET AND SCHEDULE INFORMATION
Night games start at 6:35 P.M. until the last week of June, 7:05 P.M. thereafter. Day games start at 1:35 P.M.

Colorado's season starts in the first week of April and ends in early September.

Ticket prices: $6 box seats, $5 children and seniors; $4 general admission, $3 children and seniors.

# EDMONTON TRAPPERS

### OAKLAND ATHLETICS

The Trappers occupy a new stadium this season, erected at the same site as their last one, and much more sophisticated than the old, rickety ballpark it replaces. John Ducey Park, jocularly dubbed Rob Ducey Park after a Canadian fringe player in the majors, features luxury suites at field level. While many luxury boxes in the last few years have been built at nosebleed altitudes, the Trappers had the wisdom to build them so the high-rollers within can actually see the game from a prime location. This will make little difference to an out-of-town visitor: you won't be able to get luxury-suite tickets, anyway.

Another popular section is the Home Plate Lounge, a dining area at field level right behind home plate. It will require a special ticket, but that can be obtained on a game-day basis, if it's not sold out.

Another unusual aspect of the new ballpark worth checking out is the surface. It is artificial in the infield, grass in the outfield.

There will also be grass in the outfield stands, called "the berm," a seating area for families and sunbathers.

## ◆ LOCAL AND TEAM HISTORY
Peter Pocklington was already making a name for himself in Edmonton with the hockey Oilers when Wayne Gretzky came along and began pushing the Oilers to the top of the NHL. Pocklington wanted to branch out, so he bought a PCL team in Ogden, Utah, in 1981, plopped it down in Edmonton, in Renfrew Park, and named it the Trappers.

Edmonton is the northernmost city in North America to have a major professional franchise. It is also a center for trappers who bring pelts and furs in from the frigid Northwest Territories and other parts of Canada. The real endangered species in this area is the animal-rights activist, so Trappers is an appropriate name.

*OTHER FAMOUS ALUMNI*

Babe Herman, Wally Joyner, Devon White, Dick Schofield and Gary Pettis all played here.

They became PCL champions in 1984, the same year the Oilers won their first of five Stanley Cups in seven years. The Trappers were the first Canadian team to win the Pacific Coast League championship.

Edmonton had its first minor-league team in 1907, and the city has been home sporadically to teams in the Western Canadian League and the Western International League.

Two future American League Rookies of the Year made big impacts here before moving to the big leagues. Ron Kittle had the greatest season of his pro career for Edmonton in 1982 when he was named the PCL's MVP after leading the league with 50 homeruns, 144 runs batted in, 121 runs scored, 355 total bases and a .752 slugging percentage. As a sign of the fear he put into pitchers that year, Kittle was hit by pitches 10 times, tied for most in the league. Ten years after Kittle played here, Tim Salmon topped the PCL with 29 four-baggers, 105 runs batted in, 101 runs scored, 275 total bases, and a .672 slugging percentage.

## ◆ BALLPARK EXTRAS
Concession fare in the new stadium was still under discussion at press time, but because of the heavy concen-

tration of Eastern European immigrants in Edmonton, pirogi, potato latkes and the like might make the bill.

Because of Edmonton's proximity to the Arctic Circle, you might see a real treat after you drive from a game—now and then the northern lights are visible at night.

### ◆ ATTRACTIONS

Attention, shoppers: Edmonton is famous for the West Edmonton Mall, the original megamall that was the model for the Mall of America in Bloomington, Minnesota. A 10-minute drive from the ballpark, West Edmonton Mall includes an amusement park, ice rink, wave pool and every kind of store you might imagine, in numbers beyond belief.

Fort Edmonton Park, right downtown, recreates the original fort and recalls the days when the Hudson's Bay Company (real trappers) settled the Canadian frontier.

For more information about the Edmonton area, call the Chamber of Commerce, (403) 426-4620.

### ◆ DINING

Barry T's is a popular spot for pregame and postgame food and drink, about 15 minutes away. It is located at 104th Street and 61st Avenue, within a three-block area known for a wide variety of nightclubs and dining spots. (403) 438-2582.

### ◆ LODGING

The ballpark is downtown, so you have a wide variety of accommodation choices, from the pricey (Four Seasons or Westin) to the economy brands.

Visiting teams stay at the Holiday Inn–Crowne Plaza, about five minutes away. 10111 Bellamy Hill, Edmonton, (403) 428-6611/(800) HOLIDAY.

### ◆ DIRECTIONS

From Highway 2, take Calgary Trail for about 6 miles through downtown. Turn right at the end of the trail and turn left at the first traffic light onto Queen Elizabeth Road. The ballpark will be less than a mile away on the right.

From Highway 16, go to the City Center and take the Groat Road exit. Groat turns into River Valley Road, which will take you to the ballpark.

Parking is plentiful and costs C$3.

---

**EDMONTON STADIUM**
10233 96th Avenue
Edmonton, Alberta T5K 0A5
(403) 429-2934

Capacity: 10,000
LF 335, CF 425, RF 330

---

### ◆ TICKET AND SCHEDULE INFORMATION

Games start at 2:05 P.M. or 7:05 P.M.

The Trappers season begins in early April and ends the first week of September.

Ticket prices: C$9.50 reserved grandstand chair; C$8.50 reserved grandstand bench; C$6.50 general admission. Seniors 65 and over and children under 14 receive a C$2 discount.

## LAS VEGAS STARS

### SAN DIEGO PADRES

They ought to play Glenn Frey's hit *The Heat Is On* at Las Vegas Stars games. The reason is simple: At 36 of 39 Stars home games in 1994, the game-time temperature was 100 degrees or more—even with the 7 P.M. starts.

The Stars make light of it all by offering 200 "Hot Ticket" seats to every game. The seats are painted with bright red flames, and the higher the temperature at noon that day, up to 115 degrees, the lower the cost of the seats. It is so hot—though it's a dry heat—that the Stars are considering installing a misting system like the one in Scottsdale.

This ballpark is part of the Cashman Field Center, a large facility with meeting rooms and space for conventions. Exhibit halls are next to the ballpark's grandstand, while an auditorium can be found behind it. In addition to the Field Center, the Stars' home is also bordered by a residential area plus children's and natural-history museums. Inside the ballpark, fans can escape the heat in the Club Level Restaurant, which is behind home plate, fully enclosed and air-conditioned. Beyond the park's 20-foot-high wooden outfield fence, fans are treated to a view of a Nevada state office building.

The national anthem is often more interesting here than elsewhere. Artists who are doing shows on the Strip often drop in to do the anthem. You might hear Huey Lewis or the Four Tops or the Turtles on a given night. Sorry, no Streisand yet.

### ◆ LOCAL AND TEAM HISTORY

Las Vegas had a pro team in the Sunset League from 1947 to '50, the Southwest International League ('51-52), the Arizona-Mexico League (1957) and the California League (1958). Those games were played in an old, wooden park right off the Strip.

Las Vegas joined the PCL in 1983, the same year the

franchise began its current affiliation with San Diego. The Stars' owner, Ken Stickney, has shown a decided affinity for astronomical and meteorological names when it comes to the sports teams he owns. Besides the Stars, they include the Las Vegas Thunder of the International Hockey League and the Class A California League's Lake Elsinore Storm and Rancho Cucamonga Quakes.

In 1984, Ozzie Guillen led all PCL shortstops in assists and total chances while batting .296. Five years later, Sandy Alomar Jr. had a big season for the Stars when he led the PCL with 523 at-bats, while hitting .306 with 13 homers and 101 runs batted in. Anything can happen in Las Vegas: Last year both Keith Lockhart and Kevin Higgins of the Stars each played all nine positions in one game, and slugger Dave Staton hit a ball 80 feet high off the scoreboard, 474 feet from home plate.

**OTHER FAMOUS ALUMNI OTHER FAMOUS ALUMNI**

Tony Gwynn, Carlos Baerga, Shane Mack, Benito Santiago, Kevin McReynolds and Bip Roberts have all played here.

### ◆ BALLPARK EXTRAS
In keeping with the Vegas atmosphere, you can get a martini at the ballpark. Cashman Field also has a sausage house with fresh grilled Italian sausages, bratwurst and similar items. Frozen yogurt is big, too. "Anything cold sells," says a Stars official.

### ◆ ATTRACTIONS
Las Vegas is becoming much more than the gaming/gambling capital of the USA, though of course you can play roulette, the slots or anything else you desire, bet on sports events, etc. You have hundreds of shows to see. There are rides and shows for children. Theme parks. Water parks. You get the idea.

Hoover Dam is a ride of 40 to 60 minutes east. It is a magnificent view, especially as you pass Lake Meade on the way. Take the Hoover tour. For further information, call (702) 293-8321.

For more information about the Las Vegas area, call the Chamber of Commerce, (702) 735-1616.

### ◆ DINING
There is no one must-eat place in Vegas. You can dine like a king or emir, or you can eat on a budget. Nearly all the casinos have cafeterias or buffets. The air-conditioned, massive, club-level restaurant at Cashman Field

has three-tiered seating with a field view. It is quite popular for the food and the AC.

### ◆ LODGING
You can choose from expensive accommodations or cheap ones. Options are endless. Shop for midweek specials.

### ◆ DIRECTIONS
Take I-15 to the Las Vegas Boulevard exit. Go 4 blocks north on Las Vegas Boulevard. The field is on the right. Parking is plentiful and costs $2.

**CASHMAN FIELD**
**850 Las Vegas Boulevard North**
**Las Vegas, NV 89101**
**(702) 386-7200**

**Capacity: 9,334**
**LF 328, CF 433, RF 328**

### ◆ TICKET AND SCHEDULE INFORMATION
Most games start at 7:05 P.M. During April and May, selected Sunday games begin at 1:05 P.M.

The Stars' season begins in early April and ends the first week of September.

Ticket prices: $7.50 club-level; $6 field level from dugout to dugout; $5 Plaza seats; $4.50 reserved behind the dugout; $4 general admission is for adults, $3 children, seniors and military.

# PHOENIX FIREBIRDS

## SAN FRANCISCO GIANTS

Ritzy Scottsdale packs in the tourists, and Scottsdale Stadium packs in the fans. Opened in 1992 when the team moved from aging Phoenix Municipal Stadium, Scottsdale Stadium is another of the nifty designs by HOK, the architectural firm that came up with Camden Yards in Baltimore and many other admired parks. It is snugly located a block from Scottsdale Road, the main drag in Scottsdale.

Seats are quite close to the action. In fact, they are so close, the owners had to erect some protective screens because fans had so little reaction time on foul balls. On one occasion in a spring game, before the changes, the infant child of San Francisco Giants pitcher Bryan Hickerson was saved from a potentially fatal lined foul to the head when Hickerson's wife deflected the ball with her hand. The same is true for the dugouts. In the stadium's first year, pitcher Matt Keough was sitting in the visitors' dugout when he was nailed in the head by a foul. It was nearly fatal.

Nice wide concourses near the concession stands make for easy access to bathrooms and food. Spillover crowds can sit on the grassy slopes beyond the outfield fence. The summer heat is very intense in the Arizona desert. The ballpark has a misting system that sprays water continuously into the air over the stands. It cools the air 10 to 15 degrees.

The only "problem" is that beautiful Camelback Mountain, the focal point of Scottsdale, is not visible from the stands.

### ◆ LOCAL AND TEAM HISTORY

Phoenix or Scottsdale has had baseball off and on since 1928 when Phoenix debuted in the Class D Arizona State League (1928-30), and then played in the Arizona-Mexico League (1931-32). Phoenix played in three Class C leagues: Arizona-Texas (1947-50, '52-54), Southwest International (1951) and Arizona-Mexico (1955-57).

Phoenix or Scottsdale has had a team since 1958, with the exception of a '60-65 franchise stint in Tacoma. In 1959, Phoenix won the PCL championships, its first year in the PCL, and again in '77.

The team changed its name from the Giants to the Firebirds in 1986.

Hall of Famer Willie "Stretch" McCovey hit 14 home runs for the Phoenix Giants in 1958, the year his team also set a new PCL record with 205 four-baggers. The following season, McCovey led the PCL with 29 homers while hitting .372 in just 95 games. He was brought up for the rest of season and hit .354 for the San Francisco Giants, earning Rookie of the Year honors.

OTHER FAMOUS ALUMNI

George Foster, Bobby Bonds, Felipe Alou, Chili Davis, Steve Stone, Garry Maddox, Dave Kingman, Dusty Rhodes, Dan Gladden, Terry Mulholland, Jack Clark and Dave Dravecky have played here.

Matt Williams played parts of three seasons (1987-89) here. His best was '89 when in just 76 games, he hit 26 homers and drove in 61 runs.

### ◆ BALLPARK EXTRAS

The spray is an unusual feature. The concession fare includes Italian and other brands of sausage made locally. They are quite popular.

### ◆ ATTRACTIONS

Bring your golf clubs!!! There are many who say the best golfing in the nation is concentrated in the Scottsdale area. Dazzling courses include but are not limited to Troon and Desert Mountain (both private), Troon North, TPC Scottsdale Stadium Course and the Phoenician. Generally you can get on, but be aware that the greens fees tend to run high.

Phoenix and Scottsdale are also a delight for a shopper or hiker. The old-Scottsdale shopping area is a five-minute walk from the ballpark, and the Grand Canyon is on almost anyone's Arizona intinerary. It is a scenic, four-hour drive away. Sedona is another delightful drive. The stunning red rocks country must be seen at sunrise or sunset to fully appreciate its beauty. Expect a two-hour drive.

For more information about the Phoenix area, call the Chamber of Commerce, (602) 254-5521.

### ◆ DINING

You must make it to Don & Charlie's on East Camelback Road in Scottsdale, about ½ mile East of Scottsdale Road. This Chicago-style ribs, chops and seafood emporium is *the* place in Scottsdale, if not the whole Valley, especially for baseball fans. Don Carson, the owner, is a friend of many, many baseball people, and they flock to his spot. 7501 E. Camelback Road, Scottsdale, (602) 990-0900.

Los Dos Molinos is the best Mexican spot in an area famous for them. There are three locations. The one on Alma School Road in Mesa is closest, a 15-minute drive from the ballpark. They use Hatch chilies in their food, so it's hot, authentic and delicious. Try the Adovada pork. 260 Alma School Road, Mesa, (602) 535-5356.

### ◆ LODGING

Scouts stay at The Fifth Avenue, a reasonably priced hotel in Scottsdale just a couple of minutes away. 6935 5th Avenue, Scottsdale, (602) 994-9461.

Visting teams stay at the Days Inn about 5 minutes away. 4710 N. Scottsdale Road, Scottsdale, (602) 947-5411/(800) 325-2525.

### ◆ DIRECTIONS

From the 202 Loop, take the Scottsdale Road exit. Go north for about 4 miles. Turn right on Osborn. The ballpark will be on the left, next to a hospital. Parking is unavailable at the ballpark. You can park on the street or in city-owned lots, which are free.

### ◆ TICKET AND SCHEDULE INFORMATION

Starting times are 7:05 P.M. through May, 6:05 P.M. June-September.

The Firebirds' season begins the first week of April and ends in early September.

Tickets are: $7 field box seats; $6 reserved seats; $4 general admission; $3 adults 55 and over and children under 12.

# SALT LAKE BUZZ

**MINNESOTA TWINS**

Anyone who has seen Baltimore's Camden Yards will notice similarities between Franklin Quest Field and its eastern cousin; both were designed by the same architect. This ballpark opened in 1994, on the same site where Derks Field once stood and where baseball has been played since the 1930s. With lots of red brick and forest-green seats, Salt Lake's ballpark has an old-time baseball feel. Two brick towers straddle the entrance to the park, and two more are located down each foul line. The outfield in this asymmetrical stadium has its share of quirks. The right-field foul pole is a scant 315 feet from home. But only about 20 feet to the right of the pole, the 10-foot high cement outfield wall with forest-green padding takes a quick step back, making it 345 feet from home plate. There is a grass hill, known as "the Berm," surrounding the fence where there is open seating for fans wanting to watch the game from blankets and folding chairs.

With the Wasatch Mountains visible beyond the outfield fence, the view here is one of the most spectacular in baseball, especially when the sun sets over the snow-capped peaks.

### ◆ LOCAL AND TEAM HISTORY

The Buzz moved into Salt Lake City last season and broke a PCL record for single-season attendance. The Buzz drew 714,000. This was simply a return to the successes of some previous Salt Lake City PCL entries.

In 1869, the Cincinnati Red Stockings introduced the Utah Territory to baseball when they staged an exhibition game in Salt Lake City against the Eurekas. Organized baseball here dates back to 1903 when the Salt Lake City Elders began a three-year association (1903-05) with the Pacific National League. Besides the Pacific National, Pioneer and PCL, Salt Lake City teams have also been associated with three other circuits. Antonio Bordetski, better known as Bunny Brief, led the PCL with 33 homers in 1916. He compiled career totals of 2,963 hits, 342 homers and eight home-run titles, tied with Ken Guettler for No. 1 in minor-league history in the latter category. One of his teammates in '16 was Paul Fittery, the pitching staff's ironman, who topped the circuit in games (65), innings pitched (448) and strikeouts (203) while posting a 29-19 record and 2.97 ERA for the third-place Salt Lake City Bees.

The Salt Lake City Bees moved into Bonneville Park, a real hitter's park, in 1915 and stayed for 11 years. In 1922-23 Paul Strand, an outfielder, won back-to-back Triple Crowns, a feat no one in the majors has achieved. When Lefty O'Doul played here in 1925, he had one of the hottest touches of any batter in PCL history, recording an amazing 19 hits in 21 at-bats. Hall of Famer Lefty Gomez made his pro debut in Salt Lake in 1928 when his 14 losses topped all pitchers in the Utah-Idaho League.

The minors came back to Salt Lake City in 1958 at Derks Field (now gone). That team moved to Calgary in 1985, and in its place came a Pioneer League team. The 1987 squad won 29 consecutive games as an unaffiliated team. That record is especially noteworthy because it is hard to be a minor-league power without big-league help. It remains a minor-league record.

Speaking of records, the Salt Lake City Bees lost to Vernon 35-11 in a 1923 game that set a PCL record for totals runs in one game.

But nothing quite matches the numbers Tony Lazzeri put up as a 21-year-old on the 1925 Salt Lake team in a 200-game season. The future Hall of Famer hit .355, scored 202 runs, hit 60 home runs and had 222 RBI. The runs scored is a pro record. The RBI total is third all time, believe it or not. Bob Crues of Amarillo (Texas) in

**OTHER FAMOUS ALUMNI** — Dick "Dr. Strangeglove" Stuart, Sam McDowell, and Claude "Lefty" Williams all played here.

the Class C West Texas–New Mexico League had 254 RBI in 1948.

## ◆ BALLPARK EXTRAS

This team's nickname, the Buzz, is the closest Salt Lake City could come to its old nickname, the Bees, dating back to the early years of this century. Since there were concerns about two minor-league teams carrying the same name (the Midwest League's Burlington franchise is known as the Bees), Salt Lake City opted for the Buzz, a name not surprisingly thought up by owner Joe Buzas.

## ◆ ATTRACTIONS

Salt Lake City is the international headquarters of the Church of Jesus Christ of Latter-day Saints (the Mormons). The original Mormon temple is a five-minute drive from the ballpark. For information, call (801) 240-3171.

Skiing in Utah is available even in April and May. Park City is the skiing hot spot, including the U.S. Olympic skiing team training center. Park City is a 35-minute drive. Call the Park City Ski Education Center for information. (801) 649-8749.

For more information about Salt Lake City, call the Chamber of Commerce, (801) 364-3631.

## ◆ DINING

Cafe Pierpont offers a variety of imaginative dishes, including fajitas and numerous seafood selections. This restaurant is also enjoyable for children. Anyone small enough to walk through the iron cactus at the front door can eat for free. 126 W. Pierpont Avenue, (801) 364-1222, about 10 minutes from the ballpark.

## ◆ LODGING

Visiting teams use the Red Lion Inn, a couple minutes away. 255 South West Temple, Salt Lake City, (801) 328-2000/(800) 547-8010.

## ◆ DIRECTIONS

The park is at 1300 South West Temple, 3 blocks east of I-80. Plenty of parking is available in a city-owned lot for $5.

```
FRANKLIN QUEST FIELD
77 West 1300, South
Salt Lake City, UT 84105
(801) 485-3800
─────────────────
Capacity: 12,000
LF 340, CF 420, RF 315
```

## ◆ TICKET AND SCHEDULE INFORMATION

Games are at 7 P.M.; 2 P.M. Sundays.

Salt Lake City's season begins in early April and ends the first week of September. Ticket availability is quite limited because season-ticket sales are substantial. The best seats, $7, are very limited and might be sold out. The other seats are $5 and $6. All seats are assigned locations, except those on the grassy terrace.

# TACOMA RAINIERS

### SEATTLE MARINERS

Cheney Stadium is a symmetrical, one-tier stadium named for Ben Cheney, a local philanthropist.

But Cheney donated more than his name and money to this ballpark, built in just 100 days in 1960. At that time, Cheney was a minority owner of the San Francisco Giants. When the Giants moved into Candlestick Park from Seals Stadium, Cheney shipped some of the Seals Stadium seats to Tacoma for use in the new ballpark. Several of these vintage wood seats, complete with old-fashioned metal armrests, can still be found in the grandstand here. Although they have been painted many times over the past decades, these seats will wear yet another new coat of paint in '95, one of teal and red. Once you have found a place to sit inside the ballpark, look up to see another portion of Seals Stadium now in the Pacific Northwest. When Cheney shipped those seats north, he also sent along the Seals' former light towers, which can still be found in this ballpark.

Cheney Stadium's playing field is particularly close to the stands so there is not much foul territory here—so little, in fact, that there is barely enough room for two warm-up mounds in the bullpens, which are located down each foul line. Fans benefit from this closeness by getting a good view of the field in one of AAA's best ballparks when it comes to sightlines. Over the years, Cheney has become known as a pitcher's ballpark, with a 32-foot-high wall in centerfield, 425 feet from home plate. In 1985 during batting practice, Jose Canseco became the only player in Cheney Stadium history to blast a home run over that wall.

## ◆ LOCAL AND TEAM HISTORY

Tacoma's team was formerly known as the Tigers. Now it is the Rainiers, named for the mountain range, not the beer or the royal family of Monaco. When nearby Seattle had a team in the Northwest League and the PCL, it was called the Rainiers, so the nearby cities now share more than an airport (SEA-TAC).

Baseball came to Tacoma in 1874, according to the book *The Pacific Coast League, 1903-1988*, when the Tacoma Invincibles proved vincible in their only game, losing 29-28. Tacoma's first pro team debuted in 1890 in the Pacific Northwest League. Tacoma was in the PCL in 1904-05, then from 1960 on. Its active, unbroken run in the PCL is longer than that of any other active league franchise.

Tacoma has been a PCL affiliate of San Francisco, the Chicago Cubs, Minnesota, the New York Yankees, Cleveland, Oakland and now Seattle. The new association with a major league team a 30-minute drive away will make the scutiny of young players much more intense and provide a chance for Mariners fans to see the club's future.

**FAMOUS ALUMNI**

Juan Marichal, Mark McGwire, "Ironman" Joe McGinnity, Clark Griffith, Jose Canseco, Gaylord Perry, Willie McCovey, Tom Haller, Jose Rijo, Juan Berenguer, Walt Weiss, Burt Hooton, and Jesus and Matty Alou all played here.

#### ◆ BALLPARK EXTRAS
The Seattle-Tacoma area is the coffee capital of the USA. It is no wonder, then, that Cheney Stadium offers espresso, cappuccino and *caffe latte*. They serve a fine chicken sandwich as well as premium sausages and fajitas.

#### ◆ ATTRACTIONS
Mt. Rainier is a 1½-hour drive. Mount St. Helens is a 2½-hour drive. Excellent fishing is available nearby. Tacoma is right on Puget Sound, with all the fishing and boating and other diversions that offers, and between the majestic Cascade and Olympic mountain ranges and their hiking, sightseeing and camping.

The Tacoma Dome houses concerts, trade shows and the NBA Seattle SuperSonics for the 1994-95 season. For information, call (206) 283-3865.

For more information about the Tacoma area, call the Chamber of Commerce, (206) 627-2175.

#### ◆ DINING
Harbor Lights, about 10 minutes from the ballpark, is known for seafood and big portions. Popular items include crab legs, steamed clams and King salmon. 2761 Ruston Way, (206) 752-8600.

#### ◆ LODGING
Visiting teams stay at the Tacoma Sheraton, about 10 to 15 minutes away. 1320 Broadway Plaza, Tacoma, (206) 572-3200/(800) 325-3535.

The Days Inn, about five minutes away, is also a reasonable choice. 6802 Tacoma Mall Boulevard, Tacoma, (206) 475-5900/(800) 325-2525.

#### ◆ DIRECTIONS
From I-5 take exit 132 (Washington Highway 16 W). Take the 19th Avenue East exit from that, and the stadium is on the right. Parking is plentiful and costs $3.

**CHENEY STADIUM**
2502 S. Tyler Street
Tacoma, WA 98405
(206) 752-7707

Capacity: 10,106
LF 325, CF 425, RF 325

#### ◆ TICKET AND SCHEDULE INFORMATION
Game time is 7:05 P.M., 1:35 P.M. on Sundays and holidays. There are some midweek, midday (12:35 P.M.) starts.

The Rainiers' season starts the first week of April and ends in early September.

Ticket prices: $8 premium seats; $5 economy seats. There is a 50-cent discount for seniors, children under 12 and military.

# TUCSON TOROS
### HOUSTON ASTROS

I f you saw the movie *Major League*, you saw Hi Corbett Field. It was also used for an episode of the television show *Highway to Heaven*.

The ballpark was built in 1937. A 1972 remodeling gave Hi Corbett Field—named for Hiram Corbett, who brought pro baseball back to Tucson in 1969—more of a Southwestern flavor with a white-stucco covering on the ballpark's outside walls. Inside this largely concrete ballpark with a partially covered grandstand, you will find a grassy area available for private picnics down the right-field line. The field is also quite close to the grandstand, giving the ballpark an intimate flavor.

There was yet another renovation before the 1993 season, which included new bleachers in right field, a new press box, a new home-team clubhouse, and a tripling in size of both dugouts. These improvements were made to appeal to the Colorado Rockies, who made Hi Corbett their spring-training home, replacing the departed Cleveland Indians.

Despite the fact that Hi Corbett has the shortest center field in the PCL, this ballpark is far from a power hitter's haven. Over the past few seasons, fans here have seen fewer home runs than in any other PCL ballpark, largely because of the deep power alleys and the 40-foot-high Green Monster in center field. Outfielders have also learned the hard way to avoid any collisions with the double-decked outfield fence, which is solid concrete block on the bottom and metal on top.

Although the field does not face the mountains, Hi Corbett is plopped down in Reid Park, an attractive, sprawling Tucson recreational area.

### ◆ LOCAL AND TEAM HISTORY

Tucson's first league games were played in 1907. One of the players for a local railroad squad then was Hi Corbett, who would later become Tucson's Mr. Baseball and have the city's ballpark named after him. Organized baseball first came to Tucson in 1915 when the Old Pueblos spent their first and only year in the Class D Rio Grande Valley Association, which folded before the season was over. Subsequently, Tucson teams have been associated with five other minor leagues: Arizona State (1928-30), Arizona-Texas ('31-32, '37-41, '47-50, '52-54), Southwest International ('51), Arizona-Mexico ('55-58) and Pacific Coast ('69-to date).

OTHER FAMOUS ALUMNI OTHER FAMOUS ALUMNI

Craig Biggio, Glenn Davis, Phil Garner, Ken Caminiti, Curt Schilling, Darryl Kile, Eric Anthony, James Mouton and Charlie Kerfeld have all played here.

In 1991, Kenny Lofton had a PCL all-star season for the Toros and was promoted to Houston in September. He led the PCL in at-bats (545), hits (168) and triples (17) while batting .308 and stealing 40 bases. With Lofton's help, Tucson won the PCL championship, beating Calgary three games to two in the finals.

As a PCL team Tucson has been affiliated with the Chicago White Sox (1969-72), Oakland ('73-76), Texas ('77-79) and Houston (1980-to date).

### ◆ BALLPARK EXTRAS

The most popular item is Eegee's fruit slush. It's available only in Tucson and environs.

### ◆ ATTRACTIONS

In the immediate vicinity of the stadium, five minutes away, is the El Con Mall (off 22nd and Broadway).

Old Tucson (602-883-0100) has been used as a location for many, many Westerns. It doubles as a theme park. It is a 20-minute drive from the ballpark.

Tucson has a nice zoo. The zoo (602-791-4022) and the Sonoran Desert Museum (602-883-2702) are brief drives from the ballpark.

Also, Sabino Canyon, with a tram ride and good hiking, is a 15-minute drive and the Biosphere is 45 minutes away. For more information about the Tucson area, call the Chamber of Commerce, (602) 792-1212.

### ◆ DINING

There are many superior Mexican spots. Many fans go to the Javelina Cantina, five minutes away from the ballpark in the Doubletree Hotel. 445 S. Alvernon Way, (602) 881-4200.

### ◆ LODGING

The Doubletree Hotel is about five minutes away. 445 S. Alvernon Way, Tucson, (602) 881-4200.

The Ramada Inn–Foothills lodges visiting teams and is a worthy choice from the many available. It's about 15 minutes away. 6944 E. Tanque Verde, Tucson, (602) 886-9595/(800) 228-2828.

### ◆ DIRECTIONS

Head East on 22nd Street off I-10. Go approximately three miles. The stadium is on the left. Parking is free, but limited. Overflow parking is available on the street. The Toros also run a shuttle to the ballpark from El Con Mall on weekends.

**HI CORBETT FIELD**
**3400 E. Camino Campestre**
**Tucson, AZ 85716**
**(602) 325-2621**

**Capacity: 8,000**
**LF 366, CF 392, RF 348**

### ◆ TICKET AND SCHEDULE INFORMATION

Night games start at 7 P.M. (7:30 P.M. on Friday and Saturday and 6 P.M. on Sunday) in April and May. June-September starts are 7:30 P.M.

The Toros' season opens in early April and ends the first week of September.

Ticket prices: $5 reserved; $4 general admission, $3 seniors, students and children.

# VANCOUVER CANADIANS

## CALIFORNIA ANGELS

**N**at Bailey Stadium opened in 1951 for the PCL Mounties and was named after Nat Bailey, who was a leader in the effort to bring baseball to Vancouver. The Mounties left in 1968, but in 1978, the Canadians joined the PCL.

Vancouver is possibly the most beautiful major city in North America, but there is no great skyline view from the ballpark seats. In fact, you are essentially looking away from downtown when seated. Instead, you get an attractive view of majestic Queen Elizabeth Park, a nice park and the highest point in the city.

The stadium has a quaint feel. Plenty of teams have bleacher bums, but Vancouver's are especially vocal— they sit high up near third base. They even have a newsletter, "The Bum Report." Get a copy if you can.

### ◆ LOCAL AND TEAM HISTORY

Professional baseball in this northwest Canada city goes all the way back to 1904 when Vancouver played in the Class D Oregon State League, which disbanded after only one season. Vancouver did not even make it past the halfway point that year, as the franchise left town in May. Since that ill-fated beginning, Vancouver has spent significantly more time in four other minor leagues: Northwestern (1905, '07-17); Pacific Coast International ('18-21), Western International ('22, '37-42, '46-54), and Pacific Coast ('56-62, '65-69, '78-to date).

OTHER FAMOUS ALUMNI

OTHER FAMOUS ALUMNI

Jack McDowell, Sammy Sosa, Pete Vukovich, Ted Higuera, Wilson Alvarez, B.J. Surhoff, Jose Lind, Chris Bosio, Tom Candiotti, and Roberto Hernandez all played here.

The Canadians arrived in 1978. Ownership has been colorful, including over the years Harry Ornest, Nelson Skalbania and Jim Pattison, three of the most tempestuous sports figures in Canada. The Canadians have been a flighty partner to major-league clubs. Since '78

they have been affiliated with five organizations: Oakland ('78), Milwaukee ('79-86), Pittsburgh ('87), the Chicago White Sox ('88-92) and California ('93-to date).

Hall of Famer Brooks Robinson played 42 games for Vancouver in 1959, batting .331 before being promoted to Baltimore. Pam Postema, the longest-serving female umpire in baseball history (1977-89), never made it to the big leagues, but she did have a memorable game as a PCL ump in Portland in 1984. In a game between the visiting Canadians and the Portland Beavers, she tossed four members of the home team out of the game, including manager Lee Elia for throwing a chair onto the field and the Beavers' batboy for not retrieving Elia's chair. Future big-league managers George Bamberger (1958, 2.45 ERA, best in PCL), Jack McKeon (1962, 72-79 record as skipper) and Tony La Russa (1968, .240) all spent time in Vancouver.

The Canadians won PCL championships in 1985 and '89. In the '89 season, left-hander Tom Drees threw three no-hitters, including two back-to-back.

In 1991 Canadians outfielder Rodney McCray earned highlight-reel immortality when he literally ran through the wooden outfield fence in Portland while trying to make a catch.

### ◆ BALLPARK EXTRAS

Coffee is a favored drink in the Pacific region of Canada. Nat Bailey has an espresso stand to cater to those tastes. You can also get a *latte* or a cappuccino. On a chilly or wet night, it goes down well. Salmon is the special food people clamor for when they visit Vancouver, but it's not available at Nat Bailey.

Check out the Canadians players when they take the field. From a distance, the uniforms make them look like nine Molson's Canadian beer bottles.

### ◆ ATTRACTIONS

Vancouver is almost universally considered the most beautiful major city in North America. The cleanliness of the streets, the immediacy of the snowcapped mountains and the water all around could give it an edge over San Francisco. And there is plenty to do.

Start in Stanley Park. Famed travel writer Jan Morris calls it the finest urban park in the world. We cannot argue. Stanley Park is right on the edge of the downtown.

Whistler Blacksomb Ski Resort is often called the finest skiing facility in North America. It is a two-hour drive. For information, call (604) 932-3434.

The new basketball/hockey arena, GM Place, opens this year, replacing Pacific Coliseum. For information, call (604) 681-2280.

For more information about the Vancouver area, call the Board of Trade, (604) 681-2111.

### ◆ DINING

A chain of popular sports bars, Fog & Suds, has five locations. The one at Broadway and Cambie is closest to the ballpark. 500 W. Broadway, (604) 872-3377.

Nearby, there's also Belair Sports, a comparable spot. 950 W. Broadway, (604) 736-2438.

### ◆ LODGING

The Coast Vancouver Airport Hotel is 15 to 20 minutes away. 1041 S.W. Marine Drive, Vancouver, (604) 263-1555.

The Westin Bayshore is pricey and between 30 and 45 minutes away, but it's right on the water. 1601 W. Georgia, Vancouver, (604) 682-3377/(800) 228-3000.

### ◆ DIRECTIONS

Take Highway 99 to Oak Street, turn right on 41st Avenue, then left on Ontario Street. Parking is plentiful and costs C$2.

**NAT BAILEY STADIUM**
**4601 Ontario Street**
**Vancouver, BC V5V 3H4**
**(604) 872-5232**

**Capacity: 6,500**
**LF 330, CF 407, RF 330**

### ◆ TICKET AND SCHEDULE INFORMATION

Most games are at 7:05 P.M., but the Canadians also have 13 12:15 P.M. starts, businesspeople's specials that are very popular.

The Canadians play from early April to the first week of September.

Ticket prices: C$7.50 box seats, which are essentially sold out; C$6.50 lower reserved. Upper reserved, at C$5.50, are the most available. Safeways in Canada are the exclusive outlet for bleacher seats (C$2).

# EASTERN LEAGUE

The Eastern League has been in continuous operation since 1923, when it was known as the Class B New York–Pennsylvania League (not to be confused with today's New York–Penn League). The EL acquired its current name in 1938 and its Class AA designation in '63. Over the years, many Hall of Famers have played in the Eastern League, including Warren Spahn, Juan Marichal, Early Wynn, Ralph Kiner, Bob Lemon, Jim Palmer and Ken Strong, who eschewed a baseball career for one in football and is now a member of the Pro Football Hall of Fame.

Today in the EL, there are 10 teams spread over seven states—Maryland, New York, Ohio, New Jersey, Connecticut, Maine and Pennsylvania. Each team plays 140 games, with the regular season beginning April 8 and ending September 5. In 1994, the Eastern League set an all-time attendance record, drawing 2,554,570 fans.

• • •

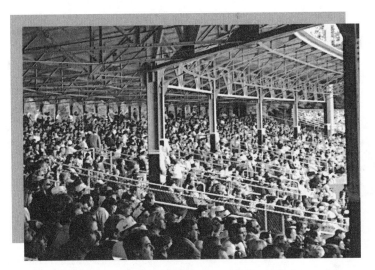

*A packed house watches the Ravens wind up their inaugural season at Yale Field.*

# BINGHAMTON METS

## NEW YORK METS

Fans coming to Binghamton Municipal Stadium, built in 1992, have no trouble figuring out that the New York Mets are the big league parent of the local team—the whole ballpark is painted blue and orange. This is an unspectacular stadium, but there's enough here to make it a good place for a ballgame. The fans are well-informed and beyond the outfield wall there's a terrific view of some upstate New York mountains. Train tracks run behind the fence, but unlike some other minor-league parks, Binghamton does not have a version of "The Longest Home Run in History." Still, El Paso's Tim Unroe came close in the 1994 AA All-Star Game, when he clanked a 400-foot homer off the tracks. On some spring nights, thousands of mayflies inundate the stadium, and though they tend to get into everything, they're more of a curiosity than a nuisance.

### ◆ LOCAL AND TEAM HISTORY

The Binghamton Bingos played several seasons in the New York State, Central and Eastern leagues in the late 19th century, beginning in 1885. In 1902, the Bingos began a 16-year association with the Class B New York State League. This city also spent time in the International (1918-19) and New York–Penn Leagues (1923-37, '64-66). Binghamton was in the Eastern League from 1938 to 1963, then from 1967 to '68, and began its current affiliation with the New York Mets in 1992.

OTHER FAMOUS ALUMNI OTHER FAMOUS ALUMNI

Bert Campaneris and Ken Harrelson also played here.

In 1892, Binghamton beat Providence to capture the EL title. The team was lead by a 19-year-old-rookie outfielder named Wee Willie Keeler. Whitey Ford topped the league in 1949 with a 1.61 ERA while winning 16 games. Future big-league managers Cito Gaston and

Tony La Russa both spent their first summers as pro ballplayers in Binghamton.

In 1955, the club posted an impressive streak in which 18 pinch-hitters in a row either reached base safely or delivered a sacrifice fly.

Overall, Binghamton has brought home 12 league titles during its time in the Eastern League, four more than any other team in the circuit's 71-year history.

### ◆ BALLPARK EXTRAS

Along with the ballpark staples, Binghamton offers a local favorite called the Spiedie, which is cubed marinated chicken breast served on a toasted roll. Some of the best food in the park can be found at the grill down the left-field line. In 1994, a local pool company sponsored a hot tub next to the left-field bullpen.

One favorite nightly promotion is the Go kart race, when a child is chosen from among the fans to try to run the bases before a motorized Go kart can drive from foul pole to foul pole. The players often get involved by dousing the Go kart rider from the dugout to keep him from beating the kids to the finish.

### ◆ ATTRACTIONS

Known as the Carousel Capital of the World, Binghamton and its suburbs are home to six carousels donated to local parks by benefactor George Johnson. They spin from Memorial Day to Labor Day, free of charge. Binghamton's carousel at Ross Park on Morgan Road is the oldest of the group, having been installed in 1920. The park also features a zoo with exotic inhabitants, the Carousel Museum, a playground and a sheltered picnic area in a wooded setting. For information on all of the parks and carousels, call (607) 772-7180.

Cooperstown and the Baseball Hall of Fame is only 76 miles northeast of Binghamton. For information, call (607) 547-9988.

For more information about the Binghamton area, call the Chamber of Commerce, (607) 772-8860.

### ◆ DINING

Cortese, just a couple minutes from the park, offers Italian cuisine in a casual setting. 117 Robinson Street, Binghamton, (607) 723-6440

Scott's Oquaga Lake House is one of the fine restaurants in the area and its scenic setting in the Oquaga Lake resort hotel also sets it apart. It's about 30 minutes from the ballpark. Oquaga Lake, Deposit, (607) 467-3094.

### ◆ LODGING

Holiday Inn Arena is about five minutes from the ballpark. 2-8 Hawley Street, Binghamton, (607) 722-1212/(800) HOLIDAY.

Comfort Inn is about 10 minutes from the park. 1156 Front Street, Binghamton, (607) 722-5353/(800) 4-CHOICE.

## ◆ DIRECTIONS

I-81 to exit 4S. Merge with traffic through one light and over an overpass to Route 11. Follow through two traffic lights to Henry Street. Parking is plentiful and costs $3.

**BINGHAMTON MUNICIPAL STADIUM**
211 Henry Street
Binghamton, NY 13902
(607) 723-6387

Capacity: 6,064
LF 330, CF 400, RF 330

## ◆ TICKET AND SCHEDULE INFORMATION

Game times are generally at 7 P.M. weeknights and 1:30 P.M. Saturdays and Sundays. Saturday home games move to 7 P.M. after July 1.

The Mets open their schedule in early April and they close out the first week of September.

Ticket prices: $10 luxury box seats, which provide waitress service; $6.50 box seats; $5.50 reserved grandstand; $4.50 general admission, sold day of game only. Children 14 and under and seniors 60 and over receive $1 off all tickets.

# BOWIE BAYSOX

### BALTIMORE ORIOLES

To call Prince Georges County Stadium a work in progress in 1994 would have been a serious understatement. Throughout the winter of 1993-94, the Baysox endured innumerable weather-related construction delays, causing the team to push back the opening date for their new ballpark several times. Although the first game at the stadium was played on June 16, much work still remained to be done before everything would be finally in place. On Opening Day, there was an unpaved parking lot, no permanent rest rooms, no clubhouses, no running water in the trailers used as the players' changing rooms, and no permanent concession stands. But the Baysox braved their 1994 stadium difficulties, eventually ending up with an attractive new ballpark.

The stadium, built in a slight depression, with the

outfield fence ringed by lush trees, offers an excellent setting for baseball. In PG Stadium's inaugural summer, several players also remarked that on certain nights, a light mist would roll across the outfield, perhaps aided by the ballpark's location in the bottom of a bowl. The Baysox and their fans can now enjoy this team's fully completed ballpark, the largest and most appealing minor-league stadium in the Washington area.

## ◆ LOCAL AND TEAM HISTORY

The Baysox are the first organized-baseball team to be located in Bowie. From 1989 to '92, the franchise was based in Hagerstown, Maryland (where the team was known as the Suns), before moving to Baltimore for the 1993 season. That was the first year a big-league and a minor-league team had shared a city since 1915, when the Indians and the Spiders (an American Association franchise) both played in Cleveland. While in Baltimore, the Baysox played baseball at Memorial Stadium, the Orioles' home before that team moved downtown to Camden Yards. Bowie's tenure at Memorial makes the Baysox the last organized-baseball team to play at this venerable stadium, which is now home to a Canadian Football League squad.

## ◆ BALLPARK EXTRAS

Since Chesapeake Bay is nearby, you should not be surprised to find some good crab cakes on the menu here. The grilled sausages and Italian ices are noteworthy as well. The Baysox also have a local microbeer on sale. Down each foul line, on both sides of the uncovered grandstand, there are two grassy embankments. Fans bring blankets and chairs to spread here for a comfortable view of the action. These hills are also prime foulball territory. As such, they are well patrolled by the kids who have come out to the ballgame. PG Stadium features two scoreboards, one for the inning-by-inning score and the second to display various player, team and promotional graphics.

## ◆ ATTRACTIONS

Bowie Race Track features Thoroughbred horse racing. For further information, call (410) 741-1355.

Washington is fewer than 20 minutes away. For information about the many sites in the capital, call (800) 422-8644 or (202) 789-7000.

Annapolis, with such attractions as the U.S. Naval Academy, the Maryland State House and the historic quarter, is about 10 miles west of Bowie. For further information, call (410) 268-TOUR.

For additional information about this area, call the Prince Georges County Conference and Visitor's Bureau, (301) 925-8300.

## ◆ DINING

Rip's Country Inn, adjacent to the ballpark, offers a variety of seafood and chicken dishes. Ask about the daily seafood special. U.S. 301, (301) 805-5900.

La Gringada, about a ¼ mile south of Rip's, offers moderately priced Mexican food, including such novel dishes as a Burrito del Mar stuffed with crabmeat and a seafood quesadilla. U.S. 301, (301) 262-5454.

### ◆ LODGING

Comfort Inn is near the intersection of U.S. 301 and U.S. 50 on State Route 3, across the street from the park. (301) 464-0089/(800) 4-CHOICE.

Rip's Country Inn is located behind Rip's Restaurant. (301) 805-5900/(800) 359-RIPS.

### ◆ DIRECTIONS

From U.S. 50, exit at Collington Road/State Route 197. Go south on 197. After about one mile, turn left at the traffic light on U.S. 301 north. Turn right at the first traffic light and drive into the ballpark's parking lot. There is plenty of free parking available.

> **PRINCE GEORGES COUNTY STADIUM**
> P.O. Box 1661
> Bowie, MD 20717
> (301) 805-6000
> ———————————
> Capacity: 10,000
> LF 309, CF 400, RF 309

### ◆ TICKET AND SCHEDULE INFORMATION

Most games are played at night, starting at 7:05 P.M. Sunday and doubleheaders begin at 2:05 P.M. and 6:05 P.M. respectively. Verify all game times with the Baysox.

The Baysox' home opener is usually in early April, and the season ends in the first week of September.

Ticket prices: $7 reserved box seat; $5 general admission, $3 seniors 60 and over and children 5 to 14. Children under 5 are free.

# CANTON/ AKRON INDIANS

## CLEVELAND INDIANS

This ballpark, built in 1989 and visible from the nearby interstate highway, is not particularly memorable. The grandstand, roof and floor in this horseshoe-shaped stadium are all made of metal. Foul balls can make a loud, lasting impression on nearby fans when the balls strike any part of the metal structure. There is a picnic pavilion down the first-base line, with tables reserved for groups of 25 or more. Canton's proximity to Cleveland is the biggest plus here, since big-league Indians fans have an easy time keeping close track of their team's hottest AA prospects.

Thurman Munson Memorial Stadium was named in honor of the town's most famous baseball native son, who was killed here in August 1979 while practicing takeoffs and landings in his private plane. Munson's widow still lives in the Canton area.

### ◆ LOCAL AND TEAM HISTORY

Canton spent several seasons in the Tri-State League in the late 1880s. After the turn of the century, Canton was associated with the Central (1905-07, '12, '28-30, '32) and Ohio-Pennsylvania leagues (1905, '08-11). This city also fielded teams in the Interstate (1913), Buckeye (1915) and Middle Atlantic leagues (1936-42). Through many of these years, Canton and nearby Akron, just minutes away to the north, were rivals in the same leagues. Canton and Akron joined forces in 1989, the same year this franchise began its current affiliation with Cleveland.

Cy Young made his pro debut with Canton in 1890.

**OTHER FAMOUS ALUMNI**

Rube Marquard, Bill McKechnie, Jim Thorpe, Manny Ramirez, Albert Belle, and Charles Nagy all played here.

On April 30, he defeated Wheeling 4-2 for his first win in organized baseball, and less than three months later he threw his first no-hitter, beating McKeesport 4-1. The latter turned out to be his last game for Canton. After winning 15 games and striking out 201 in 260 innings, his contract was bought by the Cleveland Spiders.

Though the team housed at Thurman Munson Memorial Stadium bears the name of both cities, it is situated in Canton. That may not be the case for many more years, however.

The team will be moving from Canton to Akron as club officials are not thrilled with the current facility, citing dissatisfaction with such items as poor drainage. The mayor of Akron has pledged that his city will build a $10 million, 8,500-seat stadium there that could be ready for the Indians as early as 1997. Negotiations continue regarding the details of the move. It's no surprise that despite sharing a club since 1989, there is once again some animosity between the two cities when it comes to their ballclub.

### ◆ BALLPARK EXTRAS
Check out the Bases Loaded Grill, an enclosed area on the concourse behind first base. The best food in the ballpark is right here, including specialty items like kielbasa, steak sandwiches and chili dogs.

### ◆ ATTRACTIONS
The Canton area offers many cultural highlights to visitors such as its art institute, ballet, symphony orchestra and civic opera, all located at 1001 Market Avenue NW. These are all part of the city's Cultural Center for the Arts, which you can call at (216) 452-4096 for more information.

The Canton Classic Car Museum is located at 555 Market Avenue S and can be reached at (216) 455-3603.

Canton may be most famous for being the home of the Pro Football Hall of Fame, fittingly located at 2121 George Halas Drive NW. For further information, call (216) 456-8207.

For more information about this area, call the Canton Chamber of Commerce, (216) 456-7253.

### ◆ DINING
Damon's is a family restaurant with a casual atmosphere, about 10 minutes from the ballpark. 4220 Belden Village Avenue NW, Canton, (216) 492-2413.

Mulligan's Pub has award-winning food, and it's also about 10 minutes away. 4118 Belden Village Avenue NW, Canton, (216) 493-8239.

### ◆ LODGING
Parke Hotel is about 20 minutes from the park. 4343 Everhard Road, Canton, (216) 499-9410.

Holiday Inn–Belden Village is at exit 109 off I-77, about 20 minutes away. (216) 494-2770/(800) HOLIDAY.

### ◆ DIRECTIONS
From I-77, take exit 103/Cleveland Avenue. Turn right at the traffic light and then left onto Mill Road. Turn left at the stop sign onto Allen Avenue. The ballpark, less than a mile from the highway, will be immediately visible. Plentiful parking is available for $1 a car.

---

**THURMAN MUNSON MEMORIAL STADIUM**
**2501 Allen Avenue SE**
**Canton, OH 44707**
**(216) 456-5100**

**Capacity: 5,500**
**LF 330, CF 400, RF 330**

---

### ◆ TICKET AND SCHEDULE INFORMATION
Games starts at 7:15 P.M.; 1:35 P.M. on Sundays.

The Indians' season opens in early May and ends the first week of September.

Ticket prices: $5 reserved seats; $4 general admission; $3 children under 14.

## HARDWARE CITY ROCK CATS

### MINNESOTA TWINS

Ninety miles from New York City, New Britain is a blue-collar city in the middle of Connecticut and is home to the Stanley Works, a major manufacturer of tools that led to the city's nickname, "Hardware City." Beehive Field is not a high-tech place, with the look and feel of a much older, quaint ballpark. But a new era appears to be beginning this season as the former New Britain Red Sox club has switched not only affiliation, to the Minnesota Twins, but a lot of other things as well. The red socks are gone, replaced by team colors of red, purple, gold and black and a logo featuring a cat with an earring, leather coat, shades and electric guitar.

### ◆ LOCAL AND TEAM HISTORY
New Britain's organized-baseball debut came in 1909 when this city began a three-year relationship with the

Class B Connecticut League, followed by a one-season (1914) membership in the Eastern Association. New Britain joined the Eastern League in 1984. This is the city's first year of affiliation with the Minnesota Twins. Future Boston Red Sox skipper Butch Hobson managed New Britain in 1989 and '90. In 1990, two of his players had significant seasons. Jeff Bagwell was the Eastern League MVP, leading the circuit in total bases (220), hits and doubles while batting .333. Kevin Morton pitched the third perfect game in EL history on August 25, beating Reading 1-0.

OTHER FAMOUS ALUMNI OTHER FAMOUS ALUMNI

Roger Clemens, Ellis Burks, Steve Lyons, Greg Blosser and Mo Vaughn have all played here.

Beehive Field will be replaced in 1996 by a new stadium, also in the Willow Brook Park Complex. The prospect of a new stadium helped keep the team in town as New Britain came close to losing its team to Springfield, Massachusetts, where the former Boston brass wanted the team. After much consideration, club owner Joe Buzas decided to keep the team in New Britain, though he knew that would in effect signal the end of the team's Red Sox affiliation, which had lasted 38 years and dated back to the club's previous locations.

### ◆ BALLPARK EXTRAS

New Britain's games are called by the radio team of Jim Lucas and Don Wardlow, who have been partners since their days together at Glassboro State College (now Rowan College). Lucas does the play-by-play while Wardlow, who has been blind since birth, does the color commentary. They are joined by one of the most popular visitors to the ballpark, Gizmo the Wonder Dog—Wardlow's guide dog, a beautiful black Labrador. The two announcers invite fan participation, and on Saturday home games fans are invited to join them for an inning of "fantasy play-by-play."

### ◆ ATTRACTIONS

Bishop Farms in nearby Cheshire is a 200-year-old working farm with apple orchards, cider press, fruit winery and farm animals. It's open through mid-June and then reopens in early August. 500 S. Meriden, Route 70, Cheshire, (203) 272-8243.

The New Britain Museum of American Art is the oldest museum collection devoted exclusively to American art and has a permanent collection of more than 3,000 works, including some particularly notable murals by

Thomas Hart Benton. 56 Lexington Street, New Britain. (203) 229-0257.

For more information about this area, call the Chamber of Commerce, (203) 229-1665.

### ◆ DINING

Portofino's, just a minute away, offers Italian food, including pizza. 246 New Britain Road, Kensington, (203) 826-6374.

Hawthorne Motor Inn is just a few minutes from New Britain and has an award-winning restaurant famous for its prime rib. 2387 Wilbur Cross Highway, Berlin, (203) 828-4181.

### ◆ LODGING

Ramada Inn is about 15 minutes from the park. 65 Columbus Boulevard, New Britain, (203) 224-9161/(800) 228-2828.

### ◆ DIRECTIONS

I-84 to exit 39A, Route 9 South. Take to exit 25 (Ellis Street) then left at next light onto S. Main Street. Ballpark is a mile up on the right. From I-91 or Route 15 (the Wilbur Cross Parkway), take to Route 9 North to exit 24 for Route 71. First exit will be for Willow Brook Park. Parking is plentiful and free.

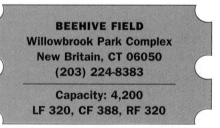

**BEEHIVE FIELD**
**Willowbrook Park Complex**
**New Britain, CT 06050**
**(203) 224-8383**

**Capacity: 4,200**
**LF 320, CF 388, RF 320**

### ◆ TICKET AND SCHEDULE INFORMATION

Games start at 7:15 P.M. and 2 P.M. Sundays, with Saturday 2 P.M. starts in April.

The Rock Cats open their season in early April and finish the first week of September.

Ticket prices: $5 box seats; $4.50 reserved seats; $4 general admission, $2 seniors, $1.50 children 12 and under.

# HARRISBURG SENATORS

## MONTREAL EXPOS

The best aspect of Riverside Stadium is its setting on City Island Park in the middle of the Susquehanna River. As you walk to the stadium, you can watch boats sail along the Susquehanna, or gaze at the gold-domed State Capitol on the other side of the river and the many hills which mark Harrisburg's environs. The stadium, which opened in 1987, is bordered by a football/soccer field containing statues of a pitcher and umpire. The Little Grabber Railroad stops right outside Riverside's front gate and offers tours of City Island. Although the ballpark itself is not the most architecturally interesting in the minors, it features a covered metal grandstand, and its surroundings make this a great place to spend an evening.

### ◆ LOCAL AND TEAM HISTORY

Harrisburg fielded a pro baseball team as early as 1883 when this city was associated with the short-lived Inter-State Association, a league that disbanded following the '83 season. Several other pro teams played here through the remaining years of the 19th century. In 1907, Harrisburg began a relationship with organized baseball laregly uninterrupted over the next 45 years, which saw Pennsylvania's capital city belong to five different minor-league circuits: Class B Tri-State League (1907-14); Class AA International League (1915); Class B New York State (1916-17); Class B New York–Pennsylvania (1924-35) and Class B Interstate (1940-42, '46-52). Following a 34-year absence, baseball returned here in 1987 when Harrisburg joined the Eastern League. Harrisburg also hosted the Giants of the Eastern Colored League for four years (1924-27). The Senators

**OTHER FAMOUS ALUMNI**

Moises Alou, Rondell White, Cliff Floyd, Wes Chamberlin, Rafael Belliard, Orlando Merced, and Mike Lansing have all played here.

began their current affiliation with the Expos in 1991. From 1991 to '94, the Senators' record of 347-207 was the best among all minor-league teams.

Frank Grant, considered one of the best African-American ballplayers of the 19th century, batted .333 for Harrisburg in 1890. Hall of Famer Oscar Charleston, who was a player or manager in the Negro leagues from 1915 to '54, was one of the greatest players to come out of segregated baseball. He was known for his aggressiveness and tremendous intensity. There is a legend that Charleston once even ripped the white hood from the head of a Klu Klux Klansman and then dared him to speak his mind. Charleston was the player/manager for the Harrisburg Giants from 1924 to '27. In '25, he led the Eastern Colored League with an almost unbelievable .445 batting average. Fellow Hall of Famer "Sliding Billy" Hamilton played two seasons for Harrisburg (1905-06). In '05, he batted .342 for the Tri-State League's Senators. Art "The Great" Shires, a former pro wrestler and boxer who had one bout with a center for the Chicago Bears, finished his 10-year baseball career here in 1935 with a .244 batting average.

### ◆ BALLPARK EXTRAS

A two-tiered picnic area overlooks the Senators' bullpen. Riverside has several good concession items at the Hot Corner Grill, which is not behind third base, as its name would suggest, but instead is in back of first. While burgers and hot dogs are sold here, check out the revolving menu, which changes each home stand. Noteworthy choices include cheese steaks and Italian sausages.

### ◆ ATTRACTIONS

The Pride of the Susquehanna, an old-fashioned paddle wheeler, docks on City Island next to the ballpark. Various river cruises are available. For further information, call (717) 234-6500.

The State Museum of Pennsylvania has several historical exhibits including an enormous painting that depicts the Battle of Gettysburg. There is also a planetarium. For further information, call (717) 787-4978.

For additional information about Harrisburg, call the Mayor's Office, (717) 255-3040.

### ◆ DINING

In Riverside Park, immediately adjacent to the stadium, you will find picnic tables and food kiosks featuring several items, including grilled burgers, chicken and surprisingly good crab cakes. Come to the ballpark early, grab a meal here and watch a variety of boats sail by on the Susquehanna River.

### ◆ LODGING

Harrisburg Hilton & Towers is located off the 2nd Street exit of I-83, about 10 minutes from the ballpark. (717) 233-6271/(800) HILTON.

Comfort Inn East is located at exit 29 off I-83, about

15 minutes from the ballpark. (717) 561-8100/(800) 4-CHOICE.

◆ **DIRECTIONS:**
Take the 2nd Street exit from I-83. Stay on 2nd until Market Street and turn left. Take the Market Street Bridge over the Susquehanna. Take your first right on the bridge at the sign for City Island Park. After parking, walk under the pedestrian bridge and the ballpark will be in front of you. Island parking costs $1 and is plentiful. If you present your Senators' ticket at selected downtown lots, you can park for $1 and take the pedestrian bridge over the river to Riverside Stadium.

**RIVERSIDE STADIUM**
P.O. Box 15757
Harrisburg, PA 17105
(717) 231-4444
_____

Capacity: 6,300
LF 335, CF 400, RF 335

◆ **TICKET AND SCHEDULE INFORMATION:**
Most games are played at night, starting at 7:05 P.M. Sunday games begin at 2:05 P.M.

The Senators' season opens in early April, and it ends in the first week of September.

Ticket prices: $7 box seats; $6 reserved seats; $5 general admission, $3 seniors 55 and over and children 12 and under.

# NEW HAVEN RAVENS

## COLORADO ROCKIES

**S**teel columns and concrete arches reminiscent of the original Comiskey Park give Yale Field—still the home of Yale's varsity squad—the look and feel of a comfortable, old-time ballpark; it's not surprising, since it opened in 1927. But after renovations by the Ravens in preparation for their inaugural '94 season, all that remains of the original structure are the concrete outside wall, the center-field Green Monster and those columns. The center-field wall

here, 25 feet high and 405 feet from home plate, is a local conversation piece for reasons other than its dimensions. It was built after World War II of steel from ships that sailed during that conflict. In 1994, the so-called Green Monster also contained a hand-operated scoreboard. The wall and scoreboard have been refurbished for '95, although the board remains at least in part manually operated, preserving one of this park's most attractive features. In the nearly 70-year history of Yale Field, only three balls have been hit over the monster. One came in 1994 when New Britain's Jose Malave belted a home run to center that traveled nearly 500 feet.

Moving in from the outfield, find a seat in Yale Field's metal-floored grandstand. You won't have a hard time finding some shade because the grandstand is completely covered from first to third by a roof of interlocking steel beams. Also, the foul territory here is unusually large.

◆ **LOCAL AND TEAM HISTORY**
Professional baseball in New Haven dates back to 1894, when this city fielded a team in the Connecticut League. From 1902 to '14, New Haven teams were associated with the Connecticut State League and Eastern Association. After a 16-year stint in the Eastern League (1916-32), organized baseball left town until 1994 when the Ravens returned to the Eastern League as an expansion team. From 1972 to '82, the adjacent town of West Haven had its own team in the EL.

"Bird Dog" Hopper, who did not win a single game during his three years in the majors, led all minor-league hurlers with 31 wins while pitching for New Haven in 1913. New Haven native Pop Foster did double duty as a batter and pitcher for his hometown team in 1912. He led the Class B Connecticut League in home runs (9) and winning percentage (15-5, .750). Hall of Famer Albert "Chief" Bender pitched three seasons in New Haven (1920-21, '24) following the end of his big-league career. In 1920, the first of his two-year stint as New Haven's player-manager, Bender led the Eastern League in games (47), innings pitched (324) and wins (25). Fellow Hall of Famer Joe Cronin batted .320 in 66 games for New Haven in 1926.

OTHER FAMOUS ALUMNI
OTHER FAMOUS ALUMNI
Ron Darling, George Bush, Smokey Joe Wood and Ken McKenzie either played or managed here.

## ♦ BALLPARK EXTRAS

The fans here are among the league's loudest and most knowledgeable. When one of the Ravens gets a hit or makes a good play, the fans stomp their feet on the metal floor; it can be deafening when things are going well for the home team. There's not much room in the concession concourse below the grandstand, so it can get crowded here.

Among the menu selections, try a Hummel hot dog and Elm City beer, both made in New Haven. There is a picnic area down the right-field line and behind the right-field wall. The team also stages a Closest-to-the-Pin promotion. A golf flagstick is placed in center field, and from a mini-green behind first base fans hit golf balls at it.

## ♦ ATTRACTIONS

Yale University held its first classes here in 1701. For further information about the campus and its museums, call (203) 432-2300. Outside of New Haven is West Rock Ridge State Park and Nature Center, near Merritt Parkway exit 60. Admission is free. For further information, call (203) 787-8016.

For additional information about this area, call the New Haven Chamber of Commerce, (203) 787-6735.

## ♦ DINING

Michelangelo Pizza & Restaurant is about five minutes from the ballpark. Michelangelo's features a large variety of very good homemade breads and unique pizza toppings such as eggplant and tomato, and tomato, spinach and pesto, plus stuffed white pizza. 425 W. Derby Avenue, New Haven, (203) 389-1603.

## ♦ LODGING

Holiday Inn at Yale is about 10 minutes from the ballpark on Whalley Avenue, in New Haven. (203) 777-6221/(800) HOLIDAY.

Days Hotel New Haven/West Haven is at exit 42 from I-95 in West Haven, about 15 minutes from the ballpark. (203) 933-0344/(800) 325-2525.

## ♦ DIRECTIONS

From I-95, take exit 44, State Route 10/Kimberly Avenue. Follow signs to the Yale Bowl on Route 10 North. At the first light after I-95, turn left. After about 2½ miles turn left on Derby Avenue, Route 34. The ballpark is about ¼ of a mile further up on your left. Parking is available in several area lots. The premium lot is on X/Y Drive, with a fee of $3 per car. Parking is available for $1 inside the Yale Bowl and in Lot A north, adjacent to Volvo Stadium. On-street parking may be found on Yale Drive across Derby Avenue from the ballpark.

---

**YALE FIELD**
63 Grove Street
New Haven, CT 06511
(203) 782-1666

Capacity: 6,200
LF 335, CF 405, RF 315

---

## ♦ TICKET AND SCHEDULE INFORMATION

Most games are played at night, starting at 7:05 P.M. Sunday games begin at 2:05 P.M.

The Ravens' home opener is usually in early April, and the season ends in the first week of September.

Ticket prices: $12.50 luxury box seats; $7 box seats; $5 reserved seats; $3 general admission, $2 seniors and children. Children 5 and under are free.

# NORWICH NAVIGATORS

## NEW YORK YANKEES

The as-yet-unnamed stadium being built in the Norwich industrial park for an estimated cost of $9.3 million will feature most of the state-of-the-art accoutrements being provided at the new parks such as sky boxes and a 46-by-56-foot scoreboard. The scoreboard will include instant replay—a minor-league first.

## ♦ LOCAL AND TEAM HISTORY

The Navigators revive a long-gone tradition of baseball in Norwich—the town was a member of the Connecticut League from 1902 to '07 and a member of the Connecticut Association during that circuit's only season, 1910.

Although the current team's history is brief, the enthusiasm generated has been great. The club received more than 600 entries for its "name-the-team" contest, and the name was chosen to reflect the region's nautical ties. The team colors, however, bear no resemblance to the parent club's staid pinstripes—look for green and purple at the ballpark.

## ♦ BALLPARK EXTRAS

There is an outdoor grill which serves up hot dogs, burgers, and barbecued chicken. Such accompaniments as baked beans and cole slaw are also available.

## ◆ ATTRACTIONS

Norwich is just 15 miles from the Mystic Seaport and its shops and museum as well as its Seaquarium, all of which reflect the great nautical history of the area (203-572-5315). It is also 15 miles from New London and its beaches.

The Foxwoods High Stakes Bingo and Casino is less than 8 miles from the stadium, in Ledyard. For information, call (800) FOXWOOD.

Despite the attractions in the surrounding towns, Norwich itself is quite lovely and its history is filled with lore from Revolutionary days. There are several annual fairs held in the summer, such as the Cherry Blossom Festival in May, the Rose Arts Festival in June and the Antique Auto Show in July.

The Norwich Tourism Commission can be reached at (203) 886-2381, ext. 228.

## ◆ DINING

Americus on the Wharf (1 American Wharf, 203-887-8555), Bella Fiore (543 W. Thames Street, 203-887-9030) and Old Tymes Restaurant (360 W. Main Street, 203-887-6865) are all within a few minutes' drive of the stadium site in the town of Norwich. There are also several pizza parlors in town on West Main Street, including Mystic Pizza, which claims to be the restaurant that inspired the film of the same name.

## ◆ LODGING

If you want to make this a completely idyllic experience and spend the extra dollars, check out the Norwich Inn & Spa, a unique combo of New England inn, luxury villa and modern spa, about 10 minutes from the ballpark. Options include skin-care treatments, fitness classes and all the other spa pleasures. 607 W. Thames Street (Route 32), Norwich, (203) 886-2401.

The Norwich Motel is between 10 and 15 minutes from the ballpark. 181 W. Town Street, Norwich, (203) 889-2671.

Ramada Inn of Norwich is 15 to 20 minutes away. 10 Laura Boulevard, Norwich, (203) 889-5201/(800) 228-2828.

## ◆ DIRECTIONS

From the south, take I-395 north to exit 81W, Routes 2 & 32. Follow Route 32 to Willimantic exit; right onto New Park Avenue; left on Wisconsin Avenue; right onto Stott Avenue. Stadium is at top of hill. From the north, I-395 south to exit 82. Right onto West Town Street. Right onto Connecticut Avenue. Left on Wisconsin Avenue and follow previous directions. Parking is plentiful and costs $2. Overflow parking is also available at the ballpark.

## ◆ TICKET AND SCHEDULE INFORMATION

Most games are played at night, beginning at 7 P.M. Sunday games start at 2 P.M., as do the first four Saturday games of the season.

The Navigators begin their season in early April and end it the first week of September.

Ticket prices: $8 premier seats; $7.50 box seats; $6 reserved seats; $5 general admission; $3.50 for seniors over 62 and children under 16.

# PORTLAND SEA DOGS

### FLORIDA MARLINS

The Sea Dogs began play in 1994 with a bang, drawing 375,187 fans to shatter the old Eastern league mark of 324,003 set back in 1985 by the Albany Yankees. Among that record attendance were such luminaries as former president George Bush and his wife, Barbara, novelist Stephen King and rock star Bruce Hornsby.

The ambience at the ballpark is much friendlier than its hot-selling logo, a fierce-looking Slugger the Sea Dog chomping a baseball bat. Hadlock Stadium, though brand-new and state-of-the-art, has the type of old-time facade that has become so popular since the advent of Baltimore's Camden Yards. It fits in nicely with Portland.

The state's maritime history is honored by a spinning lighthouse that appears on the electronic scoreboard every time a Sea Dogs player hits a home run.

## ◆ LOCAL AND TEAM HISTORY

Portland was the site of minor-league baseball off and on between 1907 and '49 in several different leagues. After that there was no pro ball in Maine until the Maine Guides of Old Orchard Beach played in the International League between 1984 and '88.

Willard "Grasshopper" Mains, who pitched from 1887 to 1906, was the first minor-league pitcher to win

300 games. His 318-179 record (.640) is the third-best all-time among minor-league hurlers. Mains won a total of 18 games in two seasons (1893-94) with Portland.

From 1913 to '16, the Portland team was owned and managed by Hugh Duffy, who called the team the Duffs. His .438 batting average in 1894 is still the major-league single-season record.

Baseball returned to the state in 1994 when the Eastern League expanded by two cities to make room for affiliates of the most recent expansion franchises, the Florida Marlins and the Colorado Rockies. Portland was not only the smallest market (just over 64,000) of the 13 finalists for a new Eastern League franchise but the last one to put in its entry as well, so it was something of an upset when it received the Marlins' AA team.

One of the movers and shakers among the current Portland baseball cognoscenti is Dan Burke, former CEO of CBS.

Opening Day 1994 was a sellout—6,274 fans squished in—and a trio of ticketless local boys built a treehouse to watch the game, near the elevated railroad tracks that run behind left field.

### ◆ BALLPARK EXTRAS
It would be wrong to go to a ballpark in New England and not get some good seafood, so the team offers a Sea Dog, a tasty fish-fillet sandwich. Other offerings include steak-and-cheese and meatball subs.

### ◆ ATTRACTIONS
There's a reason people call Maine "America's vacationland." From its beaches to its pine-forest parks, there are few places more beautiful. Located near the Atlantic Ocean in southern Maine on a peninsula jetting into Casco Bay, Portland is within 15 miles of coastal landscapes and quaint country villages.

There are shopping outlets galore for the bargain hunter, including the famous L.L. Bean factory in Freeport, north of Portland (800-341-4341), and The Old Port, a shopping square of more than 100 stores located on the Portland waterfront.

For more information about Portland, call the Chamber of Commerce, (207) 772-5800.

### ◆ DINING
There are countless seafood restaurants in the area and if there is a place to splurge on lobster, Portland is it.

Sportsman's Grill advertises itself as being "just a foul ball from Hadlock Field" and is one of the top spaghetti/sports bars (!) in Maine. They also offer a full menu of burgers, chicken, wings and Boston-style barbecue, and have five satellite TVs. 909 Congress Street, (207) 772-9324.

The Snow Squall is about 10 minutes from the park, and features such delicacies as lobster fettuccine and grilled salmon fillets. South Portland Waterfront, (207) 799-2232.

### ◆ LODGING
Sonesta Portland Hotel is about two minutes from the ballpark. 157 High Street, Portland, (207) 775-5411.

Embassy Suites is between five and 10 minutes away. 1050 Westbrook Street, Portland, (207) 775-2200/(800) 362-2779.

### ◆ DIRECTIONS
Take I-295 to exit 5A, Congress Street East. Merge onto Congress, stay left. Turn left at St. John Street, the first light. Stay right and merge onto Park Avenue. Parking is limited, but free. Parking is also available in area lots and on the street. The team runs shuttle buses from parking areas elsewhere in Portland.

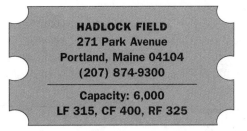

**HADLOCK FIELD**
**271 Park Avenue**
**Portland, Maine 04104**
**(207) 874-9300**

**Capacity: 6,000**
**LF 315, CF 400, RF 325**

### ◆ TICKET AND SCHEDULE INFORMATION
Weeknight games vary between 6 P.M. and 7 P.M. starts, mostly 7 P.M. after mid-May, while weekend games vary among 1 P.M., 4 P.M. and 7 P.M.

The Sea Dogs open their 1995 season in early April and close out the first week of September.

Ticket prices: $6 box seats, $5 seniors (62 and older) and children (16 and under); $5 reserved seats, $4 seniors and children; $4 general admission, $2 seniors and children.

# READING PHILLIES

## PHILADELPHIA PHILLIES

A 1992 renovation to this classic ballpark, first opened in 1950, made it even more comfortable and attractive than it was before while improving upon its historical qualities. The stadium's new front entrance, with brick arches and a plaza, evokes memories of old-time stadiums. As you walk through the plaza and into the park, there is a display case to the right with replicas of bats used by such former Reading Phillies as Larry Bowa, Ryne Sandberg, Julio Franco and Greg "The Bull" Luzinski. Turn right on the concourse to view several pictures of past Phillies' teams plus a display listing all Reading players who have reached the majors since Philadelphia began its affiliation with this city in 1967. Check out the nearby plaques honoring members of the Reading Hall of Fame. Walk out beyond the grandstand and look up to the roof. The flag with the No. 24 honors Mike Schmidt, the only player to have had his number retired by Reading. Look beyond the outfield fence and you will see a brick wall nearly 500 feet from home plate. It is said that Luzinski's home runs often reached this barrier when he played here in 1970.

### ◆ LOCAL AND TEAM HISTORY

Reading was a charter franchise in the Interstate League back in 1883. In the early part of the 20th century, this city had several organized-baseball teams in four different circuits—Class B Tri State (1907-12, '14), Class B New York State (1916-17), Class B Interstate (1940-41) and Class AA International (1919-31). Reading first joined the Eastern League in 1933.

Hall of Famer Frank "Home Run" Baker was in his second pro season in 1908 when he slugged six homers (three behind the league leader) for Reading in 1908. Fellow Hall of Famer Bucky Harris was Reading's second baseman nine years later. Fred Merkle, who committed the infamous baserunning miscue known as the Merkle Boner in 1908 while with the New York Giants, managed Reading in 1927. Merkle's bad luck continued as his club lost 31 straight games and finished 68 games out of first with a record of 43-123, the worst in organized baseball that year. In 1953, Rocky Colavito helped the Reading Indians to an Eastern League pennant by pacing the circuit with 28 home runs and 121 runs batted in. Two years later, Roger Maris hit 19 homers for Reading. More recently, Greg Luzinski tore up the EL in 1970, leading the league in games (141), runs scored (94), runs batted in (120) and batting average (.325). He narrowly missed the Triple Crown as his 33 homers were one behind league leader Richie Zisk's 34. The next year, Mike Schmidt was a 21-year-old rookie when he hit .211 for Reading. Ryne Sandberg and Julio Franco both hit over .300 when they played here in the early 1980s,

OTHER FAMOUS ALUMNI

OTHER FAMOUS ALUMNI

Jim Perry, Dallas Green, Bob Boone, Carl Furillo, Kevin Stocker and Kevin Gross all played here.

and Darren Daulton hit 19 home runs for Reading in 1983.

### ◆ BALLPARK EXTRAS

Behind the left-field wall is an area known as the Deck. Here, fans can get something to eat or drink plus an outfielder's view of the ballgame. While on the Deck, try Yuengling beer, made in nearby Pottsville at one of the oldest breweries (circa 1829) in the USA. The Phillies sell a large variety of good concession items. In the right-field food-court area, you can sample grilled chicken, burgers and sausage. Other noteworthy items are meatball heroes, pizza, "hat full of fries," funnel cakes and locally made Berks hot dogs, which compare very well with the competition in other ballparks. Since Philadelphia is not far away, the fans here are definitely Phillies loyalists. Like their Philadelphia counterparts, they can also turn on hometown players, although not as vociferously as the Veterans Stadium regulars. In 1994, Reading fans came down hard on a perennially struggling Jeff Jackson, a Phillies former No.1 draft pick. The clubhouses here are located at opposite ends of the concourse. To get to and from the dugouts, the players must walk through the crowd, creating prime autograph and vegetable-throwing opportunities.

### ◆ ATTRACTIONS

Several large manufacturers' outlet malls are located in and around Reading. For further information, call (800) 772-8336.

The Berks County Heritage Center, housed in a restored 19th-century factory, contains several historical displays with an industrial perspective. Admission is $2.50, $2 for seniors over 60, $1.50 for children 7 to 18. For further information, call (610) 374-8839.

For additional information about the Reading area, call the Berks County Visitors' Bureau, (800) 443-6610.

### ◆ DINING

The Peanut Bar, in business since the 1920s and about 15 minutes from the ballpark, is a Reading institution. Watch out for the peanut-shell-covered floor. 332 Penn Street, (610) 376-8500.

Mike's Sandwich Shop is down the street from the stadium and offers a wide selection of good sandwiches and hoagies. 1755 Centre Avenue, (610) 374-2626.

### ◆ LODGING

Comfort Inn is on U.S. 222 near U.S. 422, about 15 minutes from the ballpark. (610) 371-0500/(800) 4-CHOICE.

Dutch Colony Inn is on U.S. 422, about 15 minutes from the ballpark. (610) 779-2345/(800) 828-2830.

### ◆ DIRECTIONS

From the Pennsylvania Turnpike, take U.S. 222 north for about 15 miles to U.S. 422 west. Stay on 422 and exit at U.S. 61 south. The stadium will be on your right. For other directional information, call the Phillies and listen to their recorded directions. There is plenty of free parking available.

```
MUNICIPAL MEMORIAL STADIUM
P.O. Box 15050
Reading, PA 19610
(610) 375-8469

Capacity: 8,000
LF 330, CF 400, RF 330
```

◆ TICKET AND SCHEDULE INFORMATION

Most games are played at night, starting at 7:05 P.M. Doubleheaders begin at 6:05 P.M. Sunday games begin at 1:05 P.M.

The Phillies' home opener is usually in early April, and the season ends in the first week of September.

Ticket prices: $6.50 box seats; $5 reserved seats; $3.50 general admission, $2 seniors 62 and over and children 5 to 14. The grandstand seats are largely covered, and all of the seats in the ballpark have backs, a comparative rarity in the minors.

# TRENTON THUNDER

### BOSTON RED SOX

**M**ercer County Waterfront Stadium officially opened May 9, 1994, following a last-minute 26-game road trip to open the season for the Thunder. Horrible weather during the winter of 1993-94 had caused construction delays on the stadium and resulted in a hastily-installed playing field.

Poor drainage and unexpected flooding caused 11 rainouts in 1994, but that should not be a problem in 1995 as the field has been carefully resodded.

Construction delays aside, Mercer County Waterfront Stadium—less than an hour's drive from New York City—is beautiful and well-designed. The open concourse allows fans to roam the concession stands without missing a pitch. The Delaware River is adjacent to the stadium and makes evenings at the ballpark especially picturesque. You can gaze past the right-field wall

at the river. One symbol of Trenton's past that can be viewed from the seats is the old Champale factory, which can be seen over the center-field wall. Though no longer in use, it is a reminder of the days when Trenton was one of the top manufacturing cities in the Northeast—and when you drive into the city you can still see the sign "Trenton Makes—The World Takes."

◆ LOCAL AND TEAM HISTORY

Trenton fielded pro teams as far back as the 1880s. This city joined the Inter-State Association as a charter member in 1883 and remained in that league through '84 and most of '85. In 1889, the Trenton Cuban Giants played in the Middle States League. Despite the name, there were no Cubans or other Latin Americans on this team, which consisted entirely of African-Americans. Instead, the name was used as a cover, allowing them to play against white teams.

Trenton had pro baseball from 1907 to '14 as a member of the Tri-State League and again from 1936 to '50, but was then without a pro team until the Thunder came to town in 1994. In fact, the state of New Jersey had been without a minor-league franchise since 1961 (when Jersey City finished up its two-year stint in the International League) until Trenton and the New Jersey Cardinals of the short-season New York–Penn League opened shop last summer.

*OTHER FAMOUS ALUMNI OTHER FAMOUS ALUMNI*

Goose Goslin and George Case played here.

In Trenton's final year before its hiatus, 1950, it featured Willie Mays, who was making his National Association debut.

In 1994, it didn't take long for imposing 6-foot-8 slugger Tony Clark to make his mark felt when it comes to team lore. The Tigers—Trenton switched to the Red Sox organization in the off-season—didn't have a lot of exciting prospects, but they made up for it in the soft-spoken, power-hitting Clark, who had been Detroit's first-round draft pick in 1990. Clark made history on June 7 when he deposited a 475-foot grand slam over the right-field wall and into the Delaware. The ball was believed to have been retrieved by a passing fisherman, but some of Clark's teammates insist it was seen paying the toll heading out of New Jersey and over the state line into Pennsylvania.

The first member of the Thunder to make it to the majors was relief pitcher Phil Stidham, who was promoted from Trenton to Toledo after a few games, and then up to Detroit in July 1994.

### ◆ BALLPARK EXTRAS

Not surprisingly, the Thunder's mascot is called Boomer. He's a blue thunderbird with oversized sunglasses. Among the more unusual favorite items at the concession stands are pork-roll subs. There is also a stadium restaurant that offers a full buffet meal. The Thunder Dugout, a souvenir store behind home plate on the concourse level, is the first full-service souvenir store designed by Major League Baseball at the minor-league level.

### ◆ ATTRACTIONS

Sesame Place, just 8 miles from the stadium in Langhorne, Pennsylvania, is one of the top theme parks in the country for kids. It offers several play areas, water-park-type rides and multimedia hands-on offerings. As you would expect from a park sponsored by the folks at Children's Television Workshop, it is clean and beautiful. You can meet your favorite Sesame Street characters daily. For parents who have enjoyed this show for 25 years, a visit to Sesame Place can be as much fun as it is for the kids. For information, call (215) 757-1100.

Six Flags Great Adventure, in Jackson, New Jersey, is just 20 miles east of the stadium and features not only top amusement-park rides but also a drive-through safari (keep those windows rolled up and replace that For information, call sunroof first). (908) 928-1821.

For more information about the Trenton area, call the Chamber of Commerce, (609) 393-4143.

### ◆ DINING

The Chambersburg Restaurant district, a mile from the ballpark, is known as "the Little Italy of New Jersey" and has several top spots.

Also, half an hour away, there's Oakley's which offers country-style fare including a special Sunday brunch. It's also a country-music club and features free dance lessons every night. Route 1 South at the Ramada Princeton, (609) 452-2044.

### ◆ LODGING

Palmer Inn is 20 to 25 minutes from the ballpark. 3499 Route 1 S, Princeton, (609) 452-2500.

### ◆ DIRECTIONS

From the Jersey Turnpike and Route 195, exit turnpike at 7A and get on Route 195 West toward Trenton. Get off at exit 2 (S. Broad Street and Arena Drive) and stay left for South Broad Street. This will merge with Route 206; follow it for about 2 miles to Lalor Street. Make a left on Lalor and go 2 miles to the end. Turn right and the stadium will be on your left. Parking costs $1 at the ballpark. On-street parking is also available.

---

**MERCER COUNTY WATERFRONT STADIUM**
**410 Riverview Executive Plaza**
**Trenton, NJ 08611**
**(609) 394-8326**

**Capacity: 6,453**
**LF 330, CF 407, RF 330**

---

### ◆ TICKET AND SCHEDULE INFORMATION

Game times are generally 7:05 P.M. from Monday through Saturday and 1:35 P.M. on Sunday, with the occasional 12:35 P.M. midweek businessperson special.

Trenton opens its schedule in early April and closes out the season the first week of September.

Ticket prices: $7 club seats; $6.50 loge seats; $6 pavillion seats; $5 terrace seats, $3 children 5 to 14 and seniors 61 and over. Children under 5 are free.

# SOUTHERN LEAGUE

The Southern League has operated as a Class AA circuit since 1964. But a predecessor of the current league debuted almost 80 years earlier, in 1885 (staying in business until 1899 and then somewhat sporadically until 1964), making the Southern League one of the oldest in baseball. Birmingham and Chattanooga are the only charter members who are still in operation. Today, there are 10 teams in mid-size cities spread over five states: Alabama, Florida, North Carolina, South Carolina and Tennessee. Each team plays 140 games, with the regular season beginning April 7 and ending September 3. In 1994, the Southern League continued its reign as the leading AA circuit in overall attendance, with a total of 2,596,339.

• • •

*The front entrance to Chattanooga's Engel Stadium features a distinctive brick facade.*

# BIRMINGHAM BARONS

## CHICAGO WHITE SOX

**H**oover Metropolitan Stadium, built in 1988, is a symmetrical ballpark with a partially covered grandstand, surrounded by a residential area and some undeveloped land. There are two areas down each foul line called the Grassy Knolls, where fans bring blankets and lawn chairs to sit on while watching the ballgame. The big story here in 1994 was Michael Jordan. His presence as a Barons player created an electric atmosphere at Hoover, as fans came from across the country to watch Jordan try his hand at baseball. After each home game, several hundred fans waited in the grandstand hoping for a glimpse of Jordan while he and his bodyguard walked out of the dugout and across the field to his car, parked all alone under the roof of a maintenance shed behind the outfield wall.

### ◆ LOCAL AND TEAM HISTORY

Birmingham has a particularly interesting baseball past. In 1887, the Birmingham Coal Barons played at a place called the Slag Pile. Fans who could not find seats in the ballpark's tiny grandstand sat atop the slag pile behind the outfield fence. After the turn of the century, Birmingham joined the successively Class A, A1 and AA Southern Association, where the city remained for 60 years, from 1901 to '61. After a two-year absence, pro baseball returned in 1964 when the Barons joined the Southern League. With two short exceptions (1966, '76-80) when there was no organized baseball here, Birmingham has remained in this circuit ever since. The Barons began their current affiliation with the White Sox in 1986.

Rickwood Field, built in 1910 and the Barons' home until 1987, is one of the oldest standing ballparks in the USA. The field, located about 15 minutes from Metropolitan Stadium and today used by amateur and school teams, is on the National Register of Historic Places. The first minor-league park of concrete and steel, Rickwood was designed to resemble the Baker Bowl in Philadelphia and Pittsburgh's Forbes Field. Originally, Rickwood's center field was 470 feet from homeplate, making it one of the deepest in baseball. This ballpark was also the home of the Birmingham Black Barons, which produced several of the greatest teams in the Negro leagues. In '43, '44, and '48 they won the Negro

American League title but lost the championship to the Homestead Grays. In the 1950s the Black Barons remained one of the Negro leagues' better teams.

Rickwood is rumored to be the site of one of the longest home runs in baseball history. According to the tale, Babe Ruth hit a homer over Rickwood's right-field wall during an exhibition game. His ball supposedly landed in a boxcar of a Tennessee-bound freight train and proceeded to travel some 200 miles before stopping. Although this story is considered by many to be apocryphal, it nevertheless remains part of Rickwood's lore.

Hall of Famer Burleigh Grimes pitched two full years for Birmingham (1915-1916), winning a total of 37 games before moving up to Pittsburgh in '16. Fellow Hall of Famer Pie Traynor batted .336 for the Barons in 1921, the same year a tornado demolished Rickwood's outfield fence and bleachers. Hall of Famer Satchel Paige began his pro career here in 1927 with the Black Barons of the Negro National League. He won eight games that year.

OTHER FAMOUS ALUMNI OTHER FAMOUS ALUMNI

Darrell Evans, Mike Henneman, Bo Jackson, and Bob Wickman also played here.

In the 1940s, several other great players became part of the Black Barons' history. Lorenzo "Piper" Davis was one such player. In his nine seasons (1942-50) with Birmingham, Davis batted .350 or better four years in a row ('47-50) and led the Negro American League with 69 runs batted in in the Barons' pennant-winning season of 1948. That year, Davis had two famous teammates, one of whom was 17-year-old future Hall of Famer Willie Mays, who hit .262 in his first year of pro ball. Mays played two more seasons in Birmingham before being signed by the New York Giants in 1950 and moving on to Trenton of the Interstate League. Shortstop Artie Wilson was the third member of this group. Wilson led the Negro American League with a .402 average and 134 hits in 1948. Three years later, he and Mays were playing for the New York Giants, but unlike his teammate's Wilson's stay in the majors was brief—just 19 games, in which he batted .182.

More recently, Hall of Famers Reggie Jackson and Rollie Fingers were Barons teammates in 1967 when Birmingham won the Southern League championship. One of their Birmingham teammates in '67 was future A's manager Tony La Russa who batted .230 for the Barons. Jackson and Fingers, together with such other Barons alumni as Bert Campaneris (1964, .325, Southern League leader with 11 triples) and Vida Blue (1969, 10 wins), were Oakland A's teammates.

In 1986, Ron Karkovice was the first of five players to play for Birmingham who later became prominent regulars for the Chicago White Sox. That year, Karkovice batted .282 with 20 homers. The next season, Jack McDowell won only one of his four decisions while posting a 7.84 ERA. In 1989, Robin Ventura was in his first season of pro ball when he helped lead the Barons to a championship by batting .278 and topping all third basemen in fielding percentage. The next season, Frank Thomas and Alex Fernandez were Birmingham teammates. Thomas gave fans a taste of what he would do in the majors by leading the circuit in slugging percentage (.581), walks (112) and on-base percentage (.487) while also batting .323 with 18 home runs. Fernandez appeared in only four games after being promoted from Sarasota. He posted a 3-0 record and 1.08 ERA, and was in Chicago before the season ended.

### ◆ BALLPARK EXTRAS
Check out the grilled chicken sandwiches and the choices at the Barons' ice-cream stand, which made its debut in 1994. Jordan's presence here in '94 helped boost the Barons' attendance by almost 200,000 to 467,867, best among all AA teams. This gave Birmingham the distinction of being one of only two AA clubs in minor-league history to attract more than 400,000 fans at least three times.

### ◆ ATTRACTIONS
The Alabama Sports Hall of Fame has various displays highlighting stars and events in Alabama sports history. Admission is $5, $4 for seniors over 59 and $3 for children 7 to 20. For further information, call (205) 323-6665.

The Arlington Antebellum Home and Gardens features a Greek-revival home dating to the 1840s. Admission is $3, $2 for children 6 to 18. For further information, call (205) 780-5656.

For additional information about Birmingham, call the Visitors' Bureau, (205) 254-1654.

### ◆ DINING
Dreamland Restaurant, about 15 minutes from the ballpark, is a popular local barbecue joint that ships its famous sauce all across the country. Dreamland's motto is, "We have spareribs and white bread. Don't ask for anything else." 1427 14th Avenue S, (205) 933-2133.

### ◆ LODGING
Riverchase Inn at the Galleria is in Hoover near the intersection of I-459 and U.S. 31, about 10 minutes from the ballpark. (205) 985-7500/(800) 239-2401.

Courtyard by Marriott is also about 10 minutes from the park, in Hoover at exit 13 off I-459. (205) 988-5000/(800) 443-6000.

### ◆ DIRECTIONS
From I-459, take exit 13, the Galleria Mall exit. Turn left off the ramp and then turn right onto Trace Crossing. Follow this road to the ballpark, which is located in suburban Hoover. Plentiful parking is available for $2 per car.

---

**HOOVER METROPOLITAN STADIUM**
P.O. Box 360007
Birmingham, AL 35236
(205) 988-3200

Capacity: 10,800
LF 340, CF 405, RF 340

---

### ◆ TICKET AND SCHEDULE INFORMATION
Most games are played at night, starting at 7:10. Doubleheaders and Sunday games begin at 2 P.M. and 6 P.M., respectively.

The Barons' home opener is usually in early April, and the season ends in the first week of September. Purchasing tickets on the day of the game should be no problem, unless Michael Jordan plays here in 1995.

Ticket prices: $6 box seats; $4 general admission. Seniors 55 and over and children 14 and under get $1 off each ticket.

# CAROLINA MUDCATS

**PITTSBURGH PIRATES**

This ballpark is nearly impossible to miss. Sitting amid fields near the intersection of two highways in tobacco country, it is the most prominent building for miles around, especially during night games when the stadium's lights illuminate the dark sky. Five County Stadium is within shouting distance of four counties that border its own Wake County, hence its name. This expansive steel ballpark, painted bright red with an uncovered grandstand, has what is reputed to be the largest scoreboard in the minors, at 56 feet by 85 feet. During Carolina rallies, the team illuminates the word MUDCATS at the top of the scoreboard. Fireworks are shot off from behind the scoreboard when the team wins or a home player hits a home run. The fans here respond well, helping to make Five County Stadium a lively, fun place for baseball. Though it was built in 1991, the Mudcats are still in the process of completing their ballpark, including plans to convert the numerous trailers that serve as clubhouses, offices and concession stands into permanent structures.

### ◆ LOCAL AND TEAM HISTORY

When the Mudcats relocated to Zebulon from Columbus, Georgia, for the 1991 season, they became the first organized-baseball team based in this town. Although Zebulon's baseball past is rather brief, the sport has a long history in the surrounding areas of Raleigh, Rocky Mount and Wilson. Raleigh's baseball past dates back to 1902 when the city played in the Class C North Carolina League. After spending time in three other circuits through the 1930s, Raleigh joined the Carolina League in 1945. From 1968 to '71, Raleigh shared a Carolina League franchise with nearby Durham. To the northeast in Edgecombe County, Rocky Mount fielded teams in six circuits, beginning in 1909 with the Class D Eastern Carolina League. In 1980, the Carolina League's Rocky Mount Pines closed out the city's pro baseball history. Wilson lies to the southeast. Organized baseball made its first appearance here in 1908, when the Wilson Tobacconists won the Eastern Carolina League title. Baseball continued in this county seat through the 1973 season, when the Wilson Pennants finished last in the six-team Carolina League.

OTHER FAMOUS ALUMNI

OTHER FAMOUS ALUMNI

Dick Radatz, Greg Luzinski, Bob Boone, Manny Sanguillen, Jon Matlack, Al Oliver, Cesar Tovar, Jim Leyland and Lee May all played in this area.

Four Hall of Famers spent a portion of their careers playing baseball in Raleigh. Slugger Hank Greenberg belted 19 home runs while batting .314 and driving in 93 runs for the Raleigh Capitals in 1930. Carl Yastrzemski, then a second baseman, had a Carolina League MVP season for the Caps in 1959, leading the circuit with a .377 average and 34 doubles, while also hitting 15 home runs and driving in 100 runs. Joe "Ducky" Medwick and Enos "Country" Slaughter also played for Raleigh at the end of their careers.

In 1940, shortstop Johnny Pesky began his professional career with a bang in Rocky Mount; Pesky led the Piedmont League in at-bats (576), hits (187) and triples (16) while batting .325. Despite Pesky's stellar season, Rocky Mount lost to Durham in the league championship series, four games to two. In 1909-10, Olympian Jim Thorpe batted .247 overall for the Rocky Mount Railroaders. When the Olympic authorities discovered Thorpe's professional baseball exploits here, he was stripped of his Olympic medals. Tony Perez spent the 1962 season in Rocky Mount, batting .292 with 18 home runs and 74 runs batted in.

Hall of Famer Rod Carew spent his third pro season with the Wilson Tobacconists in 1966. That season, the Tobs' second baseman batted .292.

### ◆ BALLPARK EXTRAS

The concession stands here are in trailers and tents beneath and behind the grandstand. One of the team's best concessions, a fried catfish sandwich, is a play on the Mudcats' nickname. The Mudcats also sell fries in a fish bait cup, which bears some resemblance to a can of worms. For something different, try some grilled bologna. As for souvenirs, Carolina's logo has become one of the most popular in the minors, ranking No.1 in 1992 and '93.

### ◆ ATTRACTIONS

In nearby Raleigh, you can visit the North Carolina Museum of History, which has exhibits on early American history, including the Colonial period and the Civil War. Admission is free. For further information, call (919) 733-7450.

Imagination Station is a hands-on museum in Wilson with several exhibits designed for kids. Admission is $3.50, $3 for seniors 62 and over and children 4 to 17. For further information, call (919) 291-5113.

For additional information about this area, call the Capital Area Visitors Center in Raleigh, (919) 733-3456.

### ◆ DINING

Parker's Barbecue, about 25 minutes from the ballpark, serves good North Carolina pork barbecue. U.S. 301, Wilson, (919) 237-0972.

### ◆ LODGING

Holiday Inn North is located at exit 11B off I-440 in Raleigh, about 30 minutes from the ballpark. (919) 872-7666/(800) HOLIDAY.

Red Roof Inn is located near the intersection of U.S. 64 and I-440 in Raleigh, about 20 minutes from the ballpark. (919) 231-0200/(800) THE-ROOF.

### ◆ DIRECTIONS

From I-95, take U.S. 264 west to U.S. 64. The ballpark is near the intersection of U.S.64 and State Route 39. From I-440, take U.S. 64 east to State Route 39. Plentiful parking is available for $1.50 per car.

**FIVE COUNTY STADIUM**
P.O. Drawer 1218
Zebulon, NC 27597
(919) 269-2287

Capacity: 6,000
LF 330, CF 400, RF 330

### ◆ TICKET AND SCHEDULE INFORMATION

Most games are played at night, starting at 7:35. Doubleheaders and Sunday games begin at 6:05 P.M.

The Mudcats' home opener is usually in early April, and the season concludes in the first week of September.

Ticket prices: $6 box seats; $5 reserved seats; $4 general admission. Seniors 65 and over, children 14 and under and military with identification get $1 off each ticket.

# CHATTANOOGA LOOKOUTS

## CINCINNATI REDS

Joe Engel Stadium evokes memories of baseball's early days. Built in 1929 and remodeled in 1990, it has green grandstand seats modeled after those of the 1930s, and red-brick walls. The stadium also features one of the game's most unusual center fields. A small hill rises behind the warning track up to the outfield wall. For years, this oddity made catching a deep fly ball in Engel Stadium an adventure, at least until Cincinnati began its affiliation with Chattanooga in 1988. The Reds, concerned about players' getting hurt while running uphill in center field, insisted that Chattanooga install the fence in front of the hill, where it stands today. All told, Joe Engel Stadium's many distinctive features combine to make this one of the most attractive ballparks in the minors.

### ◆ LOCAL AND TEAM HISTORY

The Chattanooga Lookouts (named after this city's Lookout Mountain, site of an 1863 Civil War battle) played their first game in 1885. Nine years later, on July 3, 1894, night baseball was tried here with the aid of electric arc lights, one of the first such attempts in history. The home team won that game 9-0.

But these tidbits are only part of Chattanooga's baseball story. The local ballpark is named for the central figure in this franchise's past, Joe Engel, the Lookouts' former president and baseball's version of P.T. Barnum. In true circus tradition, he staged innovative promotional events to attract people to his ballpark, including a house giveaway in 1936 that drew more than 24,000 fans and a faux big-game hunt in 1938 complete with papier-maché animals.

**FAMOUS ALUMNI**

Harmon Killebrew, Rogers Hornsby, Burleigh Grimes, Kiki Cuyler, Calvin Griffith, Ferguson Jenkins, Satchel Paige, Danny Tartabull, Reggie Jefferson, Mark Langston and Reggie Sanders all played here.

In 1931, Engel signed 17-year-old Jackie Mitchell to a Lookouts' contract, the first offered to a woman. As a promotion, Engel had Mitchell pitch in an exhibition game against the New York Yankees. In the first inning, she struck out Babe Ruth and then Lou Gehrig before being replaced. A film of Mitchell's unique feat can be seen at Chattanooga's Regional History Museum. Engel's exploits are memorialized on plaques located to the left as you enter the stadium.

### ◆ BALLPARK EXTRAS

Popular food items include bratwurst and Pasquali pizza, made fresh at the ballpark in three varieties—sausage, pepperoni and cheese. There is a picnic area in left field reserved for groups of 25 or more. Joe Engel Stadium also has a souvenir shop under the grandstand behind third base with an extensive selection of Lookouts paraphernalia.

### ◆ ATTRACTIONS

Chickamauga and Chattanooga National Military Park contains the sites of two of the Civil War's most decisive battles. Admission to the park is free. The Chickamauga Visitor Center can be reached at (706) 866-9241.

Chattanooga Choo-Choo and Terminal Station showcases the legendary Chattanooga Choo-Choo railroad car, part of which has been converted into a restaurant and hotel. Admission is free. For further information, call (615) 266-5000.

Chattanooga Regional History Museum features exhibits detailing this city's past. The museum also contains an exhibit about the Lookouts that includes the Jackie Mitchell videotape. Admission is $2, $1.75 for seniors and $1.25 for children 5 to 18. For further information, call (615) 265-3247.

To obtain additional information about Chattanooga, call the Visitors' Bureau, (800) 322-3344.

### ◆ DINING

While there are several good restaurants in the Chattanooga area, don't miss Smokey's Barbecue, at exit 183 eastbound and exit 183A westbound off I-24. Smokey's is a casual place that serves excellent chicken and ribs. Check out their three all-you-can-eat specials: beef on Monday, pork on Tuesday and chicken on Wednesday. 3850 Brainerd Road, (615) 622-8996.

### ◆ LODGING

Comfort Hotel River Plaza is five minutes away at the 4th Street exit off I-24. (615) 756-5150/(800) 4-CHOICE.

Holiday Inn Chattanooga Choo-Choo is five minutes away, right off exit 178 westbound on I-24, or the Broad Street exit eastbound. (615) 266-5000/(800) HOLIDAY.

### ◆ DIRECTIONS

Take I-24 to U.S. 27 north. Take exit 1C and turn right. The ballpark is about 1½ miles up on the right. Turn right at the park on Third Street. Ample parking is available for $2.

---

**JOE ENGEL STADIUM**
**1130 E. 3rd Street**
**Chattanooga, TN 37403**
**(615) 267-2208**

---

**Capacity: 7,500**
**LF 355, CF 415, RF 318**

---

### ◆ TICKET AND SCHEDULE INFORMATION

Most games are played at night, starting at 7 P.M. Doubleheaders begin at 6 P.M. There are selected Wednesday afternoon games starting at 12:30 P.M., and Sunday games begin at 2 P.M.

The Lookouts' home opener is usually in early April, and the season ends in the first week of September.

Ticket prices: $7 VIP box seats (5 rows behind dugouts, with waitress service), terrace section (tables behind third-base dugout); $5 box seats; $3 general admission. Children 6 to 12 get $1 off each ticket. Children aged 5 and under are free.

The first six rows of general admission seats are sold as reserved seats on selected nights when box seats have sold out in advance. Reserved seats cost $4, $3 for children.

# GREENVILLE BRAVES

**ATLANTA BRAVES**

When you visit Greenville, there is little doubt this is Braves country; Atlanta is only about 2½ hours away via interstate. This makes for an unusually close relationship between fans of the major-league team and one of its farm teams; many Atlantans make the drive north in the summer to see some of the Braves' future stars.

Municipal Stadium opened in 1984. The ballpark has no covering over the stands, which get hot in the sticky summer months. A no-nonsense, basic ballpark with the game on the field the prime focus, it rests in a bucolic setting, surrounded by trees and low hills, and the team is a consistent winner. If you can't get tickets to do the tomahawk chop at Fulton County Stadium, a visit to Greenville might be the next best thing.

### ◆ LOCAL AND TEAM HISTORY

In 1907, the Greenville Mountaineers, this city's first pro team, played in the Class D South Carolina League. The Mountaineers dropped out of the league on July 26 after posting a 26-28 record. Greenville fielded another team in the Class D Carolina Association from 1908 to '12. After that, Greenville was associated with four other leagues until baseball left town following the '72 season: a rather lengthy affiliation with the Sally League (1919-30, '38-42, '46-50, '61-62) during which it was designated variously as a Class A, B and C circuit; Class D Palmetto, which lasted only season, 1931; Class B Tri-State (1951-52, '54-55); and Class D Western Carolinas, the predecessor to today's South Atlantic League, (1963-72). In 1984, Greenville joined the Southern League as Atlanta's AA affiliate. In 1992, the G-Braves won 100 games, the most in the minors. From 1991 to '94, this

**OTHER FAMOUS ALUMNI**

Tom Glavine, David Justice, Steve Avery, Jeff Blauser, Mark Lemke, Duane Ward and Bill Taylor all played here.

team's 336 wins ranked Greenville second among all minor-league teams, behind Harrisburg's 347.

Meadowbrook Park, built in 1938 and this area's first lighted ballpark, proved to be ill-fated. It was badly damaged by fire in 1948, which eventually forced the Greenville Spinners out of the South Atlantic League after the 1950 season. In 1972, Meadowbrook burned to the ground on Valentine's Day, the year baseball left town again.

Shoeless Joe Jackson, a native of nearby Brandon Mills, South Carolina, had a big year for Greenville in 1908. He led the Carolina Association with a .346 batting average and 120 hits, but it wasn't enough to lead his team to a pennant. Greenville finished second, 1/2 game behind Greensboro. Smead Jolley was one of the greatest hitters in minor-league history. His .366 career average places him third among all minor-league players. Jolley also won more batting titles (six) than any other minor leaguer. On the minors' all-time list, he ranks 18th in hits (3,037) and ninth in runs batted in (1,631). Jolley began his career with Greenville in 1922 as a pitcher. That season, he had 86 at-bats and hit .314. In his pitching career, he appeared in 97 games, compiling a 41-34 record. By the time Jolley was promoted to the majors in 1930, his pitching career had ended. He enjoyed four productive seasons (1930-33) in the big leagues with the White Sox and the Red Sox, batting .305 for his career. Jolley made a splash in his rookie big-league season when he hit .313 with 16 home runs and 114 runs batted in. In 1938, Mickey Vernon, two-time AL batting champ who batted .286 over his 20-year career in the majors, hit .328 with 72 runs batted in for Greenville.

In 1966, Greenville had a 19-year-old fireballing right-hander in his second pro season, Nolan Ryan. He made mincemeat of the competition in the Western Carolinas League. Ryan led the circuit with 17 wins (he lost twice), 28 starts, 272 strikeouts and 127 walks. His ERA was 2.51. One year before, Jerry Koosman, a very productive left hander with 222 career major-league victories and 2,556 strikeouts, began his career in Greenville by posting a 5-11 record and 4.71 ERA. Two future big-league managers, Cito Gaston (1964, .230 average, 16 runs batted in) and Tommy Lasorda (1949, 7-7, 2.93 ERA), played in Greenville at the beginning of their baseball careers.

### ◆ BALLPARK EXTRAS
The Braves offer several good concession items sold by area businesses. Down the left-field line, try some boiled peanuts, a true Southern tradition. Down the right field line, check out chief's wings (stuffed with jalapeños), chicken fingers, burritos and grilled build-your-own burgers.

### ◆ ATTRACTIONS
The Greenville County Museum of Art has several exhibits relating to early Colonial history in the South. For further information, call (803) 271-7570.

The Cherokee Foothills Scenic Highway runs northwest of Greenville and offers a variety of historic sites and scenic vistas. For further information, call the South Carolina Parks Department, (803) 734-0127.

For additional information about this area, call the South Carolina Tourism Department, (803) 734-0235.

### ◆ DINING
Blazin' Bill's BBQ, about five minutes from the ballpark, offers a good buffet with barbecue chicken, pork, ribs, fried chicken, salad and several vegetables. Bill's two barbecue sauces, tomato-based and mustard-based, are homemade. 701 W. Butler, (803) 299-1571.

### ◆ LODGING
Comfort Inn I-85 is at the Mauldin Road exit from I-85, about 10 minutes from the ballpark, in Greenville. (803) 277-6730/(800) 221-2222.

Ramada Inn South is at the Mauldin Road exit from I-85, about 10 minutes from the ballpark, in Greenville. (803) 277-3734/(800) RAMADA.

### ◆ DIRECTIONS
From I-85, take exit 46, Mauldin Road. Go left, southeast on Mauldin. The ballpark is about two miles away on your right. Plentiful parking is available for $2 per car.

```
MUNICIPAL STADIUM
P.O. Box 16683
Greenville, SC 29607
(803) 299-3456

Capacity: 7,500
LF 335, CF 405, RF 335
```

### ◆ TICKET AND SCHEDULE INFORMATION
Most games are played at night, starting at 7:15 P.M. Doubleheaders begin at 6:15 P.M.

The Braves' home opener is usually in early April, and the season ends in the first week of September.

Ticket prices: $6.50 prime box seats; $5.75 box seats; $5.25 reserved; $4.50 general admission, $3 for children 14 and under.

# HUNTSVILLE STARS

## OAKLAND ATHLETICS

"The Mausoleum." "The Three Rivers Stadium of the Minor Leagues." These nicknames for Joe W. Davis Stadium accurately tell the story of this large, cold, concrete ballpark, one of the minors' least attractive facilities. Built in 1985 at the end of an old airport runway, Davis has an uncovered grandstand and bleachers in left center field to the left of the foul pole. Its concrete structure quite literally dampens the spirit of local fans by muffling whatever noise is generated by the usually reserved crowd. The front office does little on its part to generate excitement. During one game in 1994, the Stars staged Mascot Races, a popular minor-league promotion in which the local mascot races a young fan around the bases to the cheers of the crowd. But there's no mascot here, so an overalls-clad grounds-crew member was the designated team representative, and his lackluster effort generated little response from the grandstand. On the vast majority of nights, Joe W. Davis Stadium can be a strangely quiet place to watch a ballgame.

### ◆ LOCAL AND TEAM HISTORY

The Stars moved here from Nashville in 1985. Prior to that, Huntsville had only an intermittent connection with professional baseball that dates back to 1903. This city operated two organized-baseball teams before the Stars arrived: 1911-12 in the Class D Southeastern League and 1930 in the Class D Georgia-Alabama League. In 1991, Huntsville hosted the minors' first Joint-AA All-Star Game.

OTHER FAMOUS ALUMNI

Tim Belcher, Greg Cadaret, Kevin Tapani, Felix Jose and Troy Neel all played here.

Since 1985, several of the most prominent members of the Oakland A's have played here, including consecutively, three players who were eventually named American League Rookie of the Year: Jose Canseco, Mark McGwire, and Walt Weiss. In '85, Jose Canseco was named the Southern League's Most Valuable Player after batting .313 with 25 home runs and 80 runs batted in for Huntsville. The following year, Mc-Gwire belted 10 homers and compiled a .303 batting average here. Weiss batted .285 for Huntsville in 1987.

### ◆ BALLPARK EXTRAS

Look for the heartburn special—Nachos for Two, featuring chips topped with cheese, jalapeños, salsa and sour cream, plus two beers or soft drinks. Complimentary antacids are provided by the concessionaire upon request. Smoked Polish hot dogs and pizza are also available.

### ◆ ATTRACTIONS

The U.S. Space and Rocket Center is Huntsville's most popular attraction. You can see various exhibits here related to the USA space program, including an Apollo 16 command module. Admission is $11.95, $7.95 for seniors 60 and over and children 3 to 12. For further information, call (205) 837-3400.

U.S. Space Camp provides "astronaut" training for kids of various ages. For further information, call (800) 63-SPACE.

For additional information about this area, call the Huntsville/Madison County Convention & Visitors Bureau, (800) SPACE-4-U.

### ◆ DINING

Tim's Cajun Kitchen, about 10 minutes from the ballpark, serves up some very good Cajun food in an informal restaurant whose brick interior walls are decorated with animal skins. The bargain-priced lunch special features a choice among several entrees: gumbo, jambalaya, crawfish étouffée, red beans and rice and *boudin* (blood sausage), plus side dishes. 114 Jordan Lane, (205) 533-7589.

There are several national chain and fast-food restaurants on University Drive, and along U.S. 231.

### ◆ LODGING

La Quinta Inn/Huntsville Research Park is 10 minutes away on University Drive, west of U.S. 72, in Huntsville. (205) 830-2070/(800) 531-5900.

Radisson Suite Hotel is about 10 minutes from the park on South Memorial Parkway, in Huntsville. (205) 882-9400/(800) 333-3333.

### ◆ DIRECTIONS

Take I-65 to I-565 East. Exit at Memorial Parkway/U.S. 231 South. Stay on 231 and take the Drake Avenue exit. The ballpark is on the west side of the Parkway, about a mile from the exit on a strip with several stores and other businesses. There is plenty of parking for $2.50 per car, one of the highest rates among AA teams.

### ◆ TICKET AND SCHEDULE INFORMATION

Most games are played at night, starting at 7:05 P.M. Doubleheaders begin at 6:05 P.M. Sunday games begin at 2:05 P.M. from April through June and at 7:05 P.M. in July and August.

The Star's home opener is usually in early April, and the season ends in the first week of September.

Ticket prices: $6 box seats; $4 general admission. Seniors 65 and over get in free on Mondays. Children 12 and under receive $1 off the price of general-admission tickets for selected games.

# JACKSONVILLE SUNS

### DETROIT TIGERS

The Suns' ballpark has a comfortable, old-time flavor. The grandstand is completely covered, and its roof is dotted with several relatively small, round white lights for night games. The bullpens here are behind a fence beside the grandstand and next to the dugouts, within easy shouting distance of the managers. An old brick outfield wall is still standing, but now a wooden barrier stands several feet in front of it. Jacksonville's 25-foot-high center-field wall is known as Bragan's Blue Monster, because of its height, color and the Suns' president, Peter Bragan Sr., whose brother Jimmy retired in 1994 as Southern League president.

On June 3, 1955, 7,123 fans, then the largest crowd to see a South Atlantic League game in Jacksonville, were here for the opening of Wolfson Park.

### ◆ LOCAL AND TEAM HISTORY

This city's first baseball game was played in 1874. On March 21, 1898, Jacksonville was the site of what is thought to be the first spring training exhibition game, between the New York Giants and the Washington Statesmen. After the turn of the century, Jacksonville joined the South Atlantic League, where it remained for most of the next 60 years (1904-17, '36-42, '46-61). Interspersed with Jacksonville's Sally tenure, the city also was associated with the Class C Florida State League (1921-22) and the Class B Southeastern League ('26-30). Jacksonville also had a seven-year stint as a AAA team in the International League, 1962-68. Following a one-season hiatus, baseball returned here in 1970 when Jacksonville joined the Southern League. This is the Suns' first year of affiliation with the Detroit Tigers. Jacksonville also hosted three different negro leagues teams, in 1886, 1920, '38 and '41-42. The Negro American League's Jacksonville Red Caps (1938, '41-42) played at Red Cap Stadium, which eventually became the home of the Sally's Tars & Braves, who played in the late 1940s and early '50s, before Wolfson opened.

Hall of Famer Henry Aaron broke the South Atlantic League's color line with Jacksonville in 1953. The 19-year-old Aaron endured many racial taunts that season. But in the end, his bat spoke the loudest. Aaron led the SAL in most offensive categories—runs (115), hits (208), doubles (36), runs batted in (125) and average (.362). He also hit 22 home runs as Jacksonville wound up in first but lost the championship series to Columbia, four games to three. Several prominent pitchers began their careers here. Phil Niekro posted a 6-4 record and 2.79 ERA for the Jacksonville Braves in 1960. Three years later, "Sudden" Sam McDowell, arguably the hardest-throwing pitcher of his day, pitched 12 games for Jacksonville and won three while striking out 84. Tommy John, winner of 288 games in his 26-year big-league career, won eight for Jacksonville in 1962-63. Hall of Famer Tom Seaver was a 21 year-old rookie when he won 12 games for Jacksonville in 1966. The next season, Nolan Ryan breezed through town at the end of the year, winning one game while striking out 18 in seven innings.

### ◆ BALLPARK EXTRAS

Try the grilled burgers or hot dogs. You can also get Wolfson Park's sausage and barbecue pork. At the pizza stand, fruit salad and mixed green salad are available. A picnic area and playground are located in right field. John Leard, the Suns' public address announcer and a former radio disc jockey, likes to put on a good show for

**OTHER FAMOUS ALUMNI OTHER FAMOUS ALUMNI**

Bret Saberhagen, Andres Galarraga, Randy Johnson, Larry Walker, Delino DeShields and Marquis Grissom all played here.

the crowd; whenever one of the Suns hits a homer, Leard will draw out his call of the player's name during the home-run trot.

### ◆ ATTRACTIONS
On nearby Fort George Island, you will find Kingsley Plantation National Historic Site, one of the few remaining cotton plantations from the years before Florida became a state. Admission is free. For further information, call (904) 251-3537.

Amelia Island, north of Jacksonville, has great beaches, golfing and horseback riding. For further information, call (800) 2-AMELIA.

For additional information about this area, call the Visitors' Bureau, (904) 353-9736.

### ◆ DINING
The Landing is located along Jacksonville's riverfront about 15 minutes from the ballpark at Two Independent Drive. You'll find a variety of good restaurants here, such as Fat Tuesday (904-353-0444) and Kuco's (904-355-6334). For more information about The Landing, call (904) 353-1188.

### ◆ LODGING
Comfort Inn South is just off I-95 at the Emerson Street exit, about 10 minutes from the ballpark, in Jacksonville. (904) 398-3331/(800) 4-CHOICE.

Ramada Inn South is at the West University exit from I-95, about 15 minutes from the ballpark, in Jacksonville. (904) 737-8000/(800) 272-6232.

### ◆ DIRECTIONS
From I-95 south, take the 20th Street Expressway. The expressway leads right into the end zone of the Gator Bowl, which is next to the ballpark. From I-95 north, take the Emerson Street exit and turn right. Go over the Hart Bridge. Follow signs to the Gator Bowl and Wolfson Park. Plenty of parking is available for $2 per car, $3 if there is an event at the Gator Bowl.

---

**SAM M. WOLFSON PARK**
P.O. Box 4756
Jacksonville, FL 32201
(904) 358-2846

Capacity: 8,200
LF 320, CF 395, RF 320

---

### ◆ TICKET AND SCHEDULE INFORMATION
Most games are played at night, starting at 7:35 P.M. Selected weekday games begin at 12:15 P.M. Sunday games begin at 3:35 P.M. and 5:35 P.M.

The Suns' home opener is usually in early April, and the season ends in the first week of September.

Ticket prices: $6 lower box seats; $5 upper box seats;

$4 general admission. Seniors 65 and over, children 4 to 14 and military with identification get $1 off the prices of all tickets.

# KNOXVILLE SMOKIES

## TORONTO BLUE JAYS

**B**aseball has been played on this site since 1921. The current ballpark was destroyed by fire in 1951 and rebuilt two years later. In 1957, Neil Ridley Field at Bill Meyer Stadium received its current name in honor of Knoxville native and former Pittsburgh Pirates manager Bill Meyer, who was National League Manager of the Year in 1948. Neil Ridley was a previous owner of the Knoxville team responsible for bringing baseball back to town in the 1960s and '70s. A large popcorn popper in the stadium's foyer begins popping at about 5 P.M., so by the time the gates open, Bill Meyer Stadium is filled with the pleasing scent of freshly made popcorn. The largely covered grandstand here contains about 4,000 of the stadium's original wood seats with metal armrests, which have been here since 1953. Behind the left-field wall, you will notice a large warehouse, which has experienced many broken windows over the years from home-run balls striking its facade. The blue batters' backdrop in center is one of the minors' tallest, at 28 feet.

For some local flavor, the team decided to drop the name Blue Jays in 1993 and adopt its current nickname and attractive logo: the Knoxville skyline together with the nearby Blue Ridge Mountains.

### ◆ LOCAL AND TEAM HISTORY
In 1896, the Knoxville Indians joined the Southeastern League as a charter member. After the turn of the century, Knoxville teams began an association with seven different organized-baseball leagues when the Appalachians joined the Sally League in 1909. Knoxville also spent time in the Class D Southeastern League (1910), Class D Appalachian League (1911-14, '21-24), Class A Southern Association (1932-44), Class B Tri-State League (1946-52, '54-55), Class D Mountain States League (1953), Class B and A South Atlantic League (1925-19, '56-63), and Class AA Southern League (1964-67, '72-to date). In 1945, Knoxville also fielded a

team in the Negro Southern League. The Smokies began their current affiliation with Toronto in 1980.

Hall of Famer Hoyt Wilhelm won 13 games for the Smokies in 1948 while also posting a 3.62 ERA. Eight years later, Knoxville fired its manager in August 1956 and asked the team's second baseman to step in as the Smokies' skipper. That player was 26-year-old Earl Weaver, who guided his team to a 10-24 record over the remainder of the season in his first professional baseball managerial job. In 1978, another future big-league manager got his first assignment in Knoxville. Tony La Russa's team won the Southern League's first half Western Division title, shortly after which he joined the Chicago White Sox as a coach. Johnny Pesky managed Knoxville in 1959 and led the team to the regular season pennant, but the Smokies lost in the playoffs to Charleston.

**OTHER FAMOUS ALUMNI**

Pat Borders, Manny Lee, Jesse Barfield, Carlos Delgado, Glenallen Hill, Jeff Kent, Jim Northrup, Mike Timlin, Ryan Thompson, Junior Felix, Denny McLain, Mickey Stanley, and Dick McAuliffe have all played here.

When Knoxville was a Detroit Tigers' farm team in the early 1960s, several players who would have prominent roles on Detroit's world championship team in 1968 played in Knoxville. Willie Horton, who belted 36 homers in 1968, hit 14 for Knoxville five years earlier. Mickey Lolich won three games for the Smokies in 1961, and catcher Bill Freehan was his battery mate.

In 1983, Jimmy Key went 6-5 for Knoxville before being promoted to Syracuse. Five years later, Juan Guzman, another important pitcher for Toronto's 1992 world championship team, won four games for Knoxville in the first of his three seasons here. In 1984 and '85, Knoxville featured two future big-league home-run champs. Cecil Fielder was just another minor leaguer when he hit a combined 27 home runs for Knoxville over those two seasons. One of Fielder's teammates in 1984 was Fred McGriff, who hit nine homers and batted .249 for the Smokies.

◆ **BALLPARK EXTRAS**
Check out the grilled burgers and hot dogs; the Polish dogs are especially worth a try. There is a picnic area in left field.

◆ **ATTRACTIONS**
Governor William Blount Mansion was one of the first frame houses built west of the Allegheny Mountains in 1792. Admission is $3, $2.50 for seniors and $1.50 for children 6 to 12. For further information, call (615) 525-2375.

The Knoxville Zoological Gardens features a Marine Animal Complex and one of the largest collections of big cats in the USA. Admission is $6.50, $4 for seniors 65 and over and children 3 to 12. For further information, call (615) 637-5331.

For additional information about Knoxville, call the Chamber of Commerce, (615) 637-4550.

◆ **DINING**
Calhoun's, about five minutes from the ballpark, overlooks the Tennessee River. This restaurant, a former National Ribs Cook-off winner, specializes in good barbecue pork and ribs. 400 Neyland Drive, (615) 673-3355.

◆ **LODGING**
Howard Johnson Motor Lodge is at exit 108 off I-75, about 15 minutes from the ballpark. (615) 688-3141/(800) 654-2000.

Hampton Inn North is also at exit 108 from I-75, about 15 minutes from the ballpark. (615) 689-1011/(800) 426-7866.

◆ **DIRECTIONS**
From I-40, take the James White Parkway exit. Stay on the Parkway until Summit Hill Drive. Follow signs to the ballpark. Take Summit Hill and turn right at the first traffic light. Turn right on Willow and the ballpark will be immediately visible. Free parking at the ballpark and on-street parking in the area are available.

**NEIL RIDLEY FIELD AT BILL MEYER STADIUM**
**633 Jessamine Street**
**Knoxville, TN 37917**
**(615) 637-9494**

**Capacity: 6,412**
**LF 330, CF 400, RF 330**

◆ **TICKET AND SCHEDULE INFORMATION**
Most games are played at night, starting at 7 P.M. Sunday games begin at 2 P.M. or 7 P.M.

The Smokies' home opener is usually in early April, and the season ends in the first week of September.

Ticket prices: $5.50 box seats; $4.50 general admission, $3.50 for seniors 55 and over and children 14 and under.

# MEMPHIS CHICKS

## SAN DIEGO PADRES

**MEMPHIS CHICKS**™

A quick glance at Tim McCarver Stadium's playing field may leave you scratching your head: The infield is artificial turf while the outfield is natural grass. This schizophrenic difference is the result of requests made by the Kansas City Royals when Memphis was a K.C. farm team from 1984 to '94. The Royals wanted their AA ballplayers to become accustomed to a turf infield in preparation for playing on the artificial surface in Kansas City's Kauffman Stadium, and although Memphis is no longer a Royals affiliate, the turf/grass field remains. McCarver Stadium is named for former big-league catcher and Memphis native Tim McCarver, who batted .347 for the Chicks in 1960 and is now one of the celebrity owners of his former team. McCarver's partners include Ron Howard, Bob Costas and Maury Povich.

The team's nickname, honoring the Chickasaw Indians, dates back to 1912.

### ◆ LOCAL AND TEAM HISTORY
Memphis has a distinguished baseball past. In 1877, this city's first pro team, the Red Stockings, went 25-6 before disbanding. Several other pro and semipro teams played in Memphis through the remaining years of the 19th century. In 1902, Memphis began a 59-year membership in the Class A/A1/AA Southern Association. After 1960, Memphis fielded teams in the AA Texas League (1969-73), AAA International League (1974-76) and AA Southern League (1978-to date). This is the first year of Memphis' affiliation with San Diego.

Memphis was also the home of several Negro league teams. In 1886, the Memphis Eclipses of the Southern League of Colored Baseballists, arguably the first organized Negro league, played here. In 1938, the Memphis Red Sox won the Negro American League's first-half title and were managed by Ted "Double Duty" Radcliffe, who had a long and distinguished career (1928-50) in the Negro leagues as a player and manager.

Over the years, Memphis teams have played in several unique ballparks that have long since disappeared. Russwood Park, built in 1896, was oddly shaped with an inner fence in left, behind which stood a hand-operated scoreboard, and a short right-field porch a scant 301 feet from home. In 1906, with one out in the ninth inning of an exhibition game here between the Memphis

Leaguers and the Philadelphia A's, Philadelphia pitcher Rube Waddell, famous for his many eccentricities, sent all his fielders to the dugout except for the catcher and one infielder, and then proceeded to strike out the next two batters as the A's won the game 5-2. After Russwood burned down in 1960, the Chicks played at Hodges Field, a high-school ballyard. A ball had to travel only 204 feet down the left-field line to land in the seats at Hodges, so the number of homers hit here threatened to reach astronomical proportions. The Southern Association eventually ruled that balls hit over this short fence were to be ground-rule doubles.

**OTHER FAMOUS ALUMNI**

Art Howe, Ted Kluzewski, Tom "Flash" Gordon, Ken Singleton, and Kevin Appier all played here.

Hall of Famer Kid Nichols won 11 games here in 1888, and one of his teammates was fellow Hall of Famer Buck Ewing. Two other Hall of Famers were teammates in 1917. Waite Hoyt won just three of 12 decisions before being promoted to Montreal, while Dazzy Vance fared slightly better, going 6-8.

In 1955, Luis Aparicio, a future Hall of Fame shortstop, led the Southern Association with 48 steals, 314 putouts and 44 errors while also batting .273. In 1944, his second season with Memphis, one-armed outfielder Pete Gray was named the Southern Association's MVP after leading the league with 68 stolen bases while also batting .333. In 1982, 9,000 fans were on hand when Gray returned to Memphis to throw out the first pitch at McCarver Stadium on Opening Day.

In 1986, Bo Jackson made his professional baseball debut with Memphis. He batted .277 with seven home runs and 81 strikeouts in 184 at-bats before being promoted to Kansas City later that season. Brian McRae (.268, 10 homers and 64 runs batted in) and Jeff Conine (.320 and 95 runs batted in) were teammates with the 1990 Chicks, winners of the Southern League championship. Bob Hamelin, 1994 AL Rookie of the Year, spent 1989 and '92 here, hitting 22 home runs overall.

### ◆ BALLPARK EXTRAS
There is a picnic area in left. Among the best concession items here are barbecue pork sandwiches and good grilled barbecue ribs.

### ◆ ATTRACTIONS
Beale Street is the birthplace of the Memphis blues. You can visit the Beale Street Blues Museum and the clubs

that line this historic street. For further information, call (901) 526-0110.

The biggest tourist attraction in Memphis is Graceland, former home of Elvis Presley. Admission prices vary according to what sights you wish to see here, such as the Lisa Marie Jet, the *Sincerely Elvis* film or just the mansion itself. For further information, call (901) 332-3322/(800) 238-2000.

For additional information about Memphis, call the Visitors' Information Center, (901) 543-5333.

### ◆ DINING

B.B. King's Blues Club and Restaurant, about 20 minutes from the ballpark, offers tasty Southern food to go along with the blues. Noteworthy menu selections include red beans and rice, grilled catfish, and black-eyed pea dip. B.B. King's also has a good buffet lunch special. 143 Beale Street, (901) 524-KING.

### ◆ LODGING

Holiday Inn–Medical Center is on U.S. 70 near the intersection with U.S. 72, about 10 minutes from the ballpark. (901) 278-4100/(800) HOLIDAY.

Hampton Inn Medical Center is at exit 30 off I-240, about 15 minutes from the ballpark. (901) 276-1175/(800) 426-7866.

### ◆ DIRECTIONS

From the south, take I-240 east to the Airways Boulevard exit and go north. This turns into East Parkway. Turn right off the parkway onto Central Avenue. The ballpark will be on the right. From the west, take I-240 south and exit at Madison Avenue. Go east on Madison and turn right on East Parkway. Then turn left on Central. The ballpark will be on the right. From the east, take the Sam Cooper/Broad Street exit off I-240. Turn left on Hollywood and then right on Central. The ballpark will be on the left. Tim McCarver is located next to the Liberty Bowl, so plenty of parking is available at $2 per car.

---

**TIM McCARVER STADIUM**
**800 Home Run Lane**
**Memphis, TN 38104**
**(901) 272-1687**

**Capacity: 9,841**
**LF 323, CF 398, RF 325**

---

### ◆ TICKET AND SCHEDULE INFORMATION

Most games are played at night, starting at 7:15 P.M. Sunday games in April and May begin at 2:15 P.M. and 6:15 P.M.. the rest of the year.

The Chicks' season opener is usually in early April, and the season ends in the first week of September.

Ticket prices: $6 box seats; $5 general admission; and $1.96 bleachers, priced to fit a promotion by a radio station whose frequency corresponds to this price. Seniors 60 and over, children 12 and under and military with identification pay $4 for box seats and $3 for general admission. The team will award as yet undetermined prizes in 1995 to the lucky patron determined to be the 12 millionth fan in Memphis baseball history.

## ORLANDO CUBS

**CHICAGO CUBS**

In the high-tech entertainment land of Disney, Tinker Field's old-time flavor seems oddly out of place. It first opened in 1914 and was renamed in 1921 to honor Hall of Famer Joe Tinker, who had retired to Orlando after his playing career ended. A bust of Hall of Famer Clark Griffith greets those who enter Tinker Field. Griffith was the former owner of the Washington Senators, who conducted spring training in Orlando for many years, beginning in 1936. In the largely uncovered grandstand, approximately 1,500 of the seats originated in the Senators' old home in Washington, Griffith Stadium, which was torn down following the 1961 season. Besides a coat of gold paint, these historic seats are still in their original condition. The grandstand also features one of pro baseball's few open press boxes.

Above Tinker's home dugout, you can find the small building constructed by Clark Griffith, complete with a bathroom and a deck so he could watch his team in relative comfort. Today, tables and folding chairs atop the Cubs' dugout afford fans an unusual view of the diamond. The unpadded outfield fence here is made of metal, which you will be reminded of every time a ball thuds against it. Over the years, Tinker's fence has picked up dents from the countless fly balls and line drives that have caromed off it. The Citrus Bowl is located behind the right-field wall, and part of that stadium's stands hang over Tinker's fence. Any ball hitting the Citrus Bowl counts as a home run.

### ◆ LOCAL AND TEAM HISTORY

Organized baseball first appeared here in 1919 when Orlando began a 54-year (1919-24, '26-28, '37-41, '46-61, '63-72) association with the Florida State League.

Orlando spent the 1942 season in the Class D Florida East Coast League, which folded in May of that year. The city joined the Southern League in 1973 and began its current affiliation with the Chicago Cubs in 1993.

Joe Tinker effectively ended his playing career in 1917. After serving as team president for Columbus of the American Association in 1919-20, Tinker moved to Orlando, where he became Orlando's manager and owner in 1921. In Tinker's only season as the Orlando Tigers' field manager, the team responded to his leadership by winning the Class C Florida State League title with a record of 73-42. That same season, Tinker penciled himself into the lineup for two games, his last as a player.

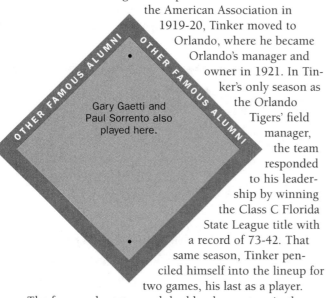

Gary Gaetti and Paul Sorrento also played here.

OTHER FAMOUS ALUMNI

The former shortstop and double-play partner in the famous Tinker-to-Evers-to-Chance trio, made the most of his final at-bats, going 1 for 3 while scoring a run. Rod Carew played for the Orlando Twins 44 years later. In 1965, Carew batted .303 but the Twins finished in third, eight games out of first place. Four years later, Bert Blyleven, Carew's future Minnesota teammate, won all five of his decisions while also posting a 1.45 ERA. The next season, Blyleven began his 22-year big-league career in which he won 287 games and amassed 3,701 strikeouts. Frank Viola, another future pitching star for Minnesota, went 5-4 with a 3.43 ERA as a 21-year-old rookie for Orlando in 1981. Three years later, Mark Portugal won 14 games but also walked 113 batters in 196 innings.

The 1990 Orlando Sunrays won the Southern League's Eastern Division title behind Chuck Knoblauch (.289) and Scott Erickson (8-3, 3.03 ERA). Minnesota's manager Tom Kelly spent two years in Orlando (1981-82) as the O-Twins' skipper, winning the league championship in '81 with a record of 79-63.

### ◆ BALLPARK EXTRAS

The Twins are operating a grill for the first time in 1995. Philadelphia cheese steaks, Italian sausages, chicken and burgers are some of the items that will be available. There is a picnic area in left field.

### ◆ ATTRACTIONS

Walt Disney World includes EPCOT Center, The Magic Kingdom and Disney-MGM Studios Theme Park. Admission fees vary depending on which attractions you wish to see. For further information, call (407) 824-4321.

Universal Studios Florida recreates several famous movies. Admission is $31, $28.50 for seniors over 50 and $25 for children 3 to 9. For further information, call (407) 363-8000.

For additional information about Orlando, call the Tourist Information Center, (407) 363-5871.

### ◆ DINING

Straub's Seafood Restaurant, about 15 minutes from the ballpark, is somewhat pricey but the fare is good. There is a selection of grilled fish as well as Cajun-style seafood. Ask about the daily specials. 5101 E. Colonial Drive, (407) 273-9330.

### ◆ LODGING

Holiday Inn Centroplex/Orlando Arena is on U.S. 17/92, just east of I-4, about 20 minutes from the ballpark. (407) 843-1360/(800) HOLIDAY.

Ramada Orlando Central is on State Route 50, about 2 miles west of I-4 and about 10 minutes from the ballpark. (407) 295-5270/(800)228-2828.

### ◆ DIRECTIONS

From I-4, take the East-West Expressway west. Take the first exit, Orange Blossom Trail, and get on Frontage Road instead of the Trail. Go to the second stop sign and turn right. The ballpark will be immediately visible. Parking is available for $2 per car at the ballpark and is also available in several area lots.

**TINKER FIELD**
**287 Tampa Avenue S**
**Orlando, FL 32805**
**(407) 872-7593**

**Capacity: 5,104**
**LF 340, CF 425, RF 320**

### ◆ TICKET AND SCHEDULE INFORMATION

Most games are played at night, starting at 7 P.M. Sunday games begin at 2 P.M.

The Cubs' home opener is usually in early April, and the season ends in the first week of September.

Ticket prices: $6 box seats; $4 reserved seats; $3 general admission. Seniors and children receive a $1 discount on each ticket.

# TEXAS LEAGUE

The Texas League was an original member of the National Association, which began in 1902, and it has been in operation since, with the exception of the war years of 1943-45. There was no league champion crowned in 1971, however, as the league played that one season in what was known as the Dixie Association, with an interlocking schedule with the Southern League. One of the best offensive seasons in the league's history was had by Clarence "Big Boy" Kraft, who drove in 196 runs for Fort Worth in 1924, setting league marks which still stand in runs batted in, extra-base hits (96) and total bases (414). Ken Guettler holds the league home-run mark, hitting 62 for Shreveport in 1956. Dizzy Dean tossed a league-best 11 shutouts for Houston in 1931.

The league plays 136 games. The defending champion is El Paso, the Brewers affiliate. League attendance for 1994 was 2,108,405 overall, up more than 216,000 from 1993 and a single-season record for the circuit. San Antonio drew 411,959 to set a league record. Tulsa (344,764), El Paso (327,542) and Jackson (148,647) also set team records for season attendance.

• • •

*A mountain sunset highlights this scenic view of El Paso's Cohen Stadium.*

# ARKANSAS TRAVELERS

## ST. LOUIS CARDINALS

Ray Winder Field was built in 1932 and has been the home of the Travelers ever since. About 2,000 seats at Ray Winder Field are the original wooden seats installed that year. The stadium is located in War Memorial Park, which also houses the Little Rock Zoo, War Memorial Fitness Center and War Memorial Stadium, the Little Rock home of the Arkansas Razorbacks football team.

The park has been completely renovated during the past 15 years. Travelers General Manager Bill Valentine takes pride in having the "cleanest ballpark in all of baseball."

One unusual feature here is a 60-foot screen above the outfield fence, from left-center past the right-field foul pole. Its job is to protect traffic on adjacent I-630.

### ◆ LOCAL AND TEAM HISTORY

Little Rock joined the Southern Association in 1901 as a charter member and remained in the league off and on for more than 50 years. Before entering the Texas League in 1966, Little Rock spent time in two Class AAA leagues, the International in 1963 and the Pacific Coast in 1964-1965. The Travelers' current affiliation with St. Louis began in 1966, the longest term with one big-league team in the Texas League. On July 21, 1946, Travelers' outfielder Lew Flick had one of the best days in Southern Association history, recording nine straight hits in the first game of a doubleheader. He went 12 for 13 for both games. In 1908, Tris Speaker was the Southern Association's leading hitter with a .350 average, while also topping the loop in runs and hits. Rube Robinson, who won 314 games—273 in the minors over his 22-year pro career—may be the greatest pitcher in Little Rock history. He spent 13 seasons (1916-28) here and was the Southern Association's top pitcher from 1919 to '22, when he won 92 games and led the league in wins three times.

In 1963, Dick Allen became the first African-American to play for Little Rock, when segregation was still the rule. Allen endured much abuse that summer, but he ended the season as the International League's top slugger, with 33 home runs, 263 total bases and 97 runs batted in. The next season he was the National League Rookie of the Year.

The team's nickname comes from an Arkansas legend about a 19th-century trader who rode throughout the northern part of the state telling stories and selling his wares.

### ◆ BALLPARK EXTRAS

Brown Packing Company makes hot dogs and Polish sausages especially for the Travelers. One unique feature is that beer is sold by the can, yet fans seldom litter the empty containers. The popular promotions include Clunker Car Night and Captain Dynamite's self-demolition act. (501) 868-5806.

### ◆ ATTRACTIONS

Pinnacle Mountain, which has hiking and other outdoor activities, is off I-430, about 20 minutes from the ballpark.

Old State House/Arkansas Territorial Restoration is where President Bill Clinton made his victory speech in November 1992. The restoration exhibit features restored cabins. It's downtown, about 10 minutes away. (501) 324-9685.

Hot Springs is one hour south on I-30 and Route 70. It features Bill Clinton's old home, turn-of-the-century bathhouses and Oaklawn Race Track (501) 623-4411.

For more information about the Little Rock area, call the Chamber of Commerce, (501) 374-4871.

### ◆ DINING

Food Court at University Mall and Food Court at Park Plaza Mall are across the street from each other at University and Markham and feature primarily fast-food chains.

Your Mama's Good Food is a couple of minutes from the field. 2811 Kavanaugh Avenue, (501) 663-6333.

### ◆ LODGING

Little Rock Hilton is five minutes from the ballpark. I-630 and University, Little Rock, (501) 664-5420/(800) 445-8667.

La Quinta Inn is just two minutes away. Fair Park and 12th Street, Little Rock, (800) 531-5900.

### ◆ DIRECTIONS

From Memphis, take I-40 across the Arkansas River Bridge to I-630 exit on right. Proceed to Fair Park Boulevard. Take first right and follow signs.

From Dallas, take I-30 to I-430 South, then get off at

OTHER FAMOUS ALUMNI OTHER FAMOUS ALUMNI

Fergie Jenkins, Pat Gillick, Travis Jackson, Bill Dickey, Dallas Green, Paul "Daffy" Dean, Keith Hernandez, Al Hrabosky, Jose Cruz, Garry Templeton, Jim Bunning, Eddie Lopat, Leon Durham, Jim Riggleman, Andy Van Slyke, Bernard Gilkey and Ray Lankford all played here.

I-630 East exit. Exit at Fair Park Boulevard on left. Take first right and follow signs.

From downtown Little Rock, take Markham Avenue and turn south on Monroe Street. Stadium is ½ mile away. Parking is free at the ballpark and somewhat limited. Additional parking is available in the area.

```
RAY WINDER FIELD,
WAR MEMORIAL PARK
Little Rock, AK 72205
(501) 664-1555
─────────────────
Capacity: 6,781
LF 330, CF 390, RF 345
```

### ◆ TICKET AND SCHEDULE INFORMATION

Single games start at 7:30 P.M., doubleheaders at 6:30 P.M. and Sunday games at 3 P.M.

The Travelers' season begins the second week of April and ends the last week of August.

Ticket prices: $6 box seats; $4 general admission. Children 14 and under get $2 discounts. Military personnel get $1 discounts.

# EL PASO DIABLOS

## MILWAUKEE BREWERS

**C**ohen Stadium is a state-of-the-art facility with 20 luxury sky boxes. The color-graphics scoreboard measures 24 feet by 18 feet and is surrounded by four 17-by-10 foot panels.

In June 1994, 174 giant palm trees were planted to provide a spectacular backdrop beyond the outfield fence, as well as around the main entrance and parking areas, giving this ballpark a decidedly non-El Paso appearance since palm trees are not commonplace in this area. But the outside of Cohen Stadium, painted in desert-like colors, does have a distinctively Southwestern feel. The landscaping will be completed this spring with a waterfall adorning the main gate. The Franklin Mountains lie directly behind the stadium, creating the setting for great sunsets—and tricky winds on the field as the sun goes down.

The ballpark is named for Syd and Andy Cohen, former major-league players who also played for El Paso

and were local civic leaders. Syd, who was the last pitcher to both strikeout and yield a home run to Babe Ruth when he was still a New York Yankee, ended his 37-year pro career in El Paso as a coach in 1965.

### ◆ LOCAL AND TEAM HISTORY

Although amateur baseball in El Paso dates back to the 1880s, it was not until the El Paso Mackmen joined the Class D Rio Grande Valley Association in 1915 that this city had its own organized-baseball team. Since the Association folded during the summer of '15, El Paso has fielded teams in eight other minor leagues. El Paso first joined the Texas League in 1962 and has belonged to this circuit continuously since 1972. The current affiliation with Milwaukee began in 1981.

**OTHER FAMOUS ALUMNI**

Jose Cardenal, Chuck Tanner, Tom Brunansky, Carney Lansford, Greg Vaughn, Gary Sheffield, Jesus Alou, Manny Mota, Frank Tanana, Mickey Rivers, John Jaha, Chris Bosio, Tom Candiotti, Ted Higuera and Ken Schrom, currently a co-owner of the team, all played or managed here.

El Paso teams formerly played at Dudley Field, built in 1924. This quirky ballpark featured perhaps professional baseball's only grandstand built of adobe bricks and equipped with giant venetian blinds to ward off the sun. There was also a rise in center field designed to prevent flooding from a canal just beyond the outfield fence. The dimensions of Dudley Field, 300 feet down the left-field line and 305 to right, coupled with El Paso's high elevation and thin air, made this ballpark a hitters' paradise and the site of many high-scoring games. One such affair occurred on April 30, 1983, when El Paso defeated Beaumont 35-21. El Paso scored in every inning, with six runs in the first, fourth, fifth and sixth, and both teams collected 56 hits on the way to setting the all-time Texas League record for most runs scored in a single game. This old ballpark, nicknamed the "Dudley Dome," also produced six consecutive Texas League batting champs from 1973-1978, as well as in 1980, 1982 to '83 and 1985 to '87.

### ◆ BALLPARK EXTRAS

El Paso is so well-known for its promotions that each year team president Jim Paul sponsors a popular seminar on promotions for fellow minor-league entrepreneurs. El Paso is especially proud of its year-long "Baseball Buddies" program, where area Little League players accompany the Diablos onto the field for the National Anthem.

The most popular concessions are the 25-cent hot-dog nights each Sunday. The Diablos also sell *churros* (crullers) and egg rolls.

### ◆ ATTRACTIONS

Juarez, Mexico, is a bargain hunter's paradise. Just go across the I-10 downtown bridge.

There's also casino gambling at the Tigua Indian Reservation. I-10 at Zaragosa. (915) 859-7913.

Fort Bliss is one of the country's biggest U.S. Army bases. I-54 at Fort Bliss. (915) 568-2121.

For more information about the El Paso area, call the Chamber of Commerce, (915) 534-0500.

### ◆ DINING

Cappetto's has good Italian food, between 10 and 15 minutes from the ballpark. Montana and Piedras streets, (915) 566-9357.

San Francisco Grill is downtown, 15-20 minutes away. I-10 and Kansas, (915) 545-1386.

### ◆ LODGING

Marriott Hotel is 15 minutes away. I-10 at Airport Way and Montana, El Paso, (915) 778-6611/(800) 228-9290.

Embassy Suites is also 15 minutes from the park. I-10 at Gateway East and Airport Way, El Paso, (915) 779-6222/(800) 362-2779. Parking is ample and costs $2.

### ◆ DIRECTIONS

Take I-10 to Patriot Highway (U.S. 54) North. Go six to eight miles to Diana exit (note signs for Cohen Stadium). Go on Diana through one traffic light. Stadium is on right.

---

**COHEN STADIUM**
**9700 Gateway North Boulevard**
**El Paso, TX 79924**
**(915) 755-2000**

---

**Capacity: 9,776**
**LF 340, CF 410, RF 340**

---

### ◆ TICKET AND SCHEDULE INFORMATION

From Opening Day to Memorial Day, games Sunday through Thursday start at 6:30 P.M. and games Friday and Saturday start at 7 P.M. After Memorial Day, Monday through Saturday games start at 7 P.M., Sunday games at 6:30 P.M.

El Paso's season begins the second week of April and runs until the last week of August.

Ticket prices: $6 box seats; $5 reserved seats; $4 general admission.

# JACKSON GENERALS

**HOUSTON ASTROS**

**S**ettle into your seat at Smith-Willis Stadium, built in 1975, and enjoy this ballpark's best feature: a forest of verdant southern pine trees behind the outfield fence. The largely brick construction and those trees make this an attractive, if not particularly unique, venue for baseball. Renovations here in 1991 resulted in new lights, new seats and a picnic area in right field. Outside the ballpark there is an athletic field as well as a true hidden gem unknown to many baseball fans—the Dizzy Dean Museum, just on the edge of Smith-Willis' parking lot. The museum details the Hall of Famer's pitching and broadcasting careers, while also housing several items of memorabilia. There are plans to transfer the contents of this museum to a planned Mississippi Sports Hall of Fame, which is to be built next to the ballpark in the near future.

### ◆ LOCAL AND TEAM HISTORY

In 1904, the Jackson Senators debuted as this city's first pro team, in the Class D Delta League, which folded after its first and only season. The Senators returned the next year, beginning a sporadic 21-year association (1905-08, '10-13, '22-32, '36, '53) with the Class D Cotton States League. Jackson also fielded teams in five other leagues: Mississippi State, Dixie, East Dixie, Southeastern and Texas. Jackson began its current association with the Astros in 1991.

In 1927, Bill Dickey was the top catcher in the Cotton States League, as he compiled the best fielding average among receivers while also batting .297. Fred Singon, an All-American football player in 1929 and '30 at the University of Alabama, played 50 games in the outfield for the 1931 Cotton States League champion

**OTHER FAMOUS ALUMNI   OTHER FAMOUS ALUMNI**

Mookie Wilson, Jody Davis, Darryl Strawberry, Lenny Dykstra, Kevin Mitchell, Roger McDowell, Kevin Tapani, Chuck Carr, Gregg Jefferies, Mike Scott, Jeff Reardon, Jesse Orosco, Rick Aguilera, Brian Hunter and Tony Eusebio have all played here.

Jackson Red Sox, batting .276. In 1981, manager Davey Johnson led the Jackson Mets to their first Texas League title.

### ◆ BALLPARK EXTRAS
The favorite concessions include Big Smokey grilled sausage and grilled chicken. There is a no-smoking, no-alcohol family section. Top promotions are fireworks, Diamond Dig and the annual youth clinic.

### ◆ ATTRACTIONS
About an hour away in Vicksburg, check out the National Military Park where Union troops commanded by U.S. Grant won a decisive victory over the Confederates on July 4, 1863. Admission is $4 per car. For further information, call (601) 636-0583.

In Jackson, the Mississippi Museum of Natural Science features several hands-on exhibits and an aquarium highlighting Mississippi River aquatic life. Admission is free. For further information, call (601) 354-7303. The Dizzy Dean Museum has several trophies, autographed baseballs and jerseys donated by the Dean family. Admission is just $1, one of the best baseball bargains around. For further information, call (601) 960-2404.

For more information about Jackson, call the Visitors' Bureau (601) 960-1891/(800) 354-7695.

### ◆ DINING
At the Cafe Creole, about 15 minutes from the ballpark, you can look through the kitchen door and see a variety of hot sauces and spices stacked neatly on the shelf. These condiments are used liberally in the preparation of several good menu choices, including crawfish étouffée and redfish suzette. Try the chocolate silk pie for dessert. 5852 Ridgewood Road, (601) 956-4563.

### ◆ LODGING
The Hampton Inn is about five minutes from the ballpark. 465 Briarwood Drive, (601) 956-3611/(800) HAMPTON.

Holiday Inn is also about five minutes away. 5775 I-55 North, (601) 366-9411/(800) HOLIDAY.

### ◆ DIRECTIONS
From I-55, take Lakeland Drive East exit and go ¼ mile. Stadium is on the left. Parking is ample and free.

---

**SMITH-WILLS STADIUM**
**1200 Lakeland Drive**
**Jackson, MS 39216**
**(601) 981-4664**

---

**Capacity: 5,200**
**LF 330, CF 400, RF 330**

---

### ◆ TICKET AND SCHEDULE INFORMATION
Games are at 7 P.M. from Monday through Saturday and at 2:30 P.M. Sunday (April-July), with 6 P.M. starts for doubleheaders and Sunday games in August.

The Generals' season begins the second week of April and closes the last week of August.

Ticket prices: $5 reserved seats; $4 general admission, $3 students/seniors/military personnel.

# MIDLAND ANGELS

## CALIFORNIA ANGELS

The wind here at Christensen Stadium whips in from the flat lands and open fields surrounding it, creating excellent hitting conditions. These gales, coupled with the light west Texas air and the ballpark's intimate size, can make this place a pitcher's nightmare. Many a confident prospect has felt his self-assurance disappear after watching his pitches being propelled by Midland's wind over the outfield fence. One game here was even "winded-out" when consistent 60-70 mph gusts on May 1, 1993, forced a postponement. Other natural forces can also play a big role in Midland. A 1977 night game at Christensen (then called Angels Stadium) was called after a large mass of grasshoppers swarmed into the ballpark. The stadium is surrounded by farms and a golf course, and its small size results in good views of the action on the field. The seating area down the third-base line is largely covered, while the remaining seats have no roof overhead. There are picnic areas down each foul line. In a longstanding local tradition, the Angels' staff collects dollars from the crowd whenever an Angel hits a home run. Fans contribute singles, and sometimes bigger bills if the blast is particularly prodigious, which are given to the home-run-hitting player. Collections can range up to about $250.

### ◆ LOCAL AND TEAM HISTORY
Organized baseball first came here in 1928 when Midland began a two-year stint in the West Texas League. This city has fielded teams in five other circuits, including West Texas-New Mexico League (1937-40), Longhorn League (1947-55), Southwestern League (1956-57) and Sophomore League (1958-59). Midland has been a member of the Texas League continuously since joining

in 1972; the current affiliation with California began in 1985. In a testament to this park's batter-friendly atmosphere, only one Midland pitcher has won the league ERA title since this franchise entered the Texas League.

Dan Corder accomplished the feat in 1973 with a 2.33 ERA. Lee Smith, baseball's all-time saves leader, was a struggling starting pitcher when he threw for the Midland Cubs in 1978, posting an 8-10 record, a 5.98 ERA and a league-leading 128 walks.

OTHER FAMOUS ALUMNI

Joe Carter, Tim Salmon, Bryan Harvey, Bert Blyleven, Shawon Dunston, Jim Edmonds, Mel Hall, Billy Hatcher, Mark McLemore, Eduardo Perez, Bruce Sutter, Fernando Valenzuela and Devon White played here.

Smith recalls how he became a relief pitcher while playing for Midland the following season: "We were in Little Rock, Arkansas, and I was imitating [Kansas City Royals' reliever] Al Hrabosky. I was throwing sidearm in the bullpen on my day to throw on the side. [Midland manager Randy] Hundley saw me and asked if I'd ever thought of throwing sidearm. I said, 'No, man. I ain't nobody's relief pitcher. I'm a starting pitcher.' That same night, he brought me into the game in relief. We were up by one run in the ninth inning. I came in, threw sidearm and punched out two of the three guys I faced."

One of the Texas League's signature high-scoring games occurred here in 1990 when Wichita defeated Midland 33-17. The teams combined for 47 hits and nine errors in the league's biggest offensive explosion since El Paso topped Beaumont 35-21 seven years earlier. In 1991, Midland and El Paso played the longest nine-inning game in league history. The visiting Angels defeated the Diablos 20-18 in a game that lasted four hours and 17 minutes, eclipsing the Midland-Wichita 1990 marathon by two minutes, and featured 45 hits by both teams off nine pitchers.

### ◆ BALLPARK EXTRAS

The most popular concessions are pizza; Frito pies, which are corn chips topped with chili and cheese; and nachos. The top promotions are the annual Fourth of July celebration, Turn Back the Clock Game and appearances by the Phillie Phanatic and The Famous Chicken. Christensen Stadium has a family section.

### ◆ ATTRACTIONS

The Petroleum Museum is about 15 minutes from the stadium on I-20 West in Midland. (915) 683-4403.

For more information about Midland, call the Chamber of Commerce, (915) 683-3381.

### ◆ DINING

There's a Chili's, five minutes away from the park, for reliable family fare. 2100 W. Loop 250 N, (915) 687-3745.

Outback Steak House is also just five minutes away. 2314 W. Loop 250 N, (915) 684-1152.

### ◆ LODGING

Midland Hilton and Towers is on Wall Street downtown, five minutes away. 117 W. Wall Street, Midland, (915) 683-6131/(800) 445-8667.

Plaza Inn is just a couple minutes away from the park. 4108 N. Big Spring, Midland, (915) 686-8733.

### ◆ DIRECTIONS

From the Rankin Highway, take the Big Spring exit to Loop 250 and exit right on Lamesa Road. Parking is plentiful and free.

**CHRISTENSEN STADIUM**
**4300 N. Lamesa Road**
**Midland, TX 79705**
**(915) 683-4251**

**Capacity: 5,000**
**LF 335, CF 392, RF 335**

### ◆ TICKET AND SCHEDULE INFORMATION

Games are at 7 P.M. from Monday through Saturday and at 6 P.M. on Sunday.

The Angels' season begins in mid-April and runs through the end of August.

Ticket prices: $6 box seats; $5 reserved seats; $4 adult general admission, $2 children 6 to 12 and seniors.

# SAN ANTONIO MISSIONS

## LOS ANGELES DODGERS

Missions Stadium was opened April 18, 1994, and is located in a metropolitan area of more than one million people. The stadium is acclaimed for its design, which accents a Southwestern flavor. In addition, a prevailing breeze from center field to home plate, combined with the sunsets behind the stadium, creates a pleasant Texas evening.

The stadium is adjacent to Kelly and Lackland Air Force bases, so Missions fans are treated to impromptu "air shows" every night.

### ◆ LOCAL AND TEAM HISTORY

The Missions are the lone remaining charter member of the Texas League from 1888, though they have not played continuously since that time. The city's other nicknames over the years include Missionaries, Bears, Shamrocks and Broncos. San Antonio spent four seasons (1903-06) in the South Texas League. In 1907, this city renewed its association with the Texas League.

Ike Boone had one of the greatest seasons in Texas League history with San Antonio in 1923. That year, Boone led the league in almost every batting category, including a .402 average, 135 runs batted in, 26 triples, 53 doubles, 241 hits and 134 runs scored. Boone also had a 37-game hitting streak. He is the all-time minor league batting leader, with a .370 average. He also set an organized-baseball record with 553 total bases in 1929. Despite Boone's titanic season in '23 San Antonio finished in second, 13½ games out of first. Joe Morgan was the Texas League MVP in 1964 when he batted .323, with 90 runs batted in and a league-best 42 doubles. Ten years later, Dennis Eckersley was named the Texas League's Right Handed Pitcher of the Year after he led the circuit with 163 strikeouts, and a .824 winning percentage, while tying for the lead in wins (14) and shutouts (five).

OTHER FAMOUS ALUMNI OTHER FAMOUS ALUMNI
Billy Williams, Steve Sax, Orel Hershiser, Sid Fernandez, Sid Bream, Tom Niedenfuer, Ryne Duren, Brooks Robinson, Eric Karros, Mike Piazza and Raul Mondesi all played here.

### ◆ BALLPARK EXTRAS

The stadium has two no-alcohol, no-smoking family sections, as well as a catered picnic area. Fans sit on lawn chairs and blankets on a grassy berm beyond the left-field fence.

At the concession stands, the beef and chicken fajitas are the class of the league. Or you can try a "catcher's mitt" featuring pita bread and *picadillo* combined with roasted ears of corn and a locally brewed beer.

*Baseball Weekly* has touted the Missions' Puffy Taco as one of the premier mascots in the game.

### ◆ ATTRACTIONS

San Antonio features Riverwalk downtown, with its plethora of shops, restaurants and clubs; Fiesta Texas amusement park, on I-10 (210-697-5050); Sea World of Texas, on Highway 151 (210-523-3611); the Alamo, downtown, (210-225-1391); the new Alamodome, home of the NBA's Spurs, on I-7 downtown (210-207-3663); and more than 250 years of history. None of those attractions is more than 20 minutes from Municipal Stadium.

For more information about San Antonio, call the Visitors' Bureau, (210) 270-8748/(800) 447-3372.

### ◆ DINING

The Zuni Grill, about 20 minutes from the ballpark, in the heart of Riverwalk, serves the kind of imaginative Southwestern fare San Antonio is known for. (210) 227-0864.

The San Antonio International Airport area, located along Loop 410 W, is about 20 minutes away and offers a wide range of choices.

### ◆ LODGING

Holiday Inn Market Square (318 W. Durango) is located downtown about 10 minutes from the ballpark. (210) 225-3211/(800) HOLIDAY.

### ◆ DIRECTIONS

Municipal Stadium is located in southwest San Antonio at the intersection of Highway 90 West and Callaghan Road. Take Loop 410 West to 90 East, then go two miles to the Callaghan exit. From downtown, take I-35 South to 90 West, then go five miles to the Callaghan exit. I-35, I-37 and Highway 281 all intersect with Highway 90 West.

MUNICIPAL STADIUM
5757 Highway 90 W
San Antonio, TX 78227
(210) 675-7275

Capacity: 6,300
LF 310, CF 402, RF 340

### ◆ TICKET AND SCHEDULE INFORMATION

Games are at 7:05 P.M. Monday through Saturday and at 6:05 P.M. on Sunday. Exceptions: 12:05 P.M. on April 25 and May 17.

San Antonio's season begins the second week of April and runs through the last week of August.

Ticket prices: $8 executive box seats; $7 box seats; $6 upper box seats; $5 reserved seats; $4 general admission and $2 children 12 and under.

# SHREVEPORT CAPTAINS

## SAN FRANCISCO GIANTS

Given the name of this ballpark, built in 1986, it should come as no surprise that it is located on the Louisiana State Fairgrounds. Hirsch Coliseum, home of the Continental Basketball Association's Shreveport Crawdads, is about ¼ mile away, across a wide expanse of concrete. The site of college football's Independence Bowl is also nearby. An interstate highway runs behind the right-field fence. When this ballpark first opened, there was concern that passing cars on the highway were in danger of being struck by home-run balls off the bats of left-handed hitters, but since a home run needs to travel more than 500 feet to reach the highway, such concerns have proved groundless. The heavy, humid air here in the summer plus deep power alleys of 385 feet, a 12-foot-high outfield fence and a 24-foot-high wall in center field, combine to make Fair Grounds Field a pitchers' ballpark. Even a steady wind blowing out to the fences does not help hitters here, who get frustrated with their inability to hit the ball out of this park even in batting practice. The grandstand behind home plate is uncovered, but you will have a roof over your head if your seats are on the first- and third-base sides.

### ◆ LOCAL AND TEAM HISTORY

This season marks the 100th anniversary of pro baseball in Shreveport. Since the turn of the century, Shreveport has been associated with five minor leagues, beginning with a nine-year membership (1902-1907, 1959-1961) in the Southern Association. This city first joined the Texas League in 1895 and has been in this circuit continuously since 1968. Shreveport began its current affiliation with San Francisco in 1979. Beginning in 1903, several big-league teams, including the Detroit Tigers, the New York Yankees and the Cincinnati Redlegs used Shreveport as their spring-training bases in the early years of the 20th century. Hall of Famer Al Simmons had an excellent season for Shreveport in 1923, batting .360, 42 points behind the .402 mark of San Antonio's Ike Boone, plus 12 homers and 99 runs batted in.

But as good as Simmons' season was, it paled in comparison to the year enjoyed by Ken Guettler in 1956. In his only season with Shreveport, Guettler led all of baseball with 62 home runs, tied for the sixth best single season total in organized-baseball history, while also leading the Texas League with 115 runs scored and 143 runs batted in. He was named the 1956 Texas League Player of the Year. The accomplishments of Guettler, known for his thick eyeglasses, were all the more impressive because of this city's ball-deadening humidity, the 20-foot-high outfield walls at Shreveport's old Texas League Park and the fact that Guettler played only 140 games in '56. During his 15 years in professional baseball, all in the minors, Guettler belted 330 career four-baggers and won an all-time-best eight home-run titles.

**OTHER FAMOUS ALUMNI**

Bill Terry, George Sisler, Zack Wheat, Cito Gaston, Dick Howser, Tony Pena, Darrell Evans, Rod Beck, Ralph Garr, Rob Deer, Dusty Baker, Smead Jolley, Jack Brillheart, John Burkett, Dan Gladden and Terry Mulholland played here.

This franchise holds the Texas League record for most consecutive playoff appearances—nine—representing every season the Captains have played in this ballpark since it opened in 1986.

### ◆ BALLPARK EXTRAS

There is a Beer Garden near the home bullpen down the left-field line. This is a popular place for local fans to congregate, grab a brew and watch the game. Grilled chicken and burgers are available here. There is a deli area behind first base where fans can build their own roast beef, turkey and ham sandwiches. Shreveport is the site of the 1995 Joint AA All-Star Game.

### ◆ ATTRACTIONS

The Louisiana State Exhibit Museum features various displays, relics, and paintings with a state history theme. Admission is free. For further information, call (318) 227-5196.

In April, Shreveport hosts a 10-day festival commemorating the Louisiana Purchase. For additional information about Shreveport, call the Tourist Bureau, (318) 222-9391/(800) 551-8682.

### ◆ DINING

Ralph & Kacoo's, about 15 minutes from the ballpark, specializes in Cajun cuisine and seafood. When you visit this informal restaurant, try the crawfish étouffée, seafood gumbo, creole stuffed crab and fried oysters. 1700 Old Minden Road, (318) 747-6660.

### ◆ LODGING

Ramada Inn Airport is at exit 13 off I-20, about 10 minutes from the ballpark. (318) 635-7531/(800) 284-0224.

Best Western Chateau Suite Hotel is at exit 19A off

I-20, about 15 minutes from the ballpark. (318) 222-7620/(800) 528-1234.

◆ **DIRECTIONS**

From I-20, take the Hearne Avenue exit right into the State Fairgrounds. The ballpark will be immediately visible. Plenty of free parking is available.

> **FAIR GROUNDS FIELD**
> P.O. Box 3448
> Shreveport, LA 71133
> (318) 636-5555
> ———
> Capacity: 6,200
> LF 330, CF 400, RF 330

◆ **TICKET AND SCHEDULE INFORMATION**

Most games are played at night, starting at 7:05 P.M. in April and May and at 7:35 P.M. the rest of the year. Sunday games begin at 6:05 P.M.

The Captains' home opener is usually in early April, and the season ends in the first week of September.

Ticket prices: $10 sky boxes; $6 field box seats; $4 general admission, $2 seniors, children 2 to 12 and military with identification. The Captains have a rather unique ticket offer. They sell some seats in their sky box behind home plate on a per-game basis for $10 apiece.

# TULSA DRILLERS

### TEXAS RANGERS

Drillers Stadium is located on the Tulsa County Fairgrounds in the central part of the city; left field runs parallel to bustling 15th Street. The stands here angle out toward the field behind the corner bases, so there is little room between the foul line and the stadium's concrete retaining wall. This feature, coupled with the short outfield dimensions here, help give the Drillers' home a cozy feel, even though it has the largest capacity of any in the AA. A number of home runs end up on 15th Street or in a supermarket parking lot across the street. A night game in 1989 ended in the 12th inning when current Chicago Cubs star Sammy Sosa hit a shot that kept rolling and stopped 550 feet away, at

the feet of a shopper exiting the market with a sack of groceries. Rob Deer, though, gets credit here for what is probably the longest home run in stadium history. His shot carried more than 500 feet out of the park, bounced once and then came to rest on the roof of the Homeland supermarket.

◆ **LOCAL AND TEAM HISTORY**

The franchise was founded in 1977 and has been affiliated with the Texas Rangers the entire time.

FAMOUS ALUMNI

Frank Robinson, Dizzy Dean, Juan Gonzalez and Ruben Sierra all played here.

Professional baseball was first played in Tulsa in 1905. Tulsa was previously home to the AA and AAA Tulsa Oilers, who played in the Texas League, Pacific Coast League and American Association. Affiliations included the St. Louis Browns (1921-29), Pittsburgh Pirates (1933), Chicago Cubs (1940-47, '56), Cincinnati Reds (1948-54), Cleveland Indians (1955), Philadelphia Phillies (1957-58) and St. Louis Cardinals (1959-76). In 1924, Lyman Lamb batted .373 and amassed 100 doubles, an organized-baseball record. Tulsa's "Pound 'em Paul" Easterling led the Texas League with 29 homers in 1934. Over his career, Easterling hit 261 home runs, 257 in the minors.

◆ **BALLPARK EXTRAS**

Concessions include pizza, Mexican fajitas and frozen yogurt. Best promotions are fireworks, bat night and jersey night.

◆ **ATTRACTIONS**

Gilcrease Museum (918-596-2700), Philbrook Museum (918-748-5325), River Parks (918-596-2001), Oral Roberts University (918-495-6161) and Tulsa University (918-631-2000) are within a few minutes of the stadium.

For more information about Tulsa, call the Chamber of Commerce at (918) 585-1201.

◆ **DINING**

Jamil's Steakhouse is about 10 minutes from the ballpark. 2833 E. 51st Street, (918) 742-9097.

Atlantic Sea Grill is about 20 minutes away. 8321-A E. 61st Street, (918) 252-7966.

◆ **LODGING**

Holiday Inn is about 10 minutes from the ballpark,

3131 E. 51st Street, Tulsa, (918) 743-9811/(800) HOLIDAY.

The Ramada Hotel is about five minutes away. 5000 E. Skelly Drive, Tulsa, (918) 622-7000/(800) 228-2828.

### ◆ DIRECTIONS
The stadium is 1½ miles south of I-244 and three miles north of I-44, at 15th Street and Yale Avenue. Parking is free and somewhat limited at the ballpark. If space is unavailable, you can park elsewhere on the fairgrounds or on the street.

```
DRILLERS STADIUM
4802 E. 15th Street
Tulsa, OK 74112
(918) 744-5901

Capacity: 10,814
LF 335, CF 390, RF 340
```

### ◆ TICKET AND SCHEDULE INFORMATION
Games are at 7:35 P.M. Monday through Saturday and at 2:05 P.M. Sunday on April and May; from June through August, Sunday games are at 6:05 P.M. There are 1:05 P.M. starts on April 25 and May 16.

The Drillers' season begins the second week of April and goes through the last week of August.

Ticket prices: $7 box seats; $5 reserved seats; $4 general admission. Children 14 and under get a $1 discount for most Sunday-Thursday games, seniors a $1 discount for most Monday-Tuesday games.

# WICHITA WRANGLERS

## KANSAS CITY ROYALS

One of the oldest parks in the minor leagues, Lawrence-Dumont Stadium was built in 1934 to host the National Semi-Pro Baseball Congress tournament, an event won by Satchel  Paige's team from Bismarck, North Dakota. Paige still holds the tournament record of 60 strikeouts. Lawrence-Dumont is one of the oldest parks still in use, and still hosts the National Baseball Congress World Series each summer. The stadium features a beautiful setting, across the Arkansas River from downtown Wichita. The best view of the skyline at night is from high in the grandstand. The stadium has undergone $6 million in renovations since 1989. There is now a play area for children, an open-air restaurant seating 200, a hot tub and public batting cages. The infield here is artificial turf, while the outfield is grass.

### ◆ LOCAL AND TEAM HISTORY
The Wichita Jobbers, this city's first pro team, spent four seasons (1905-08) in the Western Association. Subsequently, Wichita was associated with the Western League (1909-33), American Association (1956-58, '70-84) and Texas League (1987 to date). In 1907, the Jobbers won the Western Association title with a 98-35 record, one of the best for a full-season team in minor-league history. After playing 23 years in the majors, Bobby Wallace was Wichita's player-manager in 1917. In 1932, Arky Vaughan began his career with the Wichita Aviators by leading the Western League with 145 runs scored. Jocko Conlon was an outfielder for Wichita before beginning his career as an umpire.

**OTHER FAMOUS ALUMNI**
Roberto Alomar, Sandy Alomar Jr., Tony La Russa, Tom Browning, Larry Gura, Buddy Bell, Chris Chambliss, Carlos Baerga, Andy Benes, Dave Hollins and Ricky Bones played for Wichita teams. The NBC World Series has sent more than 600 players to the major leagues, including Billy Martin, Tom Seaver, Dave Winfield, Tony Gwynn and Roger Clemens.

Bob and Mindy Rich of Buffalo purchased the old AAA Wichita Aeros in 1984, and moved the franchise to Buffalo. Three years later, Larry Schmittou moved his AA Beaumont, Texas, franchise to Wichita and nicknamed it the Pilots. The Richs bought the Pilots in 1989.

### ◆ BALLPARK EXTRAS
The stadium features the Hard Ball Cafe, with char-broiled chicken and sausages. The park has a no-smoking, no-alcohol family section, an arcade and a play area.

Top promotions include Wilbur's Birthday Bash in mid-July, a party for the team mascot with 20 visiting mascots and a 360-foot ice-cream sundae. The NBC World Series features round-the-clock baseball for 56 consecutive hours. Fans who "survive" the entire tournament win sleeping bags and other prizes. More than 250 fans "survived" last year.

### ◆ ATTRACTIONS
Cowtown, a reproduction of Wichita in the cattle-drive era of the 1880s (316-264-6398); Old Town, a warehouse district converted to restaurants, shops and night-

clubs; and the Wichita Zoo (316-942-2213) are within 15 minutes of the stadium.

For more information about the Wichita area, call the Chamber of Commerce, (316) 265-7771.

### ◆ DINING
Old Town has fine restaurants, including River City Brewery, Rowdy Joe's Steakhouse (try the rattlesnake appetizer), and Heroes Sports Bar and Deli. Take the Washington Street exit off U.S. 54 and go north one mile to Douglas. Go west one block to Mosley and you will be in the heart of Old Town.

The Grape is a fine restaurant about 15 minutes away on the east side of town. 550 N. Rock Road, (316) 634-0113.

### ◆ LODGING
The Ramada Broadview, about five minutes from the ballpark, overlooks the stadium at the intersection of Douglas and the Arkansas River. 400 W. Douglas, Wichita, (316) 262-5000/(800) 228-2828.

Howard Johnson's is midway between the stadium and Old Town, about 10 minutes away. 125 N. Market, Wichita, (316) 263-2101/(800) 654-2000.

### ◆ DIRECTIONS
From I-35 or I-135, take the U.S. 54 (Kellogg) exit. Go west through downtown Wichita. Take the Seneca/Sycamore exit and go north ¼ mile to Maple. Take Maple back east ½ mile to Sycamore. The stadium is on the corner. Parking is somewhat limited and is free. Priority parking close to the ballpark costs $1. On-street parking is also available.

**LAWRENCE-DUMONT STADIUM**
**300 S. Sycamore Street**
**Wichita, KS 67213**
**(316) 267-3372**

**Capacity: 6,792**
**LF 344, CF 401, RF 312**

### ◆ TICKET AND SCHEDULE INFORMATION
All games are at 7:15 P.M., except for 2:15 P.M. starts on Sundays in April and May, and 6:15 P.M. Sundays in June-August. There are occasional business workers' games at 12:15 P.M. in June and schoolkids' games at 11:15 A.M. in May.

The Wranglers' season opens in the second week of April and ends the last week of August.

Ticket prices: $8 Club box seats (including waiter service); $7 box seats; $6 reserved chair-back seats; $4 general admission bleacher seats. There are $1 discounts for seniors, military personnel and children 12 and under.

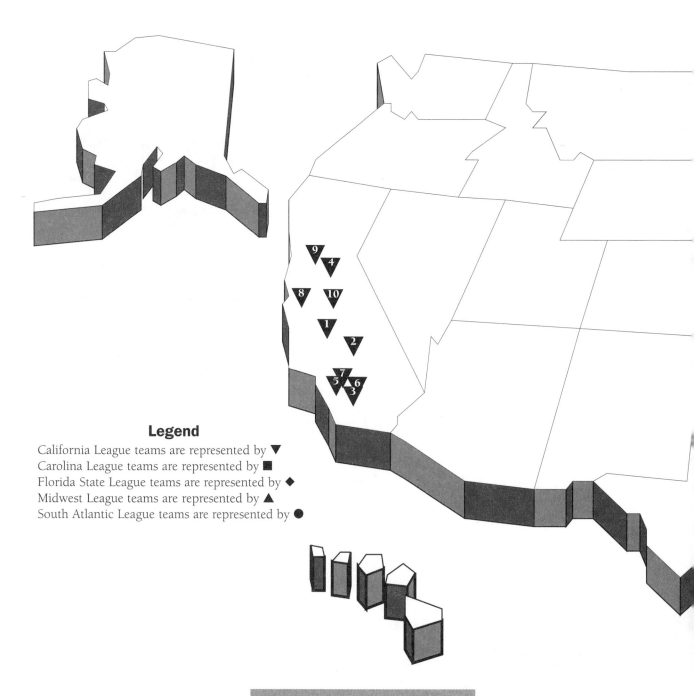

### Legend

California League teams are represented by ▼
Carolina League teams are represented by ■
Florida State League teams are represented by ◆
Midwest League teams are represented by ▲
South Atlantic League teams are represented by ●

## CLASS A

### CALIFORNIA LEAGUE

1. Bakersfield Blaze/Bakersfield, Calif.
2. High Desert Mavericks/Adelanto, Calif.
3. Lake Elsinore Storm/ Lake Elsinore, Calif.
4. Modesto A's/Modesto, Calif.
5. Rancho Cucamonga Quakes/
    Rancho Cucamonga, Calif.
6. Riverside Pilots/Riverside, Calif.
7. San Bernardino Spirit/
    San Bernardino, Calif.
8. San Jose Giants/San Jose, Calif.
9. Stockton Ports/Stockton, Calif.
10. Visalia Oaks/Visalia, Calif.

### CAROLINA LEAGUE

1. Durham Bulls/Durham, N.C.
2. Frederick Keys/Frederick, Md.
3. Kinston Indians/Kinston, N.C.
4. Lynchburg Hillcats/Lynchburg, Va.
5. Prince William Cannons/Woodbridge, Va.
6. Salem Avalanche/Salem, Va.
7. Wilmington Blue Rocks/Wilmington, Del.
8. Winston-Salem Warthogs/
    Winston-Salem, N.C.

### FLORIDA STATE LEAGUE

1. Brevard County Manatees/Melbourne, Fla.
2. Charlotte Rangers/Port Charlotte, Fla.
3. Clearwater Phillies/Clearwater, Fla.
4. Daytona Cubs/Daytona Beach, Fla.
5. Dunedin Blue Jays/Dunedin, Fla.
6. Fort Myers Miracle/Fort Myers, Fla.
7. Kissimmee Cobras/Kissimmee, Fla.
8. Lakeland Tigers/Lakeland, Fla.
9. Sarasota Red Sox/Sarasota, Fla.
10. St. Lucie Mets/Port St. Lucie, Fla.
11. St. Petersburg Cardinals/St. Petersburg, Fl

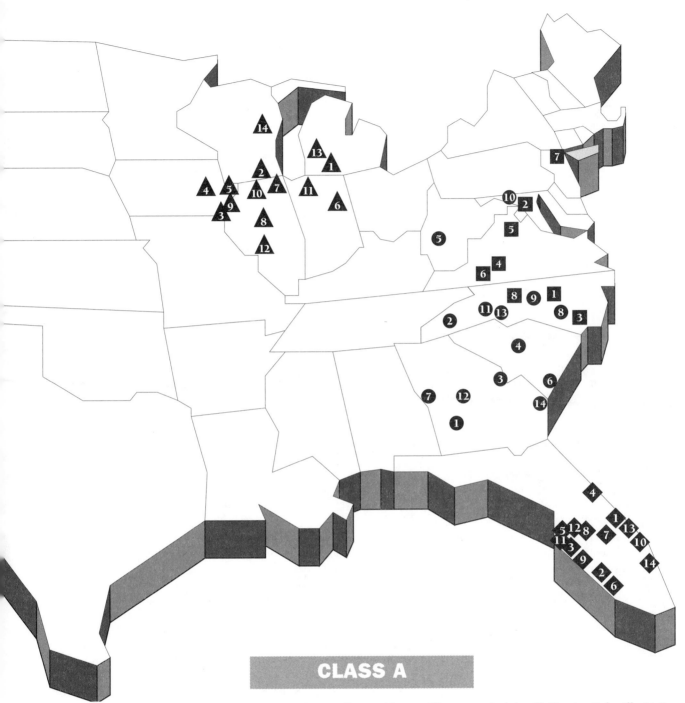

## CLASS A

12. Tampa Yankees/Tampa, Fla.
13. Vero Beach Dodgers/Vero Beach, Fla.
14. West Palm Beach Expos/West PalmBeach, Fla.

### MIDWEST LEAGUE

1. Battle Creek Golden Kazoos/
   Battle Creek, Mich.
2. Beloit Snappers/Beloit, Wis.
3. Burlington Bees/Burlington, Iowa
4. Cedar Rapids Kernels/Cedar Rapids, Iowa
5. Clinton Lumber Kings/Clinton, Iowa
6. Fort Wayne Wizards/Fort Wayne, Ind.

7. Kane County Cougars/Geneva, Ill.
8. Peoria Chiefs/Peoria, Ill.
9. Quad Cities River Bandits/Davenport, Iowa
10. Rockford Cubbies/Rockford, Ill.
11. South Bend Silver Hawks/South Bend, Ind.
12. Sultans of Springfield/Springfield, Ill.
13. West Michigan Whitecaps/
    Comstock Park, Mich.
14. Wisconsin Timber Rattlers/Appleton, Wis.

### SOUTH ATLANTIC LEAGUE

1. Albany Polecats/Albany, Ga.

2. Asheville Tourists/Asheville, N.C.
3. Augusta Greenjackets/Augusta, Ga.
4. Capital City Bombers/Columbia, S.C.
5. Charleston (W.Va.) Alley Cats/Charleston,W.Va.
6. Charleston (S.C.) RiverDogs/Charleston, S.C.
7. Columbus Redstixx/Columbus, Ga.
8. Fayetteville Generals/Fayetteville, N.C.
9. Greensboro Bats/Greensboro, N.C.
10. Hagerstown Suns/Hagerstown, Md.
11. Hickory Crawdads/Hickory, N.C.
12. Macon Braves/Macon, Ga.
13. Piedmont Phillies/Kannapolis, N.C.
14. Savannah Cardinals/Savannah, Ga.

# MINOR LEAGUE MEMORIES

### BOWIE

*Rick Forney, on going into the record books as the winning pitcher (14-6 over the Binghamton Mets) in the first organized-baseball game at Bowie's Prince Georges Stadium:*

"The other day I was thinking, 'Damn, I'm going to throw the first pitch here at this stadium.' But I wasn't thinking anything about getting that first win. But I'll take it. It's always nice to get that win."

*Later in '94, Forney had another first, pitching the first perfect game in Baysox history when he bested the Trenton Thunder 8-0 in the second game of a July 30 doubleheader in Trenton.*

### COLUMBUS

*Joe Citari was a big, left-handed, dead-pull-hitting first baseman who spent nine seasons (1981-89) in the minor leagues. His high-water mark came in 1988 when his 22 home runs for the AAA Omaha Royals tied for the team lead. But before moving to AAA, he was in Columbus for a 1985 Southern League game when an inventive soul came up with a clever way to cancel the ballgame, three years before this same method was popularized by the film BULL DURHAM.*

"I think we were the only team in baseball playing, because it was the All-Star night. Everybody's got the day off. It's like a baseball national holiday. Columbus, Ga., is always 110 [degrees] and 110 humidity and it never rains. Somebody just went up and took a hose, placed it on home plate, left it there, turned it on and just let it run for about 15 minutes. We were rained out. We can't play. And we went home. It was great."

### JACKSON

*Through eight innings, the Western division led the East in the 1992 Texas League All-Star game in Jackson. With two outs in the ninth, the West appeared on the verge of victory. Tim Barker of the West's San Antonio Missions had been* selected as the game's MVP, and Texas League president Tom Kayser was waiting to present the award to him when the East's Adell Davenport hit a grand slam that changed everything. Kayser recalls:

"[Jackson Generals principal owner] Con Maloney and I were standing in the opposing dugout to give the Most Valuable Player Award to the shortstop from the Dodgers [Barker]. We were watching the game, joking and having by-play with Barker. [With Davenport up], all of a sudden there was a crack of a bat like a pistol shot. When the ball carried over the fence, Con Maloney turned to me and said, 'I guess he [Davenport] is the MVP.'"

### WICHITA

*Texas League president Tom Kayser recalls that the 1993 Texas League All-Star game in Wichita ended in a rather novel way after both teams had run out of pitchers and were unable to continue with the score tied 3-3 after nine innings:*

"The last thing we wanted was a tie game, because each team has a limited number of pitchers on each squad. So, by golly, the game got tied late. What do we do? They made the announcement that the game would end after the ninth inning because neither side had any pitchers. The fans didn't like that at all. I didn't want to put managers and coaches out there because I think that debases an All-Star game. I was standing with my foot on the top step, thinking this is a fine mess. We're doing this just as the last out is happening. [Then] he asked me, 'Has an All-Star Game ever ended with a home-run-hitting contest?' I said, 'Why not? I'll take this side and you take that one.' It was an inspiration born of Dwayne Hosey, a last-minute replacement who hit two home runs in one game and a home run in the [Joint] AA All-Star game. He hit one right down the line, and everyone looked at me to make the call. I stood up and wondered who they were looking at. But his ball was foul. It would have been incredible if he won the home-run contest. It was an interesting way to end an All-Star game."

# CALIFORNIA LEAGUE

The league began in 1941, and Santa Barbara won back-to-back title in 1941-42. After a hiatus of three seasons, it picked up again in 1946 for good. Several record-holders are still active in pro ball, such as Mark Dewey, who set a league mark with 30 saves for San Jose in 1989; Bill Wegman, who posted a 1.30 ERA for Stockton in 1983; and Chris Cron, who was hit by pitches 27 times when he played for Palm Springs in 1988. The league plays 136 games and is split into Northern and Southern divisions. No team can have more than two players and one player-coach with six or more years of pro experience. Rancho Cucamonga is the defending league champion. The Quakes went on to beat heavily favored Modesto in the finals. The A's had led the minor leagues in victories in 1994 with 96. League attendance for 1994 was 1,691,286, up 337,831 from 1993, for a league record. Four teams set individual single-season records: Rancho Cucamonga (386,633), which broke its own league record; Modesto (109,314); Central Valley (92,756); and Riverside (85,358).

• • •

*A capacity crowd fills Herbert Field to watch the hometown Sockton Ports.*

# BAKERSFIELD BLAZE

## INDEPENDENT

Sam Lynn Park is one of the smallest in the minors, with one of the shortest centerfields in baseball. But these very dimensions, plus a breeze blowing in from right and 21-foot-high fences down the lines, help prevent this ballpark from being a hitting mecca. With such short distances to the fences, outfielders here play much shallower than in other ballparks. In most ballparks, a runner on second should score on a line-drive hit to the outfield, but here, he's likely to be thrown out. Visiting managers who are unaccustomed to Sam Lynn Park's idiosyncrasies learn about them the hard way.

Ever since this ballpark was built in 1941, the setting sun over the center-field wall has caused big problems for hitters. Game times were often pushed back to after 8 P.M. to avoid the most blinding effects of the sun, but this all changed in 1994 when the team built what is maybe the biggest wall in the minors in hopes of solving this problem. A steel sunscreen 50 feet high and 120 feet long was erected about 15 feet behind the wood, outfield fence. Stretching from left field to center, it has apparently done its job.

### ◆ LOCAL AND TEAM HISTORY

Although there are reports of amateur baseball being played here as early as the 1870s, Bakersfield's organized-baseball involvement began in 1910 when this city spent its first and only season in the Class D San Joaquin Valley League, winning the league championship. Bakersfield spent one season in the Class D California State League (1929) before joining the Class C California League in 1941. Bakersfield has been a member of this circuit continuously since 1982. The Los Angeles Dodgers ended their 10-year affiliation with Bakersfield after the 1994 season.

In 1949, Bakersfield won the regular-season pennant with the help of Jess Pike, who set a then all-time league record with 156 runs batted in while also scoring 167 runs and hitting 37 homers. Hall of Famer Don Drysdale was 18 years old when he began his career with Bakersfield in 1954. That season, he was 8-5 while compiling a 3.45 ERA. Rich Wilson was Bakersfield's main power threat in 1956 and '57 when he slugged 60 homers and drove in 242 runs overall, leading the Cal League with 27 four-baggers in '57. In his 15-year minor league career, Wilson batted .322 while hitting 285 homers. Donell Nixon's 144 steals in 1983 place him second all-time for most stolen bases in a single season, behind Vince Coleman's 145, which he also stole in '83 while playing for Macon. Nixon also batted .321 in '83 and scored 115 runs. Nixon's talent for stolen bases did not end in Bakersfield; the following season, he set a Southern League record by stealing 102 bases for Chattanooga.

### ◆ BALLPARK EXTRAS

The concessions here are for the most part unremarkable, but the pizzas are popular and the ice-cream sundaes are worth a try. The biggest promotions are fireworks and full-sized bats.

### ◆ ATTRACTIONS

The Pioneer Village Museum is adjacent to the stadium. For information, call (805) 861-2132.

For more information about Bakersfield, call the Chamber of Commerce, (805) 327-4421.

### ◆ DINING

The Barbecue Factory is about five minutes away from the ballpark. 3401 Chester Avenue, (805) 325-3700.

Rosemary's Family Creamery is about 10 minutes from the ballpark. 2733 F Street, (805) 395-0555.

### ◆ LODGING

Ramada Inn is about 15 minutes from the park, at the corner of 99 Freeway and Rosedale Highway. 3535 Rosedale Highway, Rosedale, (805) 327-0681/(800) 228-2828.

### ◆ DIRECTIONS

From 99 Freeway, take the Rosedale exit and proceed to Chester Avenue. Turn left and go two miles to stadium.

OTHER FAMOUS ALUMNI OTHER FAMOUS ALUMNI

Rick Sutcliffe, Ron Cey, Bill Russell, Johnny Callison, Larry Bowa, Mark Langston, Pedro Martinez, Jose Offerman, Mike Piazza, Raul Mondesi, and Eric Karros played here.

**SAM LYNN PARK**
**4009 Chester Avenue**
**Bakersfield, CA 93301**
**(805) 322-1363**

**Capacity: 4,300**
**LF 328, CF 354, RF 328**

### ◆ TICKET AND SCHEDULE INFORMATION

Games begin at 7:15 P.M.

Bakersfield's season begins in early April and ends the first week of September.

Ticket prices: $5 reserved seats; $3 general admission.

# HIGH DESERT MAVERICKS

### BALTIMORE ORIOLES

**M**averick Stadium, built in 1991 when the Mavericks began their first season, is located in the Mojave Desert, one of the most unusual ballpark sites in organized baseball. Maverick Stadium is also about 2,700 feet above sea level, so the relatively thin air here helps batted balls carry well. The high altitude and desert location also help explain the roots of this team's name. In keeping with its location, the stadium has been nicknamed the "Diamond in the Desert." There is not much in the immediate vicinity around the ballpark, except for a truck stop, some Joshua trees, plenty of sand and attractive sunsets on summer nights. This is also one of the few teams with no tarp on hand in case of rain, because precipitation is simply not a problem out here. Inside the ballpark, there is an open concourse where fans can see the field from the concession stands or watch the game on closed-circuit televisions. A wooden bull wearing a Mavericks jersey stands next to the right-field foul pole; his eyes light up and smoke comes out of its ears when he's struck by a High-Desert home run.

### ◆ LOCAL AND TEAM HISTORY

The Mavericks are the first organized-baseball team to be based here. In the 1991 inaugural season, High Desert won the California League championship and set a new attendance record for the circuit by drawing 204,438 fans. San Diego Padres manager Bruce Bochy was the Mavericks' skipper that season. In 1993, the Mavericks, then a Florida Marlins affiliate, won their second league championship, the first title won by a Marlins' farm team. The '93 High Desert team featured the minors' runs batted in leaders, Tim Clark (126), John Toale (125) and Bryn Kosco (121). Clark, named the Marlins' Minor League Player of the Year, also

topped the minors' with a .363 batting average while Toale won the circuit's home-run crown with 28 round-trippers. All three Mavericks were named to the Cal League's All-Star team. In keeping with the Mavericks' desert location, the team's 1991 and 1993 championship rings featured Joshua trees. This franchise's fortunes changed dramatically in 1994 when High Desert, then an independent team after Florida ended its affiliation, finished last in the league with a 45-91 record, at one point enduring an 18-game losing streak.

**OTHER FAMOUS ALUMNI**

Carl Everett, Ray Holbert, Tim Worrell and Scott Sanders played here.

### ◆ BALLPARK EXTRAS

You can sample several grilled items including chicken, burgers, and Polish and Italian sausages. There is a two-tiered picnic area behind third base. The Mavericks have staged several interesting promotions, including an on-field wedding in 1994. For an unscheduled tie breaker game in 1993, fans were admitted to the park for the price of a coin of their choice. Proceeds were donated to charity.

### ◆ ATTRACTIONS

The Roy Rogers-Dale Evans Museum is in nearby Victorville. Here you can find several displays and mementos from the careers of these stars. Admission is $4, $3 for senior citizens over 65 and children 13 to 16, $2 for children 6 to 12. For further information, call (619) 243-4547.

The ballpark is also about 80 miles northeast of Los Angeles. For information about L.A., call the Visitors' Bureau, (213) 689-8822.

For additional information about this area, call the Adelanto Chamber of Commerce, (619) 246-5711.

### ◆ DINING

Marie Callender's, about 30 minutes from the ballpark in Victorville, has a good selection of salads and sandwiches and also offers several picnic combos. Full turkey and steak dinners plus barbecue ribs are also available. 12180 Mariposa Road, Victorville, (619) 241-6973.

### ◆ LODGING

Best Western Green Tree Inn is just east of I-15 in Victorville, about 30 minutes from the ballpark. (619) 245-3461/(800) 528-1234.

Holiday Inn is on State Route 18 off I-15 in Victorville,

about 30 minutes from the ballpark. (619) 245-6565/(800) HOLIDAY.

### ◆ DIRECTIONS
From I-15, take U.S. 395 north for about eight miles and exit at Adelanto Road. The stadium will be immediately visible. Plenty of free parking is available.

```
MAVERICK STADIUM
12000 Stadium Way
Adelanto, CA 92301
(619) 246-6287
—————————————
Capacity: 3,500
LF 330, CF 400, RF 310
```

### ◆ TICKET AND SCHEDULE INFORMATION
Most games are played at night, beginning at 7:05 P.M. Sunday games start at 1:05 P.M.

The Mavericks' home opener is usually in early April, and the season ends in the first week of September.

Ticket prices: $5 reserved seats, $4 seniors 65 and over, children 12 and under, military with ID; $3.50 general admission, $3 seniors, children, military.

# LAKE ELSINORE STORM

**CALIFORNIA ANGELS**

Nestled on the bank of Lake Elsinore and at the base of the Ortega Mountains, the Diamond is a gem among modern ballparks. The classic red brick, green steel design evokes images of Camden Yards and Forbes Field. The 90-foot-high clock tower that greets visitors is similar to that of the old Wrigley Field in Los Angeles, while a 36-foot-high wall in right turns cheap home runs into long singles, à la Fenway Park.

There is a Diamond Club, a 400-seat restaurant and sports bar, down the left-field line. The club includes terrace seating for the game, as well as a patio overlooking the lake. This is just the second year for the Diamond. The Storm drew a Cal League single-game record of 7,907 fans on September 2, 1994.

### ◆ LOCAL AND TEAM HISTORY
This is the team's second season. The Storm drew 357,000 fans in its inaugural season. The franchise moved to Lake Elsinore from Palm Springs, where it had been an Angels affiliate since 1986.

### ◆ BALLPARK EXTRAS
The Storm has its own microbrewed beer, Class A Ale. It is brewed for the team by The Blind Pig microbrewery. The Diamond Club offers gourmet sandwiches and burgers, steaks, prime rib, seafood and other items. The team features the normal minor-league promotional giveaways and appearances.

### ◆ ATTRACTIONS
Lake Elsinore is the largest natural inland lake in southern California and is home to boating, fishing and water-skiing.

Southern California's wine country is located in Temecula Valley, 15 miles south on I-15. There are more than 10 wineries, with many tours available.

San Diego is one hour south on I-15, while Los Angeles is 1½ hours north on I-15 and the 60 Freeway.

For more information about Lake Elsinore, call the Chamber of Commerce, (909) 674-2577.

### ◆ DINING
Fast-food restaurants line the I-15 corridor in Lake Elsinore, Murrieta and Temecula.

There's also Chili's, which is 15 minutes away. 27645 Ynez Road, Temecula, (909) 694-0099.

Tony Roma's is also 15 minutes from the park. 27464 Jefferson Avenue, Temecula, (909) 676-7662.

### ◆ LODGING
The Lake View Inn is within walking distance of the Diamond. 31808 Casino Drive, Lake Elsinore, (909) 674-9694.

Lake Elsinore Resort and Casino is also just a few minutes away. The casino offers limited gambling, including various card games. 20930 Malaga, Lake Elsinore, (909) 674-3101.

### ◆ DIRECTIONS
From San Diego, take I-15 north to Diamond Drive. Turn left on Diamond Drive and proceed to the stadium. The Diamond is visible from the interstate.

From Los Angeles, take I-10 or the 60 Freeway east to I-15, then proceed south on 15 to Diamond Drive. Turn right on Diamond Drive.

From Orange County, take the 91 Freeway east to I-15 and take 15 south to Diamond Drive. Turn right on Diamond Drive.

### ◆ TICKET AND SCHEDULE INFORMATION

Game time is 7:05 P.M. from Monday through Saturday and 2:05 P.M. on Sundays through June 4; it's 5:05 P.M. on Sundays after June 4.

The Storm's season begins in early April and ends the first week of September.

Ticket prices: $5 box seats; $4 reserved seats; $3 general admission, $2.50 children and seniors. Tickets for the 1995 California League All-Star Game at the Diamond go on sale in March.

# MODESTO A'S

## OAKLAND ATHLETICS

Thurman Field, built nearly 40 years ago, is currently undergoing a large-scale renovation for the 1995 season. The stadium is in a park-like setting, with soccer fields and other recreation facilities behind the 12-foot-high, wooden outfield fence. There is also a golf course next door. This franchise is owned by the same group that controls the Sacramento Gold Miners of the Canadian Football League.

### ◆ LOCAL AND TEAM HISTORY

Organized baseball first came here in 1914 when Modesto began a two-year association with the Class D California State League. Modesto joined the California League in 1946 and has been part of this circuit continuously since 1966. The A's current affiliation with Oakland began in 1975. In 1950 and '51, Rich Wilson was the Modesto Reds' main power threat, leading the Cal League with 30 and 40 home runs, respectively. In '50, when the Reds won the Cal League championship, he also topped the loop with 154 runs batted in, and the next year, his .371 batting average led the league. Tony Freitas was one of Wilson's teammates during both seasons. In 1950, at age 42, Freitas was released by the

PCL's Sacramento Solons after appearing in nine games for them. He then signed with Modesto and won 20 games here while leading the California League with a 2.56 ERA. In 1951, Freitas returned to Modesto as player-manager and led the Cal League with 25 wins. He also compiled a 2.99 ERA. Freitas, arguably the greatest left-hander in minor-league history with 342 wins, No. 4 on the all-time list, spent parts of only five seasons in the majors, posting a 25-33 record and 4.48 ERA. Rickey Henderson not only batted .345 for Modesto in 1977, he also was part of an unusual promotion in which he raced a horse. Henderson lost.

**OTHER FAMOUS ALUMNI**

Reggie Jackson, Tony La Russa, Joe Morgan, Rollie Fingers, Joe Rudi, Mickey Tettleton, Jose Canseco, Mark McGwire, Walt Weiss and Brent Gates played here.

### ◆ BALLPARK EXTRAS

Top promotions include a monthly fireworks series, postgame concerts, Turn Back the Clock Day and a local trade show. There are three concession spots, including a barbecue area that offers hot dogs, chicken, steak, burgers, Italian sausage and spicy sausage. Ribs will be served for the first time in 1995.

### ◆ ATTRACTIONS

Modesto is home to the Julio Gallo Wineries. You also can "cruise" some of the same streets where *American Graffiti* was filmed.

For more information about Modesto, call the Chamber of Commerce, (209) 577-5757.

### ◆ DINING

Aside from the usual fast-food choices, there's Mallard's Inn, about 20 minutes away. 1720 Sisk Road, (209) 522-3825.

### ◆ LODGING

Best Western is about five minutes away. 909 16th Street, Modesto, (209) 524-7261/(800) 528-1234.

Vagabond Inn is about 20 minutes away. 1525 McHenry, Modesto, (209) 521-6340.

### ◆ DIRECTIONS

From Highway 99, take Tuolomne Boulevard/B Street exit. Turn right onto Tuolomne and proceed one block west to Neece Drive (at the golf course). Turn left and the stadium is ¼ mile down the driveway, on the right.

### ◆ TICKET AND SCHEDULE INFORMATION

Games are at 7:15 P.M. from Monday through Saturday and at 1:15 P.M. Sundays in April and May; they move to 5:15 P.M. Sundays from June through August.

Modesto's season begins in early April and ends the first week of September.

Ticket prices: $5 box seats; $3.50 general admission, $2.50 seniors 65 and over and children 12 and under.

# RANCHO CUCAMONGA QUAKES

**SAN DIEGO PADRES**

The Epicenter is located at the foot of the picturesque San Gabriel Mountains, 45 miles east of Los Angeles. Built in 1993, it offers wide seats in the grandstand and 13 luxury sky boxes above. A full-color graphics board in right field supplies information and entertainment.

### ◆ LOCAL AND TEAM HISTORY

The Rancho Cucamonga Quakes' first season was 1993. The franchise originated in Lodi, California, in 1966. The team, affiliated with five different parent clubs, remained in Lodi until 1984. The franchise moved to Ventura County in 1986 and was purchased by current owner Hank Stickney the following year. He moved the team to San Bernardino, where it remained through the 1992 season. The Quakes won the California League championship in 1994.

### ◆ BALLPARK EXTRAS

The team offers sausages, barbecue beef, chicken wings and fingers, deli sandwiches and cappuccino, in addi-tion to standard ballpark fare. There are nine varieties of beer, including the team's own special Shakin' Ale lager.

### ◆ ATTRACTIONS

Disneyland (714-999-4565) and Anaheim Stadium (714-254-3100) are 35 minutes away. Hollywood and Universal Studios (818-622-3801) are 45 minutes away.

For more information about Rancho Cucamonga, call the Chamber of Commerce, (909) 987-1012.

### ◆ DINING

Claim Jumper is five minutes away. The specialty here is ribs with homemade sauce. Prime rib is big on the weekend, as well as burgers and pasta. 12499 Foothill Boulevard, Rancho Cucamonga, (909) 899-8022.

There's also a strip of fast-food and family restaurants five minutes away along Foothill Boulevard, west of the stadium.

### ◆ LODGING

Best Western is within five minutes of the park. 8179 Spruce Avenue, Rancho Cucamonga, (909) 466-1111/(800) 528-1234.

### ◆ DIRECTIONS

From the intersection of I-10 and I-15, take I-15 north to the second exit (Foothill Boulevard). Proceed west to the first light (Rochester Avenue). Turn left. Stadium is on the right. Parking is plentiful and costs $2.

### ◆ TICKET AND SCHEDULE INFORMATION

Games start at 7:15 P.M. from Monday through Saturday; there are 1:15 P.M. Sunday starts through June 11 and 5:15 P.M. Sunday times from June 25 to the end of the season.

Ticket prices: $6 super box seats; $5 box seats; $4 view seats; $3 terrace seats.

# RIVERSIDE PILOTS

**SEATTLE MARINERS**

The Sports Center is on the edge of the University of California-Riverside campus and is also used by the college's baseball team. Several university buildings are located behind the right-field fence while distant hills span the entire outfield. A large net, similar to the one in Fort Wayne and approximately 40 feet high, was erected behind the left-field fence to protect cars on the street behind the ballpark from being struck by home runs. Although several balls have soared over the net, there are no reports of injuries caused by California League home runs. The ballpark's location in a residential area also creates a unique problem for this franchise because according to California law, no alcohol can be sold at a facility within 100 feet of a residence. The Pilots' efforts to obtain area residents' permission to sell alcoholic beverages at the Sports Center have been unsuccessful because unanimous consent of local citizens is required.

### ◆ LOCAL AND TEAM HISTORY

Riverside made its organized-baseball debut in 1941 when this city first joined the California League. After five years without pro baseball, Riverside began a four-year association with the Sunset League in 1947. Following the 1950 season, baseball left town again, not returning until 1988 when Riverside rejoined the Cal League for three years. After the 1990 season, this franchise moved to Adelanto and became the High Desert Mavericks. Riverside rejoined the California League in 1993, which was also the beginning of the current affiliation with Seattle. Riverside captured the 1988 California League championship by beating Stockton three games to none in the playoffs' final round.

OTHER FAMOUS ALUMNI — OTHER FAMOUS ALUMNI

Ricky Bones, Tim Davis, Dave Staton, Luis Lopez and Jose Valentin played here.

Warren Newson provided much of the offensive firepower that year, topping the circuit with 22 homers and seven triples while batting in 91 runs. Another important contributor to Riverside's success was Dave Hollins, who batted .304 and drove in 92 runs for the Red Wave. The following season, Rafael Valdez pitched the second nine-inning perfect game in league history, beating Reno 2-0 on July 20. Valdez was promoted to AA before the end of the month. This no-hitter was the second tossed by Riverside hurlers in 1989. Darrin Reichle and Bill Marx combined to no-hit Modesto in April.

### ◆ BALLPARK EXTRAS

There is a barbecue area with two grills where you can sample some specialty sausage, burgers and chicken. In 1995, the team will make further attempts to gain permission for the sale of alcoholic beverages at the ballpark. The Pilots are partially owned and operated by the same group that controls the Pioneer League's Lethbridge Mounties.

### ◆ ATTRACTIONS

The Mission Inn was built to resemble California's Spanish missions. There are several Tiffany windows here and an 18th-century gold altar. Admission is $6. Reservations are needed. For further information, call (909) 781-8241.

The Joshua Tree National Monument is a federally protected desert park with many interesting plants and rock formations. Campsites are also available. Admission is $5 per car. For further information, call (619) 367-7511.

Los Angeles is about 60 miles west of Riverside. For information about L.A., call (213) 689-8822.

For additional information about Riverside, call the Chamber of Commerce, (909) 683-7100.

### ◆ DINING

Coco's, about 15 minutes from the ballpark, offers a variety of imaginative dishes, including the Sunrise burrito, the Haystack barbecue burger and Louisiana (Cajun-style) steak and shrimp. 3640 Central Avenue, (909) 683-3962.

### ◆ LODGING

Days Inn is just west of I-215, about 15 minutes from the ballpark. (909) 359-0770/(800) 325-2525.

Hampton Inn is on University Avenue, about 15 minutes from the ballpark. (909) 683-6000/(800) 426-7866.

### ◆ DIRECTIONS

From Highway 60, take the Blaine Street exit. Go north on Blaine for about three blocks. The ballpark will be on your right. Parking is limited at the ballpark, but overflow parking is available in a nearby church parking lot.

◆ **TICKET AND SCHEDULE INFORMATION**

Most games are played at night, starting at 7:15 P.M. Sunday games begin at 1 P.M in April and May and at 6 P.M. the rest of the season.

The Pilots' home opener is usually in early April, and the season ends in the first week of September.

Ticket prices: $5 box seats; $3 general admission. These are subject to change for 1995.

# SAN BERNARDINO SPIRIT

## LOS ANGELES DODGERS

SAN BERNARDINO SPIRIT
PROFESSIONAL BASEBALL CLUB

Originally built as a WPA project in the 1930s, Fiscalini Field, which was remodeled in the 1980s, is scheduled to close in mid-summer 1995, when the Spirit move into a new ballpark in San Bernardino. The new $12 million park, designed by the same architects responsible for Cleveland's Jacobs Field, will resemble an old Spanish mission with its outside wall made of red-brick tiles. The promise of having their minor leaguers play in a new ballpark helped convince the Los Angeles Dodgers to begin an affiliation with San Bernardino in 1995. This decision was undoubtedly helped by the fact that the Spirits' owner also controls the Dodgers' AA team in San Antonio.

From the uncovered grandstand in Fiscalini Field, fans can see Perris Hill, a small promontory covered with trees that looms about 200 feet past the right-field fence. Perris Hill was also the old name of this ballpark. There are picnic areas down each line.

◆ **LOCAL AND TEAM HISTORY**

San Bernardino's early pro baseball years were somewhat ill-fated. The Kittens, this city's first pro team, spent 1913 in the Class D Southern California League, which folded before the season ended. San Bernardino did not do much better the next time this city had an organized baseball team, in 1929, when the Padres entered the Class D California State League, which folded in mid-June. Baseball returned here in 1941 when San Bernardino joined the California League as a farm club of the Pacific Coast League's Hollywood Stars, who ended this affiliation midway through the '41 season. From 1948 to '50, San Bernardino was associated with the Class C Sunset League. Following the '50 campaign, this circuit merged with the Arizona-Texas League to form the Southwest International League, which San Bernardino was not part of. This city has been a member of the California League continously since 1987. In 1989, Ruben Gonzalez became the first Cal League player to win the Triple Crown since 1963. He compiled a .308 average, 27 homers and 101 runs batted in. Gonzalez clinched the batting title on the last day of the season by going two for two to edge out Bakersfield's Eric Karros, who finished with a .303 average. In 1993, Makato "Mac" Suzuki was an 18-year-old Japanese pitcher with the independent San Bernardino Spirit whose 12 saves, four wins and 3.68 ERA earned him a $750,000 signing bonus from the Seattle Mariners.

**OTHER FAMOUS ALUMNI**

Ken Griffey Jr., Mike Hampton, Jeff Nelson, John Cummings, Dave Fleming and Roger Salkeld played here.

◆ **BALLPARK EXTRAS**

In right field, such fare as brats, grilled chicken, ribs and spicy sausages are served at the Spirit Cafe, while the left-field area offers several specialty beers. The new ballpark will feature individual pizzas and Buffalo wings.

◆ **ATTRACTIONS**

San Bernardino is near several popular resort areas. Lake Arrowhead, Big Bear Lake and the San Bernardino National Forest, which contains some of the tallest mountains in southern California, are all within an easy drive of this city. For further information, call (909) 383-5588.

Los Angeles is about 65 miles away. For information about this city, call (213) 689-8822.

For additional information about San Bernardino, call the Chamber of Commerce (909) 885-7515.

## ◆ DINING

Guada La Harry's, about 15 minutes from the ballpark, serves a good assortment of Mexican food, including shrimp burritos, shrimp enchiladas and the Guada La Harry special, a taco stuffed with beef, plus chicken enchiladas and chiles rellenos. 280 E. Hospitality, (909) 889-8555.

## ◆ LODGING

Best Western Sands Motel is at the 5th Street exit off I-215, about 15 minutes from the ballpark. (909) 889-8391/(800) 528-1234.

Radisson Hotel is at the 2nd Street exit off I-215, about 15 minutes from the ballpark. (909) 381-6181/(800) 333-3333.

## ◆ DIRECTIONS

From I-215 north, take the Highland Avenue exit. Go east for about three miles. Turn right into the ballpark's parking lot from Highland. To the new ballpark, take the Mill Street exit off I-215 north. Go east for about three blocks. The ballpark is located between E and G streets, with Rialto Street to the north and Mill Street to the south. Parking at Fiscalini Field is free but somewhat limited. You can also park on the street.

---

**FISCALINI FIELD**
**1007 E. Highland Avenue**
**San Bernardino, CA 92404**
**(909) 881-1836**

**Capacity: 3,600**
**LF 330, CF 387, RF 330**

---

## ◆ TICKET AND SCHEDULE INFORMATION

Most games are played at night, starting at 7 P.M. Sunday games in April and May begin at 2 P.M and start at 6 P.M the rest of the year.

The Blaze's home opener is usually in early April, and the season ends in the first week of September. Purchasing tickets in the new ballpark may be difficult since new stadiums tend to generate much local excitement.

Ticket prices: $6 superbox seats (with cup holders); $5 box seats; $4 reserved seats; $3 general admission. Seniors 65 and over and children 12 and under receive a $1 discount off the price of each ticket.

# SAN JOSE GIANTS

## SAN FRANCISCO GIANTS

**M**unicipal Stadium is in the heart of San Jose's sporting community. Spartan Stadium, where the San Jose State football team plays, is next door, and the Ice Arena, home of the NHL 's Sharks, is less than two miles away. This ballpark has an uncovered grandstand and an unusual outfield fence. It is double-tiered, about 12 feet high. The bottom portion is eight feet tall and made of unpadded metal. Whenever a fly ball or player hits this part of the wall, the resulting clang can be heard throughout the stadium. San Jose Municipal Stadium, built in 1942 as a WPA project, has undergone extensive renovations over the past few years. Nearly $1.5 million was spent in 1994 on a new parking lot, restrooms, home clubhouse and improved seating.

When you enter this attractive ballpark, which has a scenic grove of trees and a mountain range behind home plate, turn left and check out San Jose's baseball mural. About 200 feet long, it extends from near the front gate to past third base. The first 25 feet or so are devoted to San Jose's baseball past and feature a list of old team names plus players who have gone from here to the big leagues. There is also a depiction of all National Association team logos.

## ◆ LOCAL AND TEAM HISTORY

Pro baseball in San Jose dates from the late 1890s. In 1910, San Jose began a four-year membership in the California State League. San Jose first joined the California League in 1942 and has been continuously associated with this circuit since 1979. San Jose began its current affiliation with San Francisco in 1988. In 1891, George Harper had probably the most remarkable single season of any pitcher in baseball history. While pitching for the San Jose Gardeners, Harper was a true workhorse, lead-

**OTHER FAMOUS ALUMNI**

George Brett, Frank White, Brian Harper, Dave Dravecky, Dave Henderson, Steve Howe, Royce Clayton, Rod Beck, Kevin Rogers and Bud Black played here.

ing the league with 80 games started while also pitching a phenomenal 704 innings. Harper posted a 47-32 record, struck out 313 batters and compiled an almost unbelievably low ERA of 0.96. The latter two statistics led the league. In 1892, Harper returned to San Jose and had an off-year for him, pitching 697 innings while winning just 37 games with an ERA of 1.21. He retired in 1901 with 290 victories, 2,492 strikeouts and a 1.72 ERA in the minors. Harper pitched two years in the majors, winning only 10 games.

The 1991 San Jose Giants led all minor-league teams with a 92-44 record. The Giants' 2.67 team ERA led the loop and Rick Huisman was named the league's Pitcher of the Year after posting a 16-4 record with a 1.83 ERA and 216 strikeouts, the latter the No. 1 total in the minors. He also had a 36-inning scoreless streak, four short of the league record. Closer Gary Sharko set an all-time league mark with 31 saves, a record which was broken the next season. But despite the Giants' regular-season success, the team lost to Stockton in the first round of the playoffs.

### ◆ BALLPARK EXTRAS

Turkey Mike's Barbecue Area was created in 1989; it features chicken, ribs, baked beans and turkey burgers. The Giants also offer one food not found in most ballparks—fish kebabs. The stand is named in honor of Turkey Mike Donlin, the captain of the 1906 New York Giants, who began his career here in San Jose and was known for his turkey-like strut.

The Giants stage a highly popular promotion called Smash for Cash. An old bread truck is driven onto the field where three players, each representing two fans, have two chances apiece to smash out the truck's front headlights with thrown baseballs. The players enjoy this stunt, making it into a lively competition among themselves. The whole stadium goes wild when the lights are broken. There were 20 winners in 1994; successful players and fans received $25 each.

### ◆ ATTRACTIONS

San Francisco is about an hour away, via Highway 101 or I-280 north, and downtown San Jose is about five minutes from the park, using the 11th Street exit off I-280.

For the family, there's Raging Waters theme park, on Senter Road south, 20 minutes away. (408) 270-8000.

Paramount's Great America theme park is 20 minutes away, on Highway 101 north to the Great America Parkway exit. (408) 988-1776.

For more information about San Jose, call the Visitor's Bureau, (408) 295-9600.

### ◆ DINING

Tied House, about five minutes from the ballpark, offers a good variety of entrees, such as blackened catfish, ribs and smoked salmon. 65 N. San Pedro, (408) 295-2739.

### ◆ LODGING

Biltmore Hotel is about 20 minutes away, near the airport. 2151 Laurelwood Road, Santa Clara, (408) 988-8411.

Best Western-Gateway Inn is also near the airport and 20 minutes from the park. 2585 Seaboard Drive, San Jose, (408) 435-8800/(800) 528-1234.

### ◆ DIRECTIONS

From Highway 101, take the Tully Road exit and proceed to Senter Street. Turn right on Senter. Go through three traffic lights and turn left on Alma. The ballpark will be immediately visible.

From I-280, take the 10th and 11th streets exit. Proceed south on 10th to Alma Avenue (two lights past the freeway overpass). Turn left on Alma and stadium is on the right, behind the Ice Centre of San Jose.

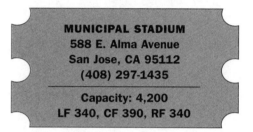

**MUNICIPAL STADIUM**
588 E. Alma Avenue
San Jose, CA 95112
(408) 297-1435
_____
Capacity: 4,200
LF 340, CF 390, RF 340

### ◆ TICKET AND SCHEDULE INFORMATION

Games start at 7:15 P.M. Monday through Friday; at 5 P.M. on Saturday; and at 1:30 P.M. on Sunday from April through June; there are 5 P.M. starts on Sunday from July through September and 6:30 P.M. games on June 30 and July 4.

The Giants' season begins in early April and ends the first week of September.

Ticket prices: $7 box seats; $6 general admission; $3 children 4 to 10. Children under 4 are free.

# STOCKTON PORTS

## MILWAUKEE BREWERS

**B**uilt in the 1930s, Billy Hebert Field is one of the oldest in the Cal League. The original wood grandstand here was destroyed by fire in the 1950s and replaced by the present concrete structure. This is an attractive ballpark facing towards the northwest, with the sun setting at such an angle between left field and the bleachers down the line that it does not get into the batters' eyes.

Billy Hebert is located in Oak Park, named for the hundreds of oak trees that fill this 61-acre recreation complex. Picnic tables and basketball courts can be found in front of the ballpark. The outfield wall is about 12 feet high and made of unpadded concrete, so players trying to catch fly balls always are very cautious. Wind gusts known locally as Delta Breezes frequently blow through at night, making home runs hard to come by.

### ◆ LOCAL AND TEAM HISTORY

Baseball has been played here since the 1850s. Stockton also fielded teams in several minor leagues in the late 1880s and the '90s. After the turn of the century, Stockton spent four seasons (1910, '13-15) in the California State League. This city first joined the California League in 1941 and has been continuously associated with this circuit since 1978. Stockton began its current affiliation with Milwaukee in 1979.

This city's greatest baseball claim to fame is that Stockton is the Mudville in Ernest Thayer's famous poem, *Casey at the Bat*. In the 1880s, because gold mining in this area made the local rivers and channels quite muddy, the city was nicknamed Mudville by river-barge captains. Cooney, Barrows and Flynn, all of whom played for Stockton in the late 1880s, are also the fielders men-

> **OTHER FAMOUS ALUMNI**
> Don Baylor, Pat Listach, Al Bumbry, Paul Blair, Dave LaPoint, Vince DiMaggio, Gary Sheffield, Doug Jones, Pat Gillick and Ron Shelton (writer/director of *Bull Durham* and *Cobb*) all played here.

tioned in *Casey at the Bat*. Casey himself is thought to have been John Patrick Francis Parnell Cahill, a former Stockton player who left town to seek his fame and fortune in the major leagues, where he pitched for parts of three seasons. The popular Cahill/Casey returned here to play in an 1880s all-star game against his former teammates. That game's 4-2 score was the same as in the fictional game in the poem.

George B. Harper was a West Coast pitching star in the latter part of the 19th century. He won 21 games for Stockton in 1889 and also led the California League with 212 strikeouts. The following year, Harper won 41 of the 70 games he appeared in for Sacramento while posting a 1.22 ERA and pitching an amazing 596 innings. Harper is the top pitcher in league history, with more than 200 wins. Tony Freitas, another great minor-league pitcher, spent the last two seasons of his career with Stockton in 1952 and 1953. At age 45, Freitas led the '53 Cal League with 22 wins and 279 innings pitched while also compiling a 2.38 ERA. Mike Epstein barely missed winning the 1965 Triple Crown here in his first pro season. His 30 home runs and .338 batting average led the league, but Epstein's 100 runs batted in were second to Bobby Etheridge's 107. Stockton won the league championship that season.

The Ports have been affiliated with Milwaukee for 16 years and recently extended their working agreement four more years, through 1998. Stockton's previous California League affiliations were with Baltimore and California.

### ◆ BALLPARK EXTRAS

The Ports hark back to their heritage twice a year to honor their Mudville roots. Players dress in 1880 uniforms, and the souvenir shop sells special Mudville caps and jerseys.

Another big promotion is Mascot Mania, in which several area companies send their mascots. There are also Baseball Buddies, The Famous Chicken, Bash for Cash and U-Pick-Em souvenir nights.

There are three main concession areas here. The Hardball Cafe serves hot dogs and sausages. Such specialty items as churros, pizza and chili are available at the Mudville Eatery. The Casey BBQ Area is a three-tiered picnic area with some of the best food in the park, including grilled chicken, burgers and tip steak. Dinner platters, including one of the above plus baked beans, potato salad, cole slaw, watermelon and hot peppers, are also available.

### ◆ ATTRACTIONS

The Haggin Museum features local as well as international art. (209) 462-4116. Stockton also is within one hour of the State Capitol in Sacramento (I-5 and the 99 Freeway) and within two hours of San Francisco (I-5 and I-580), Lake Tahoe (99 Freeway to Route 50), Reno

(I-5 to I-80) and Yosemite National Park (99 Freeway to Route 120).

The San Joaquin County Fair is held annually in Stockton, along with the Stockton Asparagus Festival in April.

For more information about these and other events in Stockton, call the Chamber of Commerce, (209) 547-2770.

#### ◆ DINING

The Pacific Baking Company is within 20 minutes of the stadium. 3286 Pacific Avenue, (209) 462-7939.

Red Robin is also 20 minutes away. 5084 West Lane, (209) 472-9184.

#### ◆ LODGING

The Stockton Inn is 20 minutes away. 4219 E. Waterloo, Stockton, (204) 931-3131.

Stockton Hilton is also 20 minutes from the park. 2323 Grand Canal Boulevard, Stockton, (204) 957-9090.

#### ◆ DIRECTIONS

From the Bay Area, take I-580 East to I-5, exit at March Lane east, take a right on El Dorado Street and a left on Alpine. Stadium is in the middle of Oak Park.

From Sacramento, take 99 Freeway south to Wilson Way. Go south on Wilson to Alpine, then right on Alpine to Oak Park. Stadium is in the middle of Oak Park.

From south of Stockton, take 99 Freeway north to Crosstown Freeway (Highway 4). Proceed west to El Dorado Street, and north on El Dorado to Alpine. Stadium is in the middle of Oak Park. Plenty of free parking is available.

---

**BILLY HEBERT FIELD**
Alpine and Alvarado Streets
Stockton, CA 95204
(209)-944-5943

Capacity: 3,750
LF 325, CF 392, RF 325

---

#### ◆ TICKET AND SCHEDULE INFORMATION

Games start at 7:05 P.M. from Monday through Saturday and at 5 P.M.on Sunday; the lone exception is 6 P.M. on July 4.

The Ports' season begins in early April and ends the first week of September.

Ticket prices: $6 for MVP reserved seats; $5 general admission; $2.50 children and seniors. The Casey BBQ Area (redwood deck with tables) is $7.50 for the meal and $5 for the seat.

# VISALIA OAKS

### INDEPENDENT

**R**ecreation Park was originally built entirely of wood in the 1920s before being reconstructed as a concrete ballyard some 40 years later. Located in a city-owned park, the Oaks' home is in an attractive setting, with trees behind the outfield fence and a high school football field about two blocks away. The uncovered grandstand is rather distinctive because it was built into the slope of a hill. Recreation's playing field is so close to the grandstand, about 25 to 30 feet in some places, that this franchise had to secure a waiver from compliance with the ballpark-standards provision of the Professional Baseball Agreement.

#### ◆ LOCAL AND TEAM HISTORY

Visalia's baseball tradition goes back more than 100 years, to the 1870s, when several amateur teams played here, decades before the first pro team arrived in 1910. In April 1879, the Two Orphans Baseball Club of Bakersfield defeated the Empire Club of Visalia 31-6 in a game played at the Empires' Recreation Grounds ballpark. According to reports of the match, no uniforms were worn and no gloves were used. Visalia first joined the California League in 1946. After being called the Central Valley Rockies, this franchise reverted to being the Visalia Oaks for 1995, a name which originated in 1977. On May 20, 1985 at Visalia, Modesto's Kevin Stock and Bob Loscalzo each hit for the cycle as the visiting team won 23-4. That was apparently the first time in organized-baseball history that two players hit for the cycle in the same game. Few ballplayers end their careers in such dramatic fashion as Bud Heslet did for Visalia in 1956. That year, Heslet led the California League with 51 home runs and 172 runs batted in, both league records, and 147 runs scored. Heslet retired

OTHER FAMOUS ALUMNI

Kirby Puckett, Chuck Knoblauch, Scott Erickson, Vada Pinson, Mark Portugal and Jay Bell all played here.

after the season with 314 career homers in the minors. Kent Hrbek had the best season of his pro career here in 1981 when he batted .379, seventh-best in Cal League history, with 27 homers and 111 runs batted in.

### ◆ BALLPARK EXTRAS

The team's concessions boast barbecued quarter-pound burgers and Haagen-Dazs ice cream. The most popular promotions are the annual bat giveaway and fireworks.

### ◆ ATTRACTIONS

The giant sequoias in the Sierra Nevada range are just 1½ hours away on Highway 198 East. Yosemite National Park is about two hours north. For information, call (209) 372-0200.

For more information about Visalia, call the Chamber of Commerce, (209) 734-5876.

### ◆ DINING

The Wagon Wheel has pit-cooked steaks and ribs, and it's about five minutes from the park. Goshen Avenue and Willis Street, (209) 627-8325.

The Vintage Press is an acclaimed dining spot, also five minutes away. Center Avenue and Willis Street, (209) 733-3033.

### ◆ LODGING

Radisson Hotel is about 10 minutes from the park. 300 S. Court Street, Visalia, (209) 636-1111/(800) 333-3333.

Holiday Inn is also 10 minutes away. Highways 99 and 198, Visalia, (209) 651-5000/(800) HOLIDAY.

### ◆ DIRECTIONS

From Highway 99, take Highway 198 East to the Mooney Boulevard exit. Turn left on Mooney and proceed to Giddings Avenue. Turn left on Giddings, and stadium is three blocks ahead on the right. Parking is free but limited at the ballpark. On-street parking is also available.

**RECREATION PARK**
440 N. Giddings Avenue
Visalia, CA 93291
(209) 625-0480

Capacity: 2,000
LF 320, CF 405, RF 320

### ◆ TICKET AND SCHEDULE INFORMATION

Games are at 7:05 P.M. Monday through Saturday and at 6:05 P.M. on Sunday.

The Oaks' season begins in early April and ends the first week of September.

Ticket prices: $6 executive box seats; $5 box seats; $4 reserved; $3.50 adult general admission, $3 students 13 to 20, $2.50 children 6 to 12, $1.50 senior citizens.

# MINOR LEAGUE MEMORIES

### SAN JOSE

*In 1986, Mike Verdi was managing the San Jose Bees, an independent team with such former and future big leaguers as Mike Norris, Ken Reitz and Steve Howe. Verdi recalls one particularly memorable road trip that season.*

"I didn't have a coach. I didn't have a trainer. I didn't have much of anything. [But] we did have a lot of Japanese kids [on the team]. We were going to Palm Springs. It's supposed to be a 7½-hour drive. We were 16 hours in the bus. It would overheat every mountain we came to, which in California is every 300 feet. We had no money to fix the bus. [But] we had a Japanese kid who would pour rubbing alcohol on a piece of bread and light it. Dancing and chanting some stuff, he would throw the bread on the engine and the damn bus would run. I kept thinking the engine would catch fire [but it didn't]. We would go about another hour and I'll be damned, it would overheat. We'd pull over. He'd go out and start chanting stuff [and the bus would start again]. We got there five minutes before the ballgame. We got off the bus and Howe threw a shutout. We used that bus all year."

### PRINCE WILLIAM

*New York Yankees second baseman Pat Kelly recalls the 1989 season with Prince William when he was a Carolina League All-Star and the Cannons won the Carolina League championship:*

"Stump Merrill was our manager. That was our first affiliation with somebody [who had already been] in the big leagues. We were kind of in awe of it but then he turned us around and showed us what it was to win. I learned how to win and have fun as opposed to [saying], 'Ah, we've got another game today.' That's how it was the first half. We were just losing. Stump came in and we started winning. [I'll] never forget the last out of that championship. Even in Single A, it was unbelievable."

### DURHAM

*Hall of Famer Joe Morgan recalls his season with the Durham Bulls in 1963, when he batted .332 with 13 home runs and 43 runs batted in. Before the season was over, he was playing in the major leagues for the Houston Colt .45's:*

"I was not one of [Houston's] big bonus babies. When I went to spring training, I made a good impression on [Durham manager] Billy Goodman. I was sent to Modesto to start the season. They sent me to Durham to kind of hide me, hoping they could slip me through the draft. They didn't think I'd do so well. When I came to Durham, things kind of clicked. I did so well they had to protect me in the draft. I could remember my first at-bat here like it was yesterday. I pinch-hit in the ninth inning and hit a home run that won the game. From then on, I was a hero in Durham."

### DURHAM

*Johnny Vander Meer started his 1936 season with the Durham Bulls slowly but then came on strong, compiling a 19-6 record with 295 strikeouts:*

"I was wild and I threw real hard. Johnny Gooch was the manager. Gooch said, 'I'll slow him up.' My first 10 starts here in Durham, I pitched with two days' rest. I was a big strong kid so I didn't mind. The first game I played was a doubleheader. I went in for relief in the 10th and got beat. I started the second game and got beat. So I started off losing two ballgames in the first day I was here. I lost only four after that."

### REIDSVILLE

*Leo "Muscle" Shoals recalls the 1949 season when he played for the Reidsville Luckies, broke the Carolina League home-run record, almost got called up to the big leagues and eventually led all of baseball with 55 home runs.*

"When I hit No. 42, I broke the record. I had one of those years. There was a woman in Durham who told me that if I hit 60 home runs, she'd bake me a pineapple upside-down cake. I had about 48 then. I said, 'My God, lady!' She said, 'Well, make it 50.' When I hit 50, she did."

# CAROLINA LEAGUE

T he Carolina League made its organized-baseball debut in 1945 as a Class C circuit with two teams in Virginia and six in North Carolina. The league received its Class A designation in 1963. Over the years, several Hall of Famers, including Rod Carew, Willie McCovey, Johnny Bench and Carl Yastrzemski, played in this league, while fellow Hall members Ducky Medwick, Heinie Manush and Enos Slaughter managed teams here. Today, there are still eight teams now in four states—Maryland, Virginia, North Carolina and Delaware. In contrast to 1945, only three teams today are based in North Carolina. Each team plays 140 games, with the regular season beginning April 7 and ending September 4. In 1994, Carolina League teams attracted 1,687,596 fans, led by the Frederick Keys who drew 344,563.

• • •

*The Wilmington Blue Rocks take batting practice at their home park, Judy Johnson Field.*

# DURHAM BULLS

## ATLANTA BRAVES

**D**urham's new ballpark makes its much-anticipated debut in 1995. After much wrangling among politicians and local citizens about whether to build this stadium and after a one-year delay that caused some embarrassment to the team (the Bulls staged a yearlong goodbye to their old ballpark in 1993, only to find that their new home would not open in '94 as expected), the team is ready. The stadium, built in the middle of a downtown warehouse district, was designed by the architects responsible for Jacobs Field and The Ballpark in Arlington. It resembles an old-time ballyard, with lots of brick and steel and a brick facade. The grandstand is covered, and there is an old tobacco warehouse behind the third-base seats. Like Fenway Park's, the left-field wall here is tall, 26 feet high, and close, only about 315 feet from home plate, and it has a manually operated scoreboard.

### ◆ LOCAL AND TEAM HISTORY

Organized baseball made its debut here in 1902 when the Bulls joined the Class D North Carolina League, which only lasted one season. After a 10-year absence, baseball returned in 1913 when Durham began a five-year association with the Class D North Carolina State League. Over the last 75 years, Durham has spent time in two circuits, the Piedmont League (1920-33, '36-43) and the Carolina League (1945-67, '80-to date). The Bulls began their current affiliation with the Braves in 1980.

The term "bullpen" is thought by some to have originated in Durham back in the early years of the 20th century. In order to escape the summer heat at the ballpark, pitchers at that time sought refuge in the shade provided by a large wooden bull, advertising locally produced Bull Durham tobacco. After a while, an association is thought to have been made between the place where pitchers sat (the pen) and that giant bull.

Durham Athletic Park, known affectionately as the DAP, was one of the USA's most historic ballparks. It was built in 1938 and featured a short right-field wall, 290 feet from home, that was the friend of left-handed hitters. When it first opened, the DAP's outfield fence was atop an embankment, resulting in many fly balls' hitting the elevated wall and then bouncing back into play. Perhaps DAP's most singular claim to fame was its starring role in the 1988 film *Bull Durham*, which focused national attention on the Bulls and minor-league baseball. The mechanical bull that sat in right field will also be moving to the new ballpark. Whenever a Durham player hits a home run, the bull's tail spins, its eyes blaze red and smoke spews from its snout. Originally just a prop in the film, it became a fixture at Bulls games after it was left behind by the movie's crew and then adopted by the real Durham baseball team. In 1990, as a result of their celluloid-driven popularity, the Bulls became the first team in league history to draw more than 300,000 fans to their ballpark.

Johnny Vander Meer's career was on the fast track when he played for Durham in 1936. That season, he lost his first two games but only four more the rest of the year en route to a 19-6 record and 295 strikeouts. The next season, he was pitching for the Cincinnati Reds. In '38, Vander Meer became the only pitcher in major-league history to hurl two straight no-hitters. Norman Small batted .320 and belted 336 homers in his 17-year minor-league career. While playing for the Bulls in 1937-38, Small batted .275, hit seven four-baggers and was married at home plate before one of the Bulls' games. Clarence "Ace" Parker played for and managed the Bulls during his four seasons (1949-52) in Durham. Parker, a star NFL quarterback, running back and defensive back in the 1930s and '40s, was inducted into the Pro Football Hall of Fame in 1972. He is one of the few players to homer in his first big-league at-bat, which he did in 1937 while pinch-hitting at Fenway Park as a member of the Philadelphia A's. That same season, he also played for the NFL's Brooklyn Dodgers. Parker, together with other such two-sport stars as Bo Jackson and Deion Sanders, is one of six players to hit a home run and score a touchdown in the same season. Crash Davis became a nationwide star by association when Kevin Costner took Davis' name for his character in *Bull Durham*. In real life, Davis batted .317 for the Bulls in 1949 and led the Carolina League with 50 doubles. He played three years (1940-42) in the majors for the Philadelphia A's.

Mickey Lolich, winner of 217 big-league games and the star of the 1968 World Series for the Detroit Tigers, compiled an 11-17 record here from 1959 to '61. In 1963, Joe Morgan, Durham's only Hall of Famer, batted

**OTHER FAMOUS ALUMNI**

Pat Dobson, Jon Matlack, Gates Brown, Duane Ward, Javy Lopes, Mark Lemke, Steve Avery, Kent Mercker, Ryan Klesko, Rex Barney, Rusty Staub and Charley Grimm all played here.

.332 for the Bulls with 13 home runs and 43 runs batted in. Later that season, he was playing for the NL's Houston Colt .45s. Greg "The Bull" Luzinski and Bob Boone were Durham teammates seven years later. Luzinski led the league with 31 homers and 92 runs batted in while Boone, a future big-league catcher, tied for the Carolina League lead among third basemen with 18 double plays, while also batting .300.

More recently, Brett Butler batted .366 and stole 36 bases for Durham in 1980, when the Bulls lost to the Peninsula Pilots in the league championship series, three games to one. The 1986 Bulls featured three future Atlanta stars: Ron Gant, David Justice and Jeff Blauser. Despite the presence of these high-profile players, the Bulls failed to qualify for the postseason playoffs.

### ◆ BALLPARK EXTRAS

Durham's new ballpark has a larger concession area than the old park did. The Bulls continue to serve Flying Burrito Brothers burritos (made with beans, beef and even Polish sausage), among the best fare in the minor leagues. You can also find barbecue sandwiches plus such items as chicken wings, Italian sausage and steak sandwiches. The Bulls' logo, a snorting bull jumping through a brown D, is one of the minors' most recognizable, another legacy of the movie that made Durham famous. There are picnic areas down each foul line.

### ◆ ATTRACTIONS

Duke University is located in Durham. On campus, there is a good art museum (919-684-5135) and the Sarah Duke Gardens, with a large collection of flowers, trees and other shrubbery. For further information, call (919) 684-3698.

The North Carolina Museum of Life and Science features several science and nature exhibits. Admission is $5, $3.50 for seniors and children 3 to 12. For further information, call (919) 220-5429.

For additional information about Durham, call the Visitors' Information Center, (919) 687-0288/(800) 446-8604.

### ◆ DINING

Parizade, about 10 minutes from the ballpark, offers surprisingly well prepared and imaginative Italian food in a fashionable setting. Erwin Square on Main Street, (919) 286-9712.

### ◆ LODGING

Best Western University Inn at Duke is just south of State Route 147, about 10 minutes from the ballpark. (919) 286-4421/(800) 528-1234.

Fairfield Inn by Marriott is at the Cole Mill Road exit off I-85, about 15 minutes from the ballpark. (919) 382-3388/(800) 348-6000.

### ◆ DIRECTIONS

From I-85, take the Downtown Durham/Mangum Street exit. Stay on Mangum for about two miles through downtown. Follow signs to the ballpark. From I-40, take the Durham Freeway/State Route 147 exit. Go about eight miles to Roxboro Street exit. Turn left on Dillard and left on Mangum. Follow signs to the ballpark. Parking is free at the ballpark. Parking is also available in area lots.

> **DURHAM BALLPARK**
> P.O. Box 507
> Durham, NC 27702
> (919) 688-8211
>
> Capacity: 7,500
> LF 305, CF 400, RF 327

### ◆ TICKET AND SCHEDULE INFORMATION

Most games are played at night, starting at 7:30 P.M. Sunday games begin at 6:05 P.M.

The Bulls' season opener is usually in early April, and the season ends in the first week of September. Purchasing tickets on the day of the game may be difficult because the Bulls, perennially a big draw, now have a new, state-of-the art ballpark that should attract lots of fans.

Ticket prices: $6.25 box seats; $5.25 reserved seats; $4.25 general admission, $3.25 seniors, children and students with identification. Children under 5 are free.

# FREDERICK KEYS

## BALTIMORE ORIOLES

**H**arry Grove Stadium, built in 1989, quickly became a favorite around the Carolina League with visiting players. Frederick fans enjoy the stadium, too. The Keys have been one of the top draws in Class A ball ever since the stadium opened, and only part of that popularity is due to the convenient fact that its parent club is also the local major-league team—the Baltimore Orioles are less than an hour's drive away.

The stadium has an uncovered grandstand and an open concourse. Some players contend this is a tough ballpark to hit in at twilight, when the ball gets lost against multi-tiered outfield fence. Located in the foothills of the Catoctin Mountains, the stadium sits right behind a local cemetery, giving new meaning to the expression "dead center field." (Actually, the cemetery would be in foul territory behind home plate.)

### ◆ LOCAL AND TEAM HISTORY

Pro ball was played in Frederick in the Blue Ridge League from 1915 to '17 and again in that circuit from 1920 to '30 before finally returning in 1989 to tiny McCurdy Field, an American Legion park. The Keys last won the Carolina League title in 1990.

The Keys are named for a former local resident, Francis Scott Key, who wrote the *Star Spangled Banner*. The name was chosen from a name-the-team contest. A losing but noteworthy entry was the Frederick Flintstones.

When current Orioles ace Ben McDonald made his professional debut on the McCurdy Field mound in August 1989, after protracted and bitter negotiations following his selection as the first player overall in the '89 draft, the announced attendance was more than 8,000 even though the park only held about 2,500.

OTHER FAMOUS ALUMNI OTHER FAMOUS ALUMNI

Brady Anderson, David Segui, Mike Oquist and Arthur Rhodes played here.

The Keys' theme song, *We're the Frederick Keys,* is a nightly highlight at the games as fans pull out their key chains and jangle along with the record by Holly and Lou. The song is even a hit with opposing players; Yankees farmhand Jason Robertson cited the Keys as having the best ballpark music in the league simply because he loved this theme song.

### ◆ BALLPARK EXTRAS

Along with the standard concession lines, the stadium also features vendor carts. One especially popular item is the Italian sausage. The fresh-squeezed lemonade is also a don't-miss. If you want, you can eat at The Keys Cafe, a dining room overlooking the field where for $24 per ticket, you get a large buffet dinner, hot dogs and popcorn after the fourth inning and a great view as well. The Keys have offered some special theme weekends, such as 1994's Magic Weekend, which started, ironically, on the day the major-league strike began and featured magicians, jugglers and face-painting. Among the tentatively planned weekends for 1995 are Carnival Weekend, Oldies Weekend and Fiesta Weekend.

If both teams are in contention—and sometimes even

if they're not—games against nearby Prince William have become big tickets because of the local rivalry. The two clubs are less than an hour apart, and the two booster clubs have gotten into the act with occasional pregame softball contests.

### ◆ ATTRACTIONS

The Frederick area should appeal to shoppers, nature lovers and history buffs. Several wineries offer tours and tastings, such as the unique Linganore Plantation, which specializes in such wines as blueberry and raspberry, as well as mead, and often hosts music-and-wine fests (Glisans Mill Road, Mount Airy).

For shoppers, the streets of Frederick are filled with countless boutiques, craft shops and antique stores. If you don't feel like walking to get to a bunch of them, check out the Antique Station, a dealer mall with more than 130 booths that range from fine art to sports collectibles. 194 Thomas Johnson Drive, (301) 695-0888.

McCutcheon's Factory Store gives you the chance to sample some of Maryland's delicious natural resources with its homemade apple products such as apple butter, preserves and jellies and cider. South Wisner Street, (301) 662-3261.

There are also several Civil War sites within an easy drive. For more information about Frederick, call the Chamber of Commerce, (301) 662-4164.

### ◆ DINING

Dutch's Daughter, less than 10 minutes from the ballpark, has great crab cakes and other seafood specialties. 5901 Old National Pike, (301) 663-0297.

Griff's Landing, five to 10 minutes from the park, has overstuffed sandwiches and fresh-cut steaks on the menu. 43 S. Market Street, (301) 694-8696.

### ◆ LODGING

Comfort Inn is about five minutes away. 420 Prospect Boulevard, Frederick, (301) 695-6200/(800) 4-CHOICE.

There are also several lovely inns and B&B's in Frederick's old town and the surrounding area.

### ◆ DIRECTIONS

From I-70, take exit 31A/Market Street and turn left at the traffic light. Make the next left on New Design Road. The ballpark will be visible on the right. From I-270, take the Market Street/State Route 355 exit and turn right. After about one mile, turn left at the traffic light and then left again on New Design Road. The ballpark will be on the right. Parking is plentiful and free.

### ◆ TICKET AND SCHEDULE INFORMATION

Most games start at 7 P.M. Sundays from April through June, games begin at 2:05 P.M.; July and August at 4 P.M.

The Keys' season begins in early April and ends the first week of September.

Ticket prices: $7 box seats; $5 general admission; $2 for seniors over 60 and children 5 to 14.

# KINSTON INDIANS

## CLEVELAND INDIANS

**G**rainger Stadium was built back in 1949 and was named for Jesse Grainger, who introduced tobacco farming to eastern North Carolina. While not the most politically correct distinction, it's an important one in this part of the country.

In 1994, the ballpark got a face-lift that included a new grandstand roof, office, clubhouse building and fresh paint. Other major improvements have been made in the last few years, including better lights and steps and an improved sound system. Prior to the 1994 season, the clubhouse facilities were improved as well—a relief to visiting players, who used to bump their heads on the low dugout ceilings and shower at the hotel because of the lack of hot water.

Despite the major renovations, though, Grainger still retains its historic old-time baseball feel, and a new entranceway was added that features old-fashioned brick work and wrought-iron details.

### ◆ LOCAL AND TEAM HISTORY

Kinston had pro ball in town off and on between 1908 and 1952 before joining the Carolina League in 1956. It played sporadically in that circuit until 1974, then rejoined for good in 1977.

The land upon which Grainger Stadium is situated was donated by the Kinston school board, and to this day it remains a city-owned stadium. In addition, a local ownership group took control of the club in 1994.

### ◆ BALLPARK EXTRAS

The Tribe Dog is a big seller for those with big appetites; it's covered with chili, mustard and onions. Chili cheese fries are also messy and popular, and half-price beer nights on Thirsty Thursday bring out the "vocal crowds."

### ◆ ATTRACTIONS

There are many beautiful beaches within an hour's drive, the most lovely of which is Emerald Isle, about 45 minutes away. Morehead City is also popular but a bit farther and more crowded.

**FAMOUS ALUMNI** · **FAMOUS ALUMNI**

Dock Ellis, Fred McGriff, Albert Belle, Cecil Fielder, Tony Fernandez, Jesse Barfield, Charles Nagy and Ron Guidry all played here.

New Bern, about halfway between Kinston and Emerald Isle, is definitely worth a stop to check out Tryon Palace's gardens and stop for lunch in one of the quaint cafes or restaurants.

For more information about Kinston, call the Chamber of Commerce, (919) 527-1131.

### ◆ DINING

Many will argue that North Carolina barbecue is better than its Texas counterpart; and at Buddy's Bar-Be-Que in Grifton, just 10 minutes from Kinston, you'll be treated to some of the best North Carolina barbecue available. Route 2, Highway 11, ¼ mile north of Dupont, Grifton, (919) 524-5044.

House of Wang, about five minutes from the park, is a popular Chinese restaurant. 710 W. Vernon Avenue, Kinston, (919) 527-7897.

### ◆ LODGING

Sheraton-Kinston is less than 10 minutes from the ballpark. 1403 Richlands Road, Kinston, (919) 523-1400/(800) 325-3535.

Holiday Inn is a couple of minutes from the park. 208 E. New Bern Road, Kinston, (919) 527-4155/(800) HOLIDAY.

### ◆ DIRECTIONS

From I-95, take Business Route 70 East exit and go three blocks beyond the Queen Street intersection. Turn left onto East Street. Parking is free but limited. On-street parking is also available.

### ◆ TICKET AND SCHEDULE INFORMATION

All games are at 7 P.M. except five selected 3 P.M. dates and a July 1 doubleheader against Durham, which begins at 6 P.M.

The Indians season begins in early April and ends the first week of September.

Ticket prices: $5 box seats; $4 reserved seats; $3 general admission, $2 seniors, military and students. Children under 5 are free.

# LYNCHBURG HILLCATS

## PITTSBURGH PIRATES

City Stadium opened in 1939, and with new stadiums in Salem and Durham opening this year, it now reigns as the oldest park in the league. But don't let the urban sound of the stadium name fool you; when you're sitting in the stands at City Stadium, the view past center field features Norman Rockwellesque church spires and the rolling green fields of the Virginia countryside.

A hot ticket will be July 19, when City Stadium hosts this year's Carolina League All-Star game, but try to avoid attending a game on a Friday night during high school football season (usually only one or two coincide in late August or early September). The football stadium is next door, and the two sites share parking. We're talking big-time traffic jams.

The Rev. Jerry Falwell's Liberty Baptist University is located in Lynchburg, and his brother Calvin is the club owner.

### ◆ LOCAL AND TEAM HISTORY

Lynchburg joined the Carolina League in 1966 after having been a site for teams in five other leagues off and on since 1906, though some argue that the Lynchburg Hill Climbers of 1894 were the city's first pro team. Most recently a farm club of the Boston Red Sox and before that of the New York Mets, this year the club welcomes the Pittsburgh Pirates as its parent team. Maybe the greatest season in Lynchburg history was had by Dwight Gooden in 1983, when he went 19-4, with more than 300 strikeouts in less than 200 innings.

However, this year also marks the first time that the team has not shared its nickname with that of its parent club since entering the Carolina League. The name Hillcats was chosen through a name-the-team contest, but one of the more unusual suggestions was the Bibbies, in honor of long-time pitching coach Jim Bibby. The last time a Lynchburg team had carried its own nickname had been in 1939, when it was known as the Grays.

**OTHER FAMOUS ALUMNI**

Dave DeBusschere, Lenny Dykstra, Randy Myers, Phil Plantier, Gregg Jefferies, Red Schoendienst, Rick Aguilera, Kevin Mitchell, Jeff Reardon and Darryl Strawberry all played here.

One major piece of Lynchburg baseball history is now gone, as Harvey's Hotel was recently torn down. The city's host hotel for visiting Carolina League teams for several years, Harvey's was a far cry from the spiffier Sheratons and even Days Inns of the road. New York Yankees farmhand Bubba Carpenter once said it was his favorite road hotel: "Everybody else hates it, but I like it because it reminds me of my grandma's house." You'll be hard-pressed to find a player who came through the league in the Harvey's era who doesn't remember it well.

### ◆ BALLPARK EXTRAS

New to Lynchburg in 1994 was its mascot Socko, a 6-foot-7 furry animal. The corn dogs and hot dogs are the best choices out of a standard selection of concessions.

### ◆ ATTRACTIONS

For Civil War buffs, a trip to Appomattox Court House is a must. It's 30 miles from the city and is the site where Gen. Robert E. Lee surrendered the Army of Northern Virginia to Gen. Ulysses S. Grant. For further information call (804) 352-8987.

Poplar Forest, Thomas Jefferson's former summer home, is about five miles away. For further information call (804) 525-1806.

For more information about the Lynchburg area, call the Chamber of Commerce, (804) 845-5966.

### ◆ DINING

Rumors Sports Bar & Grill, about five minutes from the park, offers 13 TVs, including a 60-inch-wide screen, and has all the basic burger fare you could want to eat with your sports. 6001 Fort Avenue, (804) 239-8230.

Gatsby's, five minutes away, is one of the top restaurants for postgame eats and calls itself "Lynchburg's ultimate nightspot." 2034 Lakeside Drive, (804) 385-5052.

#### ◆ LODGING
Best Western is about 10 minutes from the park. 2815 Candlers Mountain Road, Lynchburg, (804) 237-2986/(800) 528-1234.

Howard Johnson's is on U.S. 29, about 10 minutes from the ballpark. (804) 845-7041/(800) 654-2000.

#### ◆ DIRECTIONS
From U.S. 29, take the City Stadium exit. Go up the hill, pass the Econo Lodge to the stop sign. The ballpark will be on the right. Parking is plentiful and free.

---

**CITY STADIUM**
**Fort Avenue and Wythe Road**
**Lynchburg, VA 24506**
**(804) 528-1144**

---

**Capacity: 4,000**
**LF 325, CF 390, RF 325**

---

#### ◆ TICKET AND SCHEDULE INFORMATION
Weeknight and Saturday games are at 7:05 P.M., with Sunday games at 2:05 P.M. from April through June and at 6:05 P.M. in July and August. There will also be two weekday matinees during the season.

The Hillcats open their season in early April and close it out the first week of September.

Ticket prices: $5 reserved seats; $4 general admission.

# PRINCE WILLIAM CANNONS

### CHICAGO WHITE SOX

Over the years, some Carolina League players have disparagingly referred to Prince William County Stadium, which opened in 1984, as The

Erector Set. This sobriquet accurately describes Prince William's all-metal grandstand and its silver girders, screws and planks. Despite this stadium's rather unspectacular appearance and two uninspiring mascots, it does have some saving graces. Located off the main road in a government office complex, it is in a rather peaceful setting, with an outfield wall framed by an attractive array of trees and other foliage. When the noise level inside the ballpark is low, you can hear the sounds of crickets coming from the surrounding brush. On most nights, while the pros play inside Prince William Stadium, the softball fields in front of the ballpark are illuminated and filled with the sights and sounds of amateur games.

#### ◆ LOCAL AND TEAM HISTORY
Organized baseball first came to this suburb of Washington in 1984, when the franchise shifted south from Alexandria, Virginia, just across the Potomac River from the nation's capital, to Prince William County. The Cannons' most memorable season was 1989. That year, Stump Merrill (New York Yankees manager in 1990 and '91) took over a Cannons' team with an 18-23 record and led it to Prince William's only Carolina League championship. This franchise also won the title in '82 while based in Alexandria.

Despite the short tenure of minor-league baseball here, Prince William has sent an impressive list of players to the big leagues. Barry Bonds made his pro debut here in 1985, batting .299 with 13 home runs and 37 runs batted in. As a hint of what he would subsequently do in the big leagues, Bonds homered in three straight at-bats in a game against the Durham Bulls. Bonds' once and future teammate that year was Bobby Bonilla, who hit .262 in 39 games. Although these two players could not prevent the '85 Prince William Pirates from finishing under .500, they would eventually lead the Pittsburgh Pirates to three straight National League East titles (1990-92).

The team's name and its logo, a cannon firing baseballs instead of cannonballs, are references to the nearby Manassas battlefield, site of the Civil War's first major land confrontation.

**OTHER FAMOUS ALUMNI**
Bernie Williams, Pat Kelly, Hensley "Bam-Bam" Meulens, Jose Lind, John Smiley, Rafael Belliard and Jeff King all played here.

#### ◆ BALLPARK EXTRAS
The Cannons' operate two grills, found behind each corner base, that offer good grilled chicken sandwiches. Burgers, hot dogs and sausages are also available. There

is a picnic area down the right-field line, but there is no covering over the grandstand. When the hot summer sun reflects off the stadium's metal benches, it can be somewhat blinding here and also quite warm.

◆ ATTRACTIONS

Washington and its many sights are about 30 miles north of here. For information about Washington, call (202) 789-7000/(800) 422-8644.

Manassas National Battlefield Park, located along U.S. 29 near I-66, commemorates the first and second Civil War battles of Manassas/Bull Run. Admission is $2. Seniors 61 and over and children 17 and under are free. For further information, call (703) 361-1339.

Potomac Mills Mall, located off I-95 in Dale City, is one of the largest discount shopping areas on the East Coast. For further information, call (703) 643-1770.

For additional information about this area, contact the Prince William County Tourist Office, (703) 491-4045.

◆ DINING

Durango Steakhouse, about five minutes from the ballpark, serves a good assortment of steaks, chicken and ribs, plus southwestern fare. Old Bridge Road in the Glen Shopping Center, (703) 680-0599.

◆ LODGING

Comfort Inn is at exit 161 from I-95, about 20 minutes from the ballpark. (703) 494-5644/(800) 4-CHOICE.

Days Inn Potomac Mills is at exit 156 from I-95, about 15 minutes from the ballpark. (703) 494-4433/(800) 325-2525.

◆ DIRECTIONS

Take exit 160 from I-95 south. Turn left at the second traffic light, Davis Ford Road. Stay on Davis Ford for about six miles. Look for the park on your right, about 1 mile past The Glen Shopping Center. From I-95 north, take exit 156, Dale Boulevard. Stay on Dale for about four miles. Turn right on Hillendale Drive. Turn left at the first traffic light, Davis Ford Road, and left again at the next light. The ballpark is about ½ mile away on your right. There is plenty of parking available for $1.50.

**PRINCE WILLIAM COUNTY STADIUM**
P.O. Box 2148
Woodbridge, VA 22193
(703) 590-2311
_____
Capacity: 6000
LF 315, CF 400, RF 315

◆ TICKET AND SCHEDULE INFORMATION

Most games are played at night, with weekday games starting at 7:30. Saturday and Sunday games begin at 7 P.M. and 1:30 P.M., respectively. The Memorial Day game begins at 1:30 P.M., while the one on July 4 is at 6:30 P.M.

The Cannons' home opener is usually in early April, and the season ends in the first week of September.

Ticket prices: $7.50 field box seats; $6.50 box seats; $5.50 reserved grandstand; $4.50 general admission, $3.50 for seniors and children 6 to 14.

# SALEM AVALANCHE

## COLORADO ROCKIES

The new as-yet-unnamed stadium opens this year, replacing Municipal Field, which had stood since 1932. Although details weren't all available at press time, some  planned features include wider concourses, team clubhouses designed to AAA specifications, picnic areas near the bullpens and the increasingly popular sky boxes.

Salem is considered one of the more beautiful sites in the Carolina League by visiting players who praise the rolling hills and mountains. Pitchers hated Municipal Field's short fences in left and right fields, though, so look for deeper lines at the new digs.

In fact, there were so many jokes about the dimensions of the old outfield lines, officially listed at 316 to left and 302 to right, that some visiting players once brought measuring tapes from home and claimed that the distances were actually less than 300 feet down each line.

◆ LOCAL AND TEAM HISTORY

A member of the Carolina League since 1968, Salem also hosted an Appalachian League team in 1955 and from 1957 to '67 as well as a club in conjunction with nearby Roanoke in the Virginia League in the late '30s. The first Salem minor-league team played for a season in the Ohio-Pennsylvania League in 1912. Roanoke also hosted teams for several years, though only in 1939 did the two towns combine for a club, and they never had teams at the same time.

Municipal also featured some seats from the old Yankee Stadium stands prior to its renovation in the mid-1970s. For the final game at the stadium, 96-year-old Dewey Owen threw out the first pitch.

Not all of the team's history is happy. In 1974, a

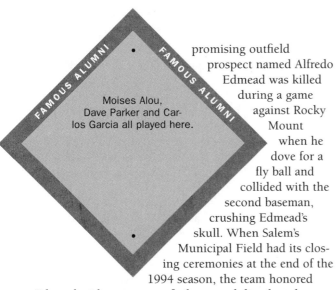

FAMOUS ALUMNI

Moises Alou, Dave Parker and Carlos Garcia all played here.

promising outfield prospect named Alfredo Edmead was killed during a game against Rocky Mount when he dove for a fly ball and collided with the second baseman, crushing Edmead's skull. When Salem's Municipal Field had its closing ceremonies at the end of the 1994 season, the team honored Edmead with a moment of silence and distributed copies of the original newspaper article detailing his death.

◆ **BALLPARK EXTRAS**

Along with the regular fare, Salem offers "burger barn" specialties such as hot-off-the-grill burgers and chicken and beer-battered onion rings, as well as Carolina-style barbecue sandwiches with fresh coleslaw.

◆ **ATTRACTIONS**

The Roanoke Valley has much to offer those who want sites of historic interest and those who simply want to browse through scenery or stores.

Attractions in downtown Roanoke and its surroundings include the Center in the Square, with such sites as the Art Museum of Western Virginia (703-342-5798); the historic Farmers' Market; Mill Mountain Zoo and Star Overlook (703-343-3241); and the Virginia Museum of Transportation (703-342-5670).

Blue Ridge Balloons offers a unique way to sightsee around the lovely Roanoke Valley. Route 1, Wirtz, Virginia, (703) 721-6092.

For more information about this area, call the Chamber of Commerce, (703) 387-0267.

◆ **DINING**

Piche's, about five minutes from the park, offers pizza, sandwiches and salads. 3404 Brandon Avenue, (703) 345-7311.

Sports Heroes, about 10 minutes away, offers hot and cold heroes and is worth the trip if only to read the menu with such items as the George Foreman (hot homemade meatloaf that clearly packs a punch), the Roger Clemens (meatballs topped with mozzarella cheese) and the Shaquille O'Neal Ragin' Cajun (savory roast beef with veggies and spices). 3232 Electric Road, (703) 989-0717.

◆ **LODGING**

Days Inn–Airport is 15-20 minutes from the ballpark.

8118 Plantation Road, Roanoke, (703) 366-0341/(800) 325-2525.

Ramada Inn Central is 15 to 20 minutes away. 1927 Franklin Road SW, Roanoke, (703) 343-0121/(800) 228-2828.

---

**SALEM BASEBALL STADIUM**
**1004 Texas Street**
**Salem, VA 24153**
**(703) 389-3333**

**Capacity: 6,000**
**LF 330, CF 401, RF 330**

---

◆ **TICKET AND SCHEDULE INFORMATION**

Weeknight and Saturday games are at 7 P.M.; Sunday games are at 3 P.M. through mid-June and then at 7 P.M.

Salem begins its 1995 season in early April and closes out the first week of September.

Ticket prices: $6 box seats; $5 reserved seats; $3 general admission. Seniors and children under 12 receive $1 off on box seats and reserved seats for most events.

# WILMINGTON BLUE ROCKS

## KANSAS CITY ROYALS

The name of the Blue Rocks' ballpark honors Negro league star Judy Johnson, a Wilmington native, and Dan Frawley, a former mayor who helped bring pro baseball back to Wilmington in 1993. The stadium, with an attractive red-brick facade, features an uncovered grandstand from which fans get a view of the Wilmington skyline and I-95. This highway passes just beyond and above the outfield wall on an elevated roadway, so it is not unusual for motorists driving by to peer from their cars into the ballpark. The wide concourse here is open, and you can follow the game from the concession stands. Fans here also have a unique local tradition. Once the game starts, everyone in the ballpark stands and applauds until the Wilmington pitcher throws a strike, which can occasionally take several pitches. The Blue Rocks Cafe is behind home plate on the luxury box level. The cafe, which can accommodate up to 75 people, provides a seat for the ballgame and such fare as beer, chicken, beef and a salad bar.

### ◆ LOCAL AND TEAM HISTORY

Pro baseball in Wilmington dates from 1884, when the Delawareans opened the season as a charter member of the Eastern League. Several other minor-league teams played here through the end of the 19th century. In 1907, Wilmington began a six-year association with the Class B Tri-State League. That was also the season Hall of Famer Joe McCarthy began his pro baseball career as a member of the Wilmington Peaches. He batted .175 in 12 games. Baseball left town in 1952, following Wilmington's 13th season in the Class B Interstate League. In 1993, the Blue Rocks joined the Carolina League and began their current affiliation with Kansas City. The team's name originated in a 1940s name-the-team contest submission by a Wilmington resident named Arthur Miller, who lived in a section of the city known for its blue granite rocks. Today, former big leaguers Bud Harrelson and Rick Cerone serve as team president and vice president, respectively.

> **OTHER FAMOUS ALUMNI**
> **OTHER FAMOUS ALUMNI**
>
> Jon Lieber, Curt Simmons, Albert "Chief" Bender, Billy Southworth and Robin Roberts either played or managed here.

Last year was a big one for Wilmington fans. The Blue Rocks, led by a pitching staff with the lowest ERA (2.96) among all full-season minor-league teams, won the Carolina League championship. During the '94 All-Star game, which was held in Wilmington and featured eight players from the hometown team, a throwing error by Blue Rocks' catcher Lance Jennings in the top of the ninth allowed the Southern Division to tie the game 1-1. But in a storybook finish, Jennings atoned for his miscue by hitting a game-winning home run just inside the left-field foul pole in the bottom half of the frame.

### ◆ BALLPARK EXTRAS

Fans in Wilmington have basic ballpark taste when it comes to food; by far the most popular items on the menu are hot dogs and draft beer. Still, the Blue Rocks feature a variety of good concession items, including cheese steak, cheese sausage, Polish sausage and fries served in a mini batting helmet. They also have one of the cutest mascots in the league in Rocky Bluewinkle. He's a moose, if you hadn't guessed.

### ◆ ATTRACTIONS

Just a few minutes over the state line is Philadelphia and all its history and lore, as well as the Philadelphia Zoo. In addition, just 20 minutes further is Sesame Place—a wonderful theme park/water park for kids and their parents. (215) 757-1100.

Brandywine River Museum, housed in a 19th-century mill, features paintings by three generations of the Wyeth family. Admission is $5, $2.50 for seniors over 65 and students 6 to 12. For further information, call (215) 388-2700.

For more information about Wilmington, call the Visitors Bureau, (302) 652-4088/(800) 422-1181.

### ◆ DINING

Harry's Savoy Grill was awarded the "best prime rib" award for 1993 by a local magazine and offers an upscale gas-lit atmosphere as well as a piano bar and Sunday brunch. It's about 15 to 20 minutes away. 2020 Naamans Road, (302) 475-3000.

### ◆ LODGING

Holiday Inn Downtown is about 15 minutes from the park. 700 King Street, Wilmington, (302) 655-0400/ (800) HOLIDAY

Quality Inn Skyways at Airport is 10 to 15 minutes away. 147 N. DuPont Highway, New Castle, (302) 328-6666(800) 228-5151.

### ◆ DIRECTIONS

From I-95, take exit 6/Martin Luther King Jr. Boulevard. Turn right on Maryland Avenue. Follow signs to the ballpark, which is less than one mile away. Parking is plentiful and free.

> **JUDY JOHNSON FIELD AT FRAWLEY STADIUM**
> **801 South Madison Sreet**
> **Wilmington, DE 19801**
> **(302) 888-2015**
>
> **Capacity: 5,500**
> **LF 325, CF 400, RF 325**

### ◆ TICKET AND SCHEDULE INFORMATION

Monday through Saturday games are at 7:05 P.M., while Sunday games start at 2:05 P.M.

The Blue Rocks open their season in early April and end it in late September.

Ticket prices: $6 box seats; $5 reserved seats; $4 general admission.

# WINSTON-SALEM WARTHOGS

**CINCINNATI REDS**

A large-scale renovation to Ernie Shore Field, built in 1956, has added much to this comfortable ballpark. Down the left-field line there is a new, tree-shaded picnic deck, and new concession stands have also been added. Trees line the outfield fence, and there are two grassy hills down each line that are used primarily to accommodate overflow crowds when the stands are full. Fans can picnic here, and chase after foul balls and homers between bites of their sandwiches. The covered grandstand features wooden seats, several of which carry various coats of paint covering many years of minor-league baseball in Winston-Salem. Grove Stadium, home of the Wake Forest University football team, is adjacent to the ballpark. The ball carries well at Ernie Shore Field, as the home players' constant presence among the league's home-run leaders can attest.

The stadium was expanded by 2,000 seats in 1994, and new clubhouses were added as well. The proximity of Wake Forest University and its college-town ambience, coupled with the beautiful scenery of the region, makes Winston-Salem a favorite road stop of players and fans alike.

### ◆ LOCAL AND TEAM HISTORY

In 1905, Winston-Salem made its organized baseball debut in the Class D Virginia–North Carolina League. After being associated with three other circuits, in 1945, Winston-Salem joined the Carolina League, where this city has remained ever since. Winston-Salem, whose 10 championships lead the circuit, is the only current Carolina League franchise to have been in the league continuously since its inception. Winston-Salem began its current affiliation with Cincinnati in 1993. George Whiteman, No. 4 on the all-time minor-league list with 3,388 career hits, batted .267 and banged out 124 safeties for Winston-Salem in 1929, his final season as a player. "Handy" Andy Phillip, a member of the Basketball Hall of Fame, tried his hand at baseball as Winston-Salem's first baseman in 1949. He had a respectable season, batting .279.

Ernie Shore Field, with short distances down the lines and power alleys about 350 feet away, is a home-run hitters' paradise. In 1993 and 1994, Winston-Salem had seven players who hit at least 20 homers, including the Carolina League's home-run champions for those seasons. Bubba Smith, perhaps the most popular Carolina League player in recent years, joined Winston-Salem in June 1993. He proceeded to tear up the Carolina League for the rest of the season, hitting .301 with 27 homers and 81 runs batted in to help Winston-Salem capture the league championship. After the campaign, Smith was named the league MVP for the second straight season. In 1994, Winston-Salem set a new Carolina League record with 202 home runs, topping the former mark of 160 that it set in '93.

The team underwent a name change in the off-season, transforming itself from the patriotic Spirit to the bizarre Warthogs.

### ◆ BALLPARK EXTRAS

The park will offer a new mascot to go with the new name, but it's still under wraps. The club is hoping to give everything a new flavor, including updates on the concession menu, but it was still in planning stages at press time. The club's 1994 program offered one unique item that was hard to find—a full explanation of exactly what different pitches do, for those confused by the difference between a sinker, slider, screwball and basic curveball.

### ◆ ATTRACTIONS

Old Salem is a restored version of the town founded in 1766, which was one of the twin cities of Salem and Winston before the two merged in 1913. One of America's most authentic restored Colonial sites, it features such spots as a bakery and a shoemaker's shop. It's on Main Street, south of I-40 in downtown Winston-Salem. (910) 721-7300.

Stroh's Brewery offers a 30-minute guided tour of the facility that explains every step of the brewing and packaging process at America's largest family-owned brewery. Not surprisingly, it ends in the Hospitality Center where visitors of legal age receive a complimentary glass of the product in the Bavarian-style dining room (younger folks get a soft drink). 4791 Schlitz Avenue, Winston-Salem. (910) 788-6710.

For more information about Winston-Salem, call the Chamber of Commerce, (910) 725-2361.

### ◆ DINING

On the Fringe Pub and Grill, across the street from the ballpark, offers great burgers and half-price appetizers for baseball ticket-stub holders. The restaurant features several meet-the-players nights as well. (910) 723-3966.

Rainbow Cafe-Bookstore, about five minutes away, offers meals in a European cafe–style atmosphere with homemade soups, sandwiches, decadent desserts and a full list of wines and imported beers. You can browse the bookstore and read while you dine. 712 Brookstown Avenue, (910) 723-0858.

## ◆ LODGING
Holiday Inn North is a couple of blocks from the ballpark. 3050 University Parkway, Winston-Salem, (910) 723-2911/(800) HOLIDAY.

## ◆ DIRECTIONS
From I-40, take the Cherry Street exit. Stay on Cherry until it turns into University Parkway, about two blocks outside downtown. Stay on University, crossing Coliseum Drive and passing the Lawrence Joel Memorial Coliseum. The next street after Coliseum is Deacon Boulevard. Turn right on Deacon. The ballpark will be about ¼ mile away on the left. Parking is plentiful and free.

**ERNIE SHORE FIELD**
401 W. 30th Street
Winston-Salem, NC 27105
(910) 759-2233

Capacity: 6,280
LF 335, CF 400, RF 325

## ◆ TICKET AND SCHEDULE INFORMATION
Game times are 7:05 P.M. from Monday through Saturday; on Sunday games are at 2:05 P.M. from April through June and at 6:05 P.M. in July and August.

The Warthogs open their home schedule in early April and close out at home in the last week of August.

Ticket prices: $6 box seats; $5 reserved; $4 general admission.

# FLORIDA STATE LEAGUE

The Florida State League debuted in 1936 and ran through 1941, but was shut down for World War II. Returning in 1946, it has been a part of the minor leagues ever since. There have been 29 cities represented in Florida State League history. The league holds 14 clubs divided into Eastern and Western divisions. The reigning champions are the Tampa Yankees.

Stan Musial, Jimmy Wynn, Jose Rijo, Juan Gonzalez and Rocky Colavito rank among its many famous alumni, but some of the finer seasons in FSL history were not from ballplayers who experienced major-league success. Dan Keith hit .400 in 1955, a league record. Ed Levy set a record with 33 home runs in 1950, and Jim Fuller matched it in 1971. Scott Karpinsky won a record 29 games in 1949.

Twelve of the league's 14 ballparks also serve as a spring-training home to major-league teams. St. Petersburg hosts the St. Louis Cardinals and the Baltimore Orioles, and West Palm Beach hosts the Atlanta Braves and the Montreal Expos.

● ● ●

*A statue of Jackie Robinson and two young fans stands outside the historic ballpark in Daytona Beach that bears his name.*

# BREVARD COUNTY MANATEES

## FLORIDA MARLINS

Space Coast Stadium opened with much fanfare for the Marlins' spring training 1994. Kennedy Space Center is nearby, and the stadium makes the most of the space connection. On the plaza right outside is a replica of the X-30 NASA exploratory device, a structure about 60 feet by 30 feet. There's a countdown clock similar to the one at the Kennedy Space Center that starts three hours before game time and counts down to the first pitch. If a Manatee hits a home run, a large neon mock-baseball blasts off from the scoreboard, which emits smoke, heavy bass reverberations and blastoff sounds while the PA plays a NASA-generated tape that booms space jargon about the liftoff. The black hitting backdrop in centerfield is even called "the black hole," referring to the outer-space phenomenon, not the dungeon in Calcutta.

If it sounds like they lay the space stuff on pretty thick, it is because they do. It makes the park unique, and the fans love it. The players like the place too. The location, a three-hour drive up I-95 from the Marlins' Joe Robbie Stadium, makes it easy to reach for Marlins front-office personnel and Marlins fans.

### ◆ LOCAL AND TEAM HISTORY
The Marlins planted their FSL affiliate here last year, moving it from the California League. The first-year team won the first-half championship (the FSL season is divided into two half-season races) and reached the best-of-five finals before losing to Tampa, a Yankees affiliate. The Manatees were 78-61 in their first season. The club easily led the FSL in attendance, drawing 149,813. St. Petersburg was second with just over 108,000.

### ◆ BALLPARK EXTRAS
The space stuff reaches into concessions as well. You can dine at the Galaxy Grill or the Orbit Grill, or—new this year—buy a shuttle snack, a boxed lunch designed to look like a space vehicle. No Tang or freeze-dried astronaut food, though.

### ◆ ATTRACTIONS
Obviously there's the Kennedy Space Center, a 30-minute drive away. If you time your visit right, you might be able to watch a shuttle launch. (407) 452-2121.

Many people visit the original RonJon surf shop at historic Cocoa Beach. 4151 N. Atlantic Avenue, Cocoa Beach, (407) 799-8820.

And it's an hour to Disneyworld. (407) 824-4321.

For more information, call the Chamber of Commerce, (407) 724-5400.

### ◆ DINING
This ballpark is truly isolated. There are fast-food places nearby, but two better choices are Primavera, an Italian spot, about 10 minutes down the road (6300 N. Wickham, Melbourne, 407-242-8507), and Fresh Pasta, another Italian spot, also about 10 minutes away (1319 Cypress Avenue, Melbourne, 407-768-0200).

### ◆ LODGING
Again, isolation is an issue, but the Melbourne Hilton-Rialto Place is 40 minutes away. The Marlins use it as spring training housing. 200 Rialto Place, Melbourne, (407) 768-0200/(800) 445-8667.

### ◆ DIRECTIONS
The stadium is actually in the unincorporated town of Viera. From the North, take I-95 South to exit 73 (Wickham Road), go west ½ mile to Lake Andrew Drive, then left on St. John's and right on Stadium Parkway. From the south, take I-95 North to Exit 74 (Fiske Boulevard), then go south to Stadium Parkway. Parking is plentiful and costs $1.

---

**SPACE COAST STADIUM**
**5600 Stadium Parkway**
**Melbourne, FL 32940**
**(407) 633-9200**

**Capacity: 7,381**
**LF 340, CF 404, RF 340**

---

### ◆ TICKET AND SCHEDULE INFORMATION
All night games are 7:05 P.M. starts. Sunday games are at 1:35 P.M., and doubleheaders are 5:05 P.M. starts.

The season starts one week into April and runs a day or two into September.

Ticket prices: $4 box seats; $3 reserved; $2 general admission.

# CHARLOTTE RANGERS

## TEXAS RANGERS

This ballpark was built in 1987 expressly for the Rangers, the first organized-baseball team located in this area. Charlotte County Stadium features a grandstand that covers all but the first eight rows of seats. The cloverleaf practice fields of the Texas Rangers' spring training complex are visible beyond the right-field fence, while several small lakes plus various trees can be seen in right. A row of palm trees runs the entire length of the outfield fence, completing what is a pleasant background here. Behind the right-field bullpen, you will find a picnic area that the team is planning to cover with a tent in 1995.

### ◆ LOCAL AND TEAM HISTORY

The Rangers have been affiliated with Texas since their inaugural season in 1987. In '88, Sammy Sosa struggled, batting just .229 for Charlotte although he did manage to lead the FSL with 12 triples, still a franchise record. The Rangers' 1989 championship season had some interesting twists. Manager Bobby Jones promised his team he would shave off his mustache if Charlotte won the first half Northern Division title. The Rangers kept their part of the bargain and so did Jones, shaving his upper lip. Shortly thereafter, the Rangers went into a slump. But by the end of the season, Charlotte, a team with no .300 hitters among the regulars and only one pitcher with at least 10 wins, had won its first FSL championship and Jones had a new mustache. Barry Manuel set a new FSL record with 38 saves in 1990, his third consecutive season in Charlotte, and was also credited with the win in the league's All-Star game. One of his teammates that season was fellow FSL All-Star Ivan "Pudge" Rodriguez, who batted .287.

OTHER FAMOUS ALUMNI

Juan Gonzalez, Dean Palmer, Kenny Rogers, Kevin Brown, Rusty Greer and Jeff Frye played here.

### ◆ BALLPARK EXTRAS

At the concession stands, brats, hot dogs, grilled pretzels and super dogs are available. A large outdoor grill is used when the crowd is especially large, such as on weekends, holidays or big promotion days. The savory smell wafts into the stands at times, and naturally the lines grow longer.

### ◆ ATTRACTIONS

The tarpon fishing off the coast is some of the best in the world. Sarasota and Fort Myers, famous for their beaches, are 40 minutes away—Sarasota to the north, Fort Myers to the south. Boca Grande also has beautiful beaches; the $3.20 toll is well worth it. It's ½ hour or so from the ballpark.

For more information about Port Charlotte, call the Chamber of Commerce, (813) 627-2222.

### ◆ DINING

The Old World Restaurant is the most popular in the area. It is a family restaurant in Northport, 10 minutes from the stadium on U.S. 41 (Tamiami Trail). 14415 S. Tamiami Trail, Northport, (813) 426-1155.

### ◆ LODGING

The Palm Island Resort is upscale, and you need to take a ferry to get there. It's about 20 to 25 minutes away. 7092 Placida Road, Cape Haze, (813) 697-8989.

The Days Inn–Murdock is the choice of visiting teams, about 10 minutes away on U.S. 41. 1941 Tamiami Trail, Northport, (813) 627-8900/(800) 325-2525.

### ◆ DIRECTIONS

From I-75, take exit 32/Toledo Blade Boulevard. Go west on Toledo Blade and straight through the traffic light where the boulevard intersects U.S. 41. Turn right at the stop sign onto State Highway 776. The stadium will be about 1½ miles away on the right. Plentiful parking is available for $1.

**CHARLOTTE COUNTY STADIUM**
**2300 El Jobean Road**
**Port Charlotte, FL 33948**
**(813) 625-9500**

**Capacity: 6,026**
**LF 340, CF 410, RF 340**

### ◆ TICKET AND SCHEDULE INFORMATION

Games start at 7 P.M. from Monday through Saturday and at 6 P.M. on Sunday.

The season starts one week into April and runs a day or two into September.

Ticket prices: $4 box/reserved seats; $3 general admission.

# CLEARWATER PHILLIES

## PHILADELPHIA PHILLIES

Jack Russell Stadium, the FSL's second-oldest ballpark, had an auspicious debut on Opening Day during spring training in 1955, when the Philadelphia Phillies defeated the Detroit Tigers 4-2 in the first exhibition game played here. Since the stands are unusually close to the playing field at Jack Russell, the ballpark has an intimate feel. The stadium is structurally unremarkable save for its 25-foot-tall Green Monster in center field and a covered grandstand. Located in the middle of a residential area, the ballpark is also only about two miles from the home of the Dunedin Blue Jays, making these two cities the closest neighbors among all National Association teams. This proximity has resulted in a good local rivalry between the Blue Jays and the Phillies, especially since their big-league parents faced each other in the 1993 World Series.

### LOCAL AND TEAM HISTORY

There is a 60-year gap in this city's pro baseball past. In 1924, the Clearwater Pelicans spent almost three weeks in the Class C Florida State League after the franchise moved here from Daytona Beach. The league folded in August. Baseball returned to this city in 1985 when the Philadelphia Phillies established their FSL franchise in Clearwater. On August 23, 1992, Clearwater's Andy Carter and Winter Haven's Scott Bakkum faced each other and hurled the first double no-hitter in Florida State League history. Carter beat Bakkum 1-0 as Clearwater scored on two walks and two sacrifice bunts in a game which also featured a 30-minute rain delay. The next year also proved to be a record-setting one in Clearwater. Phil Geisler collected three home runs and a single on July 20 against St. Petersburg, tying

**OTHER FAMOUS ALUMNI**

Kim Batiste, Mickey Morandini, Marvin Freeman, Mike Lieberthal, Andy Ashby, Ricky Jordan and Kevin Stocker played here.

league records for most home runs and most total bases (13) in a game. Geisler, who had been suspended earlier that season for using a corked bat, also hit for the cycle on June 13. One day after his three-homer slugfest, he was promoted to AA Reading.

### BALLPARK EXTRAS

The Hard Ball Cafe offers a buffet with an all-you-can-eat option. It is located in the left-field section. The Phillies also offer a good selection of grilled meats, including brats, sausage and chicken. Pizza and refreshing Italian ices are also available.

### ATTRACTIONS

Busch Gardens in Tampa is a ½ hour drive away. (813) 987-5082.

Ybor City, a section of Tampa, has an old Cuba atmosphere, and Clearwater Beach is a famous white-sand stretch not far from the park.

For more information about Clearwater, call the Chamber of Commerce, (813) 461-0011.

### DINING

Capogna Dugout is less than five minutes away and is popular with the fans. 1563 Gulf Tobay, (813) 441-4791.

### LODGING

The Holiday Inn Central is 10 minutes away. 21030 U.S. 19 North, Clearwater, (813) 797-8173/(800) HOLIDAY.

Howard Johnson's is five minutes away. 20967 U.S. 19 North, Clearwater, (813) 799-1181/(800) 654-2000.

### DIRECTIONS

Take U.S. 19 to Drew Street and go west on Drew. Turn right on Greenwood to Seminole and go east. The ballpark will be directly in front of you shortly after turning onto Seminole. Plenty of free parking is available.

---

**JACK RUSSELL STADIUM**
**800 Phillies Drive**
**Clearwater, FL 34615**
**(813) 441-8638**

**Capacity: 7,195**
**LF 340, CF 400, RF 340**

---

### TICKET AND SCHEDULE INFORMATION

Starts are at 7 P.M. from Monday through Saturday and at 2 P.M. on Sunday.

The season starts one week into April and runs a day or two into September.

Ticket prices: $4 box seats; $2 general admission.

# DAYTONA CUBS

## CHICAGO CUBS

Here is a mystery for you: Even the city of Daytona Beach does not know exactly when Jackie Robinson Stadium (né City Island Ballpark) was built, according to club president Jordan Kobritz, but most estimates say the park is 55 years old. Buck O'Neil visited last year, though, and said he remembered playing there more than 60 years ago, so go figure.

Depending on how you feel about old ballparks, this one is either decrepit or quaint. It has a traditional wooden-seat grandstand. There are no modern ballpark amenities: no luxury boxes, no comfortable rest rooms and only one concession stand. The ballpark just meets the National Association standards for facilities for the players. It reaches none of the standards for fans.

The grandstand on the first-base side is divided from the grandstand on the third-base side. The third-base side has football-style no-back bleachers. The first two rows are aluminum-bench seating. On the plus side the seats are right on top of the field.

### ◆ LOCAL AND TEAM HISTORY

Daytona Beach is the senior member of the Florida State League, with more than 50 years in the circuit since first joining in 1920. Hall of Fame outfielder Stan Musial was the league's top pitcher in 1940, winning 18 games for Daytona Beach while also compiling a 2.62 ERA. Since he had the best arm on his high school team years before, Musial's coach made him a pitcher. Stan the Man pitched three seasons in the minors before an arm injury in 1941 helped to end his mound career and force his full-time move to the outfield, where he preferred to be. Musial batted .311 for Daytona Beach in 1940.

In 1947, the Daytona Beach Islanders purchased Elvin "Stubby" Stabelfield for $25. He proved to be a real bargain, leading the 1948 FSL with 28 wins, No. 2 all-time in the league, after losing 21 games in 1947. That same season, Wally Gaddis posted a 26-9 record for the Islanders while pitching 32 complete games, still the most ever in this loop. The FSL's top pitching staff helped Daytona Beach win the '48 championship. The following year, Gaddis returned here to post 25 wins.

### ◆ BALLPARK EXTRAS

Jackie Robinson is honored in a statue outside the stadium; it's popular for fan photos.

### ◆ ATTRACTIONS

Daytona Motor Speedway is five miles away. Just follow the signs. (904) 254-2700.

Daytona Beach is a two-minute drive away. Boosters call Daytona Beach "the world's most famous beach." If nothing else, the fact that you can drive on it is novel.

For more information about the Daytona area, call the Chamber of Commerce, (904) 255-0981/(800) 854-1234.

### ◆ DINING

Both nearby International Speedveard Boulevard and nearby A1A are crammed with fast-food franchises and family dining spots. No single spot stands out for local baseball fans.

### ◆ LODGING

The Ocean's Eleven Resorts provide a variety of accommodation choices, including the Mayan Inn, which is less than five minutes away. 103 S. Ocean Avenue, Daytona Beach, (904) 252-0584.

### ◆ DIRECTIONS

Take U.S. 1 South to Orange Avenue, then bear left. The ballpark is two blocks on the left. Plenty of free parking is available.

---

**JACKIE ROBINSON STADIUM**
**105 East Orange Avenue**
**Daytona Beach, FL 32114**
**(904) 257-3172**

**Capacity: 4,200**
**LF 315, CF 400, RF 325**

---

### ◆ TICKET AND SCHEDULE INFORMATION

Most games start at 7:05 P.M. Sunday games begin at 1:05 P.M.

The season starts one week into April and runs a day or two into September.

Ticket prices: $4 box seats; $3.50 general admission, $2.50 seniors and youth.

# DUNEDIN BLUE JAYS

## TORONTO BLUE JAYS

The original facility was built in 1938, named Grant Field for then–Dunedin mayor A.J. Grant. A piece of history from the Great Depression, it was erected as a WPA project. The field was used for amateur baseball for years until the Buffalo Bison, a minor-league team, conducted spring training on site in the 1960s. The Detroit Tigers then used it as a site for their Florida Instructional League team in the 1970s. The first permanent tenant was the 1977 Toronto Blue Jays, a brand-new expansion team.

Grant Field was expanded to a full complex for 1978. The field was originally little more than a grandstand and some temporary bleachers. The city rebuilt the stadium in 1990. Now it is one continuous deck with a concourse dividing the box seats from the general admission. There are 1,700 bleacher seats down the right-field line. These seats do not have backs.

### ◆ LOCAL AND TEAM HISTORY

Dunedin's organized-baseball history began in 1978, the first of two consecutive seasons in the Florida State League. Baseball left town following the 1979 season and did not return until 1987. Dunedin has been affiliated with Toronto since first joining the FSL. In 1992, Carlos Delgado had one of the greatest offensive seasons in FSL history. His 30 home runs not only topped the circuit, they were more than double the number hit (14) by the 1993 league leader and were only three shy of tying the all-time FSL record. Delgado also led the league with 100 runs batted in. Rob Butler kept his teammate from winning the Triple Crown by capturing the batting title with a .358 average, 34 points above Delgado, who was named the MVP that season. The following year, Dunedin again had the FSL's top power hitters. Rick Holifield won the home-run title with 20 four-baggers, while Chris Weinke led the league with 98 runs batted in. Both players were selected to the FSL All-Star team.

### ◆ BALLPARK EXTRAS

Canadians are famous for their love of back bacon. The Canadians and Americans who come to Dunedin can get grilled Peameal back bacon served on a bun. It's different from standard fare and well worth trying.

### ◆ ATTRACTIONS

Caladesi is a state park accessible by ferry. To get there, drive to the ferry in Honeymoon Island. (813) 469-5918.

Clearwater Beach is a 10-minute drive. Dunedin has a nice marina and waterfront, but no beaches except Honeymoon Island.

For more information about Dunedin, call the Chamber of Commerce, (813) 733-3197.

### ◆ DINING

Eddie's Bar & Grill is one favored pregame dining spot, about five minutes from the ballpark. 1283 Bayshore Boulevard, (813) 734-2300.

Sea Sea Riders is another favorite, just a few blocks away. 221 Main Street, (813) 734-1445.

### ◆ LODGING

The Howard Johnson's in Clearwater is 10 minutes away. 209647 U.S. Highway 19 North, Clearwater, (813) 799-1181/(800) 654-2000.

The Econo Lodge is next door to the ballpark. 1414 Bayshore, Dunedin, (813) 734-8851/(800) 446-6900.

### ◆ DIRECTIONS

Take U.S. 19 to Florida Highway 580, go west on 580 to Douglas Avenue, then left and go left south ¼ mile to the ballpark.

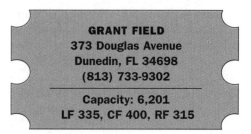

**GRANT FIELD**
**373 Douglas Avenue**
**Dunedin, FL 34698**
**(813) 733-9302**

**Capacity: 6,201**
**LF 335, CF 400, RF 315**

### ◆ TICKET AND SCHEDULE INFORMATION

Games start at 7 P.M. Sunday games in April and May begin at 2 P.M. and at 6 P.M. the rest of the season.

The season starts one week into April and runs a day or two into September.

Ticket prices: $4 box seats; $3 general admission, $2 children and seniors.

# FORT MYERS MIRACLE

## MINNESOTA TWINS

**S**ome people call Lee County Complex Stadium the nicest facility in the FSL. This stadium, built in 1991, is an attractive facility with a facade topped by a spiral tower that is somewhat reminiscent of Churchill Downs in Louisville. There is a fountain in front of the ballpark and the walkway up to the gate is lined with palm trees. Inside, only the top several rows of the grandstand are covered. The sunny side of the ballpark is the third-base side, so the bleachers here can get quite toasty on warm days. Lee County Stadium is surrounded by cow pastures. The team likes to describe its bovine neighbors as the fastest cows in baseball because the big annual fireworks show here, at which the Miracle has set all-time FSL single-game attendance records from 1992 to '94, keeps these animals hopping.

### ◆ LOCAL AND TEAM HISTORY
This franchise moved here in 1992, having previously spent 1962 to '91 in Miami, where the team won five FSL championships—1969-72 and 1978. Cal Ripken Sr. managed the 1967 Miami Marlins to a 65-76 record. Jim Fuller, a prodigious minor-league slugger who had more limited success in the majors, powered the '71 championship team by tying the FSL record for home runs (33), setting the franchise record for runs batted in (110) and league record for intentional walks (21) and leading the league with 298 total bases. Eddie Murray may be the most famous Miami alumnus. He batted .289 for the Miami Orioles in 1974 and also led the FSL with 212 total bases and 29 doubles, still a franchise record. While the Fort Myers version of this franchise has yet to have any famous alumni, it does boast two well-known owners, actor Bill Murray and singer Jimmy Buffet.

### ◆ BALLPARK EXTRAS
In 1995, the team will run the concessions for the first time. Look for a new line of offerings including Miracle lemonade in various colors, Miracle peanuts and a Miracle sandwich. Conventional pizza and ice cream will also be available. While the annual fireworks night is a big event here, fireworks are only part of the show orchestrated by General Manager Mike Veeck, whose father Bill was legendary for his eye-catching promotions. Mike has kept up the family tradition by staging such events as a postgame CD Scramble, where fans try their luck at picking out the one CD among 1,000 compact discs that contains a $1,000 certificate of deposit; a Kids Day, where children act as ticket takers and operate the concession stands and scoreboard while one serves as honorary manager; Adult Bat Boys Night; and a Field of Screams all-night horror-movie festival shown on a sail draped over the center-field scoreboard. Since Mike Veeck keeps a bust of Elvis Presley in his office, it should not be surprising that the team has an Elvis impersonator on 24-hour call. Perhaps the most unusual promotion here was a Thomas Edison seance one night in 1992. Since one of Edison's old labs is in Fort Myers, the team decided to honor the man ultimately responsible for night baseball by using one of his own straw hats in an unsuccessful attempt to summon Edison's spirit back to see what his electric light bulb had wrought. While the many attractions Florida has to offer, plus the warm temperatures, can keep people away from the ballpark, the entertaining and offbeat promotions staged by the Miracle provide plenty of incentive to visit Lee County Stadium.

### ◆ ATTRACTIONS
The winter homes of Thomas Edison and Henry Ford are in Fort Myers. They are approximately a 10-minute drive from the stadium and tours are offered. 2350 MacGregor Boulevard, Fort Myers, (813) 334-3614.

Sanibel and Captiva Islands are very popular tourist destinations. Each can be reached by bridge for swimming, clamming, first-rate seashell collecting and fishing. The area is excellent for deep-sea fishing.

For more information about Fort Myers, call the Chamber of Commerce, (813) 332-3624.

### ◆ DINING
Pott's Sports Cafe is right behind the right-field wall, abutting the ballpark. It serves Buffalo wings, oyster dishes and shrimp. (813) 768-5500.

Like grouper? It is the official fish of Florida's west coast. You can find it, as well as plenty of other fine dishes, at The Bubble Room on Sanibel Island. The building was designed in the 1940s and is packed with period memorabilia, presented in a Planet Hollywood style. It's about an hour away, but it's worth the trip. 15001 Captiva Avenue, Sanibel Island, (813) 472-5558.

### ◆ LODGING
The Wellesley Inn is the top pick, about 10 minutes from the park. 4400 Ford Street Extension, Fort Myers, (813) 278-3949.

### ◆ DIRECTIONS
From I-75, take exit 21/Daniels Road. Turn right and go west for about three miles. At the first major intersection, turn left on Six Mile Cypress Parkway at the traffic

light. The ballpark is about one mile away on the right. Ample parking is available for $1.

LEE COUNTY SPORTS COMPLEX
14400 Six Mile Cypress Parkway
Fort Myers, FL 33912
(813) 768-4210

Capacity: 7,500
LF 330, CF 405, RF 330

◆ TICKET AND SCHEDULE INFORMATION

Usual starting time is 7:05 P.M. Sunday games begin at 5 P.M.

The season starts one week into April and runs a day or two into September.

Ticket prices: $4 box seats; $3 general admission, $2 children and seniors.

# KISSIMMEE COBRAS

## HOUSTON ASTROS

Osceola County Stadium, built in 1984, has some interesting neighbors. A local Bible college is behind center field, while two other schools and the Silver Spurs Rodeo Arena are located on the opposite side of the ballpark. Rodeo performances here in early July turn this into an area filled with activity and many different types of motor vehicles. From the mostly covered grandstand inside the ballpark, you can see Houston's spring-training practice fields in left and an attractive grove of pine trees beyond the outfield fence. There are grassy areas for fans past the corner bases and picnic tables down the right-field line. The Cobras have installed an innovative enclosed playground, complete with slide and monkey bars, behind the left-field bleachers.

The stadium has become home to two noteworthy events—the Senior Little League World Series, held annually in August, and the Olive Garden Classic, a college baseball tournament held annually in March.

◆ LOCAL AND TEAM HISTORY

In 1985, the Osceola Astros, the first organized-baseball team based here, joined the Florida State League and began its current affiliation with Houston. The team adopted its current name for the 1995 season in order to give this franchise some local identity. Kissimmee's attractive new logo features a menacing cobra with its tail curled around a baseball. A stock joke in the FSL is they never dared go by the name Kissimmee Astros because it sounds too much like a vulgar challenge.

Thirty-three Kissimmee/Osceola alumni have reached the big leagues since the franchise's debut in '85. In 1990, Jeff Juden posted a 10-1 record and .909 winning percentage, the fourth-best in FSL history. Kenny Lofton, who batted .331 for the O-Astros in 1990, became the first franchise alumnus to play in the major league's All-Star game four years later when he singled and collected two runs batted in. Both of these players were named by fans to the Osceola Astros' 10th-anniversary team.

**OTHER FAMOUS ALUMNI**

Scott Servais, Ken Caminiti, Luis Gonzalez and Orlando Miller all played here.

◆ BALLPARK EXTRAS

Food fare is standard: nachos, hot dogs, hamburgers and popcorn.

◆ ATTRACTIONS

The ballpark is located right off U.S. 192, a road packed with more fast-food restaurants, miniature golf courses and kitschy attractions per square inch than any in Western civilization. Disneyworld and EPCOT Center (407-824-4321), Universal Studios (407-363-8000), Sea World (407-351-3600) and many more attractions are all within a ½ hour drive.

For more information about the Kissimmee area, call the Chamber of Commerce, (407) 847-5000.

◆ DINING

La Forchetta, about 20 minutes from the ballpark, serves good Northern and Southern Italian food. They make their own pasta here. Try the fettuccine Alfredo and lasagna. 321 S. Bermuda, (407) 933-4215.

◆ LODGING

Howard Johnson Kissimmee Lodge is on U.S. 192, near Florida Turnpike exit 244, less than 10 minutes from the ballpark. (407) 846-4900/(800) 654-2000.

Best Western Kissimmee is on U.S. 192 at Florida Turnpike exit 244, less than 10 minutes from the ballpark. (407) 846-2221/(800) 528-1234.

From the Florida Turnpike, take exit 244/U.S. 192. Turn right on Osceola Boulevard and follow signs to the ballpark, which will be about one mile away on the right. Parking is plentiful and costs $2.

**OSCEOLA COUNTY STADIUM**
1000 Bill Beck Boulevard
Kissimmee, FL 34744
(407) 933-5500

Capacity: 5,130
LF 330, CF 410, RF 330

### ◆ TICKET AND SCHEDULE INFORMATION

Game time is 6:30 P.M. in April and May and 7 P.M. June through August. Sunday games are at 2 P.M. in April and May and at 6 P.M. from June through August.

The season starts one week into April and runs a day or two into September.

Ticket prices: $3.50 general admission, $2.50 seniors, $2 children. Season ticketholders are assured of a specific seat. All other seating is open.

# LAKELAND TIGERS

**DETROIT TIGERS**

Joker Marchant Stadium, built in 1966, is named for a former city parks and recreation director. The ballpark's location on Al Kaline Drive, in honor of the Tigers' Hall of Fame outfielder, is a reminder of the extended ties between Lakeland and Detroit, which go back to 1960, the longest connection with the same big-league parent of any franchise in the Florida State League. Joker Marchant is located in downtown Lakeland, in the middle of a commercial district and right down the street from a hospital. The ballpark itself is rather plain, with a large, mostly covered concrete grandstand. At the top of the grandstand, you will find one of the most expansive press boxes in the FSL. There is also seating available down the left-field line in a sizable bleacher section. In 1994, renovations to Joker Marchant resulted in new concession stands and a new stadium marquee.

### ◆ LOCAL AND TEAM HISTORY

In 1919, Lakeland joined the original Class D Florida State League, remaining in this circuit for 15 seasons (1919-26, '53-55, '60, '62-64) before settling in for good in 1967. This city was also associated with the Florida International League from 1946 to '52. Harry Smythe, winner of 301 games in the minors, began his career here in 1922 with 16 victories. Lakeland's Ron LeFlore, who played nine years in the majors, was the FSL batting champ in 1974 with a .339 average. Over the years, Lakeland has had several prominent former big leaguers as managers, including Eddie Brinkman, Jerry Grote and Max Lanier. Future Pittsburgh Pirates skipper Jim Leyland, who played for Lakeland in 1964 and '69, returned here as manager and won two straight FSL titles in 1976-77. Johnny Lipon is the fourth-winningest manager in minor-league history, posting 2,185 victories over 30 seasons. From 1988 to '92, he managed Lakeland, leading his team to three straight Central Division titles in 1989-91 and one FSL championship in 1992, his final year as a manager. Today, Lipon is Detroit's minor-league field coordinator.

### ◆ BALLPARK EXTRAS

The concessions are straightforward. The best are in a stand behind the plate where hamburgers, chicken and sausages are grilled. Little Caesar's Pizza is available. They also have tuna sandwiches and salads, unusual at a minor-league ballpark.

### ◆ ATTRACTIONS

Cypress Gardens are in Winter Haven, a half-hour drive via Memorial Boulevard, Highway 92, into Winter Haven. Look for the signs. (813) 324-2111.

Disneyworld is a 45-minute drive away (407) 824-4321.

For more information about Lakeland, call the Chamber of Commerce, (813) 688-8551.

### ◆ DINING

Farmer Jones' Red Baron Inn, a steakhouse, is a favorite spot. 5150 New Tampa Highway, (813) 686-2754.

### ◆ LODGING

The Holiday Inn South, 10 minutes away, is the visiting-team hotel. 3405 S. Florida Avenue, Lakeland, (813) 646-5731.

### ◆ DIRECTIONS

Take I-4 to exit 19 (called Florida Highway 33 or Lakeland Hills Boulevard), turn left off ramp and go south two miles. The ballpark is on the left. Parking is plentiful and costs $2.

### ◆ TICKET AND SCHEDULE INFORMATION

Usual starts are 7 P.M. Sunday games are at 2 P.M. in April and May and at 6 P.M. thereafter.

The season starts one week into April and runs a day or two into September.

Ticket prices: $4 box seats; $3 general admission, $2 seniors and children.

# SARASOTA RED SOX

## BOSTON RED SOX

The Red Sox have become accustomed to playing FSL baseball in other organizations' ballparks. They spent the 1993 season in Fort Lauderdale, the spring home of the New York Yankees, and now the White Sox' office building behind Ed Smith's right-field line makes it clear that Chicago trains here each spring. The ballpark, located in a residential area, has few distinguishing characteristics. The upper 20 or so rows of the grandstand are covered, and the bullpens and a palm tree or two sit behind the 10-foot-high chain-link fence that serves as the outfield wall. There is a picnic area behind the left-field fence.

### ◆ LOCAL AND TEAM HISTORY

Sarasota first joined the Florida State League, then a Class D circuit, in 1926. After the '27 season, baseball left town, not to return until 1961, when a five-year stint in the FSL began. Following another gap, this one of 23 years, Sarasota rejoined the circuit in 1989. On May 16, 1964, Roger Nelson set a league record by striking out 22 batters in a 14-inning game. Three years later, Nelson began his nine-year big-league career. Frank Thomas spent 1989, his rookie year in Sarasota, first with the Gulf Coast League White Sox and then the FSL franchise. In 55 Class A games, Thomas batted .277 with four homers and 30 runs batted in.

### ◆ BALLPARK EXTRAS

Fans in the box seats get waitress service so they don't miss the action.

### ◆ ATTRACTIONS

The Ringling Museum in Sarasota is a real art museum, not a circus museum, although it was founded by John and Mabel Ringling of Ringling Brothers and Barnum & Bailey circus fame. There is a circus gallery there as well. It's at 5401 Bayshore Road, in Sarasota. (813) 355-5101.

Long Boat Key, Lido Key and Siesta are lovely public beaches 15 minutes from the ballpark. Lido Key is closest, but Siesta won a whitest sand international contest a few years ago, sponsored by the prestigious Woods Hole Oceanographic Institute.

Sarasota Jungle Gardens are botanical gardens with wildlife, including tropical birds and alligators. 3701 Bayshore Road, (813) 355-1112.

For more information about the Sarasota area, call the Chamber of Commerce, (813) 957-1877/(800) 522-9799.

**OTHER FAMOUS ALUMNI**
Alex Fernandez and Bob Wickman played here.

### ◆ DINING

The Dry Dock Waterfront Grill, about 20 minutes from the ballpark, is on Longboat Key and has some great views of Sarasota Bay. There is good seafood here, especially Gulf of Mexico grouper. Ask about the Key lime pie. 412 Gulf of Mexico Drive, (813) 383-0102.

Nick's, about 10 minutes from the ballpark, offers good Italian food. Check out the seafood and pasta. 230 Sarasota Quay, (813) 954-3839.

### ◆ LODGING

The Wellesley Inn, five minutes from the ballpark, is considered the best bet for reasonable rates. 1803 N. Tamiami, Sarasota, (813) 366-5128.

### ◆ DIRECTIONS

Take I-75 to exit 40 (University Parkway), head west three miles to Tuttle Avenue, turn left on Tuttle, then head south to 12th Street and the ballpark.

```
ED SMITH STADIUM
2700 12th Street
Sarasota, FL 34237
(813) 365-4460

Capacity: 7,500
LF 340, CF 400, RF 340
```

### ◆ TICKET AND SCHEDULE INFORMATION

Usual starts are 7 P.M.

The season starts one week into April and runs a day or two into September.

Ticket prices: $5 diamond club box seats; $4 general admission. General admission is $3, $2 on Thursdays. General admission is a two-for-one deal on Tuesdays.

# ST. LUCIE METS

## NEW YORK METS

The stadium was opened for spring training of 1988 as the St. Lucie County Sports Complex. It was renamed and dedicated to Thomas J. White in March 1992.

The stadium outfield dimensions are equal to those of Shea Stadium, the Mets' home ballpark. The stadium has more of a major-league feel than most minor-league ballyards because of its size and the up-high location of the press box.

In front of the stadium you'll find a lone tree dedicated to the late Andy Kaplan, the first general manager of the St. Lucie Mets.

OTHER FAMOUS ALUMNI

Kevin Tapani and Fernando Vina played here.

### ◆ LOCAL AND TEAM HISTORY

The Mets, who began play here in 1988, are the first organized baseball team based in St. Lucie. During that inaugural season, the Mets won the FSL championship and St. Lucie's Kevin Brown, not the Kevin Brown who pitches in the majors, led the league with a 1.81 ERA. In the St. Lucie Mets' short history, they have reached the league playoffs every season except 1994. Three St. Lucie players, Chris Donnels (1989), Nikco Riesgo (1990) and Randy Curtis (1993) have been league MVP's. D.J. Dozier, an NFL running back with the Minnesota Vikings and the Detroit Lions from 1987 to '91, tried his hand at pro baseball with St. Lucie in 1991. Dozier was an FSL All-Star that season, batting .297 with 13 home runs and 57 runs batted in. Two years later, he made it to the big leagues for the first and only time, hitting .191 in 25 games for the New York Mets.

### ◆ BALLPARK EXTRAS

The concessions are run by the county. According to some fans surveyed, the food is rather lame and served in desultory fashion.

### ◆ ATTRACTIONS

The UDT SEAL Museum, honoring our national underwater SWAT team, is right in St. Lucie County. 3300 Highway A1A, Fort Pierce, (407) 489-3595.

The Atlantic beaches are two miles from the stadium. St. Lucie County has plenty of secluded stretches with easy public access.

For more information about Port St. Lucie, call the Chamber of Commerce, (407) 595-9999/(800) 344-8443.

### ◆ DINING

Jensen's Ale House and Raw Bar, about 20 minutes away, serves standard American fare. 3611 Northwest Federal Highway, Jensen Beach, (407) 692-3293.

Conchy Joe's is a seafood emporium, also in Jensen Beach, about 20 minutes from the park. Northeast Indian River Drive, (407) 334-1130.

### ◆ LODGING

Best bet is the Holiday Inn of Port St. Lucie, 20 minutes away. 10120 S. Federal Highway, Port St. Lucie, (407) 337-2200/(800) HOLIDAY.

The Best Western is about 10 minutes away, at 7900 South U.S. 1 and Prima Vista, Port St. Lucie, (407) 878-7600/(800) 528-1234.

### ◆ DIRECTIONS

Take I-95 to exit 63-C at the 120-mile marker. Turn left on Peacock. Follow signs to the ballpark, which is ¼ mile away. Plenty of free parking is available.

### ◆ TICKET AND SCHEDULE INFORMATION

Usual starting time is 7 P.M., and Sunday games are at 2 P.M.

The season starts one week into April and runs a day or two into September.

Ticket prices: $4 reserved seats; $2.50 general admission.

# ST. PETERSBURG CARDINALS

## ST. LOUIS CARDINALS

Al Lang Field was originally built in 1921 as the spring home of the Boston Braves. Al Lang Stadium, built on the same site, opened in 1947 and has since undergone several renovations. The ballpark is located right next to Tampa Bay, and from the grandstand, fans get a good view of the water and the various craft moored at the nearby yacht basin and marina, situated behind the left-field side of the ballpark. The location also gives fans the benefit of occasional sea breezes, which can be welcome on especially hot days. Beyond the center-and right-field fences, you can watch small planes landing at a local airport. Al Lang is made primarily of concrete, with a roof over only the grandstand's top several rows.

### ◆ LOCAL AND TEAM HISTORY

St. Petersburg's first pro team played in the Florida State League in 1920. After a 26-year hiatus from the FSL, St. Petersburg rejoined the league in 1955 and has been a member ever since. From 1947 to '54, the city was associated with the Florida International League. In 1922, Babe Bigelow's third season with St. Petersburg, he was the FSL's top hitter, leading the league in average (.343), doubles (27) and triples (21). Two years earlier, he also won the circuit's home-run title with the prodigious

total of 10 round-trippers. In 1951-52, Clarence "Hooks" Iott struck out 483 batters to lead the Florida International League while also winning 46 games for St. Pete. Iott's 2,561 career strikeouts place him No. 4 all-time in the minors. Also in 1952, the St. Petersburg Saints' Nesbit Wilson led the league with 15 homers. Wilson blasted 329 home runs in his minor-league career.

This franchise began its current affiliation with St. Louis in 1966, which proved to be a very historic season for St. Petersburg. At one point that season, the Cardinals had a 22-game winning streak, the eighth longest in minor-league history. On June 14, St. Pete lost a 4-3 decision to Miami in a 29-inning game that lasted seven hours and 29 minutes, then the longest game in organized baseball history and only supplanted by the Pawtucket-Rochester marathon 15 years later. The 1966 Cardinals, managed by Sparky Anderson, also won 91 games to tie for most in the minors that season. They captured the regular-season FSL pennant but lost the championship to the Leesburg Athletics.

**OTHER FAMOUS ALUMNI**

Ozzie Smith, Willie McGee, Keith Hernandez, Andy Van Slyke, Tommy Herr, Terry Pendleton, Alex Cole, Mike Perez and Brian Jordan all played here.

### ◆ BALLPARK EXTRAS

If you sit high up in the stands, you get a marvelous view of Tampa Bay's boats and bathers. Also, the picnic area down the left-field line has been expanded this year.

### ◆ ATTRACTIONS

Busch Gardens amusement park is 15 minutes away on I-275 North. (813) 987-5082.

The Thunderdome, home of the NHL's Tampa Bay Lightning, is a few blocks away. (813) 825-3100.

For more information on St. Petersburg, call the Chamber of Commerce, (813) 821-4069.

### ◆ DINING

Bleachers, a sports bar and grill, is 15 minutes away. 10478 Roosevelt, (813) 576-2216.

Ferg's, another sports bar, is just a couple of minutes away. 1320 Central Avenue, (813) 822-4562.

### ◆ LODGING

The St. Petersburg Hilton is right next to the ballpark. Ask for a room high up facing the field, and you'll be able to look right in. 333 1st Street S, St. Petersburg, (813) 894-5000/(800) 445-8667.

### ◆ DIRECTIONS
Take I-275 to exit 9 (downtown St. Petersburg). Go east ½ mile to 1st Street South. Turn left. The ballpark is two blocks ahead on the right. Parking is plentiful and costs $2.

**AL LANG STADIUM**
**180 2nd Avenue**
**St. Petersburg, FL 33701**
**(813) 822-3384**

**Capacity: 7,004**
**LF 330, CF 410, RF 330**

### ◆ TICKET AND SCHEDULE INFORMATION
Usual starts are at 7:05 P.M., Sundays 2 P.M.

The season starts one week into April and runs a day or two into September.

Ticket prices: $4 box seats; $3 general admission. Seniors can get a gold card for free admission. Knothole-gang children get admission for five games.

# TAMPA YANKEES

## NEW YORK YANKEES

The Yankees are in temporary digs. In 1996 they move into an as-yet-unnamed stadium across the street from Tampa Stadium, home of the NFL Tampa Bay Buccaneers. The Yankees moved to Tampa in 1994 from Fort Lauderdale. Tampa is the home of Yankees owner George Steinbrenner and the home of the Yankees' minor-league administration, so Steinbrenner wanted everything consolidated.

University of South Florida Stadium is humble by FSL standards, but the Tampa Yankees make the most of it. They use tents for their souvenir and food stands, lending a real circus atmosphere to games.

### ◆ LOCAL AND TEAM HISTORY
The 1994 season marked the return of Florida State League baseball to this city for the first time since 1988,

when Tampa's string of 32 consecutive years in the league was snapped. In their first season back, the Yankees won the FSL championship. Tampa originally joined the Florida State League in 1919, the first of nine straight seasons in the FSL. From 1928 to '30, Tampa was associated with the Southeastern league. The city was next with the Florida International League, from 1946 to '54. In 1957, Harry Coe had the greatest single pitching season in Tampa history, winning 26 games, fourth-best total in FSL history, and leading the league with a 1.37 ERA; he hurled a 2-0, 18-strikeout no-hitter against Orlando on Aug. 30. The next season, Coe returned to top the FSL in strikeouts (194) and tie for the lead in wins (18). Despite his success here, Coe never pitched in the big leagues. In 1961, manager Johnny Vander Meer led Tampa to an FSL title with the help of a 19-year-old second baseman named Pete Rose, who batted .331 and set an all-time FSL record with 30 triples. He also led the league with 246 total bases.

*OTHER FAMOUS ALUMNI*

Danny Tartabull, Jimmy Wynn, Johnny Bench, Lee May, Al Lopez, Ducky Medwick and Mario Soto played here.

### ◆ BALLPARK EXTRAS
The Italian water ice is refreshing in the Gulf heat and humidity. Grilled chicken and sausage sandwiches are popular.

### ◆ ATTRACTIONS
Ybor City, an old-town part of Tampa where cigars were once king, has become a trendy spot for nightclubbing and dining. The Columbia Restaurant there is legendary for Latin American (especially Cuban) food. Ybor City is a 10-minute drive on I-275 South to I-4.

Busch Gardens is a few minutes away. Take Fowler Avenue to 30th Street, turn left and travel to Busch Boulevard. (813) 987-5082.

For more information about Tampa, call the Chamber of Commerce, (813) 228-7777.

### ◆ DINING
Beef O'Brady's is a favorite spot for fans pregame and postgame. It's all of a minute from the ballpark. 5025 E. Fowler, (813) 989-9125.

Damon's at Radisson Bay (Steinbrenner's place) on the causeway is a spot famed for ribs and is packed with Yankees and Olympic memorabilia. 7700 Courtney Campbell Causeway, (813) 281-0566.

◆ **LODGING**

The Days Inn Busch Gardens Maingate, five minutes from the park, is a good buy. 2901 E. Busch, Tampa, (813) 933-6471/(800) 325-2525.

Another option is the Holiday Inn Busch Gardens, just a couple of minutes away. 2701 E. Fowler Avenue, Tampa, (813) 971-4710/(800) HOLIDAY.

◆ **DIRECTIONS**

Take I-275 to exit 34 East (Fowler Avenue). Stay on Fowler until the campus.

From I-75, take exit 54 West (Fowler Avenue) and follow it to the campus.

From I-4 West, take the Florida Highway 581 North to Fowler Avenue, turn left and follow it to the campus. Free parking is available at the ballpark and on the street.

---

**UNIVERSITY OF SOUTH FLORIDA STADIUM**
3102 N. Himes Avenue
Tampa, FL 33607
(813) 632-9855

Capacity: 3,000
LF 340, CF 400, RF 340

---

◆ **TICKET AND SCHEDULE INFORMATION**

Usual starts are 7 P.M., while Sunday games begin at 6 P.M.

The season starts one week into April and runs a day or two into September.

Ticket prices: $4 reserved seats; $3 general admission.

# VERO BEACH DODGERS

## LOS ANGELES DODGERS

This is what Florida minor-league baseball is supposed to be all about: easy access to players, an idyllic setting of lush green grounds, shady trees, relaxed pace. You simply can't beat it.

Holman Stadium was built in 1953, the centerpiece of a complex that was the idea of Walter O'Malley, owner of the Brooklyn Dodgers at that time. (His son Peter is the main man now.)

The seating is limited to behind the plate and down the lines. Spillover fans can sit on the berm, a grassy hill beyond the cyclone outfield fence. Those spots are needed in spring training, but not by the Vero Beach Dodgers, who do not attract as many fans in the regular season as the Los Angeles Dodgers do in spring training.

The stadium held up to Hurricane David in 1979, excluding the destruction of the press box. That was restored in 1980.

This may be the only place where you can sit at a ballgame and see golfers in the distance.

◆ **LOCAL AND TEAM HISTORY**

Organized baseball has been played in Vero Beach since 1980, when this franchise joined the FSL and began its current affiliation with Los Angeles. Vero Beach was the last stop in the 37-year managerial career of Stan Wasiak. He managed here in 1980-81, one game in '82 and '83-86. In '83, Wasiak led the Dodgers to the Florida State League championship, the last title of his career. Two years later, he passed Bob Coleman (2,496 wins) to become the winningest manager in minor-league history. Terry Collins, now the Houston Astros' skipper, managed Vero Beach in 1982, which turned out to be a big year for several Dodgers. Sid Fernandez tossed two no-hitters, striking out 32 batters in the two games, while teammate Bobby Kenyon also pitched a no-hitter. This was the first time since 1952 that at least two pitchers from the same Florida State League team combined for three nine-inning no-hitters. Fernandez won eight games for Vero Beach in '82, leading the league with 137 strikeouts although he was promoted in June to AAA Albuquerque, where he finished the season. Also in 1982, Cecil Espy led the FSL with 74 stolen bases and 100 runs scored while batting .317.

*OTHER FAMOUS ALUMNI* — Mike Piazza, Dave Hanson, Ramon Martinez, John Franco and Steve Sax all played here.

◆ **BALLPARK EXTRAS**

Take the time to stroll around the grounds. You can amble along Duke Snider Street, Vin Scully Way, Sandy Koufax Lane, Don Drysdale Drive, Pee Wee Reese Boulevard, Jackie Robinson Avenue and Roy Campanella Boulevard.

The Holman Stadium lemonade ice is a refreshing item that sells well.

◆ **ATTRACTIONS**

You can drive one hour north on I-95 to the Kennedy

Space Center. Disneyworld is a 1½-hour drive. Take State Route 60 to the Florida Turpike at Yee-Haw Junction.

Vero Beach is five minutes east of Holman Stadium.

For more information about Vero Beach, call the Chamber of Commerce, (407) 567-3491.

### ◆ DINING
Bobby's, about 10 minutes from the park, is known for something called steak bits. You can also get a simple burger. Route 60, east of the stadium near the beach, (407) 231-6996.

Mr. Manatee's, also about 10 minutes away, has light seafood. Route 60 before the drawbridge, (407) 569-9151.

### ◆ LODGING
Virtually everyone stays at the Vero Beach Inn right on the beach, about 10 to 15 minutes from the ball park. 4700 N. A1A, Vero Beach, (407) 231-1600.

### ◆ DIRECTIONS
Take I-95 to the exit for Florida Highway 60, head east five miles to 43rd Avenue, turn left to head north 1 block to Dodgertown.

---

**HOLMAN STADIUM**
**4001 26th Street**
**Vero Beach, FL 32961**
**(407) 569-4900**

---

**Capacity: 6,474**
**LF 340, CF 400, RF 340**

---

### ◆ TICKET AND SCHEDULE INFORMATION
Usual starts are at 7 P.M.

The season starts one week into April and runs a day or two into September.

Ticket prices: $3.50 general admission, $2.50 seniors and children. Season ticketholders have assigned seats identified by stickers. All other seating is open.

# WEST PALM BEACH EXPOS

## MONTREAL EXPOS

Municipal Stadium, built in 1962, is one of the most attractive ballparks in the Florida State League. From the largely covered grandstand, fans can enjoy a scenic panorama of palm trees, Lake Worth, Palm Beach and, to the east, the Atlantic Ocean. The best views are from the top several rows of the grandstand, which can also be the coolest place to sit when breezes occasionally filter through to provide welcome relief on warm days. Just down the street, you will find a civic auditorium and golf course. Municipal is shared by the Montreal Expos and the Atlanta Braves in spring training, a partnership announced by a large sign over the stadium's entrance. During the summer, Municipal Stadium is home to the Class A Expos plus the Gulf Coast Rookie League teams of Montreal and Atlanta. There is plenty of room for all these squads here because several practice fields are located just in back of Municipal's outfield fence, Montreal's in left and Atlanta's in right. To reach the grandstand, you must walk up a ramp to reach the upper concourse, where you will also find concession stands and a souvenir shop. Another place for souvenirs is located near the ticket booth as you enter the ballpark.

### ◆ LOCAL AND TEAM HISTORY
Organized baseball first came here in 1928 when West Palm Beach began its association (1928, '55-56,'65 to date) with the Florida State League. West Palm Beach has also fielded teams in the Florida East Coast (1940-42) and Florida International (1946-54) leagues. West Palm Beach began its current affiliation in 1969, Montreal's first major-league season.

OTHER FAMOUS ALUMNI
OTHER FAMOUS ALUMNI

Larry Walker, Andy Pafko, Gary Roenicke, Larry Parrish and Mel Rojas played here.

Two future big-league managers struggled while playing here early in their careers. Cito Gaston batted .188 in 1965, while three years later, Dusty Baker hit .190 in six games. Felipe Alou managed seven seasons here (1977, '86-91), winning the Eastern Division title with 92 wins in '90 and the FSL championship the following year. In 1992, West Palm Beach hosted the FSL All-Star game, which was halted by rain in the third inning when the National League was leading 4-0. The next day, with the field still soaking wet and more rain on the way, this game became a baseball oddity, one of the few All-Star games to be rained out.

### ◆ BALLPARK EXTRAS

The souvenir stands this year emphasize the wide selection of minor-league caps. The food items are dull.

### ◆ ATTRACTIONS

Lion Country Safari is in West Palm Beach. 7 Boulevard West, West Palm Beach, (407) 793-1084.

So is the Henry Flagler Museum, named for the multi-millionaire whose immense wealth almost single-handedly gave South Florida its developmental kick start. Whitehall Way and Coconut Row, West Palm Beach, (407) 655-2833.

The Palm Coast beaches are a 10-minute drive to the east. They are among Florida's best.

For more information about West Palm Beach, call the Chamber of Commerce, (407) 833-3711.

### ◆ DINING

The Palm Beach Ale House is a sports bar that the players love, just two minutes away, west of I-95. 2161 Palm Beach Lakes Boulevard, (407) 683-3777.

Chili's, on the corner of Okeechobee and Military Trail, is about 10 minutes away; it's also a hot spot before or after games. 4262 Okeechobee Boulevard, (407) 689-9118.

### ◆ LODGING

The Wellesley Inn, just west of I-95, is the best pick and is used by visiting teams. It's a couple of minutes from the park. 1910 West Palm Beach Boulevard, West Palm Beach, (407) 689-8540.

### ◆ DIRECTIONS

Take I-95 to Exit 53 (Palm Beach Lakes Boulevard), then go west ½ mile to Hank Aaron Drive.

---

**WEST PALM BEACH MUNICIPAL STADIUM**
**715 Hank Aaron Drive**
**West Palm Beach, FL 33401**
**(407) 684-6801**

**Capacity: 4,404**
**LF 330, CF 405, RF 330**

---

### ◆ TICKET AND SCHEDULE INFORMATION

Usual start times are at 7:05 P.M., with Sunday games at 5:05 P.M.

The season starts one week into April and runs a day or two into September.

Ticket prices: $7 box seats; $6 grandstand, $4 bleachers.

# MIDWEST LEAGUE

The Midwest League started as an eight-team Class D circuit in 1956. Its predecessor, the Mississippi–Ohio Valley League, operated for only six seasons (1949-1955) before yielding to the Midwest circuit in 1956. The league received its current Class A designation in 1963. Today, there are 14 teams in five Midwestern states—Michigan, Indiana, Illinois, Iowa and Wisconsin. Each team plays 140 games, with the regular season beginning April 8 and ending September 2. In 1994, the Midwest League set an all-time attendance record of 2,469,999. This figure surpassed the attendance of all other Class A leagues and was sixth overall in the minors. The West Michigan Whitecaps paced the Midwest in '94 by drawing 475,212 fans.

• • •

*Sunday afternoon with the West Michigan Whitecaps at old Kent Park.*

# BATTLE CREEK GOLDEN KAZOOS

**BOSTON RED SOX**

This site has been the home of various amateur baseball tournaments, including the Stan Musial World Series and the Big Ten Championship, for years. The Stan Musial Series has taken place here since the 1950s. C.O. Brown's covered grandstand, with its steel pillars and obstructed views, is reminiscent of Detroit's Tiger Stadium, less than a two-hour drive to the east. Trees and the Kalamazoo River, which flows past the ballpark about 500 yards behind the outfield fence, form an attractive background. C.O. Brown is also located in a recreation complex that includes two other baseball diamonds and eight softball fields. The picnic area and stadium lighting have been improved for the 1995 season.

### ◆ LOCAL AND TEAM HISTORY

The Golden Kazoos became the first organized-baseball team to be based here since 1921 after the franchise moved to Battle Creek from Madison, Wis., for the 1995 season. The team's name, one of the minors' most unique, is a tribute to the Kalamazoo Kazoos, who played in Battle Creek's neighbor city intermittently from the 1880s through the 1920s. The Golden part of Battle Creek's name is meant to add a touch of nostalgia to this franchise. In this century's first two decades, these two cities fielded teams in the same leagues, resulting in a healthy local rivalry.

Battle Creek's pro baseball history dates to the 1890s, when this city was associated with the Michigan State League. Battle Creek won the league championship in 1902. This city subsequently belonged to four other circuits: Class D Southern Michigan League (1906-09); Class D/C Southern Michigan Association (1910-15), Class B Michigan-Ontario (1919-21) and Class B Central League (1916). The Belles of the All-American Girls Professional Baseball League played here in 1951 and '52 after moving from Racine. The Kalamazoo Kazoos won the Southern Michigan Association championship in 1911, while the Battle Creek Crickets captured the title two years later.

### ◆ BALLPARK EXTRAS

There are four concession stands here, with the usual hot dogs, burgers, pizza and barbecued chicken.

### ◆ ATTRACTIONS

Battle Creek is the home of Kellogg's and Ralston-Purina, but, unfortunately, tours of these cereal makers' factories are no longer given. The Binder Park Zoo is a well-maintained, attractive zoo with a variety of animals and nature trails. Admission is $4.50, $3.50 for senior citizens over 65 and $2.50 for children 3 to 12. For further information, call (616) 979-1351. The Kalamazoo Nature Center, about 25 minutes away, features an interpretive center where injured birds are cared for by the center's staff. Admission is $3, $1.50 for senior citizens over 64 and children 4 to 17. For further information, call (616) 381-1574.

For additional information about Battle Creek, call the Calhoun County/Battle Creek Visitors' Bureau, (616) 962-2240.

### ◆ DINING

Clara's on the River, about 15 minutes from the ballpark, is an attractive restaurant located in a refurbished railroad station, complete with antique portraits and lamps. An eclectic, moderately priced menu features steak, pork chops, pizza, quiche, burgers and children's offerings. 44 N. McCamly Street, (616) 963-0966.

### ◆ LODGING

Battle Creek Inn is at exit 97 off I-94, about 15 minutes from the ballpark. (616) 979-1100, (800) 232-3405.

Howard Johnson's Lodge is at exit 97 off I-94, about 15 minutes from the ballpark. (616) 965-3201, (800) 654-2000.

### ◆ DIRECTIONS

From I-94, take the Downtown Battle Creek exit and go north for about four miles on Highway 66. Go through three traffic lights, pass the YMCA and the road will change into Capital Avenue NE. About three miles after this change, the ballpark will be on your right. Parking is free and somewhat limited. The team is planning to expand its parking facilities.

**C.O. BROWN STADIUM**
**1392 Capital Avenue NE**
**Battle Creek, MI 49017**
**(616) 660-2287**

**Capacity: 6,200**
**LF 325, CF 400, RF 325**

### ◆ TICKET AND SCHEDULE INFORMATION

Most games are played at night, starting at 7:05 P.M. Sunday games begin at 2:05 P.M.

The Golden Kazoos' home opener will be in early April, and the season ends in the first week of September. Purchasing tickets on the day of the game may be difficult because this is the first team based in Battle Creek in more than 70 years.

Ticket prices: $5 box seats; $4 reserved seats; $3 general admission, $2.50 senior citizens 65 and over and children 15 and under.

# BELOIT SNAPPERS

**MILWAUKEE BREWERS**

This ballpark is located in a residential area on the edge of Telfer Park, a municipal recreation facility with tennis courts and an open-air pavilion. Houses are across the street from the stadium's third-base side, and a pasturelike open area is behind the tree-lined outfield fence. For 1995, the team has installed 400 new box seats underneath the partially covered grandstand. The most interesting feature of Pohlman Field, built in 1981, is the four-tiered wood picnic deck down the right-field line. The deck, which is open to groups as well as individuals, was built around a large tree that today is growing out of the deck's center. This tree and the shade it provides can make you feel as if you are sitting on the back porch, enjoying a weekend barbecue.

After being called the Beloit Brewers since 1982, this team felt it was time for a change in 1995. Beloit, a community-owned franchise in the Midwest League's smallest city, decided it needed an attractive, novel name to generate needed income from souvenir sales. Snappers was chosen because this area has a turtle connection, with a creek and a township named after this amphibian and with Native American burial grounds shaped like turtles near Beloit College.

### ◆ LOCAL AND TEAM HISTORY

Although amateur baseball has been played here since the 1860s, Beloit's organized-baseball history is rather brief. This city fielded its first team in the 1905 Class D Wisconsin Association. After the season, baseball left town and did not return until 1982, when Beloit joined the Midwest League and began its current affiliation with Milwaukee. Buck Weaver, banned from organized baseball for his role in the 1919 Black Sox scandal, played semipro ball here in 1920. Tim Barker set a Midwest League record in 1987 by reaching base 11 straight times. Fort Wayne's Rene Lopez tied this mark six years

later. Greg Vaughn had a 30-30 season for Beloit in 1987 when he hit 33 home runs, No. 1 in the league, and stole 36 bases while also batting .305 with 105 runs batted in. He shared the league's MVP award with Springfield's Todd Zeile. On April 15, 1994, 115 fans in Beloit saw Kelly Wunsch become the first starting pitcher in baseball history to strike out five batters in one inning against the Sultans of Springfield. The last pitcher to pull off this feat was a reliever, Ron Necciai, pitching for Bristol on May 17, 1952. Wunsch put his name into the record books in the third inning. After a leadoff walk, Wunsch fanned two before yielding a run-scoring double. Wunsch then struck out Erik Corps, who reached base on a wild pitch. The next batter swung at a pitch in the dirt for strikeout No. 4, and he reached base on another wild pitch. Wunsch then ended the inning by fanning Eduardo Cuevas for No. 5. Wunsch's hat, an autographed baseball and a picture of the young hurler were sent to the Hall of Fame, where they will remain on exhibit through 1996.

OTHER FAMOUS ALUMNI OTHER FAMOUS ALUMNI

Pat Listach, Chris Bosio, Cal Eldred, Dave Nilsson, John Jaha, B.J. Surhoff, Bill Wegman and Bill Spiers played here.

### ◆ BALLPARK EXTRAS
Since Beloit is only about 75 miles from Milwaukee, it is not surprising that beer and brats are the best items here. You can also sample some grilled chicken and grilled ribeyes.

### ◆ ATTRACTIONS
Beloit is only a short distance from Chicago, and features a small historic district and a local preforming arts theater. For information about Chicago, call the Tourism Office, (312) 793-2094. For information about Milwaukee, call the Visitors Bureau, (800) 231-0903.

For additional information about Beloit, call the Chamber of Commerce, (608) 365-8835/(800) 659-4831.

### ◆ DINING
Cartunes, about 20 minutes from the ballpark, is a casual place with a good selection of burgers and sandwiches, plus steak and blackened-chicken dinners. 2640 Prairie Avenue, (608) 362-3362.

### ◆ LODGING
Comfort Inn is at exit 185 off I-90, about 15 minutes from the ballpark. (608) 362-2666/(800) 424-6423.

Holiday Inn Express is at exit 185 off I-90, about 15

minutes from the ballpark. (608) 365-6000/(800) HOLIDAY.

### ◆ DIRECTIONS

From I-90, take the Shopierre exit. Turn right at the first traffic light, Cranston Road. After about 200 yards, you will see the ballpark. From I-43, the highway becomes Milwaukee Road. Turn right on Cranston and the ballpark will be immediately visible. Parking is free but limited at the ballpark. Alternate parking is available on the street.

---

**POHLMAN FIELD**
**P.O. Box 855**
**Beloit, WI 53512**
**(608) 362-2272**

---

**Capacity: 3,100**
**LF 325, CF 380, RF 325**

---

### ◆ TICKET AND SCHEDULE INFORMATION

Most games are played at night, starting at 7 P.M. Sunday games begin at 3 P.M.

The Snappers' home opener is usually in early April, and the season ends in the first week of September.

Ticket prices: $5 box seats; $4 reserved seats; $3 general admission. Children under 5 are free.

# BURLINGTON BEES

## SAN FRANCISCO GIANTS

Community Field, the smallest park in the Midwest League, features short outfield dimensions and a playing field that is particularly close to the stands, giving fans a close-up view of the action on the diamond. Despite the ballpark's size, Burlington nevertheless routinely outdraws other teams in the league. Trees are visible from the wood seats in the uncovered grandstand. The Bullpen, an attractive open-air concession area complete with waitress service, is behind third base. The Brat Garden picnic area is down the first-base line.

### ◆ LOCAL AND TEAM HISTORY

Burlington's professional baseball history dates back to 1889. Teams competed in the Central Interstate League, Eastern Iowa League, Western Association, Iowa State League, Mississippi Valley League and Three-I League.

The Midwest League absorbed several Three-I teams in 1962. The team almost missed the 1970 season when Community Field burned down during a road trip. However, two days later, the team returned and played as scheduled with temporary bleachers and a backstop.

Burlington has been affiliated with eight major-league clubs, but had its best success with the Milwaukee Brewers in the late 1970s, winning the league championship in '77. This is the first year of the affiliation with the Giants. Rene Lachemann won the Midwest League home-run crown in 1964 with 24 round-trippers. In 1979, Doug Jones topped the circuit with a 1.75 ERA, 16 complete games, three shutouts and 190 innings pitched.

**OTHER FAMOUS ALUMNI**

Paul Molitor, Billy Williams, Melido Perez, Mike Stanley, Kenny Rogers, Mel Rojas, Larry Walker, Vida Blue, Sal Bando, Phil Garner, Dan Ford, Javy Lopez, Chet Lemon and Ruben Sierra have all played here.

### ◆ BALLPARK EXTRAS

The Famous Chicken attracted a franchise record 4,600 fans for one game here last season. The most popular food items are pulled-pork sandwiches and the Macho Nacho. Grilled items are available in the picnic deck.

### ◆ ATTRACTIONS

*Ripley's Believe It or Not* named Burlington's Snake Alley as the most crooked street in the world, even surpassing Lombard Street in San Francisco. Burlington also is home to the Catfish Bend Mississippi River Boat for gambling and river cruises. For further information call (319) 753-2946. Both attractions are five minutes east of the ballpark, off Highway 34.

For more information about Burlington, call the Chamber of Commerce, (319) 752-6365.

### ◆ DINING

Pzazz Restaurant in the Best Western-Pzazz Motor Inn is south on Highway 61, two minutes from the stadium. 3001 Winegard Drive, (319) 753-2291.

Dillons Bar-B-Q is north on Highway 61, two minutes away. 2107 Roosevelt Drive, Burlington, (319) 752-7427.

### ◆ LODGING

Best Western–Pzazz Motel Inn is south on Highway 61, two minutes away. 3001 Winegard Drive, (319) 753-2291/(800) 528-1234.

## ◆ DIRECTIONS

Take Highway 34 west to Roosevelt Avenue (Highway 61). Turn right and proceed one block to Mount Pleasant Avenue. Parking is plentiful and free.

**COMMUNITY FIELD**
2712 Mount Pleasant Avenue
Burlington, IA 52601
(319) 754-5705
_____
Capacity: 3,500
LF 338, CF 370, RF 315

## ◆ TICKET AND SCHEDULE INFORMATION

Most games Monday through Saturday start at 7 P.M., with Sunday games at 6 P.M. Call team for details.

The Bee's home opener is usually in early April and the season ends in the first week of September.

Ticket prices: $4 box seats; $3 general admission.

# CEDAR RAPIDS KERNELS

**CALIFORNIA ANGELS**

Veterans Memorial Stadium, built in 1949, is one of those interesting ballparks with enough quirks to make it a good place for baseball. Its location on a hill came in handy during the Flood of 1993, as the ballpark stayed free of river water, but with the local interstate closed for several weeks, it was difficult for people to get to Veterans Memorial. Fans in the covered grandstand have a good view of the Cedar Rapids skyline, which is particularly attractive at night. A World War II-era airplane is on display in Veterans Memorial Park just behind the outfield fence. The large left-field fence is a double-decked wall about 10 feet behind a lower 8-foot-high barrier, over which balls must travel to be counted as home runs. The Pfaff Terrace, named after a former Cedar Rapids general manager, is a multi-tiered picnic area whose sharp swing of about 20 feet toward the left-field foul line can result in unexpected bounces when a line drive strikes its wall.

## ◆ LOCAL AND TEAM HISTORY

Pro baseball in Cedar Rapids goes back to the 1890s,

when teams played in several different leagues. Since the turn of the century, Cedar Rapids has spent time in five circuits, beginning with the Three-I League (1902-09, '20-21, '38-42, '50-61). This city has been a continuous member of the Midwest League since 1956. Cedar Rapids began its current affiliation with California in 1993. In 1890, the Cedar Rapids Canaries of the Illinois-Iowa League debuted as arguably this city's first pro team. All Illinois-Iowa teams were required to play within a $600 monthly salary cap. Teams disregarding this limit could be fined up to $1,000 by the league. The 1897 Cedar Rapids Rabbits won 84 games and captured this city's first championship by winning the Western Association title behind the pitching of King Louie Mahaffy, who won 30 games that season. Hank Edwards had perhaps the greatest single season in Cedar Rapids history in 1941 when he won the Three-I League Triple Crown. Edwards batted .364, hit 23 home runs and drove in 113 for the '41 league champions. Forty-one years later, Jeff Jones set an all-time Midwest League record by slugging 42 home runs while also driving in a franchise-record 101 runs. The 1993 Kernels became the first Midwest League team to go from first place one yea, (1992) to last place the next. Cedar Rapids has been in the Midwest League playoffs four of the past six years, winning two league championships. The '93 Kernels also featured Yevgeni Puchkov, thought to be the first Russian to play in Class A. He batted .116 in 19 games and was released at the end of the season.

The current nickname was adopted in 1993 after a name-the-team contest drew 650 entries. The team is community-owned by more than 50 stockholders.

**OTHER FAMOUS ALUMNI**

John J. McGraw, Lou Boudreau, Rocky Colavito, Tommie Aaron, Ted Simmons, Jerry Reuss, Eric Davis, Chris Sabo, Rob Dibble, Paul O'Neill, Reggie Sanders and Trevor Hoffman played here.

## ◆ BALLPARK EXTRAS

Each night, Kernels fans have their choice of a dozen flavors of hand-scooped ice cream. The Kernels feature good grilled chicken, brats and steak sandwiches. The top promotion is Kids Carnival Night, complete with carnival rides and clowns. Also, there are more than a dozen giveaway promotions during the season. There is a picnic area near the home bullpen in left field, and there is a designated handicapped seating area in front of the right-field bleachers.

## ◆ ATTRACTIONS

The Amana Colonies, a religious communal group more

than a century old, are known for their handicrafts, especially woolen items. They are located along Highway 151 South, 20 minutes from the stadium. (319) 622-7622.

For more information about Cedar Rapids, call the Chamber of Commerce, (319) 398-5317.

### ◆ DINING

The Union Station is about three minutes from the stadium. 16th Avenue SW, (319) 364-9236.

Gringo's Mexican Restaurant is five minutes away. 207 First Avenue SE, (319) 363-1000.

### ◆ LODGING

Holiday Inn is five minutes from the ballpark. Business Highway 151 and 16th Avenue SW, Cedar Rapids, (319) 365-9441/(800) HOLIDAY.

Five Seasons Center is also five minutes away, just off I-380 on 1st Avenue downtown. Cedar Rapids, (319) 363-8161.

### ◆ DIRECTIONS

From I-380, take the Wilson Avenue exit and proceed west for 1½ miles. After crossing the railroad tracks, turn right on Rockford Road. Stadium is ½ north on the left side.

---

**VETERANS MEMORIAL STADIUM**
**950 Rockford Road SW**
**Cedar Rapids, IA 52404**
**(319) 363-3887**

---

**Capacity: 6,000**
**LF 325, CF 385, RF 325**

---

### ◆ TICKET AND SCHEDULE INFORMATION

Starts are at 7 P.M. from Monday through Saturday, with games at 2 P.M. Sundays in April and May and at 5 P.M. Sundays from June 18 to the end of the season. There are noon games on May 1 and May 18, and 2 P.M. starts April 29, May 13 and May 20.

The Kernels' season begins in early April and ends the first week of September.

Ticket prices: $4 boxseats; $3 general admission; $2 children and seniors.

# CLINTON LUMBER KINGS

## SAN DIEGO PADRES

**R**iverview Stadium is aptly named since the Mississippi River flows past the ballpark, only about 200 yards from the 10-foot-high steel outfield wall. Stiff breezes from the river occasionally blow into the ballpark as was the case one year when a storm knocked down about 65 feet of Riverview's steel barrier. During the Flood of 1993, the river here rose to about 9 feet above the level of the stadium's playing field but did not flood the ballpark. However, water seeping up through the outfield grass kept the team in Waterloo for a four-game series until the stadium dried out. From the top rows of the covered grandstand, fans can look into the dining room aboard the *Mississippi Belle II*, a floating casino which is berthed outside the stadium. This comfortable old ballpark, built as a WPA project in 1937, underwent a large-scale renovation in 1994 that prompted some local controversy when the team removed Riverview's original souvenir stand, which dated back to '37, and the old-fashioned wrought-iron gate at the front entrance. This stadium was built in an area that was the hub of Clinton's old sawmill operations; in fact, Riverview sits atop a landfill filled with sawdust.

### ◆ LOCAL AND TEAM HISTORY

Clinton's first pro team was a charter member of the 1895 Eastern Iowa League. Since the turn of the century, Clinton has fielded teams in six National Association leagues and is the senior member among current Midwest League franchises, having joined the circuit in 1956. This is the first year of affiliation with San Diego. From June 16 through August 28, 1956, Arturo Miro put together an amazing streak by recording 19 consecutive wins, still a league record and identical to the single-season big-league mark held by Hall of

*OTHER FAMOUS ALUMNI* *OTHER FAMOUS ALUMNI*

Mitch Webster, Salomon Torres, Alejandro Pena, Bryan Hickerson, Orel Hershiser, Mike Scioscia, Rod Beck, John Burkett, Matt Williams, Darren Lewis, Steve Sax, Rob Deer, Dave Stewart, Jim Leyland and Tom Kelly all played here.

Famers Rube Marquard and Tim Keefe. Miro, who never pitched in the majors, finished the season with a league-leading 22 victories. Ron LeFlore reported to Clinton after his release from prison and eventually made it to the major leagues—the movie *One in a Million: The Ron LeFlore Story* was filmed at Riverview Stadium. On July 6, 1989, Clinton and Waterloo battled to a 3-3 tie in a game suspended after 20 innings. It resumed on August 17, when the teams played five more innings before Clinton won 4-3. Several Midwest League records were set in the 25-inning, 7-hour 35-minute affair, one of the longest in baseball history, including the most batters struck out on one team in a single game (31, Waterloo). The name Lumber Kings relates to Clinton's former claim to fame as the Sawmill Capital of the World back in the 1930s and 1940s, when logs were floated down the Mississippi for processing here. In its heyday, Clinton reportedly had more millionaires per capita than any U.S. city.

#### ◆ BALLPARK EXTRAS

The top-selling food item is the Johnsonville bratwurst, a spicy pork sausage made in Wisconsin and very popular in this part of the Midwest. The pizza also is popular. One of the top promotions is Elvis Karaoke Night.

#### ◆ ATTRACTIONS

*The Mississippi Belle II* casino is two minutes from the stadium. 311 River View Drive, (319) 243-9000.

For riverboat entertainment without the gambling, *The City of Clinton Showboat*, featuring the Lillian Russell Theatre, is docked right next to the casino boat. (319) 242-6760.

The Van Allen Building, designed by Louis Sullivan, arguably America's greatest architect, is along Highway 67 South, five minutes away. (319) 242-2000.

For more information about Clinton, call the Chamber of Commerce, (319) 242-5702.

#### ◆ DINING

Rastrelli's Restaurant is about five minutes from the stadium. 238 Main Street, (319) 242-7441.

Also, many fast-food restaurants are located along Highway 67, less than five minutes away.

#### ◆ LODGING

Travelodge is five minutes from the stadium. 302 6th Avenue S, Clinton, (319) 243-4730/(800)255-3050.

Ramada Inn is 15 minutes away. 1522 Lincoln Way, Clinton, (319) 243-8841/(800) 228-2828.

#### ◆ DIRECTIONS

Riverview Stadium is located 13 blocks north of the Highway 30 Bridge across the Mississippi. It is one block from the County Courthouse. Parking is plentiful and free. An overflow lot is one block away.

---

```
RIVERVIEW STADIUM
6th Avenue N and 1st Street
Clinton, IA 52732
(319) 243-3931
─────────────────────
Capacity: 3,000
LF 335, CF 393, RF 325
```

#### ◆ TICKET AND SCHEDULE INFORMATION

Games start at 7:05 P.M. from Monday through Saturday, except at 2 P.M. on Saturday and Sunday in April and May, and at 5 P.M. on Sunday from June through August.

The Lumber Kings' home opener is usually in early April and the season ends in the first week of September.

Ticket prices: $3.75 box seats; $2.50 general admission, $1.50 for students and seniors.

---

# FORT WAYNE WIZARDS

### MINNESOTA TWINS

Memorial Stadium, built in 1993, with its imposing facade and cold, concrete structure, seems more like a football facility than a ballpark. In fact, as you walk on the concourse underneath the grandstand, you will be hard pressed to find many uniquely baseball features to this stadium. But despite this structural shortcoming, there are some interesting aspects to the Wizards' home. The dugouts here are among the largest of any Class A ballpark. Atop the 16-foot-high left-field wall, stretching from the foul line to center field, there is a large net, approximately 45 feet tall, intended to protect passing cars on Coliseum Boulevard from being struck by home-run balls. Nevertheless, about six homers have soared over the net in the Wizards' two years at the stadium. Balls that hit this barrier and bounce onto the field are home runs. This local rule influenced an umpire's call in '93, when a ball that landed on the left-field warning track was ruled a home run although it hadn't hit the net. The ump, who had lost the ball in the lights, simply assumed it had hit Memorial's barrier.

#### ◆ LOCAL AND TEAM HISTORY

After a 44-year absence, organized baseball's return in

1993 was greeted enthusiastically, as 318,506 fans attended games here, but Fort Wayne had baseball as far back as 1867. Many think that the first affiliated farm club in history played here in 1896, as a member of the Interstate League. One of the players on that team was Zane Grey, who later became famous as a writer of westerns. After the turn of the century, Fort Wayne was associated with the Class B Central League intermittently until 1948. This city also had one-year affiliations with the Interstate Association (1906) and the Three-I League (1935).

Hall of Famer Jesse "Pop" Haines pitched here in 1914. Fellow Hall of Famer Chuck Klein batted .331 with 28 home runs as a Fort Wayne Chief in 1928. That year, Klein hit what is called one of the longest home runs ever. His ball cleared the fence and landed in a railroad car, which then traveled an unspecified distance with Klein's home-run ball riding the rails. In 1930, Sylvester Simon hit .364 with 15 home runs and 95 runs batted in for Fort Wayne. This is even more impressive if you consider that Simon lost four of his fingers and part of his left palm in a machine accident after the 1926 season. Subsequently, he devised a special glove and grip so he could continue playing, which he did through 1932. Rene Lopez set an all-time Midwest League record in 1993 by getting 10 straight hits. A month after setting this record, Lopez won $5,000 for himself and a new car for a fan by hitting a grand slam in the Grand Slam Inning, so designated by the team and two of its local sponsors.

The Wizards' nickname was chosen in a name-the-team contest that sparked a local controversy in 1993. Some area residents opposed the name choice because they perceived a connection between the team moniker and the grand wizard of the Klu Klux Klan which had a notoriously strong following in Indiana during the '20s. Others felt it had satanic cult overtones. But the team weathered this storm and, today, the Wizards' logo is among the minors' most popular.

### ◆ BALLPARK EXTRAS

Check out the Hard Ball Cafe near the right-field picnic area. You can get beer on tap plus a choice of two dinner platters, grilled bratwurst or a super hot dog, plus coleslaw, chips, potato salad and watermelon. Other noteworthy concession items include a barbecue chicken sandwich, a pork-chop sandwich and grilled boneless pork with barbecue sauce.

The team tries its best to enliven a usually staid crowd through various promotions. Among the zanier ones are a potato-sack race down the third-base line, a tricycle race on the main concourse behind the home-plate screen and Human Bowling, in which a fan is strapped inside a large plastic ball and then rolled down a ramp into adult-size bowling pins. The fans seem to get as excited, if not more so, about these diversions as they do about the ballgame.

### ◆ ATTRACTIONS

The Lincoln Museum features several exhibits relating to Lincoln's life and times. Admission is free. For further information, call (219) 427-3864.

The Fort Wayne Children's Zoo offers many displays of interest to kids, including Australia Adventure and African Veldt exhibits. Admission is $4.50, $3 for children under 14. For further information, call (219) 482-4610.

For additional information about the area, call the Fort Wayne Visitors Center, (219) 424-3700.

### ◆ DINING

Red River Steaks and BBQ, about 10 minutes from the park, is decorated with Western memorabilia and serves good barbecue ribs, brisket and chicken in an informal atmosphere. As you enter from the parking lot, cowbells over the door ring once you open the door. 305 E. Washington Center Road, at the Marriott Hotel, (219) 484-0411.

A large number of national chain and fast-food restaurants are located on Coldwater Road off I-69 and Coliseum Boulevard on the way to the ballpark.

### ◆ LODGING

Fort Wayne Marriott is 10 minutes away, at exit 112A (Coldwater Road) from I-69. (219) 484-0411/(800) 228-9290.

Super 8 Motel is on Coliseum Boulevard East, 10 minutes from the ballpark, near exit 112A from I-69. (219) 484-8326/(800) 800-8000.

### ◆ DIRECTIONS

Take exit 112A, Coldwater Road south from I-69. Stay on Coldwater for about 1½ miles. Turn left on Coliseum Boulevard, U.S. 30. After ¾ mile, turn right at the ballpark, adjacent to the Memorial Coliseum. Parking is plentiful and costs $2 per car.

### ◆ TICKET AND SCHEDULE INFORMATION

Most games are played at night, starting at 7 P.M. Sunday games begin at 2 P.M.

The Wizards' home opener is usually in early April, and the season ends in the first week of September.

Ticket prices: $6 box seats; $5 reserved seats; $4 general admission, $3 for seniors 60 and over and children 13 and under.

# KANE COUNTY COUGARS

**FLORIDA MARLINS**

The main focus of attention here at Elfstrom Stadium is in the outfield, where a large, approximately 60-foot-tall billboard towers over the left-field fence. Earl Cunningham, a 6-foot-2, 225-pound, right-handed, former No. 1 draft pick of the Chicago Cubs who visited here with league rival Peoria in the early 1990s, hit a homer over this sign that landed in the direction of the railroad tracks behind the outfield fence. There are bleachers in right-center field with another rather unusual addition—a large inflatable mitt atop the Wendy's sign at the back of the section. Any player who hits a home run into the mitt wins $100,000 for himself, $450,000 for a fan and $450,000 for charity. So far, the closest anyone has come to striking it rich is hitting a home run about halfway up the bleachers. Many fans enjoy watching the game from a two-tiered wood deck located behind the right-field fence. In 1994, a hot tub was installed in the area adjacent to the deck, and on the weekends, the picnic tents down the right-field line have featured such events as pig roasts and clambakes. There is an open concourse plus grassy areas down each foul line past the uncov-ered grandstand where you will find more picnic facilities.

### ◆ LOCAL AND TEAM HISTORY

Although the Cougars, who relocated here from Wausau, Wis., and began play in 1991, are the first orga-nized-baseball team based in Geneva, the histo-ry of pro ball in this area goes back much further to the 1890s, when nearby Aurora played in the Illinois-Iowa League. After the turn of the century, this city spent four seasons (1910-1912, 1915) in two minor leagues. In 1911, a 21-year-old Casey Stengel played outfield for Aurora and led the Wisconsin-Illinois League in hits while batting .352. Other neighboring cities such as Elgin and Joliet also hosted organized-baseball teams in the early years of the 20th century. Kane County set successive Midwest League attendance records in 1992 and 1993, only to see the West Michigan Whitecaps set a new mark in 1994. The Cougars '94 attendance of 417,744 ranked third among all Class A and AA teams, behind only West Michigan and Birmingham.

Will Cunnane's 1.43 ERA in 1994 ranked No. 1 among full-season minor-league pitchers. Cunnane, who also posted an 11-3 record, 106 strikeouts and just 23 walks in 139 innings, was converted into a starting pitcher in June after the promotion of one of his team-mates to AA opened up a spot in the rotation. Cunnane's 1994 achievements were in sharp contrast to Kane County's dubious pitching distinction of breaking the Midwest League record for most hit batsmen in one season twice, in 1993 and 1994, while also having the individual leader in this category in both seasons.

**OTHER FAMOUS ALUMNI**

Charles Johnson, Brad Pennington and Scott Klingenbeck played here.

### ◆ BALLPARK EXTRAS

You will find several good concession items, including locally made deep-dish pizza, pork-chop sandwiches, fajitas, enchiladas, grilled steak sandwiches, brats and burgers. The Cougars also keep things quite lively in the ballpark, staging such popular promos as the Human Bowling Ball. Fans, egged on by an energetic public address announcer, also have a good time when staff members slingshot water-soaked Nerf balls into the stands.

### ◆ ATTRACTIONS

Chicago, only a short drive from this suburban community, is the biggest tourist attraction in the area. For additional information about the Windy City, call the Office of Tourism, (312) 793-2094.

### ◆ DINING
Ristorante Chianti, less than 10 minutes from the ballpark, offers northern Italian fare plus such non-traditional and imaginative dishes as barbecued Cajun shrimp, Reuben-sandwich pasta, and lasagna stuffed with zucchini and carrots. 207 S. 3rd Street, (708) 232-0212.

### ◆ LODGING
Holiday Inn is in Elgin, at the Route 31 South exit off I-90, about 20 minutes from the ballpark. (708) 695-5000/(800) HOLIDAY.

Comfort Inn is in Aurora, about three miles south of the Route 59 exit off I-88, about 25 minutes from the ballpark. (708) 820-3400/(800) 424-6423.

### ◆ DIRECTIONS
From I-88, take the Farnsworth Avenue exit. Go north for about five miles, through Batavia to Cherry Lane, and turn left. The ballpark will be immediately visible. Parking is available for $1 per car. Overflow parking is available in the lots of area businesses.

**ELFSTROM STADIUM**
**34002 W. Cherry Lane**
**Geneva, IL 60134**
**(708) 232-8811**

**Capacity: 5,900**
**LF 335, CF 400, RF 335**

### ◆ TICKET AND SCHEDULE INFORMATION
Most games are played at night, starting at 7 P.M. Saturday. Sunday games begin at 5 P.M. and 2 P.M. respectively.

The Cougars' home opener is usually in early April, and the season ends in the first week of September. Purchasing tickets on the day of the game could be difficult for select dates because of Kane County's local popularity and the fact that this is the only minor-league team in the metropolitan Chicago area.

Ticket prices: $6 box seats; $5 reserved seats; $4 bleachers; $3 general admission/lawn.

# PEORIA CHIEFS

## ST. LOUIS CARDINALS

Having undergone a $2.3 million renovation prior to the 1992 season, Pete Vonachen Stadium is also home to Bradley University sports, as well as numerous amateur tournaments during the spring and summer. Situated next to I-74, the park is also close to a public golf course, tennis courts, softball fields and other venues. The stadium also is adjacent to a U.S. Department of Agriculture research facility (where penicillin was discovered). The Corn Stock summer theater is close by.

The stadium features the Hard Ball Cafe, where fans gather before games, and two picnic decks—Redbird Roost and Busch Gardens—for corporate parties. The Chiefs will add a full-color message screen in 1995. Luxury suites will be added in the near future.

### ◆ LOCAL AND TEAM HISTORY
Pro baseball in Peoria dates from the 1870s. Peoria also fielded teams in several minor leagues during the 1880s and '90s. Since the turn of the century, Peoria has belonged to five circuits, beginning with the Western League in 1902. This city also spent time in the Three-I League (1905-17, 1919-32, 1935, 1937, 1953-57) and joined the Midwest League in 1983. This is the first year of affiliation with St. Louis. Hall of Famer Charles "Hoss" Radbourn played for Peoria's first pro team in 1878. Radbourn's pitching record in his rookie season as a pro ballplayer is unknown, although he did bat .289 in 28 games. In 1898, fellow Hall of Famer "Iron Man" Joe McGinnity—so named because he twice hurled more than 400 innings in one season and pitched both games of five doubleheaders for the New York Giants—won 10 games

OTHER FAMOUS ALUMNI OTHER FAMOUS ALUMNI

Greg Maddux, Mark Grace, Rafael Palmeiro, Phil Cavaretta, Rick Sutcliffe, Luis Polonia, Tony Lazzeri, Dwight Smith, Shawn Boskie, Wally Joyner, Devon White, Mark McLemore and Mike Harkey all played here.

for the Western Association's Peoria Distillers in only 104 innings. In 1922, McGinnity returned to Peoria as a member of Three-I League rival Danville. In front of an overflow crowd at Peoria's Lake View Park, the 51-year-old McGinnity shut out the home team 2-0. After his big-league career ended in 1908, McGinnity pitched 13 more seasons in the minors, during which he won 20 or more games six times and compiled 207 victories. When his playing career ended in 1925, McGinnity had won 482 games, 247 in the big leagues, and a total of 235 (including 28 in 1893, '94 and '98) in the minors. The 1992 Midwest League All-Star Game was played in Peoria and featured a home-run-hitting contest which will long be remembered by many here. Clinton's Andre Keene, nicknamed Andre the Giant because he is six-foot-five and 260 pounds, won the home-run derby and gained his place in Peoria lore by hitting a homer that ripped right through a sign atop the stadium's scoreboard.

### ◆ BALLPARK EXTRAS

One of the most popular items is the butterfly porkchop sandwich. The Chiefs also feature Macho Nachos, a rib-eye steak sandwich, grilled chicken and burgers.

A popular promotion is the Kiss the Pig musical-chairs contest, involving players from each team playing that night. The player left standing must kiss a pig. Every Sunday in 1995 will be Turn Back the Clock Day, with numerous specials around the park, including Dixieland bands and dancers.

### ◆ ATTRACTIONS

Peoria is also home to Wildlife Prairie Park (309-676-0998), Lakeview Museum (309-686-7000) and other cultural venues.

There's also the Peoria Civic Center, which hosts concerts and shows. Call (309) 673-8900 for schedules.

Those less culturally inclined might enjoy the Par-A-Dice Riverboat Casino, (309) 698-7711.

For more information about Peoria, call the Chamber of Commerce, (309) 676-0755.

### ◆ DINING

The Grill on Fulton, five minutes from the stadium, is a good choice for fine dining. 456 Fulton, (309) 674-6870.

Vonachen's Old Place also features upscale dining, about 15 minutes away. 5934 N. Knoxville, (309) 692-7033.

Several fast-food places are just a few minutes away on University Street and Sterling Avenue, which both intersect with Nebraska Avenue. Also, many pubs and grills are downtown, five minutes from the ballpark.

### ◆ LODGING

Holiday Inn City Centre is five minutes from the ballpark. 500 Hamilton Boulevard, Peoria, (309) 674-2500/(800) HOLIDAY.

Best Western Mark Twain Hotel is 10 minutes away 225 N.E. Adams, Peoria, (309) 676-3600/(800) 528-1234.

### ◆ DIRECTIONS

From I-74, exit at North University Street (exit 91 or 91-B, depending on your direction). Turn left on West Nebraska at first light (USDA research facility). Stadium is on the left. The stadium is clearly visible from the interstate.

---

**PETE VONACHEN STADIUM**
**1524 W. Nebraska Avenue**
**Peoria, IL 61604**
**(309) 688-1622**

---

**Capacity: 6,200**
**LF 335, CF 383, RF 335**

---

### ◆ TICKET AND SCHEDULE INFORMATION

Games start at 7:05 P.M. from Monday through Saturday, with Sunday starts at 2:05 P.M. in April and May and at 6:05 P.M. from June through August.

The Chiefs' home opener is usually in early April and the season ends in the first week of September.

Ticket prices: $5 field boxes; $4 reserved seats; $3 general admission.

# QUAD CITY RIVER BANDITS

**HOUSTON ASTROS**

John O'Donnell Stadium, built in 1931 and remodeled in 1989, features an attractive brick facade with several vaulted arches. A walkway lined with several old-fashioned lampposts is located at the front entrance. The Mississippi River, spanned by the Centennial Bridge visible down the right-field line, flows just six yards past the eight-foot-high right-field wall. This proximity, although a scenic plus for the ballpark, caused major problems here during the Flood of 1993. On June 23, Quad City defeated Peoria 2-0 in what proved to be the last game at John O'Donnell in '93. At one point, the flood waters covered the entire field, including all but the top of a tractor placed on the pitchers mound as a rough depth gauge. For the rest of the season, the team played "home games" in a variety of other Midwest League cities and at a nearby high school. Behind each of the stadium's two scoreboards, there are two smoke-stacks that shoot off fireworks after River Bandits home runs. There are picnic areas down each foul line.

◆ **LOCAL AND TEAM HISTORY**

Quad Cities consist of Davenport, Iowa, where the team and ballpark are located; Rock Island, Ill.; Moline, Ill. and Bettendorf, Iowa. Pro baseball in this area dates from 1879, when the Davenport Brown Stockings were a charter member of the Northwestern League, one of the earliest minor leagues. After the turn of the century, Davenport was first associated with the Three-I League, which Moline also belonged to. Davenport spent time in two other minor leagues before joining the Mid-west League in 1960, where it has since remained continuously. Quad City began its current affiliation with Houston in 1993. The Davenport Cubs won the 1946 Three-I League title when the team was led by the .354 average of catcher and batting champion Albert "Rube" Walker. Walker went on to a career as pitching coach for the New York Mets. In 1961, Dennis Ribant had one of the best seasons in league history, going 17-2, still a team record for win-ning percentage, with a 1.86 ERA while also hurling the first perfect game in Midwest League annals, shut-ting out Clinton 1-0 on July 2. Ribant pitched six years in the big leagues but never equaled his '61 Midwest League season. During two games in 1963, Quad City's pitching staff experienced both ends of the pitching spectrum. On July 3, George Sherrod hurled a 16-inning shutout against Fox Cities, tying a Midwest League record. Two days later, Decatur scored 15 runs in the first inning en route to a 16-3 victory over Quad City.

**OTHER FAMOUS ALUMNI**

Frank Tanana, Rick Reuschel, Brian Harper, Chad Curtis, Jerry Remy, Jim Bunning, Dave Collins, Luis Polonia, Damian Easley, Carney Lansford, Darrin Jackson, Roberto Hernandez, Bryan Harvey, Mel Hall, Chuck Finley, Shawon Dunston and Dante Bichette have all played here.

◆ **BALLPARK EXTRAS**

The best promotions are the Fourth of July Fireworks Show, an appearance by The Famous Chicken, Bat Night, Glove Night and Beach Towel Night. The River Bandits serve several good grilled items, including brats, burgers and Polish sausage. Tacos from a local restaurant, pizza and pork-chop sandwiches, a Midwest League staple, are also available.

◆ **ATTRACTIONS**

The *Casino Rock Island* River Boat is a common sight along the Mississippi. (309) 793-4200.

The Putnam Museum of History and Natural Science has an eclectic collection of exhibits on local history and archaeological finds from Egypt and Asia. Admission is $3, $2 for seniors 65 and over and $1 for children 7 to 17. For further information, call (319) 324-1933.

For more information about the Quad Cities area, call the Chamber of Commerce, (319) 322-1706.

◆ **DINING**

Jumers Castle Lodge is 10 minutes away. 900 Spruce Hills Drive, Bettendorf, (319) 359-7141.

Circa 21 Dinner Playhouse is five minutes away. 3rd Avenue, Davenport, (319) 328-8935.

◆ **LODGING**

Jumers Hotel is 10 minutes away. 900 Spruce Hills Drive, Bettendorf, (319) 359-7141.

Blackhawk Hotel is about four minutes away. 200 E. 3rd Street, Davenport, (319) 323-2711.

◆ **DIRECTIONS**

From I-80, take the U.S. 61 S exit. Proceed to River Drive. Stadium is at River Drive and S. Gaines Street, next to Centennial Bridge. From I-74, take Grant Street exit to River Drive South. Stadium is on left at S. Gaines Street.

**JOHN O'DONNELL STADIUM**
**209 S. Gaines Sreet**
**Davenport, IA 52802**
**(319) 324-2032**

**Capacity: 5,500**
**LF 340, CF 390, RF 340**

◆ **TICKET AND SCHEDULE INFORMATION**

Game times are Monday-Tuesday 12:30 P.M.; Wednes-day-Saturday 7 P.M.; Sunday 2 P.M. (April-May) and 6 P.M. (June-August).

The River Bandits' home opener is usually in early April and the season ends in the first week of September.

Ticket prices: $6 box seats; $5 reserved seats; $4 general admission, $3 children 6 to 14 and seniors. Children under age 6 are admitted free.

# ROCKFORD CUBBIES

### CHICAGO CUBS

When you visit Marinelli Stadium, bring your sunglasses because the ballpark faces west and the sun sets over the left-field wall. But unlike in Pittsfield, the game does not stop while the sun is going down, creating tough times for batters, especially from May through July. During those months, fans accustomed to conditions here prefer to sit along the third base side to avoid having the sun in their eyes. Besides this quirk, there are many attractive attributes to the ballpark, which opened in 1988. Marinelli Stadium, with trees behind a partially covered grandstand and the Rock River beyond left and center fields, is in a very scenic location. In summertime, geese regularly fly in from the riverside to congregate in center field before batting practice begins. The playing field is particularly close to the grandstand, so there is not much foul territory here. This closeness prompted the installation of a screen that runs from third to first to protect fans from foul balls. Municipal Stadium, home of the Rockford Peaches of the All American Girls Professional Baseball League, is still standing, about four blocks from Marinelli. From 1943 to '54, the Peaches won four AAGPBL championships, the most of any franchise, and were immortalized in the film *A League of Their Own*. The Peaches' championships double the number of titles that men's minor-league teams have captured for Rockford over the years.

### ◆ LOCAL AND TEAM HISTORY

Pro baseball in Rockford goes back a long way. Four months after the Civil War ended, the Forest City Baseball Club of Rockford was formed. Hall of Famer Albert Goodwill Spalding played for this independent team from 1866 to '70. In 1871, the club joined the National Association of Base Ball Players, regarded as the game's first professional circuit and the forerunner of the National League. Hall of Famer Cap Anson played for last-place Rockford in '71, batting .352. Rockford fielded teams in several minor leagues through the remaining years of the 19th century. In 1895, Bill Krieg led the Western Association with a .452 batting average, considered the second best all-time in the minor leagues. The next season, his second with Rockford, his .350 average again led the league. In 1902, this city began an 11-year

stint in the Three-I League. Rockford spent time in three other circuits before joining the Midwest League in 1988 after 38 years without pro baseball.

Since '88, Marinelli, where the air can be heavy during the summer and where occasional wind gusts off the Rock River can influence the outcome of a ballgame, has proven to be a tough park for home runs, but Delino DeShields hit a memorable shot here in 1988. With 35-mph winds blowing into the ballpark from the northwest, DeShields blasted a grand slam into the teeth of the gale. The ball carried about 440 feet, over the center-field wall, coming to rest after hitting the flagpole.

*OTHER FAMOUS ALUMNI*

Willie Greene, Archi Cianfrocco, Kirk Reuter, Chris Nabholz and Mel Rojas played here.

The Chicago Tribune Co., parent company of the Cubs, purchased the Rockford club in autumn of 1992. Because the Cubs were committed to Peoria for two more years, Rockford signed a two-year Player Development Contract with the Kansas City Royals in 1993-94. This was the first time in professional baseball history that a major-league team owned a minor-league club with another affiliation. This season, the Cubs ended their affiliation with Peoria and will stock Rockford.

### ◆ BALLPARK EXTRAS

Pork-chop sandwiches and Polish sausages are the local favorites at the concession stand. There is also a popular picnic area known as the Bear Garden. The stadium has a no-smoking, no-alcohol section. Children's promotions include bat, jersey, baseball and lunch-bag giveaways. Adult promotions include beach-towel and sports-bag giveaways.

### ◆ ATTRACTIONS

Magic Waters, a water theme park, is located adjacent to I-90, about 15 minutes from Marinelli Stadium. Rockford also has several golf courses and family parks around the city.

For more information about Rockford, call the Chamber of Commerce, (815) 987-9100.

### ◆ DINING

The Stadium Lounge was voted as having the best burgers in Rockford. Two blocks east of the ballpark on 15th Avenue, (815) 962-7354.

### ◆ LODGING

Howard Johnson's is about 10 minutes from the stadium. 3909 11th Street, Rockford, (815) 397-9000/(800) 654-2000.

### ◆ DIRECTIONS

Take I-90 west from Chicago to exit at mile-post 61 (U.S. 20). Continue west on U.S. 20 to Illinois Route 2 (Main Street). Exit north on Main Street and continue to second traffic light (15th Avenue). Turn right. Stadium is on your right.

> **MARINELLI STADIUM**
> **101 15th Avenue**
> **Rockford, IL 61104**
> **(815) 962-2827**
> ———————
> **Capacity: 4,300**
> **LF 335, CF 400, RF 335**

### ◆ TICKET AND SCHEDULE INFORMATION

Most games are played at night, starting at 7 P.M.

The Cubbies season begins in early April and ends the first week of September.

Ticket prices: $5 box seats; $4 reserved seats; $3 general admission. There is a $1 discount for seniors, children 13 and under and military personnel. There is no admission charge for children under 3.

# SOUTH BEND SILVER HAWKS

## CHICAGO WHITE SOX

Coveleski Stadium is better known to fans as The Cove. It opened in 1987 and hosted its first Midwest League games the following year. The park is located in the southwest corner of downtown South Bend, adjacent to the dormant Studebaker auto factory—a seven-story brick-and-glass building that lends a Camden Yards–type feel to the ballpark. The Cove's beauty is attributed to 5,000 seats that are sunk below street level, making handicapped access easy. Advertising signs are located on a second fence atop a hill, giving the field a clean, classic look. The playing field has been judged best in the Midwest League for two consecutive years.

### ◆ LOCAL AND TEAM HISTORY

South Bend had a brief fling with pro baseball in the last century, fielding a team in the Indiana State League in the late 1880s. Since the turn of the century, South Bend has been associated with the Central League and the Southern Michigan Association. South Bend joined the Midwest League in 1988. Hall of Famer Max "Scoops" Carey spent his first two seasons here, in 1909 and '10, batting .249 overall. Alex "Red" McColl won 332 games over his minor-league career, sixth best in history; he posted 16 of them for the South Bend Benders in 1916.

*OTHER FAMOUS ALUMNI* Jason Bere, Domingo Jean, Bob Wickman, Scott Radinsky, Roberto Hernandez and Mike Maksudian all played here.

The club has been affiliated with the White Sox since its inception in 1988, but the team changed its nickname from White Sox to Silver Hawks after the 1993 season. The Silver Hawk was a popular model of Studebaker built in South Bend until the mid-1960s. The franchise won the Midwest League championship in 1989 and '93.

### ◆ BALLPARK EXTRAS

The park has a barbecue stand in the right-field picnic garden. The pizzas are homemade in the stadium. In addition, the team offers Silver Hawks Pilsener, brewed by the Mishawaka Brewing Co. There will be three nights of fireworks in 1995. Acts scheduled to visit include The Famous Chicken and the Philly Phanatic.

### ◆ ATTRACTIONS

The Studebaker National Museum is behind right field, across Lafayette Street. (219) 235-9714.

The University of Notre Dame is five minutes north of the stadium on Route 31/33. (219) 631-5000.

Amish Acres Musical Theater is 30 minutes southeast of the ballpark, via Routes 31 and 6. (219) 773-4188.

For more information about South Bend, call the Chamber of Commerce, (219) 234-0051.

### ◆ DINING

Tippecanoe Place is two minutes away. 620 W. Washington Avenue, (219) 234-9077.

Mishawaka Brewing Company is about 15 minutes away. 3703 N. Main Street, (219) 256-9993.

### ◆ LODGING

Holiday Inn is within walking distance of the park. 213

W. Washington, South Bend, (219) 232-3941/(800) HOLIDAY.

Marriott is also a short walk from the park. 123 N. St. Joseph, South Bend, (219) 234-2000/(800)228-9290.

### ◆ DIRECTIONS
From I-80/90 (Indiana Toll Road), take exit 77. Follow Route 31/33 south into downtown. Go through downtown, turn right at Western Avenue, then left on Taylor Street to the ballpark. Limited on-site parking is $2, but there is plenty of free parking within walking distance.

---

**STANLEY COVELESKI REGIONAL STADIUM**
**501 W. South Street**
**South Bend, IN 46601**
**(219)-235-9988**

---

**Capacity: 5,000**
**LF 336, CF 405, RF 336**

---

### ◆ TICKET AND SCHEDULE INFORMATION
Games are at 7 P.M. from Monday through Saturday and at 2 P.M. most Sundays. Exceptions: 10:30 A.M. on May 15 and 2 P.M. on June 15.

The Silver Hawks open their season in early April and finish the first week of September.

Ticket prices: $6 box seats; $4 reserved seats; $3 general admission.

# SULTANS OF SPRINGFIELD

### KANSAS CITY ROYALS

Trains pass by on the railroad tracks behind the rightfield wall so regularly that you can almost set your watch by them, much to the chagrin of many local fans who don't appreciate their games being interrupted by the rumble and whistle of passing locomotives. The railroad and Springfield baseball must have a certain ineluctable connection, since train tracks also ran past a park simply called the Ball Grounds, where baseball was first played here in the 1870s. These trains are such a part of Lanphier Field that the Sultans contemplated a contest where a fan would get a prize if a home run struck one of the trains. Unfortunately, the team was unable to secure the necessary backing for such a promotion. Trees and tennis courts combine with the train tracks to complete the scene. Fans in the uncovered grandstand have a view of the area behind the outfield fence, which also includes a center-field batters' eye consisting of several low bushes. The Robin Roberts suffix was added to this ballpark's name in 1978 to honor the Springfield native who in 1976 was inducted into baseball's Hall of Fame.

The unusual name reversal of the Sultans of Springfield can be traced both to Babe Ruth, "the Sultan of Swat," and the Dire Straits song "Sultans of Swing." Sultans was selected as the nickname by one of the team's owners, who simply opened a dictionary to the letter S and eventually found and took a liking to this moniker.

### ◆ LOCAL AND TEAM HISTORY
Pro baseball in Springfield began in the 1880s, when this city was associated with at least two minor leagues. Organized baseball made its debut here in 1903, the first of 30 seasons (1903-14, 1925-32, 1935, 1938-42 and 1946-49) in the Three-I League. This city has also spent time in five other circuits, including four (1978-81) in the AAA American Association. Springfield first joined the Midwest League in 1982. In 1994, this city thought it would have no pro baseball until about two weeks before the season when the Waterloo, Iowa, franchise moved here. This is the first year of the current affiliation with Kansas City.

**OTHER FAMOUS ALUMNI OTHER FAMOUS ALUMNI**

Jesse "Pop" Haines, Stan Musial, Juan Marichal, Manny Mota, Roy Sievers, Todd Zeile, Danny Cox, Jeff Fassero, Ray Lankford and Tom Pagnozzi played here.

The Springfield Senators won the 1926 Three-I championship and set a league attendance record by drawing approximately 128,000 fans to the ballpark. The '26 season also produced some unique on-field accomplishments, including a game on July 14 when Al Maderas hit four consecutive home runs against Quincy. One week later, Springfield defeated the Peoria Tractors 33-23 in a game that included 18 walks and 21 extra-base hits, including 10 home runs. In 1935, Lyle Judy, in his second consecutive season with Springfield, shocked the power-oriented Western Association by stealing 107 bases, 101 more than he swiped in 1934. He also batted .337. Judy's performance impressed the St. Louis Cardinals so much in '34 that they promoted him to the majors, where he went hitless in 11 at-bats but did steal two bases, his only stolen bases in the big leagues. Lyle Judy stole 442 bases over his 14 years in the minors. Mike Perez's 41 saves in 1987 set an all-time Midwest League record. Perez also won six games that season while compiling a microscopic 0.85 ERA.

## ◆ BALLPARK EXTRAS

The Sultans offer several good concession items, including the pork-chop sandwich. You can also get brats, hot dogs, chicken, burgers, corn dogs and sourdough-bread bowls that are filled with either chili or soup. You should also put to the test this team's guarantee that fans can buy a hot dog and soda here for no more than $1 apiece.

## ◆ ATTRACTIONS

Abraham Lincoln Home National Historic Site contains the only home ever owned by the 16th President; it was built in 1839. Admission is free. For further information, call (217) 492-4150.

You can also visit Lincoln's law offices, where donations are requested as the price of admission. For further information, call (217) 785-7961.

Lincoln's Tomb is a state historic site that also contains plaques with the words of the Gettysburg Address and Lincoln's second inaugural speech. Admission is free.

For additional information about Springfield, call the Visitors' Bureau, (217) 789-2360/(800) 545-7300.

## ◆ DINING

Norb and Andy's, about 20 minutes from the ballpark, is newly renovated. Although you can get a wide selection of foods here, such as Cajun chicken and vegetarian pasta, you must try the horseshoes, a Springfield specialty. Bread is toasted and then topped with meat (at Norb and Andy's, this includes hamburger, shrimp or crab), mild cheddar-cheese sauce and fries. The Sultans have plans to offer horseshoes at the ballpark. 518 E. Capital Street, (217) 523-7777.

## ◆ LODGING

Best Western Lincoln Plaza is near the State Capitol, about 15 minutes from the ballpark. (217) 523-5661/(800) 528-1234.

Hampton Inn is at exit 94 off I-55, about 20 minutes from the ballpark.(217) 529-1100/(800) 426-7866.

## ◆ DIRECTIONS

From I-55, take the 6th Street exit. Stay on 6th Street for about 15 minutes and turn right on North Grand Avenue. Stay on North Grand for about one mile, past a high school. The ballpark will be on your left. Parking is free but limited at the ballpark. Supplemental parking is available in the lot of a nearby supermarket.

## ◆ TICKET AND SCHEDULE INFORMATION

Most games are played at night, starting at 7 P.M. In April and May, Thursday and Sunday games begin at 1 P.M. Sunday games from June through September start at 6 P.M.

The Sultans' home opener is usually in early April, and the season ends in the first week of September.

Ticket prices: $5 box seats; $4 general admission, $3 for seniors and children under 12.

# WEST MICHIGAN WHITECAPS

## OAKLAND ATHLETICS

What can the Whitecaps do for an encore? In their first season here, the team smashed the Midwest League attendance record, drawing 475,212 fans, more than 100,000 over the previous mark. The Whitecaps also outdrew every other Rookie, A and AA team. This success can be attributed to several things. Old Kent Park, named for a local business, is an attractive ballpark, spacious and comfortable. The team also makes an effort to keep things lively and entertaining. Before the first pitch, the public address announcer blares a factory whistle over the loudspeakers and then gets the crowd going by saying, "It's time to go to work, gentlemen. Let's play ball!" In the fifth inning, when the grounds crew, known as the Clean Sweepers, comes out to sweep the infield, they are timed by the scoreboard. In 1994, an exuberant staff member named Hurricane Henry became a Whitecaps' institution. He walks clapping and yelling through the grandstand, exhorting fans to cheer. Henry climbs atop the home dugout in the fifth inning to sing *Happy Birthday* to children. Things are also lively in the press box, where the official scorer entertains by playing his harmonica between innings. Altogether, the enthusiasm on display at Old Kent Park should make your visit very enjoyable.

◆ **LOCAL AND TEAM HISTORY**

Organized baseball returned here in 1994 when this franchise moved from Madison, Wis. Before '94, there had not been a minor-league team in this area since 1951, when the Grand Rapids Jets were completing their 24th and final season in the Class A Central League. Pro baseball debuted in this area in 1883 when Grand Rapids fielded a team in the Northwestern League. After the turn of the century, Grand Rapids had several organized-baseball teams affiliated with three leagues until baseball left town in 1951. Grand Rapids also had a team in the All-American Girls Professional League. Nicknamed the Chicks, the franchise moved from Milwaukee after the 1944 season and remained until the league folded in '54.

Hall of Famer Rube Waddell pitched for Grand Rapids in 1899. One of his teammates was fellow Hall of Famer "Wahoo" Sam Crawford. Bill "Rasty" Wright, regarded as the first player to collect 2,000 career hits in the minors, was Grand Rapids' leading hitter in 1894 and '95. In those seasons, he hit .423 and .408, respectively. He also scored a phenomenal 217 runs in '94. But despite his prodigious hitting ability, Wright played only one season (1890) in the big leagues, batting .282 in 101 games.

◆ **BALLPARK EXTRAS**

The two grills located at the end of the concourse down each foul line offer several good items, including barbe-cued chicken sandwich, marinated chicken kebab and bratwurst. Several premium beers can also be bought here. On the concourse, kielbasa and locally made deep-dish pizza (pepperoni, sausage and cheese) are available.

Two grassy areas are available down each foul line for lawn seating. Outside Old Kent, behind the outfield wall, you will find an amusement park complete with batting cages.

◆ **ATTRACTIONS**

The Gerald R. Ford Museum in downtown Grand Rapids features exhibits about the career of the former president, who was born here. Admission is $2, $1.50 for seniors. Children under 16 are free. For further information, call (616) 456-2674.

The Splash Family Water Park, just west of I-96, has a wave pool, water slides and play areas. Admission is $14.95, $11.95 for children 4 to 8. After 4 P.M., admission is $6.95. Seniors 60 and over are free. For further information, call (616) 940-3100.

For more information about this area, call the Grand Rapids Chamber of Commerce, (616) 771-0300.

◆ **DINING**

The Grand Rapids Brewing Company, about 15 minutes from the ballpark, offers a variety of imaginative entrees such as herb chicken linguini and shrimp with angel-hair pasta. At least five home-brewed beers are available daily. 3689 28th Street, (616) 285-5970.

◆ **LODGING**

Holiday Inn Downtown is 10 minutes from the park, about two miles north of U.S. 131, in Grand Rapids. (616) 363-9001/(800) HOLIDAY.

Radisson Hotel is 10 to 15 minutes from the ballpark, at the Pearl Street exit from U.S. 131, in Grand Rapids. (616) 242-6000/(800) 333-3333.

◆ **DIRECTIONS**

From I-69, take the U.S. 131 North exit. Stay on 131 North and exit at West River Drive. Pass through the intersection and drive straight into the parking lot. Parking is plentiful and costs $1.

```
OLD KENT PARK
4500 W. River Drive
Comstock Park, MI  49321
(616) 784-4131
―――――――――――――――
Capacity: 6901
LF 327, CF 402, RF 327
```

◆ **TICKET AND SCHEDULE INFORMATION**

In April and May, games start at 6:30 P.M. The rest of the season, they begin at 7 P.M. Sunday games start at 2 P.M.

The Whitecaps' home opener is usually in early April, and the season ends in the first week of September.

Ticket prices: $6 box seats; $4.50 reserved seats; $3 general admission.

# WISCONSIN TIMBER RATTLERS

## SEATTLE MARINERS

This is a big year for the franchise because the team will have a new name (before '95, they were known as the Appleton Foxes) and a new $4.5 million ballpark. Located in a wooded area near Grand Chute outside of Appleton, this stadium has an open concourse so fans can follow the game from the concession stands. There are also picnic areas down each foul line. Grassy berms past third and first base are available for fans who prefer to watch the game from blankets or folding chairs. This ballpark could prove tough for home-run hitters: The outfield wall from left to center is about 16 feet high and the right-center field power alley is the deepest part of the park, 405 feet from home.

The Timber Rattlers' new name reflects an effort to give this team more statewide appeal, with an eye toward drawing fans from nearby Green Bay, Fond du Lac, Oshkosh and Sheboygan. The Wisconsin Timber Rattlers also have an attractive, new burgundy-and-black logo, featuring a cap-bedecked snake curled around a bat. According to one of the primary manufacturers of minor-league headwear, the Timber Rattlers' cap was the No. 1 seller during the 1994-95 off-season.

### ◆ LOCAL AND TEAM HISTORY

The first pro baseball game in Appleton took place more than 100 years ago, on May 21, 1891. About 500 fans paid 25 cents each to watch the Wisconsin-Illinois League's Appleton Papermakers defeat the Green Bay Duck Wallopers 4-0. Since the turn of the century, Appleton has been associated with four circuits. This city has been a member of the Midwest League continuously since joining in 1962. The current affiliation with Seattle began in 1993.

OTHER FAMOUS ALUMNI

OTHER FAMOUS ALUMNI

Stan Wasiak, Cal Ripken Sr., Bucky Dent, Boog Powell, Bill Melton, Harold Baines, Bobby Thigpen, Ron Karkovice, Lamar Johnson, Tom "Flash" Gordon, Candy Maldonado and Doug Drabek played or managed here.

George "Hoggy" Hogriever, the minors' all-time stolen-base king with 948, is one of Appleton's most illustrious alumni. He stole 47 bases for the 1891 Papermakers and spent the final three seasons (1910-12, the last two as player-manager) of his 24-year playing career here, adding 75 more steals to his record. After retiring, Hogriever umpired in the Wisconsin-Illinois League, the same circuit he had played in for three years. The 1941 Papermakers finished third and qualified for the Wisconsin State League playoffs. Appleton was down two games to none when rain postponed the series with the Green Bay Blue Jays for seven days. Appleton, frustrated with the wet weather, grew impatient and forfeited the series to Green Bay. But with more rain on the way, Green Bay forfeited the next round, making fourth-place Sheboygan the champs. Goose Goosage, who then still used his given name, Rich, was the 1971 Midwest League Player of the Year after posting a league-leading 18-2 record, 1.83 ERA, 15 complete games and seven shutouts in 25 games, only one of which was in relief.

### ◆ BALLPARK EXTRAS

The team is planning to have several local restaurants provide food for sale at the ballpark. Pizza will also be available.

### ◆ ATTRACTIONS

The Gordon Bubolz Nature Preserve features several miles of trails, a nature center, picnic facilities and a variety of wildlife. Admission is free. For further information, call (414) 731-6041.

For additional information about Appleton, call the Chamber of Commerce, (414) 734-7101.

### ◆ DINING

Victoria's, about 15 minutes from the ballpark, serves Italian food, with *Pollo Bianco*, which is chicken in cream and mushroom sauce, and pasta Alfredo among the most popular dishes. 503 W. College Avenue, (414) 730-9595.

### ◆ LODGING

Best Western Midway Hotel is on U.S. 41, about 20 minutes from the ballpark. (414) 731-4141/(800) 528-1234.

Hampton Inn is near the intersection of U.S. 41 and State Route 125, about 15 minutes from the ballpark. (414) 954-9211/(800) 426-7866.

### ◆ DIRECTIONS

From U.S. 41, take the Wisconsin Avenue exit and go west. Turn right on Casaloma Drive. The ballpark will be on the right. Ample parking is available for $1.

**RATTLERS STADIUM**
**P.O. Box 464**
**Appleton, WI 54912**
**(414) 733-4152**

**Capacity: 5,000**
**LF 330, CF 400, RF 330**

### ◆ TICKET AND SCHEDULE INFORMATION

Most games are played at night, starting at 7 P.M. In April and May, games begin at 6 P.M. Sunday games start at 1 P.M. Verify all game times with the Timber Rattlers.

The Timber Rattlers' home opener is usually in early April and the season ends in the first week of September. Purchasing tickets on the day of the game should be no problem, although the new ballpark here could result in limited ticket availability for certain games.

Ticket prices: $5 box seats; $4 reserved seats; $3 general admission. Ask about ½ price senior days.

# SOUTH ATLANTIC LEAGUE

The modern version of the South Atlantic (or "Sally") League began in 1980. Before that, this league had many incarnations, most recently as the Western Carolinas League (1960-79) with older versions spanning many decades back to 1904. That first season, Chris Miller led the six-team Class C League in home runs with the prodigious total of five. Today, the South Atlantic League has 14 teams, located in Maryland, West Virginia, North Carolina, South Carolina and Georgia. Each team plays 142 games, with the regular season beginning this year on April 7 and ending on September 4. The Sally League set an all-time attendance record in 1994, with a total of 1,806,495, led by the Hickory Crawdads, who drew 270,880.

• • •

*The many well-known ballplayers who have played in the Columbus, Ga., area since 1926.*

# ALBANY POLECATS

## MONTREAL EXPOS

**B**uilt in 1993, this rather undistinguished ballpark features an uncovered grandstand with metal seats. The outfield wood fence is 20 feet high all around the park except in left. Last season was a trying one for both the team and the community, as a flood devastated the area. While Polecat Park was untouched by the surging Flint River, the city of Albany was not so fortunate. The flood waters made the ballpark an island; anyone wanting to reach it from downtown needed to take a 100-mile detour around the flood area. While waiting for the river to recede, the Polecats spent almost the entire month of July (28 games) on the road, including an eight-game "homestand" in Chattanooga, Tennessee.

### ◆ LOCAL AND TEAM HISTORY

Organized baseball came to Albany in 1906 when this city played one season in the Class D Georgia State League. The Albany Nuts, named in honor of this city's claim to being the world's pecan capital, subsequently joined the Class B Southeastern League (1926-28). In 1935-42 and '46-58, the Albany Travelers/Cardinals enjoyed much success while in the Class D Georgia-Florida League, finishing first eight times, including 1958, the team's final year in the league. The league itself disappeared for a few years, and then only two more seasons (1962-63) before disbanding. In 1911, the Albany Babies (so-named because this city was the smallest in the league) began a six-year association with the South Atlantic League. In 1992, 76 years after leaving the Sally, Albany rejoined the circuit. This season marks the Polecats' renewal of their ties to Montreal. This team previously was affiliated with the Expos in 1992 before switching to the Baltimore Orioles for the 1993-94 seasons.

Jack "Nap" Kloza, a native of Poland, batted .404 for Albany in 1927 to lead the Southeastern League. By contrast, he batted just .150 in 22 games as a major leaguer in 1931-32. Throughout the late '40s, Albany benefited from solid pitching. Three hurlers, Herb Moore (1946, 1.44 ERA), Jack Frisinger ('47, 2.18 ERA, 274 strikeouts) and Donald Stephens ('48, 221 strikeouts, 2.27 ERA), led the Georgia-Florida League in one or more categories. However, none ever reached the big

leagues. Jim Hickman, a member of the original New York Mets of 1962, spent 13 years in the majors. He played for Albany in 1956 and 1957. In '57, he topped the league with 26 home runs and 113 runs batted in. Wilmer "Vinegar Bend" Mizell, who won 13 games for the Pittsburgh Pirates in 1960, helping them win the National League pennant, also played for Albany. Chase Riddle managed Albany to a pennant in 1957 after leading the league in three batting categories (142 runs batted in, .355 average, 115 runs) as player-manager the season before. While Riddle played for first-place Jacksonville in 1954, he led the SAL with 28 home runs.

More recently, Cliff Floyd had an explosive year for the Polecats in 1992. He led the Sally with 97 runs batted in, 16 triples, nine intentional walks and 261 total bases while also batting .304 with 16 homers.

### ◆ BALLPARK EXTRAS

The Polecats feature good bratwurst and pork barbecue. You can also get some boiled peanuts. There is a grill in the left field picnic area where the Polecats also have a supervised baby-sitting area. The team's logo, a black-and-white polecat (skunk) on a black background, has proven to be among the minors' most popular logos, ranking in the top 15 in 1994.

### ◆ ATTRACTIONS

The River Day Festival is held in early April and features arts and crafts. The Chehaw Indian Festival takes place in late May. This festival has exhibits of Native American life and folkore.

For further information about these festivals and the Albany area, call the Chamber of Commerce, (912) 434-8700.

### ◆ DINING

Gus' BBQ, less than 10 minutes from the ballpark, is a popular local barbecue joint serving up a good selection of meats. 2347 Dawson Road, Albany, (912) 883-2404.

### ◆ LODGING

Holiday Inn is near the intersection of U.S. 19/82 and State Route 520, about 10 to 15 minutes from the ballpark. 2701 Dawson Road, Albany, (912) 883-8100/(800) HOLIDAY.

Holiday Inn Express is on U.S. 19/82, about five minutes from the park. 911 East Oglethorpe, Albany, (912) 883-1650.

### ◆ DIRECTIONS

From U.S. 19/82, take the Blaylock Street exit. The ballpark is just off Blaylock. Ample Parking is available for $1 per car. On-street parking is also an option.

## ◆ TICKET AND SCHEDULE INFORMATION

Most games are played at night, starting at 7:05 P.M. Sunday games begin at 5:05 P.M.

The Polecats' home opener is usually in early April, and the season ends in the first week of September.

Ticket prices: $6 box seats behind the dugouts; $5.50 box seats behind homeplate; $5 box seats down the baselines; $3.50 general admission, $2.50 seniors 55 and over and children 6 to 14. Children under 5 are free.

# ASHEVILLE TOURISTS

## COLORADO ROCKIES

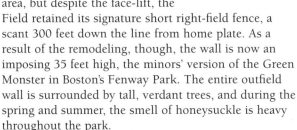

Opened in 1924, McCormick Field is one of the oldest operating minor-league ballparks in North America. A 1992 remodeling replaced the field's rickety wooden grandstand with one of steel and brick and expanded the concession area, but despite the face-lift, the Field retained its signature short right-field fence, a scant 300 feet down the line from home plate. As a result of the remodeling, though, the wall is now an imposing 35 feet high, the minors' version of the Green Monster in Boston's Fenway Park. The entire outfield wall is surrounded by tall, verdant trees, and during the spring and summer, the smell of honeysuckle is heavy throughout the park.

Looking up from the parking lot, you will notice that McCormick Field is on the side of a mountain. "There's not much level ground out here," according to General Manager Ron McKee, who has been with the Tourists since his days as a batboy in the early 1960s. Thanks to McKee and his commitment to preserving the best parts of McCormick Field, this ballpark has kept its distinctive character despite the extensive renovation. It remains a delightful place to watch a ballgame.

Detroit Tigers manager Sparky Anderson (who managed the Tourists to a first-place finish in 1968) fondly remembers McCormick Field and his time here: "The ballpark is up on a hill. It's [in] a pretty area—tremendous trees. Asheville was extra beautiful. I loved Asheville very much."

## ◆ LOCAL AND TEAM HISTORY

Pro baseball in Asheville dates back to 1897, when the city's team was called the Moonshiners. On April 3, 1924, the Asheville Skylanders opened McCormick Field by losing 18-14 to the Detroit Tigers in an exhibition game. Hall of Famer Ty Cobb hit one of the first home runs at the new ballpark during the contest.

Speaking of Cobb, he and the Tigers, plus other big-league teams such as the New York Yankees and the Brooklyn Dodgers, played several exhibitions in Asheville in the 1920s, 30s and 40s. The Dodgers and Jackie Robinson played two games here in 1948, the year after he broke baseball's color line.

During one visit to Asheville by the Yankees in 1925, Babe Ruth collapsed at the train station and was immediately taken to the team hotel under a doctor's care. The baseball world went into a panic as news of Ruth's infirmity spread. Rumors circulated that he had died. The reason for his collapse, speculated to be the flu, too many hot dogs or a surfeit of beer, was never determined and remains a mystery. Today, Ruth's so-called "Bellyache Heard 'Round the World" is part of Asheville's rich baseball history, one that also includes the Orioles' Cal Ripken Jr., who served as the Tourists' batboy when his father was the team's manager in the early 1970s.

**FAMOUS ALUMNI** Willie Stargell, Dave Righetti, Sparky Anderson, Mike Flanagan, Dave Concepcion, Tom Henke, Kenny Lofton, Orlando Miller, Craig Biggio and Andujar Cedeno all played here.

## ◆ BALLPARK EXTRAS

McCormick Field has a well-stocked souvenir shop to the right as you enter the ballpark. Check out Asheville's new logo, which debuted in 1994—a brown bear named Ted E. Tourist, decked out like his name suggests, wearing sunglasses and a flowered shirt while toting a bat and a suitcase. You can also buy a bottle of the team's private label wine, Championship White. Several food items at the concession stands are noteworthy, in particular a very good grilled chicken sandwich. Also, try the tangy chili dogs. If you sample the hot dogs without chili, be sure to at least put coleslaw on the bun—it's a North Carolina tradition.

## ◆ ATTRACTIONS

Asheville's most famous attraction is the extravagant Biltmore Estate, built by George Washington Vanderbilt. Self-guided tours allow you to visit the house, gardens designed by Frederick Law Olmsted and winery. The admission fee is $19.95 for adults and $15 for children aged 12 to 17. For information, call (704) 255-1700 or (800) 543-2961.

Because it's near the Blue Ridge Mountains, the Asheville area also features several attractions along the 470-mile scenic Blue Ridge Parkway, such as Mount Mitchell State Park, 35 miles northeast of the city, and containing the tallest peak east of the Mississippi River, and the Folk Art Center (704-298-7928), which displays a variety of local handicrafts for sale.

The Great Smoky Mountains National Park is just west of Asheville. Call the Visitor Center (615-436-1200) for information.

For more information about Asheville, call the Chamber of Commerce, (704) 258-6101.

## ◆ DINING

Cafe on the Square is about five minutes north of McCormick Field. This attractive restaurant serves a wide variety of items, ranging from burgers and pizza to pastas, seafood and grilled chicken. 1 Biltmore Street, (704) 251-5565.

Several national chain restaurants are located on Tunnel Road, north of McCormick Field and parallel to I-240.

## ◆ LODGING

American Court Motel, about a mile north of McCormick Field, is at 85 Merrimon Avenue, at exit 5A from I-240, (704) 253-4427/(800) 233-3582.

Best Western Asheville Central is at 22 Woodfin Street, exit 5A from I-240, (704) 253-1851/(800) 528-1234.

## ◆ DIRECTIONS

Take the Charlotte Street exit from I-240 and go south. The ballpark is about a mile away on your left. Parking is free but limited at McCormick Field, which has only a small lot. Fans are permitted to park in the lots of area businesses. To get a spot at the ballpark, it is best to come early.

---

**MCCORMICK FIELD**
**30 Buchanan Place**
**Asheville, NC 28801**
**(704) 258-0428**

Capacity: 3,500
LF 328, CF 406, RF 300

---

## ◆ TICKET AND SCHEDULE INFORMATION

Most games start at 7 P.M.; Sunday games start at 2 P.M. The Tourists' home opener is usually in early April, and the season ends in the first week of September.

Ticket prices: $6 box seats; $4 general admission, $3.50 students and seniors 65 and over, $2.50 children 3 to 12.

---

# AUGUSTA GREENJACKETS

## PITTSBURGH PIRATES

---

The Greenjackets will open the 1995 season in a new ballpark designed by a local architect who's taking his first crack at stadium construction. The park features a 40-foot-high scoreboard complete with a large illuminated picture of the team's logo. Approximately 3,000 seats are covered by a grandstand roof extending from third base around to first. Choosing a name for the new ballpark sparked a fair amount of local debate over the fall and winter. Many citizens liked the name Ty Cobb Stadium, in honor of the Georgia native who began his pro career in Augusta; others objected because of Cobb's unsavory reputation.

## ◆ LOCAL AND TEAM HISTORY

Augusta fielded various pro teams beginning in 1885 through the end of the 19th century. After the turn of the century, Augusta began its lengthy association with the South Atlantic League (1904-11, '14-17, '19-30, '36-42, '46-58, '62-63, '88-today), the only organized-baseball circuit this city has belonged to with the exception of a one-year membership in the Class D Palmetto League in 1931. Augusta was in first place when the Palmetto disbanded before the end of the '31 season. The Greenjackets began their current affiliation with the Pittsburgh Pirates in 1988.

Ty Cobb was 17 years old when he made his organized-baseball debut with Augusta in 1904. This future Hall of Famer was far from impressive in his first pro campaign, batting only .237 in 37 games. He was released early that season and finished out the remainder of the year with Anniston (Southeastern League) and Sheffield (Tennessee-Alabama League). The change of scenery must have appealed to Cobb, because he hit .302 overall for his new teams. In 1905, he came back to Augusta with a vengeance, batting .326 to lead the

Sally League. Ed Cicotte, one of the ballplayers banned from the game for life for his role in the 1919 Black Sox scandal, played here as well. He won 15 games in 1905, striking out 182 in 153 innings pitched. Curt Walker batted .304 in his 12-year big league career. As a 22-year-old rookie, he hit .278 for Augusta in 1919. Harry Smythe, an Augusta native, played 3½ seasons for his hometown team. In his 21-year career (1922-42, '46) Smythe amassed 306 victories, including more than 30 for Augusta and five for the National League's Phillies and Dodgers. His 301-221 lifetime minor-league record places him 19th on the all-time minors win list.

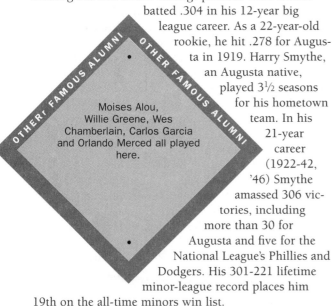

OTHER FAMOUS ALUMNI

Moises Alou, Willie Greene, Wes Chamberlain, Carlos Garcia and Orlando Merced all played here.

### ◆ BALLPARK EXTRAS

This new ballpark features the Greenjacket room, which is available for group functions and is furnished with photographs of former Augusta players. Featured concession items include grilled burgers, hot dogs and pizza. The team is also experimenting with a new, distinctively non-Southern food product, locally made bagels. Previously called the Pirates, the Greenjackets name and logo debuted in 1994 to much acclaim. According to the two companies that sell most minor-league baseball caps, Augusta's ranked No. 1 in sales. The team's name relates to the green jacket given to the winner of the Masters Golf Tournament here every April.

### ◆ ATTRACTIONS

A replica of a 19th-century paddle wheeler is available for cruises on the Savannah River. The fee is $6, $4 for children 3 to 11. For further information, call (706) 821-1300.

The Augusta/Richmond County Museum, housed in a former Civil War hospital, has several exhibits relating to that conflict, as well as ones on the American Revolution. Admission is $2, $1 for seniors over 65 and children 6 to 18. For further information, call (706) 722-8454.

For additional information about this area, call the Visitors' Bureau, (800) 726-0243.

### ◆ DINING

Sconyer's Barbecue, about 15 minutes from the ballpark, has great atmosphere and a wide selection of good menu items including chipped pork, chicken, chipped or sliced beef, ribs, tenderloin, coleslaw, potatoes and homemade barbecue sauce. After you're done eating, you won't need anything more for dessert than the mints available at the cash register. 2250 Sconyer's Way, (706) 790-5411.

### ◆ LODGING

Hampton Inn is 10 minutes away at exit 65 from I-20. (706) 737-1122/(800) 426-7866.

Best Western Bradbury Suites is 10 minutes away, across from the Georgia Medical College. (706) 733-4656/(800) 528-1234.

### ◆ DIRECTIONS

From I-20, take the Washington Road exit—the first Washington Road exit if you are coming from Atlanta and the second if from Columbia (S.C.). Stay on Washington for about three miles. Turn right on Broad Street. Turn left at the traffic light onto Millage Road. The ball park will be on your right, less than a mile away.

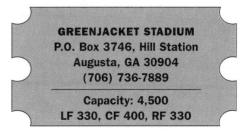

**GREENJACKET STADIUM**
P.O. Box 3746, Hill Station
Augusta, GA 30904
(706) 736-7889

Capacity: 4,500
LF 330, CF 400, RF 330

### ◆ TICKET AND SCHEDULE INFORMATION

Most games are played at night, starting at 7 P.M. Sunday games in April and May begin at 2:30 P.M.

The Greenjackets' home opener is usually in early April, and the season ends in the first week of September. Since the team is playing in a new ballpark, buying tickets on the day of the game, especially on weekends, could be difficult.

Ticket prices: $6 box seats; $4.50 reserved seats; $3.50 general admission. Seniors 65 and over and children 12 and under get a $1 discount on each ticket.

# CAPITAL CITY BOMBERS

## NEW YORK METS

Capital City Stadium is a comfortable, attractive ballpark right in the heart of Columbia's sporting community, between the Coliseum and Williams Brice Stadium. The Bombers' ballpark, built on a site where baseball has been played since 1927, underwent extensive renovations following the 1991 season. Capital City Stadium now features the Hard Ball Cafe, a triple-deck open-air picnic area behind third base and a supervised play area for kids close by. The grandstand is largely covered.

This stadium played a bit part in the football film *The Program*. Parts of the clubhouse were used in the movie while the rest of the ballpark was a staging ground for other parts of the production. The Bombers' groundskeeper has been something of a local celebrity ever since he played an assistant football coach in the movie.

### ◆ LOCAL AND TEAM HISTORY

From 1904 to '61, Columbia hosted a South Atlantic League franchise every year except for 13 seasons—1913, '18, '24, '31-35, '43-45, '58-59. In 1934, Columbia began the season in the Class B Piedmont League, but by June, the franchise had shifted to Asheville, North Carolina. Columbia rejoined the Sally in 1983 when the team began its current affiliation with the New York Mets.

Goose Goslin made his organized-baseball debut here in 1920. He hit .317 that year and returned the next season. In '21, Goslin helped Columbia win the pennant by leading the Sally League in runs (124), hits (214), runs batted in (131) and batting average (.390). Lloyd "Little Poison" Waner played the last of his three minor-league

*OTHER FAMOUS ALUMNI OTHER FAMOUS ALUMNI*

Joe Adcock and Dave Magadan played here.

seasons in Columbia in 1926. After batting .345, he was promoted to Pittsburgh the following year, when he hit .355, 25 points behind his older brother Paul, who won the National League batting title with a .380 average. Frank Robinson kept up with his future fellow Hall of Famers when he played here in 1954. That season, Robinson batted .336 with 25 home runs, 110 runs batted in and a league-leading 112 runs scored. Although he slumped in his return Columbia engagement the following year, playing in only 80 games while batting .263, Robinson made it to Cincinnati in 1956. There, he tied the record for home runs by a rookie (38) and began his 21-year big-league career.

Ted Kluszewski hit 279 home runs in his 15-year big-league career. But in 1946, he was just a rookie when he broke in with Columbia and led the league with a .352 average. Despite Big Klu's efforts, Columbia finished ½ game behind pennant-winning Columbus. More recently, Randy Myers was not yet a reliever when he played here in 1983. As a starter, Myers had a good season, with a 14-10 record and 3.63 ERA in a league-leading 28 starts. Gregg Jefferies played in 45 games over two seasons (1985-86) for Columbia, batting a combined .318. Butch Huskey was the main power threat in the SAL five seasons after Jeffries had moved on, topping the circuit with 26 home runs and 99 runs batted in while leading Columbia to a pennant.

### ◆ BALLPARK EXTRAS

A good selection of concession choices is available at the Hard Ball Cafe. Noteworthy items include chicken wings, grilled chicken sandwiches and nachos with chili and cheese. After the 1992 season, this franchise decided to adopt a different name with some local flavor. Discarding the old name—Columbia Mets—for the Capital City Bombers, the team had its new logo ready for the 1993 season. The name honors the 80 airmen who trained at Columbia Army Air Base for Doolittle's Raid, the first American bombing mission over Japan in World War II. One of the participants in that flight still lives in Columbia. In keeping with the team's name and logo, the top of the Hard Ball Cafe is called the Flight Deck and the team plays songs with a 1940s flavor at the ballpark and over the telephone to waiting callers.

### ◆ ATTRACTIONS

South Carolina State Museum, housed in a 19th-century textile mill, has several exhibits and displays on state history and industry. Admission is $4, $3 for senior citizens over 62, $1.50 for children 6 to 17. For further information, call (803) 737-4595.

The Woodrow Wilson home is where the former President was born. Admission is $3, $1.50 for students and military with identification. For further information, call (803) 252-1770.

For additional information about this area, call the Visitors' Bureau, (803) 733-8331.

### ◆ DINING

California Dreamin', about five minutes from the ballpark, is in a refurbished railroad station. Among the most interesting items here are marinated Kansas City steak, fresh fish and the California Dreamin' salad, which is a huge chef's salad. 401 S. Main Street, (803) 254-6767.

### ◆ LODGING

Holiday Inn Coliseum at USC is on Assembly Street, less than 10 minutes from the ballpark, (803) 799-7800/(800) HOLIDAY.

Columbia Marriott Hotel is downtown on U.S. 21, about 15 minutes from the ballpark. (803) 771-7000/(800) 443-6000.

### ◆ DIRECTIONS

I-126 turns into Elmwood Street. Stay on Elmwood and turn right on Assembly Street. You will see the ballpark on your right after about seven miles. Plentiful parking is available for $2. On-street parking is nearby.

> **CAPITAL CITY STADIUM**
> P.O. Box 7845
> Columbia, SC 29201
> (803) 256-4110
> ___
> Capacity: 6,000
> LF 330, CF 395, RF 330

### ◆ TICKET AND SCHEDULE INFORMATION

Most games are played at night, starting at 7:05 P.M. Sunday games and doubleheaders begin at 6:05 P.M.

The Bombers' season opener is usually in early April, and the season ends in the first week of September.

Ticket prices: $5.50 super gold box, with nameplates for season ticketholders; $5 super box, without the nameplates; $4.50 box seats, rows 6-10; $4 reserved seats and general admission. Seniors, children, military and students get $1 discount on all tickets.

# CHARLESTON ALLEY CATS

## CINCINNATI REDS

It is hard to miss Watt Powell's most prominent feature: a small hill behind the outfield fence. It slopes gradually upward in left, culminating in a rather steep peak behind the right-field wall. This lush hill, together with the railroad tracks that run between it and the park, form a highly attractive backdrop for the park, named after a popular local minor-league ballplayer. It was originally opened in 1916 as Exhibition Park before being completely rebuilt and renamed in 1948. Besides hosting the Alley Cats, this ballpark is also the home of the University of Charleston baseball team. The largely covered grandstand here is made of metal. Charleston's new ownership decided to put its own stamp on this franchise with a new moniker and logo, discarding the old nickname, Wheelers, after eight seasons.

### ◆ LOCAL AND TEAM HISTORY

Organized baseball first came here in 1910 when Charleston played in the Class D Virginia Valley League. Over the next nine decades, Charleston fielded teams in eight other leagues: Class D Mountain States (1911-12), Class D Ohio State (1913-16), Class C Middle Atlantic (1931-42), Class A Central (1949-51), Class AAA American Association (1952-1960), Class AAA International (1961, '71-83), Class A/AA Eastern (1962-1964) and Class A South Atlantic (1987-to present). The Alley Cats began their current affiliation with the Cincinnati Reds in 1990.

Exhibition Park, later renamed Kanawha Park, was a pitchers' delight with cavernous outfield dimensions of 466 feet to left center, 527 feet to center field and 528 feet to right. At one time, fans who did not take the streetcar to the game were allowed to park their cars

**OTHER FAMOUS ALUMNI**

Omar Moreno, John Candelaria, Rennie Stennett, Kent Tekulve, Terry Puhl, Denny Wailing, Ernie Whitt and Jim Bunning played here.

inside the ballpark's outfield fence. When the International League's Charleston Charlies played at Watt Powell Park from 1971 to '83, they were affiliated with the Pittsburgh Pirates, among other big-league teams. According to some local fans, there was a memorable ballgame here in the '70s when Dave Parker or Richie Zisk, depending on who is telling the story, hit two home runs in one ballgame. One of the homers allegedly carried over the right-field fence and landed in a boxcar of a passing train, a feat that Babe Ruth and Chuck Klein have been credited with in other times and other places.

Jim Kaat was 7-10 for Charleston in 1960 before moving up to Minnesota the next season. In 1962, Luis Tiant won seven of 15 decisions for Charleston while posting a 3.63 ERA. The following year, another future big-league pitching star, Tommy John, compiled a 9-2 record and 1.61 ERA for the Charleston Indians. During the 1970s, many future Pittsburgh Pirates played for Charleston. In Æ71, Richie Zisk led the league in runs batted in (109) while also batting .290 with 29 homers. The following year, Zisk returned to pace the IL with 26 four-baggers while also batting .306. In 1973, Dave Parker batted .317 with nine homers in 84 games before being promoted to Pittsburgh.

### ◆ BALLPARK EXTRAS

There is a picnic area in right field reserved for groups of 20 or more. The grill serves the best food in the ballpark, including sausages, burgers and pork-rib sandwiches. Hot dogs are available at the general concession stand. Alley Cat Amber, a beer made for the team by a local microbrewery, makes its debut in 1995.

### ◆ ATTRACTIONS

Sunrise Museums, housed in two historic houses, offer several hands-on exhibits and a planetarium. Admission is $2. For further information, call (304) 344-8035.

Tri-State Greyhound Park features dog racing. For more information, call (304) 776-1000.

For additional information about Charleston, call the Visitors Bureau, (304) 344-5075.

### ◆ DINING

The Anchor Restaurant, about 10 minutes from the ballpark, has a large selection of sandwiches, including the Anchor Boat, with roast beef or ham, banana peppers, onions, sour cream and cheese. Try some calzone or one of the good specialty pizzas, such as barbecue, chicken creole or vegetarian light. 4120 MacCorkle Avenue SE, (304) 925-5522.

### ◆ LODGING

Holiday Inn Downtown is located at exit 58C off I-64, about 15 minutes from the ballpark. (304) 344-4092/(800) HOLIDAY.

Ramada Inn is located at exit 56 off I-64, about 15 minutes from the ballpark. (304) 744-4641/(800) 228-2828.

### ◆ DIRECTIONS

From I-64, take the 35th Street Bridge exit. The ballpark is at the bottom of the ramp after you come off the highway. Drive right into the parking lot. Limited parking for $1 per car is available at the park. On-street parking in the surrounding area is also available.

---

**WATT POWELL PARK**
P.O. Box 4669
Charleston, WV 25304
(304) 925-8222

Capacity: 7,000
LF 335, CF 410, RF 345

---

### ◆ TICKET AND SCHEDULE INFORMATION

Most games are played at night, starting at 7:05 P.M. Sunday games begin at 2 P.M.

The Alley Cats' home opener is usually in early April, and the season concludes in the first week of September.

Ticket prices: $5 gold box seats; $4.50 blue reserved; $4 gold grandstand; $3.75 bleachers. Seniors 60 and over and children 12 and under receive $1 off the price of all tickets other than gold box seats.

# CHARLESTON RIVERDOGS

## TEXAS RANGERS

RIVERDOGS

This year marks the Riverdogs' final season in College Park. The ballpark, which was built in 1938, is aptly named since it is adjacent to the campus of The Citadel, South Carolina's collegiate military academy. The college's baseball team, the Bulldogs, plays its home games here. This old, intimate ballpark has several interesting features, including the deepest center field (436 feet) and shortest right-field line (290 feet) in the league. College Park's grandstand is one of the few remaining in the minors that consists almost entirely of wood. Down the right-field line, past the bullpen and picnic area, there's a replica of Durham Athletic Park's mechanical bull, which was made famous in the film *Bull Durham*. The Bull's unlikely presence in

Riverdog country is courtesy of Charleston general manager Rob Dlugozima, who is Durham's former GM.

### ◆ LOCAL AND TEAM HISTORY

Professional baseball in Charleston goes back to 1886 when the Seagulls played in the Southern League. Eighteen years later, Charleston joined the Class C South Atlantic League just in time to catch a glimpse of a 17-year-old named Tyrus Raymond Cobb, who played for the Augusta Tourists, one of Charleston's Sally League rivals. In 1907, Bugs Raymond, who later pitched six seasons in the big leagues, won 35 games for the Seagulls. This ranks Raymond sixth on the minors' all-time list for victories in a single season.

**OTHER FAMOUS ALUMNI** Willie Randolph, Carlos Baerga, Roberto Alomar, Steve Farr, Tony Pena, David Cone, Danny Jackson and Sandy Alomar Jr. all played here.

Hall of Famer Kiki Cuyler hit .309 for Charleston in 1922. One of his teammates that year was George Pipgras, who won 34 games for the New York Yankees of 1927 and '28.

### ◆ BALLPARK EXTRAS

College Park features several concession items worth trying, such as burritos, grilled burgers and grilled Italian sausage. According to the Riverdogs, the only National Association of Professional Baseball Leagues team with a canine nickname, in 1994 they ranked third in baseball-cap sales in the minors, thanks to Charleston's eye-catching, teal-and-purple cap and that feisty dog logo. Capitalizing on the popularity of its nickname, the team also has a mascot named Charlie the Riverdog, who "lives" in "The Dog Shack," a small wooden hut down the left-field line.

### ◆ ATTRACTIONS

There are plenty of non-baseball things to do in Charleston. Start downtown with some of this city's antebellum mansions. The Edmonston-Alston House, built in 1828, is located at 21 E. Battery Street. Admission is $5, with no charge for children 11 and under. For further information, call (803) 772-7171.

The Heyward-Washington House, dating to 1772, is located at 87 Church Street. Admission is $5 for adults, $3 for children 3 to 12. For further information, call (803) 722-0354.

While downtown, be sure to check out the Market Street market, which features many local foods and crafts.

You can also see where the Civil War began by taking a boat ride to the Fort Sumter National Monument. Admission to the fort is free, and boat fares are about $9. For further information, call (803) 883-3123. Across the channel from Fort Sumter is Fort Moultrie, which was used by Confederate soldiers in the Sumter bombardment. Admission to this fort is free. For information, call (803) 883-3123.

For Charleston tourist info, contact the Visitors' Bureau, (803) 853-8000.

### ◆ DINING

Charleston has a large number of excellent restaurants. For seafood, check out Hyman's, about five minutes away. Hyman's features a large variety of well-prepared fresh seafood, including scallops, shrimp and oysters. 215 Meeting Street, (803) 723-0233.

Louis' Charleston Grill, 10 minutes away, features local specialties and nightly jazz music. 224 King Street, (803) 577-4522.

### ◆ LODGING

Sheraton Inn Charleston is five minutes away on U.S. 17 South, overlooking the Ashley River. 170 Lockwood Drive, Charleston, (803) 723-3000/(800) 968-3569.

Howard Johnson Riverfront is also five minutes away on U.S. 17 South. 250 Spring Street, Charleston, (803) 722-4000/(800) 446-4656.

### ◆ DIRECTIONS

From I-26, take exit 219 A, Rutledge Avenue/The Citadel. Stay on Rutledge for about one mile. College Park will be on your right.

Parking at College Park is reserved almost exclusively for season ticketholders and handicapped fans. Unrestricted on-street parking is available in the area surrounding the ballpark.

**COLLEGE PARK**
P.O. Box 20849
Charleston, SC 29413
(803) 723-7241
_____
Capacity: 4,000
LF 315, CF 436, RF 290

### ◆ TICKET AND SCHEDULE INFORMATION

Most games are played at night, starting at 7. Sunday games begin at 5 P.M.

The Riverdogs' home opener is usually in mid-April, and the season ends in the first week of September.

Ticket prices: $6 box seats; $4 general admission, $3 for seniors 55 and over, children 12 and under, students and military with identification.

# COLUMBUS REDSTIXX

## CLEVELAND INDIANS

Anyone who has visited Golden Park before this year is in for a big surprise in 1995. This ballpark, originally built in 1926, is undergoing a nearly total face-lift in preparation for use in the 1996 Olympic Games as the women's fast-pitch softball competition venue. New grandstand seats, a six-level picnic deck and an eight-seat hot tub in right field are being added for the '95 season. A Stadium Club/Redstixx Room, down the right-field line, has a glass wall that faces onto the field. Inside you will find several pieces of Columbus baseball memorabilia donated by the team's historian. Besides the changes at the ballpark, the surrounding area is also being renovated. A river walk along the nearby Chattahoochee River and a convention center are being constructed. When you enter Golden Park, look for the large red-and-white sign welcoming you to the ballpark; it also lists the many famous players who have performed in Columbus over the years.

### ◆ LOCAL AND TEAM HISTORY

Pro baseball has been played here since 1885 when Columbus joined the Southern League as a charter member. The Columbus Babies played here in 1896 and 1897. In 1906, the Columbus River Snipes spent one season in the Class D Georgia State League. Over the next several decades, Columbus fielded teams in four other circuits: South Atlantic League (1909-17, '36-42, '46-57, '59, '91-to date), Class B Southeastern League (1926-30, '32), Class D Alabama-Florida League (1958) and Class AA Southern League (1964-66, '69-90).

Columbus has been used as a spring-training base by four big-league teams, Cincinnati Reds (1899 and 1912), St. Louis Cardinals (1913), and Pittsburgh Pirates (1917), Boston Braves (1919-20). Such future Hall of Famers as Al Lopez, Rabbit Maranville, Babe Ruth, Harry Heilmann, Joe "Ducky" Medwick, Dizzy Dean, and Grover Cleveland Alexander all played in exhibition games here.

In 1941, Golden Park was used by the St. Louis Cardinals as a spring-training base for their minor leaguers. During one exhibition game, future Hall of Famer Stan Musial, then a pitcher who had won 18 games the previous season for Daytona Beach, was on the mound against St. Louis and was rocked for long home runs by Johnny Mize and Terry Moore. Moore recently recalled what happened after the ballgame when he met with Cardinals vice president Branch Rickey. Their discussion about the minor-league pitcher whom St. Louis had faced that day turned out to have Hall of Fame implications for Stan Musial. "The funny thing was, he [Musial] also got a couple of hits against us. In the hotel, we talked to Branch Rickey. I said, 'He looks like a good hitter.' We [Cardinals' players] said we thought he'd be a better hitter than pitcher. That might have been the [reason for] of him becoming an outfielder. [When Musial was promoted to St. Louis later in 1941], Stan was sitting beside me in the dugout and said, 'You ought to remember me. You and Mize hit home runs off me.' "

Seven years later, Musial returned to Columbus as a St. Louis Cardinal outfielder and belted a 430-foot homer in an exhibition game.

Hall of Famer Enos Slaughter batted .325 with 118 runs batted in and a league-leading 20 doubles to help the Columbus Red Birds win the South Atlantic League championship in 1936. Three years later, fellow Hall of Famer Walter Alston batted .323 for Columbus. The following year, he became player-manager for Portsmouth of the Middle Atlantic League. In 1957, Bob Gibson, Columbus' third Hall of Famer, spent the month of August here. He posted a 4-3 record and 3.77 ERA in eight games for the Foxes.

Prior to the 1993 South Atlantic League All-Star game that was held here, Mike Brown, Columbus manager and also coach on the American League All-Star squad, was married in an elaborate ceremony at home plate. Several players, holding their bats aloft, formed an honor guard for Brown and his bride as they walked beneath the upraised bats and "down the aisle" to the altar at home plate.

### ◆ BALLPARK EXTRAS

The Redstixx have a larger concession menu in 1995 to complement their refurbished ballpark. Among the most noteworthy items are fried chicken, fried catfish, pork-chop sandwich and various grilled meats.

### ◆ ATTRACTIONS

The Confederate Naval Museum features several displays relating to the Confederacy's navy, including the

**OTHER FAMOUS ALUMNI**

Danny Heep, Ken Forsch, Willie Canate, Joe Sambito and Glenn Davis all played here.

remains of an ironclad warship. Donations are requested as the price for admission. For further information, call (706) 327-9798.

For additional information about Columbus, call the Chamber of Commerce, (706) 327-1566.

◆ **DINING**

Country's Barbecue, about 10 minutes from the ballpark, is an informal barbecue restaurant that serves water and ice tea in mason jars and has a variety of sauces on each table. The barbecued chicken is particularly good here. 1329 Broadway, (706) 596-8910.

◆ **LODGING**

La Quinta Inn is at exit 4 off I-185, about 20 minutes from the ballpark. (706) 568-1740/(800) 221-4731.

Holiday Inn South is at exit 1 off I-185, about 15 minutes from the ballpark. (706) 689-6181/(800) HOLIDAY.

◆ **DIRECTIONS**

From I-185, take exit 1/Victory Drive. Stay on Victory Drive for about eight miles. The ballpark will be on your left. Parking costs $1 in the expanded lot surrounding Golden Park.

**GOLDEN PARK**
P.O. Box 1886
Columbus, GA 31902
(706) 571-8866

Capacity: 5,000
LF 330, CF 415, RF 330

◆ **TICKET AND SCHEDULE INFORMATION**

Most games are played at night, starting at 7:15 P.M. Sunday games begin at 2:15 P.M.

The Redstixx' home opener is usually in early April and the season ends in the first week of September. Purchasing tickets on the day of the game should be no problem, but there may be a greater demand for tickets in 1995 because of excitement generated by the team's newly renovated ballpark.

Ticket prices: $6 box seats; $5 reserved seats; $4 general admission, $3 seniors 55 and over, children 3 to 12 and military with identification. Children under 3 are free.

# FAYETTEVILLE GENERALS

## DETROIT TIGERS

Almost from the day it opened in 1987, J.P. Riddle Stadium had the look of a temporary ballpark. Constructed quickly to be ready for Opening Day, the park's buildings were not even all in place when the first pitch was thrown. The initial plan was for J.P. Riddle to be subsequently expanded and upgraded, so there was no urgency about having everything in place. This explains why you will find a large dirt area behind the uncovered home-plate grandstand and temporary press box; the team always intended to add more seating and a permanent press box to this bare spot but never did so. Now, the Generals' expansion plans have shifted away from J.P. Riddle, which will close following the '95 season, to the team's new ballpark, which will open in 1996. Despite J.P. Riddle's somewhat unfinished character, this park, painted orange and blue like a miniature Tiger Stadium, still has a small-town intimacy that makes it worth a stop in its final season.

The Generals' name was selected in recognition of the large military presence in this area from Pope Air Force Base and Fort Bragg.

◆ **LOCAL AND TEAM HISTORY**

Since 1909, organized baseball has made several stops in Fayetteville. This city's teams belonged to five different minor leagues before joining the Sally in 1987. Despite its otherwise undistinguished history, though, Fayetteville's baseball background does include a largely unknown tidbit about Babe Ruth. In 1914, Ruth was a 19-year-old rookie with the AA Baltimore Orioles who used Fayetteville as a spring-training base that year. In one exhibition game in March, Ruth hit what is thought to be his first professional home run. A

**OTHER FAMOUS ALUMNI**

Smokey Burgess, Travis Fryman, Phil Clark, John Doherty and Milt Cuyler all played here.

plaque on Fayetteville's Highway 301 memorializes the feat. Ruth returned here in 1935, his final season in baseball, to participate in another exhibition game before approximately 15,000 fans, many of whom undoubtedly remembered the young player they had seen 21 years before.

### ◆ BALLPARK EXTRAS

Behind the third-base grandstand and the souvenir stand, you will find three batting cages available for fans to use and a children's play area. Behind the ticket booth is Kids Korner, featuring food and Generals souvenirs for children. At the concession stand, try the chili dogs with a choice of several toppings: onions, relish, coleslaw and sauerkraut. Corn dogs and pork barbecue are also available.

### ◆ ATTRACTIONS

The Museum of Cape Fear features several exhibits relating to the 19th-century life of local Native American tribes. For further information, call (910) 486-1330.

The 82nd Airborne Museum recounts this division's involvement in several historic battles in the two World Wars. For further information, call (910) 432-5307.

The John F. Kennedy Special Warfare Museum has several exhibits concerning the Green Berets and other special-forces units. For further information, call (910) 432-1533.

For additional information about this area, call the Fayetteville Chamber of Commerce, (910) 483-8133.

### ◆ DINING

Bruce & Mickey's is an informal, down-home restaurant, less than five minutes from the ballpark. A large selection of seafood is available. Check out the bargain-priced BBQ & Chicken special, featuring pulled-pork barbecue, moist and crispy fried chicken, good hush puppies and coleslaw. 2922 Legion Road, (910) 424-3688.

### ◆ LODGING

Comfort Inn I-95 is 15 minutes away, at exit 49 from I-95 at the intersection of state Routes 210 and 53. (910) 323-8333/(800) 566-5252.

Hampton Inn is also 15 minutes from the park, at exit 49 from I-95 at the intersection of state Routes 210 and 53. (910) 323-0011/(800) 426-7866.

### ◆ DIRECTIONS

From I-95, take exit 40. Take U.S. 301 North Business to Owen Drive. Turn left at Legion Road. After about one mile, the ballpark will be on your left. Parking is plentiful and free at the ballpark.

**J.P. RIDDLE STADIUM**
2823 Legion Road
Fayetteville, NC 28306
(910) 424-6500

Capacity: 4,200
LF 330, CF 400, RF 330

### ◆ TICKET AND SCHEDULE INFORMATION

Most games are played at night beginning at 7.

The Tigers' home opener is usually in early April, and the season ends in the first week of September.

Ticket prices: $6 box seats; $5 reserved seats; $3 general admission.

# GREENSBORO BATS

## NEW YORK YANKEES

Built in 1926, War Memorial is one of the oldest operating ballparks in organized baseball. Its entrance resembles a fortress, with two large turretlike structures on either side of the turnstiles. But while the ballpark has plenty of history behind it, War Memorial's most distinguishing feature is new. The Grandstand, a nine-level deck down the left-field line and also behind the outfield fence, opened in 1993. It features a 152-foot bar, private boxes, original seats from Yankee Stadium and Philadelphia's old Connie Mack Stadium and a sports-memorabilia collection. The atmosphere here, aided by music and karaoke contests that the ballplayers occasionally participate in after the game, can be quite festive. If you choose to watch the ballgame from here, you will get a good view of the action and be in the middle of several lively conversations. A smaller version of this area, called the Baby Grand, is located behind first base. The traditional grandstand, where fans sit behind home plate, is covered.

### ◆ LOCAL AND TEAM HISTORY

Organized baseball first came to town in 1902, when Greensboro was part of the Class C North Carolina League, which folded before the season ended. Over the next nine decades, this city had teams in seven other minor leagues: Class D Virginia–North Carolina (1905),

Class D Carolina Baseball Association (1908-12), Class D North Carolina State (1913-17), Class B, C, D Piedmont (1920-26, '28-34, '41-42), Carolina ('45-68), Class A Western Carolina (1979) and its progeny, Class A South Atlantic (1980-to date). The Bats began their current affiliation with the Yankees in 1990.

In 1905, night baseball came to Greensboro when an exhibition game was played at Cone Park. According to reports, a rubber ball was used that night to minimize the risk of injury to players and fans. In 1926, the Greensboro Patriots made their first year in the new War Memorial Stadium an auspicious one by capturing the Piedmont League championship. On May 15, 1966, in War Memorial, Rocky Mount's Dick Drago and Darrell Clark became the only pitchers in Carolina League history to toss back-to-back no-hitters, 5-0 and 2-0, respectively, in a doubleheader sweep over Greensboro. Drago went on to pitch 13 seasons in the majors.

**OTHER FAMOUS ALUMNI**

Stan Javier, Roberto Kelly, Curt Schilling, Bobby Murcer, Mel Stottlemyre, Mike Pagliarulo and Reggie Sanders all played here.

In 1913, Ernie Shore won 11 games while compiling a 2.05 ERA for the Patriots. Hall of Famer Johnny Mize was a 17-year-old rookie when he batted .194 for Greensboro in 1930. He came back the next season as a better ballplayer and saw his average rise almost 150 points, to .337. Fellow Hall of Famer Heinie Manush played fewer than 25 games for the Greensboro Red Sox at the end of his career in 1941 and '42.

Rube Eldridge began his 20-year pitching career with four seasons (1909-12) for Greensboro. In that time, he won 52 games while walking only 135 in 907 innings, a phenomenal average of 1.33 batters per nine innings. Eldridge returned to Greensboro in 1926 and also spent his final two seasons, 1930-31, pitching for the Patriots. When he retired, Eldridge had 285 career victories, all in the minor leagues.

Perhaps Greensboro's most famous alumnus, at least in the modern era, is Don Mattingly. The Yankees' first baseman led the league with a .358 average and 177 hits in 1980 while also driving in 105 runs, resulting in his selection as the Sally's MVP. One of Mattingly's teammates was Otis Nixon, who topped the circuit in walks (113) and stolen bases (67). Together, they helped the Hornets win the South Atlantic League championship.

◆ **BALLPARK EXTRAS**
There is a picnic area in left called Lefty's Grove. In

1994, the team dropped the name Hornets to distinguish it from the nearby NBA Charlotte Hornets. In keeping with the team's new name, souvenirs are sold at a stand known as The Bat Cave.

◆ **ATTRACTIONS**
The Blandwood Mansion was built in the 18th century and redesigned to resemble an Italian villa in 1844. Today, the house contains many of its original furnishings. Admission is $3, $2 for seniors over 60 and children 13 to 17, $1 for children under 13. For further information, call (919) 272-5003.

For additional information about Greensboro, call the Chamber of Commerce, (919) 275-8675.

◆ **DINING**
Stamey's, about 10 minutes from the ballpark, is a classic barbecue spot. The Stamey family's barbecue story, going back several decades, is told by pictures on the restaurant's walls. As for the food, the pork, coleslaw and hush puppies are all worth trying. 2206 High Point Road, (919) 299-9888.

◆ **LODGING**
Travelodge is at exit 217B off I-40, about 15 minutes from the ballpark. (919) 292-0200/(800) 255-3050.

Hampton Inn is at exit 217A off I-40, about 15 minutes from the ballpark. (919) 854-8600/(800) 426-7866.

◆ **DIRECTIONS**
From I-40, take U.S. 29 north to Sullivan Street. Stay on Sullivan and turn left on Lindsay Street. The ballpark is at the corner of Lindsay and Yanceyville streets. Parking at the ballpark is limited. Free parking is across the street, and area lots charge $1.50.

**WAR MEMORIAL STADIUM**
**P.O. Box 22093**
**Greensboro, NC 27420**
**(910) 333-2287**

**Capacity: 7,500**
**LF 330, CF 401, RF 327**

◆ **TICKET AND SCHEDULE INFORMATION**
Most games are played at night, starting at 7:15 P.M. Sunday games begin at 6:15 P.M.

The Bats' season opener is usually in early April, and the season ends in the first week of September.

Ticket prices: $7 box seats; $5 reserved seats; $4 general admission, $3 seniors, $2.50 children under 6.

# HAGERSTOWN SUNS

## TORONTO BLUE JAYS

This intimate, comfortable ball-park, circa 1931 and filled with quirks, will quickly grow on you. The outfield wall, the center-field portion of which could be called the Blue Monster given its color and height, is made of concrete. A chain-link barrier is in front of the right field wall, and behind it is the Suns' bullpen. Batting cages are kept behind another metal fence in left. There is a slight gradient in the outfield, so the center and left fielders must race uphill to chase down a fly ball hit into the gap in left center. Down the right-field line near the foul pole, you will notice a 16-by-12-foot mural. Completed in 1993, the painting honors Babe Ruth, whose sister Mary lived in Hagerstown for many years. Other Ruth relatives still reside in the community. Another painting, this one next to the third-base souvenir stand and done by local high school students in 1987, honors Hagerstown's baseball past. Located about 75 miles west of Baltimore and Washington, Hagerstown's population is about 35,000 and Municipal Stadium exudes small-town charm.

### ◆ LOCAL AND TEAM HISTORY

Organized baseball first came to the Hub City in 1915 when the Hagerstown Blues began 15 seasons (1915-18, '20-30) in the Class D Blue Ridge League. After that, Hagerstown teams spent time in three other circuits until baseball left town after the 1955 season: Class C Middle Atlantic, 1931; Class B Interstate, 1941-52; Class B Piedmont, 1953-55. Baseball returned in 1981 when the Hagerstown Suns joined the Carolina League as the Baltimore Orioles' Class A affiliate. In 1989, Hagerstown moved up to the AA Eastern League for four seasons. This city was temporarily

**OTHER FAMOUS ALUMNI**

Larry Sheets, John Habyan, Gregg Olson, Billy Ripken and Jeff Ballard all played here.

without baseball again following the '92 season when the franchise moved to Bowie, but the Myrtle Beach, South Carolina, Hurricanes stepped in to fill the void. They moved to Hagerstown, took the Suns' name for the 1993 season and joined the South Atlantic League. Hagerstown's affiliation with the Toronto Blue Jays began in 1993.

On June 23, 1950, the Trenton Giants broke the Interstate League's color line when the team's newest player, Willie Mays, sat on the bench for the final two innings of a game in Hagerstown against the Braves. In his organized-baseball debut the next night, Mays started the game against Hagerstown and went hitless.

Andy Bush was one of Hagerstown's best pitchers during his two stops here. In 1941, Bush was the Interstate League's top hurler, leading the circuit in wins (20), strikeouts (171) and ERA (1.61). In 1952, Bush returned to Hagerstown and posted a 16-9 record. Despite his minor-league success, Bush never pitched a single game in the majors. Pete Harnisch went 1-2 with a 2.25 ERA and Steve Finley batted .338 in 15 games here in 1987. Mike Mussina made his pro debut here in 1990, winning all three of his decisions. That same season, Ben McDonald also pitched for the Suns, albeit briefly. He was 0-1 with a 6.55 ERA.

### ◆ BALLPARK EXTRAS

The Suns offer several good concession items, including crab cakes and Coney Island hot dogs with chili, mustard and onions. Municipal Stadium also has "The Big Grill," which operates on weekends and major promotions. Check out the grilled burgers and Italian sausages. T.G. Gallagher, the team statistician and official scorer, has been involved with Hagerstown baseball for decades and is a local institution. He is also the unofficial musical impresario here, employing his eclectic collection of tapes to entertain the crowd between innings.

### ◆ ATTRACTIONS

Antietam National Battlefield is located in nearby Sharpsburg. The 960-acre park commemorates the 1862 Civil War Battle of Antietam. Admission is $2. For further information, call (301) 432-5124.

The Hager House, built in 1739, contains various period pieces and artifacts. Admission is $2.25, $1.25 for children 6 to 12. For further information, call (301) 739-8393.

For additional information about this area, call the Washington County Tourism Office, (301) 791-3130.

### ◆ DINING

Richardson's, about five minutes from the ballpark, is popular among locals for its buffet, offering hot and cold items for lunch or dinner. Try some ribs or fried chicken. The custard and chocolate pies are also good. On Dual Highway, (301) 733-3660.

Several national chain and fast-food restaurants are located on Dual Highway and Cleveland Avenue, within five minutes of the ballpark.

### ◆ LODGING

Holiday Inn is on Dual Highway, about five minutes from the ballpark. (301) 739-9050/(800) HOLIDAY.

Best Western Venice Inn is on Dual Highway, less than five minutes from the ballpark. (301) 733-0830/(800) 528-1234.

### ◆ DIRECTIONS

From I-70, take exit 32B, U.S. 40 West/Dual Highway. Stay on 40 for more than three miles. Turn left on Cleveland Avenue, at the Best Western. The ballpark will be about 100 yards ahead. Plenty of free parking is available.

```
MUNICIPAL STADIUM
P.O. Box 230
Hagerstown, MD 21741
(301) 791-6266
─────────────────────
Capacity: 5,140
LF 335, CF 400, RF 330
```

### ◆ TICKET AND SCHEDULE INFORMATION

Most games are played at night, starting at 7:05 P.M. Sunday games begin at 2:05 P.M.

The Suns' home opener is usually in early April, and the season ends in the first week of September.

Ticket prices: $6 box seats; $5 reserved seats; $4 general admission, $2 seniors plus students and military with identification.

## HICKORY CRAWDADS

**CHICAGO WHITE SOX**

Since the first Crawdad was spotted here in 1993, this team has taken Hickory  and the South Atlantic League by storm, leading the circuit in attendance in '93 (278,198, an all-time Sally record) and '94. L.P. Frans Stadium is an attractive ballpark built in a small valley surrounded by a highly scenic background of trees and a Blue Ridge Mountain range visible beyond the two-tiered, 30-foot-high outfield wall. L.P. Frans' outfield scoreboard, though, is large enough to bring you back to baseball from any bucolic reverie you might experience from gazing at the scenery. The stadium's entrance is built of brick and features an appealing V-shaped gate with three vaulted arches that fans pass under to enter the park. The largely covered grandstand is made of concrete.

### ◆ LOCAL AND TEAM HISTORY

When the Crawdads' franchise moved to Hickory from Gastonia, North Carolina, for the 1993 season, this marked the first time an organized-baseball team had been based in this community since 1960, when the Rebels completed the second of two years (1952, '60) in the Class D Western Carolina League. Hickory fielded teams in two other Class D leagues, Tar Heel (1939-40, '53-54) and North Carolina State (1942, '45-50). Hickory began its current affiliation with the White Sox in 1993.

Perhaps the most historic moment in Hickory's baseball past came four years before this city even had its own team. On April 11, 1935, the New York Giants and the Cleveland Indians played an exhibition game here. Residents were treated to watching future Hall of Famers Mel Ott, Travis Jackson, Carl Hubbell, Earl Averill, Walter Johnson (Indians manager) and Bill Terry (Giants player-manager). About 5,000 fans braved intermittent rain and saw New York beat Cleveland 10-6.

D.C. "Pud" Miller was probably Hickory's greatest player ever. He hit 69 homers for the Hickory Rebels in his two seasons (1950-51) here, including 40 in '51, when he was the team's player-manager and won the North Carolina State League's Triple Crown by also leading the circuit with an amazing .425 average (best in baseball that year) and 136 runs batted in. The previous season Miller's .369 batting average for Hickory was No. 1 in the league. Miller slammed 268 four-baggers in his 12-year minor-league career but never played in the majors.

One of Miller's teammates in 1951 was Norman Small (336 home runs in his minor-league career), who batted .340 with 127 runs batted in and a league-leading 35 doubles. Despite this offensive firepower, the Rebels finished second in 1951 and were swept four games to none by the Statesville Owls in the first round of the playoffs.

### ◆ BALLPARK EXTRAS

There is a large picnic area with a good view of the diamond down the left-field line. In right, check out the Crawdads' Cafe, an enclosed restaurant that serves a variety of sandwiches and appetizers. At the concession stands, foot-long hot dogs, burritos and pork barbeque are available. While you're here, check out the Crawdads' logo, one of the most popular in the minor leagues. It proved to be a hot seller even before the team played its first game. Hickory sold out of the initial shipment of a few hundred hats within a matter of days during the winter of 1993. The team has a well-stocked souvenir shop just to the left of where fans enter the ballpark.

◆ **ATTRACTIONS**

Catawba Science Center has several hands-on exhibits. Admission is free. For further information, call (704) 322-8169.

For additional information about Hickory, call the Catawba County Chamber of Commerce, (704) 328-6111.

◆ **DINING**

McGuffey's, about 10 minutes from the ballpark, is a comfortable bar and restaurant with a wide selection of burgers, salads and main courses. 1350 Highway 321 NW, Hickory, (704) 327-6600.

◆ **LODGING**

Red Roof Inn is located at exit 125 off I-40, about 15 minutes from the ballpark. (704) 323-1500/(800) THE-ROOF.

Hampton Inn is located at exit 125 off I-40, about 15 minutes from the ballpark. (704) 323-1211/(800) HAMPTON.

◆ **DIRECTIONS**

From I-40, take the State Route 321 exit. Go north towards Lenoir on 321 for about three miles. Follow signs to the ballpark and turn left on Clement Boulevard. The ballpark will be on your right in less than a mile. There is plenty of parking available for $1.

---

**L.P. FRANS STADIUM**
**P.O. Box 1268**
**Hickory, NC 28603**
**(704) 322-3000**

**Capacity: 5,100**
**LF 330, CF 401, RF 330**

---

◆ **TICKET AND SCHEDULE INFORMATION**

Most games are played at night, starting at 7:30 P.M. Sunday games in April and May begin at 2 P.M., with 6 P.M. starts the rest of the season.

The Crawdads' home opener is usually in early April, and the season ends in the first week of September. Purchasing tickets on the day of the game could be difficult on selected weekends, holidays and major promotional events, given the team's popularity.

Ticket prices: $6.25 box seats; $5.25 reserved seats; $4.25 general admission, $3.25 seniors.

# MACON BRAVES

## ATLANTA BRAVES

Located in a city park, this ballpark was built in 1929, making it among the oldest in organized baseball. Befitting its historic past, Luther Williams was the setting for the film *'Bingo Long and the Traveling All-Stars and Motor Kings*. In order to satisfy the new ballpark standards pursuant to the Professional Baseball Agreement, the Braves are upgrading the facilities by adding rest rooms and improving the teams' clubhouses. Those entering the park are greeted by a large sign that at first glance appears to have a prominent misspelling: "Macon Base Ball Park." "Base ball" is the way the word was spelled in the 19th century and, according to the Braves, in Macon as late as the 1940s. The concrete grandstand here is covered.

◆ **LOCAL AND TEAM HISTORY**

Organized Baseball in Macon goes back to 1904 when this city began its long, sporadic association (1904-17, '23-30, '36-42, '46-60, '62-63, '80-87, '91-to present) with the South Atlantic League. Macon teams have also spent several seasons in three other minor leagues: Class A Southeastern (1932), Class AA Southern Association (1961) and Class AA Southern League (1964, '66-67). The present franchise moved to Macon from Sumter, South Carolina, before the 1991 season. After the move, the team continued its affiliation with the Atlanta Braves.

Perhaps the most historic game in Macon's baseball history occurred in 1962, when the Macon Peaches beat the Greenville Dodgers 32-5. That score set a new Sally record for most runs scored in a game by one team. The Peaches had 28 hits that night, including six by a 20-year-old second baseman named Pete Rose. Rose, Art Shamsky and Larry Himes all hit home runs, and Tommy Helms had four hits. Of the seven pitchers used by Greenville that night, two were infielders and one was a catcher.

Hall of Famer Al Lopez batted .326 for the Macon Peaches in 1928 while also belting 14 home runs. In 1962, Rose tore up the Sally, leading the loop in triples (17) while also batting .330 and driving in 71 runs. One of his teammates was Tommy Helms, who topped the league with 195 hits. Helms would later join Rose on the Cincinnati Reds, a team Helms also managed in

1988 and '89. The next season, Tony Perez batted .309 for the Peaches while Lee May hit 25 home runs for Macon in 1964, driving in a league-best 110 runs. Al Oliver, who amassed 2,743 hits in the big leagues, batted just .222 in 38 games for Macon in 1967. Vince Coleman set an all-time organized-baseball record while a Macon Peach in 1983 when he stole 145 bases.

### ◆ BALLPARK EXTRAS
A picnic area with a grill is behind third base. Among the best concession items here are the bratwurst and the barbecue sandwiches, the latter courtesy of a local barbecue restaurant.

### ◆ ATTRACTIONS
Harriett Tubman Historical and Cultural Museum features several displays and exhibits relating to the history of African-Americans. Admission is free. For further information, call (912) 743-8544.

For additional information about Macon, call the Visitors' Bureau, (912) 743-3401.

### ◆ DINING
Len Berg's, about 10 minutes from the ballpark, serves up down-home food in an informal atmosphere. Try some turkey and dressing plus a slice of macaroon pie. Old Post Office Alley, (912) 742-9255.

### ◆ LODGING
Comfort Inn North is located at exit 54 off I-75, about 15 minutes from the ballpark. (912) 746-8855/(800) 4-CHOICE.

Radisson Hotel Macon is located at the Spring Street exit off I-16, about 10 minutes from the ballpark. (912) 746-1461/(800) 333-3333.

When calling either hotel, ask for the Macon Braves' special rate.

### ◆ DIRECTIONS
From I-16, take exit 4. Turn right on Coliseum Drive and go to the first light. Turn left on Riverside and stay on this street until you reach the ballpark. From the east, turn left on Coliseum and follow the rest of the above directions. Free parking is available at the ballpark.

**LUTHER WILLIAMS FIELD**
P.O. Box 4525
Macon, GA 31208
(912) 745-8943
_____
Capacity: 3,750
LF 338, CF 402, RF 338

### ◆ TICKET AND SCHEDULE INFORMATION
Most games are played at night, starting at 7 P.M. Sunday games and doubleheaders begin at 2 P.M. and 6:30 P.M., respectively.

The Braves' home opener is usually in early April, and the season ends in the first week of September.

Ticket prices: $6 box/reserved seats; $5 general admission, $4 seniors and military with identification, $3 children 5 to 12. Children under 5 are free.

## PIEDMONT PHILLIES

### PHILADELPHIA PHILLIES

Groundbreaking for the ballpark began in October 1994, shortly after this franchise left Spartanburg, South Carolina, after the '94 season ended. The grandstand here is uncovered, and the seats are made mostly of molded plastic. Lake Fisher is visible behind the third-base bleachers.

### ◆ LOCAL AND TEAM HISTORY
It has been more than 50 years since this city had its only previous organized-baseball team. From 1939 to '41, the Kannapolis Towelers, whose name relates to one of the products made by this ballpark's namesake, played in the Class D North Carolina State League. In '40 and '41, the Towelers won the circuit's regular season title but lost each season in the playoffs. In the 1950s, Kannapolis was the home of several semipro teams consisting of workers from nearby textile mills.

### ◆ BALLPARK EXTRAS
The ballpark is still being built, and concessions have not yet been determined. The team will hold a Name-the-Team Contest for fans to select a new nickname in time for the 1996 season.

### ◆ ATTRACTIONS
Cannon Village is located downtown and features several buildings built in early-20th-century style. Free guided tours of the nearby Fieldcrest Cannon plant are available. For further information, call (704) 938-3200.

For additional information about Piedmont, call the Chamber of Commerce, (704) 932-4164.

### ◆ DINING
Several national chain and fast-food restaurants are

located on Highway 29, about 10 minutes from the ball-park.

### ◆ LODGING

Best Western Lake Norman is in nearby Cornelius off I-77, about 20 minutes from the ballpark. (704) 896-0660/(800) 528-1234.

Hampton Inn Lake Norman is also in Cornelius off I-77, about 20 minutes from the ballpark. (704) 892-9900/(800) 426-7866.

### ◆ DIRECTIONS

From I-85, take exit 63. Take Lane Street west to China Grove. Turn right on China Grove, go to the next stop sign and turn right on Moose Road. The ballpark will be about a mile away on the right. Parking is plentiful.

---

**FIELDCREST CANNON STADIUM**
**P.O. Box 322**
**Kannapolis, NC 28082**
**(704) 932-3267**

---

**Capacity: 4,600**
**LF 330, CF 400, RF 310**

---

### ◆ TICKET AND SCHEDULE INFORMATION:

Most games are played at night. For game times, contact the Phillies.

The Phillies' home opener will be in early April, and the season will end in the first week of September. Purchasing tickets on the day of the game may be difficult, because Kannapolis had been without pro baseball for more than 50 years before the Phillies came to town.

Ticket prices: $7.50 premium box seats; $6.50 box seats; $5.50 reserved seats; $4.50 general admission. Seniors 65 and over and children 12 and under get a $1 discount for reserved and general-admission seating.

# SAVANNAH CARDINALS

### ST. LOUIS CARDINALS

In a league of special ballparks, Grayson Stadium, the country's largest Class A park, more than holds its own with the competition. Opened in 1941, this stadium's many unique qualities start outside the front entrance, which is surrounded by tall, verdant trees dripping with kudzu and Spanish moss. Once inside, find a place in the grandstand, a mix of steel and wood, with seating primarily in long, wooden benches. Look out to the pine-tree-framed brick outfield wall and you will see why Grayson is considered a hitters' ballpark—the left- and right-field walls are only 290 and 310 feet, respectively, from home plate. Behind the left-field wall, there's a sight uncommon in minor-league ballparks—outfield bleachers. Similar concrete bleachers can also be found down the right-field line, proof that high school football used to be played here. In fact, the old football press box still remains in the right-field stands.

### ◆ LOCAL AND TEAM HISTORY

Pro baseball made its Savannah debut in 1886. In 1904, Savannah became a charter member of the original South Atlantic League. In addition to a three-year stint (1926-28) in the Class B Southeastern League, this city belonged to the AA Southern League (1968-83) before joining the SAL in 1984.

Shoeless Joe Jackson was Savannah's leading hitter 11 years before he was banned from baseball for his role in the 1919 Black Sox scandal. Jackson led the Sally in 1909 with a .358 average, third among all minor leaguers that year. Hall of Famer Fred Clarke batted .311 for Savannah in 1894. A mere 68 years later, a young pitcher named Dave DeBusschere appeared in 15 games for Savannah, winning 10 of 11 decisions while compiling a 2.49 ERA. DeBusschere, after pitching for the Chicago White Sox in 1962 and '63, left baseball to concentrate on his NBA career with the Detroit Pistons and later, the New York Knicks. Today, he is a member of the Basketball Hall of Fame. Curt Flood, who could be considered the father of baseball free agency because of his court challenge to the reserve clause, hit .299 with 14 home runs and 82 runs batted in for Savannah in 1957.

**OTHER FAMOUS ALUMNI** Dale Murphy, Donn Clendenon, Milt Thompson, Steve Bedrosian and Bernard Gilkey played here.

### ◆ BALLPARK EXTRAS

In the left-field picnic area you will find Big Will's Grill, which features some of this park's best concession items, grilled Italian sausage and burgers. While waiting for Big Will to cook your food, take a few cuts in the nearby batting cage (12 balls for $2). The Cardinals have a "Best Seat in the House" contest in which two fans, anointed King and Queen for the night, are selected to watch the game from a couch in the grandstand behind home plate, where they are served $10 worth of complimentary food.

### ◆ ATTRACTIONS

In the historic district, check out the Owens-Thomas House and Museum, 124 Abercorn Street, where the Marquis de Lafayette stayed in 1825. Admission is $5, $4 for seniors, $3 for students with identification and $2 for children 6 to 12. For further information, call (912) 233-9743.

The Savannah History Museum, behind the Visitors' Center at 303 Martin Luther King Jr. Boulevard, offers exhibits about the city's past, including the Revolutionary War battle fought on this site in 1779. Admission is $3, $2.50 for seniors over 55 and $1.75 for children 6 to 12. For further information, call (912) 238-1779.

The Fort Pulaski National Monument, about 15 miles outside Savannah, offers displays relating to the Fort's role in the Civil War and the War of 1812. Admission is $2. Seniors over 62 and children under 17 are free. For further information, call (912) 786-5787.

For more information about Savannah, contact the Visitors' Center, (912) 944-0455.

### ◆ DINING

There are many good restaurants in downtown Savannah. One is The Shrimp Factory, about 15 to 20 minutes away from the ballpark, which features a large variety of well-prepared shrimp and other seafood dishes. 313 E. River Street, (912) 236-4229.

There are several national chain and fast-food restaurants on State Route 204 (Abercorn Street) south of the ballpark.

### ◆ LODGING

La Quinta Inn is about five miles south of the historic district, about five minutes from the park. 6805 Abercorn Street, Savannah, (912) 355-3004/(800) 531-5900.

Fairfield Inn is about five miles south of the historic district, about 15 to 20 minutes from the park. 2 Lee Boulevard, Savannah, (912) 353-7100/(800) 348-6000.

### ◆ DIRECTIONS

Take the I-16 exit from I-95 and exit at 37th Street. Turn right on Abercorn Street, (State Route 204). Stay on Abercorn and turn left on Victory Drive, U.S. 80. The ballpark will be on your right after about two miles. There is plenty of free parking.

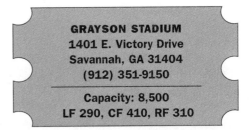

GRAYSON STADIUM
1401 E. Victory Drive
Savannah, GA 31404
(912) 351-9150

Capacity: 8,500
LF 290, CF 410, RF 310

### ◆ TICKET AND SCHEDULE INFORMATION

Most games are played at night, starting at 7:15. Doubleheaders start at 6:15 P.M., while Sunday games begin at 2 P.M.

The Cardinals' home opener is usually in early April, and the season ends in the first week of September.

Ticket prices: $5.50 box seats; $4.50 reserved seats; $3.75 general admission; $3.00 students under 18, adults 55 and over and military with identification.

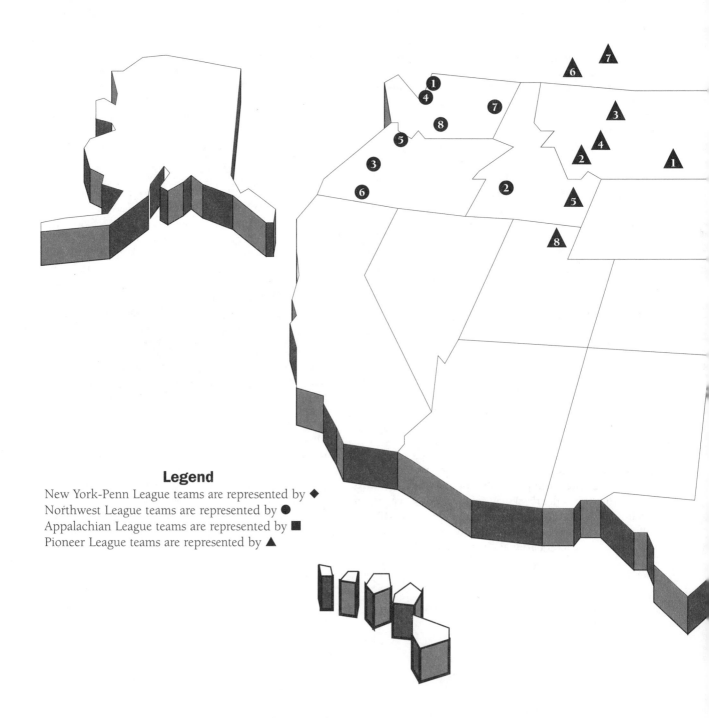

### Legend

New York-Penn League teams are represented by ◆
Northwest League teams are represented by ●
Appalachian League teams are represented by ■
Pioneer League teams are represented by ▲

## SHORT SEASON A

### NEW YORK-PENN LEAGUE

1. Auburn Astros/Auburn, N.Y.
2. Batavia Clippers/Batavia, N.Y.
3. Elmira Pioneers/Elmira, N.Y.
4. Erie Sea Wolves/Erie, Penn.
5. Hudson Valley Renegades/Beacon, N.Y.
6. Jamestown Jammers/Jamestown, N.Y.
7. New Jersey Cardinals/Augusta, N.J.
8. Oneonta Yankees/Oneonta, N.Y.
9. Pittsfield Mets/Pittsfield, Mass.
10. St. Catharines Stompers/
    St.Catharines, Ont.
11. Utica Blue Sox/Utica, N.Y.
12. Vermont Expos/Winooski, Vt.
13. Watertown Indians/Watertown, N.Y.
14. Williamsport Cubs/Williamsport, Penn.

### NORTHWEST LEAGUE

1. Bellingham Giants/Bellingham, Wash.
2. Boise Hawks/Boise, Idaho
3. Eugene Emeralds/Eugene, Ore.
4. Everett Aquasox/Everett, Wash.
5. Portland Rockies/Portland, Ore.
6. Southern Oregon Athletics/Medford, Ore
7. Spokane Indians/Spokane, Wash.
8. Yakima Bears/Yakima, Wash.

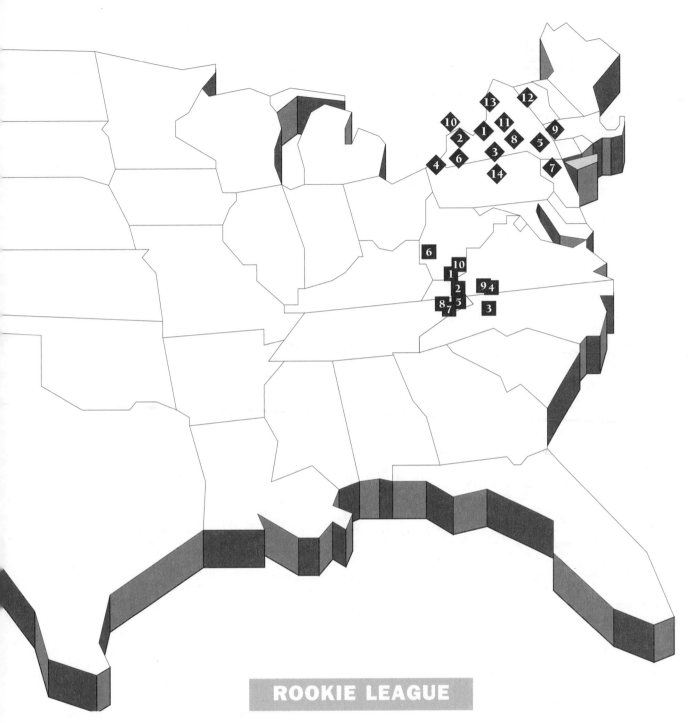

## ROOKIE LEAGUE

### APPALACHIAN LEAGUE

1. Bluefield Orioles/Bluefield, W.Va.
2. Bristol White Sox/Bristol, Va.
3. Burlington Indians/Burlington, N.C.
4. Danville Braves/Danville, Va.
5. Elizabethton Twins/Elizabethton, Tenn.
6. River City Rampage/ Huntington, W.Va.
7. Johnson City Cardinals/
   Johnson City, Tenn.
8. Kingsport Mets/Kingsport, Tenn.
9. Martinsville Phillies/Martinsville, Va.
10. Princeton Reds/Princeton, W.Va.

### PIONEER LEAGUE

1. Billings Mustangs/Billings, Mont.
2. Butte Copper Kings/Butte, Mont.
3. Great Falls Dodgers/Great Falls, Mont.
4. Helena Brewers/Helena, Mont.
5. Idaho Falls Braves/Idaho Falls, Idaho
6. Lethbridge Mounties/Lethbridge, Alta.
7. Medicine Hat Blue Jays/
   Medicine Hat,Alta.
8. Ogden Raptors/Ogden, Utah

# MINOR LEAGUE MEMORIES

## HAGERSTOWN

*Baltimore Orioles assistant director of player development Don Buford recalls a decision he made while managing the Hagerstown Suns in 1992 that had potentially serious implications for the Buford family.*

"My son [Damon Buford] was playing for us. We were losing the game by one run. This was the bottom of the ninth inning. We had the bases loaded. I pinch-hit for [my son]. [Pinch hitter] Paul Carey got a base hit and we won the ballgame. In discussing [it] with [Damon] afterward, I said, 'This can happen to you. I want you to understand that I felt maybe you would have gotten a hit, too. But I also did it for the entire ballclub. I had a left-handed hitter on the bench that could hit against a right-handed pitcher who to me, [and Carey] had a better chance of getting a base hit.' He took it very well."

## GREENSBORO

*In 1949, Leo "Muscle" Shoals led all of organized baseball, including the big leagues, with 55 home runs. He recalls one Sunday-afternoon game from that season in Greensboro when he barely missed hitting four homers in a row:*

"First time up, I doubled. Then I hit three successive home runs. I come up for the next time. We were winning by 11 to something. There was a big crowd there. The people wanted another home run. They stood up and cheered me on. I hit a pitch harder than any ball I had hit. There was a clock on top of the scoreboard. It hit the corner of the clock. Six feet either way would have been a home run. I went into my home run trot. [But] it bounced back! I got a single."

## ASHEVILLE

*Baltimore Orioles pitching coach Mike Flanagan, who played 18 years in the big leagues, recalls his 1974 season in Asheville:*

"To me, it was the breaking point of my career. [Cal] Rip[ken] Sr. was the manager. I remember coming in and there were a number of left-handers ahead of me. I won six games with Rip that summer. I was in the big leagues the next September. After you play 15, 16 years in the big leagues, you forget some of the games, some of the things that happened. But the games [in Asheville] are ingrained in there—the names of the players that played against us and for us, the towns. I remember some of those games more vividly than big-league games because [I was] making the steps. It was a learning experience."

## SAVANNAH

*In 1962, Don Buford, today a member of the Baltimore Orioles' Hall of Fame, batted .323 for the Savannah White Sox. One particular game from that season stands out very vividly in his mind:*

"We had a gentleman named Joe Shipley, a right-handed pitcher who threw pretty hard. We were losing one ballgame, and he came in. There was a home run hit by a previous batter, which meant, the pitcher was already angry in the first place. I'll never forget that the [next] hitter got into the batters' box and [Shipley] was ready to pitch. The batter stepped out, raised his hand [for] time, and started to dig a hole so that he could have better footing. The pitcher got ready again and [the batter] called time for a second time. He got back into the box, and the first pitch to this batter hit him right on the hip. The ball fell right down by his foot. The batter went to first base. Now he's on first and Joe Shipley's in a stretch. He threw over to first base and hit the batter almost in the identical spot and the ball fell right there. I'll never forget [Shipley] yelling, 'If you want to dig a hole, I'll bury you in it.' "

## HICKORY

*Chris Mader, who played for the Hickory Crawdads in 1993 and 1994, gives the ballplayer's perspective on all the new, eye-catching logos, including the Crawdads', that are sweeping the minor leagues:*

"It's a strange logo. The first time I saw it—I'm from New England—I thought it was a lobster. It's obviously strange but that's the way the minor leagues are. You've got the Polecats, the Redstixx. There are so many names, and it's a lot of fun. You turn around and you also get uniforms that are really good-looking. Everybody wants these hats."

# NEW YORK–PENN LEAGUE

I n 1939, the PONY (Pennsylvania, Ontario, New York) League was formed with six teams. Seventeen years later, the Class D PONY became the New York–Penn League, which was transformed into a Class A circuit in 1963. The short-season format was instituted four years later. Today, there are 14 teams scattered mainly throughout upstate New York, but also in Pennsylvania, Ontario, Massachusetts, Vermont and New Jersey. Each team plays 76 games, with the regular season beginning June 16 and ending September 2. In 1994, the New York–Penn League set an all-time attendance record, drawing 952,718 fans.

• • •

*The bust of Edward Joseph Dunn before it was stolen from atop its pedestal at the Elmira ball park bearing his name.*

# AUBURN ASTROS

## HOUSTON ASTROS

The original Falcon Park was one of the oldest ballparks in the minors, having been built in 1926, but it was torn down in the off-season and has been rebuilt on the same site and bears the same name. The new $3.5 million stadium features all-new facilities, from the grandstands and the restrooms to the field and the concessions. The original project was planned to comply with the NAPBL requirements, but as club president Mike Chamberlain says, "We've gone way beyond that now." Funds came from the private sector plus city, county and state coffers.

One of the high points of the 1994 season came following the final out of the team's last home game, the night cap of a doubleheader, around midnight on August 28. A bulldozer came plowing through the center-field fence and dropped its blade on the pitcher's mound to signal the end of an era—and the beginning of another for Auburn baseball.

The town of Auburn holds an unusual distinction, having been the site—in 1905—of the first execution by electric chair. There is no truth to the rumor that it was a manager in the hot seat.

### ◆ LOCAL AND TEAM HISTORY

Pro baseball has been played here for more than 100 years. In the 1870s, Auburn was a charter member of two minor-league circuits. The Auburn Maroons played in the New York State League in the 1890s. After the turn of the century, this city spent time in three minor leagues before joining the New York–Penn League in 1958.

Baseball left town after the 1980 season but returned in 1982, when Auburn rejoined the league and began its current affiliation with Houston. During the early 1960s, when Auburn was a New York Mets' farm team, several of the players who would have pivotal roles in the Mets 1969 World Series victory played here. In 1962, future Mets' first baseman Ed Kranepool hit .351, while in '63, Cleon Jones batted .360 in 14 games. Tug McGraw posted a 1.89 ERA in 19 innings pitched in 1964. Two years later, Jerry Koosman led the league with a 1.38 ERA while also winning 12 of 19 decisions. In 1971, Jack Maloof set an all-time New York–Penn League record with a .402 average, No. 2 in organized

baseball that season. He also topped the circuit with 57 runs scored for the second-place Auburn Twins. Three years later, Jorge Lebron, a 14-year-old short-stop, played two games for Auburn, making him the second-youngest player in organized-baseball history.

**OTHER FAMOUS ALUMNI OTHER FAMOUS ALUMNI**

Kenny Lofton, Jim McAndrew, Mel Stottlemyre, James Mouton, Brian Williams and Lonnie Smith played here.

### ◆ BALLPARK EXTRAS

According to club president Mike Chamberlain, "The ballpark itself will be the reason people come flocking." With its capacity only increased from 1,800 to 2,500, it's clear that Falcon Park is a cozy spot, and its family and community-focused promotions reflect that.

### ◆ ATTRACTIONS

Emerson Park, on the north bank of Owasco Lake, offers swimming, boating and fishing as well as a playground and small amusement park for the kids. There are two bathing beaches staffed by lifeguards, as well as the lake, which features trout, bass, northern pike and perch for fishermen. Also on the grounds are the Cayuga County Agricultural Museum, which features a look at farm life dating as far back as the Civil War, and the Iroquois Museum, which displays Indian artifacts. Route 38A, (315) 253-5611.

The Harriet Tubman Home is where the woman known as "The Moses of Her People" settled after the Civil War. Tubman, who escaped from slavery in the South in 1849, was a conductor on the Underground Railroad during the war, helping slaves escape to the north. When she lived in Auburn, she operated a home for aged and/or indigent ex-slaves. The home is at 180 South Street, while nearby at 17 North Street is Freedom Park, a tribute to Tubman's memory. (315) 252-2081.

For more information about Auburn, call the Chamber of Commerce at (315) 252-7291.

### ◆ DINING

Lasca's, about 20 minutes from the ballpark, serves seafood and steaks, but the specialty here is Italian food, especially the homemade pasta. Try the canneloni, ravioli and chicken parmigiana. Route 5, (315) 253-4885.

### ◆ LODGING

Days Inn is about five minutes from the ballpark. 37 William Street, Auburn (315) 252-7567/(800) 325-2525.

Holiday Inn is about 10 minutes from the ballpark. 75 North Street, Auburn (315) 253-4531/(800) HOLIDAY.

### ◆ DIRECTIONS

Take Route 5 through downtown. Go past the Holiday Inn and turn right on North Division. The ballpark is about one mile away on your right. Parking is ample and free.

---

**FALCON PARK**
**108 North Division Street**
**Auburn, NY 13201**
**(315) 255-2489**

---

**Capacity: 2,500**
**LF 330, CF 400, RF 330**

---

### ◆ TICKET AND SCHEDULE INFORMATION

Games start at 7 P.M. Sunday games and doubleheaders begin at 6 P.M.

Auburn opens its schedule in mid-June and closes out the first week of September.

Ticket prices: $4.50 premiere box seats; $4 box seats; $3 general admission; $2.50 seniors over 60 and children 14 and under. Seniors and children get a 50-cent discount off premiere box seats.

## BATAVIA CLIPPERS

### PHILADELPHIA PHILLIES

When this ballpark was being planned in 1939, the local mayor, who was apparently well connected politically, called President Franklin Roosevelt to seek his assistance. After this phone conversation, Roosevelt, so the local story goes, promptly dispatched a crew of 60 to help build Batavia's Dwyer Stadium as a WPA project. Today, this quaint ballpark set in a municipal park is one of the few remaining stadiums in organized baseball made of wood. The wood benches in the covered grandstand have been here since the late 1930s. The aisle area behind the visitors' dugout is regularly occupied by a dozen or so inveterate local fans who would rather stand here, talk and watch the ballgame than find a place to sit. You will find them leaning against a convenient wooden shelf that was designed by one creative Batavia resident as a place these regulars could put their hot dogs and scorecards. After the 1995 season, Dwyer will be torn down and a new ballpark will be built on this site for Opening Day '96; Dwyer is definitely worth a visit in its final season.

### ◆ LOCAL AND TEAM HISTORY

With the exception of the Batavia Reds' 1897 season in the New York State League, pro baseball here began in 1939 when this city joined the PONY League. This circuit, the predecessor of the New York–Penn League, was launched in Batavia's Hotel Richmond during a January 1939 meeting of baseball executives. After spending 15 years in the PONY, Batavia joined the New York–Penn League in 1957 as a charter member. Batavia has been part of this circuit continuously since 1961. The Clippers began their current affiliation with Philadelphia in 1988. In 1952, Batavia's Jim Mitchell and Bradford's Frank Etchberger pitched a double no-hitter in a game won by Bradford, 1-0. The run scored in the 8th on a walk, a sacrifice, a wild pitch and an error. Bernardo Brito captured the first of his six minor-league home-run titles here in 1984, his fourth consecutive season with Batavia, when he hit 19 four-baggers. This franchise's name originated in the 1930s when a large farm machinery manufacturer was based in Batavia. The local group responsible for bringing baseball to this city decided to name the new team after a locally made farming product that was known as the Clipper Combine.

OTHER FAMOUS ALUMNI OTHER FAMOUS ALUMNI

Cito Gaston, Kelly Gruber, Manny Sanguillen and Woody Fryman played here.

### ◆ BALLPARK EXTRAS

The hot dogs, made in Rochester, are definitely worth trying. Sausages and locally made ice cream are also available. The Batavia Rotary Club runs the concession stands here, so part of the profits from food and beverage sales are put back into the community. You may even find the local District Attorney serving up hot dogs on the night of your visit.

### ◆ ATTRACTIONS

Darien Lake Theme Park, about a 15-minute drive from Batavia, is a popular family spot. (716) 599-4641.

For information about this area, call the Genesee Chamber of Commerce, (716) 343-7440.

◆ **DINING**

Alex's Place offers charbroiled ribs, steak and shrimp and is just five minutes from the stadium. 9322 Park Road, (716) 344-2999.

Cristina's, also five minutes away, features gourmet Italian food. 230 Ellicott Street, (716) 343-1029.

◆ **LODGING**

Sheraton is five to 10 minutes from the ballpark. 8250 Park Road, Batavia, (716) 344-2100/(800) 325-3535.

◆ **DIRECTIONS**

From I-90, take exit 48. Turn left onto State Route 98 South. Turn left on Richmond. After about ¼ mile, turn left on Bank Street. The stadium is about two blocks away. Parking is plentiful and free.

> **DWYER STADIUM**
> **Deno and Bank Street**
> **Batavia, NY 14020**
> **(716) 343-7531**
>
> **Capacity: 3,000**
> **LF 326, CF 386, RF 326**

◆ **TICKET AND SCHEDULE INFORMATION**

Games are at 7:05 P.M.; doubleheaders start at 6:05 P.M.

Batavia's season begins in mid-June and runs until the first week of September.

Ticket prices: $3.50; $2.50 seniors 65 and over and students.

# ELMIRA PIONEERS

### FLORIDA MARLINS

Dunn Field, built in 1939, remains a great place for baseball. In front of the stadium, you will notice a concrete pedestal that once held a bronze bust of Edward Dunn, the man who donated the land for the stadium that bears his name. Mr. Dunn's head was stolen several years ago and has yet to be retrieved or otherwise restored,

although the Pioneers have received several suggestions for a replacement, including the head of a former team mascot who was not very popular. Dunn Field's concourse is lined with 13 flags, representing all of the major-league teams Elmira has been affiliated with over the past century. Underneath the grandstand roof, you will find wooden seats that date back to the 1940s. During renovations to Rochester's Silver Stadium in the early '80s, these seats were removed from their former home and transplanted to Elmira. The Chemung River and the surrounding hills lie beyond the ballpark's 12-foot-high wooden outfield fence.

◆ **LOCAL AND TEAM HISTORY**

Elmira has a long and distinguished baseball history. The Elmira Babies took the field in 1888 as this city's first pro baseball team. Four other squads played in Elmira through the end of the 19th century. In 1908, the Jags began a 10-year relationship with the Class B New York State League, which folded in 1917. Over the next several decades, Elmira was associated with the Eastern League (1938-55, '62-72) and New York–Penn League (1923-37, '57-60, '73-to date). Back in 1923, the old New York–Penn League was established during a meeting in a downtown Elmira hotel. Ironically, one year later in the city where the league was founded, local businessmen had to come to the financial rescue of the struggling Elmira Colonels. The Pioneers began their current affiliation with the Florida Marlins in 1993.

In 1932, Hall of Famer Johnny "The Big Cat" Mize batted .326 with eight homers for the Elmira Red Wings. Four years later, the Pioneers captured the season's second-half league championship under the guidance of Hall of Famer Rabbit Maranville, who agreed to serve as player-manager of the team following his big-league retirement in 1935. Besides leading the Pioneers into the playoffs after Elmira finished fifth in the first half of the season, Maranville helped himself on the field by batting .323. In 1950, Bill Sharman, a star NBA guard and today a member of the Pro Basketball Hall of Fame, played outfield for Elmira and batted .289 in 10 games. Future big-league player and manager Don Zimmer batted .273 for the Pioneers in 1951, the same year he was married at Dunn Field's home plate. Two years earlier, Pete Gray, the one-armed outfielder who played for the St. Louis Browns in 1945,

> **OTHER FAMOUS ALUMNI**
>
> Phil Plantier, Pete Reiser, Brady Anderson, Tim Naehring, John Valentin, Scott Cooper, Mark Belanger, Sal "the Barber" Maglie, Bo Diaz, Curt Schilling, and Oil Can Boyd all played here.

batted .291 for Elmira. One year later, he retired from baseball.

Earl Weaver spent four years (1962-65) here as the Pioneers' manager. In '64, he led the Pioneers, who included such future Baltimore Orioles as Paul Blair (.311, best in the EL) and Eddie Watt (2.86 ERA), to an Eastern League title. Besides Weaver and Zimmer, five other future big-league managers spent time in Elmira, including Roger Craig (1954, 9.00 ERA in 3 games), Joe Altobelli, Davey Johnson (1963, .326, 13 home runs), Lou Piniella (1965, .249, 64 runs batted in) and Don Baylor (1968, .333 in six games). Hall of Famer Jim Palmer pitched for Elmira in 1968, posting an 0-2 record and 4.32 ERA in six games.

Wade Boggs was the most prominent Red Sox farmhand to pass through Elmira during the Pioneers' 20-year affiliation with Boston. As an 18-year-old rookie, Boggs batted .263 in 1976, when Elmira captured the New York–Penn League title. He did not bat under .300 again until 1992, when he hit .259 for Boston. Also on that squad was Bruce Hurst (3-2, 3.00 ERA) who later spent seven seasons with Boggs in Boston. Ellis Burks (.241) and Mike Greenwell (.269, six homers) played here in 1983 and '82, respectively. In 1993, Andy Larkin became the first Florida Marlin farmhand to pitch a no-hitter.

◆ BALLPARK EXTRAS

The Pioneers have good grilled Italian sausages and hot dogs. Check out the soft ice cream as well.

◆ ATTRACTIONS

Mark Twain wrote *The Adventures of Huckleberry Finn* in Elmira. A dramatization of Twain's life is produced here each summer. Tickets range from $12 to $25. For further information, call (800) 395-MARK.

Guided tours of Twain's study on the campus of Elmira College are also available. Admission is free. For further information, call (607) 732-0993.

For additional information about Elmira, call the Chemung County Chamber of Commerce, (607) 734-5137.

◆ DINING

Light's Bakery and Coffee Shop, about 10 minutes from the ballpark, offers a variety of burgers as well as hot and cold sandwiches, but the real treat here is the bounty from the on-site bakery. Try the cheesecake or pie of the day at the restaurant, or stop by the bakery on the way out and buy some cookies. 211 W. 2nd Street, (607) 732-5600.

◆ LODGING

Holiday Inn Downtown is at exit 56 of State Route 17, about 10 minutes from the ballpark. (607) 734-4211/(800) HOLIDAY.

Howard Johnson's Lodge is at exit 52 off State Route

17, about 20 minutes from the ballpark. (607) 739-5636/(800) 654-2000.

◆ DIRECTIONS

From State Route 17, take exit 56/Church Street. Follow blue and white signs to Dunn Field. Take the first left onto Judson Street and then turn right on Water Street. Turn left on Madison Street. Stay on Madison and go over the river. Make your first left at the traffic light onto Maple Avenue. Turn left on Luce Street. The ballpark is at the end of Luce Street. There is plenty of free parking available.

```
DUNN FIELD
P.O. Box 238
Elmira, NY 14902
(607) 734-1811
─────────────────
Capacity: 5,100
LF 325, CF 386, RF 325
```

◆ TICKET AND SCHEDULE INFORMATION

Most games are played at night, starting at 7 P.M.

The Pioneers' home opener is usually in mid-June, and the season ends in the first week of September.

Ticket prices: $4.25 box seats; $3.50 reserved seats; $2.50 general admission, $1.75 seniors 65 and over and children 18 and under.

# ERIE SEAWOLVES

## PITTSBURGH PIRATES

The new, 6,000-seat stadium being built in downtown Erie has yet to be named but is expected to be finished in time for the mid-June start of the 1995 New York–Penn League season. The left-field wall will be 18 feet high to give a "green monster" effect while the stadium's downtown setting is expected to be reminiscent of the Chicago Cubs' Wrigley Field. The stadium will also be attached to the Erie Civic Center, where the locker rooms and batting cages will be housed.

◆ LOCAL AND TEAM HISTORY

Pro baseball in Erie goes back more than 100 years, to

1877, when this city was a charter member of the League Alliance, which folded before the end of the season. In the 1890s, Erie fielded teams in the New York–Penn and Eastern leagues. The Erie Fishermen joined the Interstate League as a charter franchise in 1905. Since then, this city has been associated with six other National Association leagues. Erie first joined the present New York–Penn League in 1957, winning the league championship in its first year by beating Batavia three games to one. Back in the 1940s, the Negro American League's Kansas City Monarchs played several games at Erie's

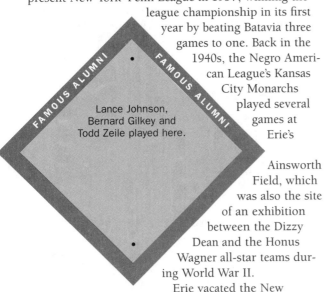

FAMOUS ALUMNI

Lance Johnson, Bernard Gilkey and Todd Zeile played here.

Ainsworth Field, which was also the site of an exhibition between the Dizzy Dean and the Honus Wagner all-star teams during World War II.

Erie vacated the New York–Penn circuit in 1994 as a new stadium was built to replace rickety Ainsworth Field, while the old stadium hosted a team in the independent Frontier League for that season. Those Erie Sailors won the league title.

### ◆ BALLPARK EXTRAS

The SeaWolves have a grill and picnic area. Try the burgers, hot dogs or barbecued chicken sandwich.

### ◆ ATTRACTIONS

Baseball fans will be sure to want to stop by the bar Jethroe's, where owner and former NL Rookie of the Year Sam Jethroe often tends bar. Jethroe, whose home was destroyed in a blaze on Thanksgiving 1994, began tending bar in Erie during the 1942 off-season when the owner of his Cleveland Buckeyes team in the Negro Leagues offered him the job tending bar at the Pope Hotel. He has owned this bar since he retired from baseball in 1958. 324 E. 18th Street, (814) 454-9433.

For the kids, the Erie Zoo is a 15-acre site that boasts more than 300 animals and includes a children's petting zoo. Route 97 and W. 38th Street, (814) 864-4091.

Waldameer Park and Water World is located at the entrance to scenic Presque Isle State Park and offers 41 rides, slides and pools, a midway, an arcade and picnic facilities. (814) 838-3591.

For more information about Erie, call the Chamber of Commerce, (814) 454-7141.

### ◆ DINING

Eagle Hotel was once the site of a stagecoach stop and is now operated as a restaurant and museum. It's about a ½ hour away. 32 High Street, Waterford, (814) 796-6990.

The Olive Garden, about 20 to 25 minutes away, is among the best of the chains, offering good-quality Italian food in dining-room comfort with quick service. 5945 Peach Street, Erie, (814) 866-1105.

### ◆ LODGING

Avalon Hotel is two blocks from the park. 16 W. 10th Street, Erie, (814) 459-2220.

Ramada Inn is about 20 minutes away. 6101 Wattsburg Road, Erie, (814) 825-3100/(800) 228-2828.

### ◆ DIRECTIONS

Take I-90 to I-79 north to the East 12th Street exit. Take 12th Street to State Street and make a left. Go to 10th Street and turn right, and you will see the ballpark on your left. There is no parking lot at the ballpark, but parking is available on the street and in area lots.

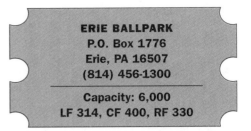

**ERIE BALLPARK**
P.O. Box 1776
Erie, PA 16507
(814) 456-1300

Capacity: 6,000
LF 314, CF 400, RF 330

### ◆ TICKET AND SCHEDULE INFORMATION

Most games are played at night, starting at 7 P.M. Sunday games begin at 2 P.M.

The SeaWolves' home opener will be in mid-June and the season ends in the first week of September.

Tickets prices: $6 box seats; $5 reserved; $3 general admission.

# HUDSON VALLEY RENEGADES

## TEXAS RANGERS

**D**utchess Stadium was finished on Opening Day 1994 and still has that brand-new atmosphere. It features eight sky box suites, but only six have been leased out to corporations—two are put aside for nightly rentals by average folks. The scoreboard is also top-quality for short-season ball, featuring color animation. Located in the bottom of a bowl, Dutchess Stadium is an attractive park that features a steel and auburn-brick facade and a green metal roof. Down each foul line past the grandstand, there are tents that serve as picnic areas.

The stadium is surrounded by some of the minors' most unusual scenery. Trees border much of the stadium, while an interstate highway overlooks right field. A mountain looms in the distance past the highway, and a large state prison, about 1,500 feet beyond the fence, completes the scene.

### ◆ LOCAL AND TEAM HISTORY

Pro ball had last been played in 1950 in Dutchess County, about an hour north of New York City, in Poughkeepsie, but the Renegades are the first organized baseball team based in Fishkill.

The Renegades' history is brief but has already created a legion of fans. Within a month of the announced arrival of the team for the 1994 season, 800 season tickets had been sold, and the packages were cut off at 1,500. Of the team's 38 home games in 1994, 22 were sellouts. Heading into 1995, there was already a waiting list of 400 on the season-ticket file.

However, the construction of the stadium didn't go quite as smoothly as the ticket sales. Ground wasn't broken until April 8, yet by Opening Day of June 18, 1994, the contractor was putting the finishing touches of bright yellow paint on the foul poles.

### ◆ BALLPARK EXTRAS

Rookie Renegade, the team's oversize raccoon mascot, leads the crowd in dances, including a famous weekly conga line through the stadium between innings of selected home games. Rookie will have a 10-inch plush doll of himself on sale in 1995 at the concession stands.

The grilled sausages and chicken are good, but save room for Carvel soft-serve ice cream, a New York institution.

### ◆ ATTRACTIONS

The United States Military Academy (a k a West Point) 25 miles from the stadium across the Hudson River in Orange County, is a major tourist attraction. The Hotel Thayer, adjacent to the site, is a favorite spot for dining when you visit the academy. (800) 247-5047.

For more information about the Hudson Valley, call (914) 897-2067.

### ◆ DINING

North Street Grill, 10 minutes from the park, offers lunch and dinner for all occasions. North and Main streets, Fishkill, (914) 896-1000.

Greenbaum and Gilhooley's, also 10 minutes away, offers steaks, chops, chicken and ribs as well as fresh seafood and all sorts of desserts, led by mud pie. Route 9, Wappingers Falls, (914) 297-9700.

### ◆ LODGING

Courtyard by Marriott is about 10 minutes away. Route 9 and I-84, Fishkill, (914) 897-2400.

Holiday Inn is between five and 10 minutes from the park. 2511 Route 9, Fishkill, (914) 896-6281/(800) HOLIDAY.

### ◆ DIRECTIONS

Take I-84 to exit 11, onto Route 9D. Go north one mile to stadium on right. Parking is available for about 1,000 cars, but the team runs a shuttle bus from an overflow parking area about ¼ mile from the ballpark.

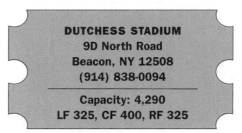

**DUTCHESS STADIUM**
**9D North Road**
**Beacon, NY 12508**
**(914) 838-0094**

**Capacity: 4,290**
**LF 325, CF 400, RF 325**

### ◆ TICKET AND SCHEDULE INFORMATION

Most games are played at night, beginning at 7:15 P.M. Sunday games start at 1:35 P.M.

The Renegades' season begins in mid-June and ends the first week of September.

Ticket prices: $7 box seats; $6 reserved seats; $4 general admission. On Mondays through Thursdays, kids under 14 and seniors over 60 receive general admission for $2.

# JAMESTOWN JAMMERS

## DETROIT TIGERS

When the Tigers moved their farm team down to Jamestown from Niagara Falls to replace the departing Expo farmhands, a local supermarket chain helped sponsor the name-the-team contest. Forty-seven of the more than 1,000 entries picked the name Jammers, though no one was quite sure what a Jammer was. The logo—a sort-of cute, sort-of fierce-looking, sharp-toothed animal with a bat on its shoulder—doesn't necessarily answer the question but that hasn't hurt its popularity.

Team attendance has increased dramatically at College Stadium, which has been open since 1941. Credit goes to the successful Rich family baseball operation, which also runs teams in Buffalo and Wichita, as much as to the fans. Among the unusual moments at the stadium in 1994 were a first pitch thrown from a helicopter, bowling with oranges and a Lucille Ball look-alike contest. In case you had forgotten, Lucille MacGillicuddy Ricardo hailed from Jamestown—actually, West Jamestown—while Lucy herself was from Jamestown.

### ◆ LOCAL AND TEAM HISTORY

Jamestown first hosted minor-league ball in the PONY League, which predated the New York–Penn League, in 1939. It remained in that loop until 1956 and stayed in the new New York–Penn League for its first season of 1957 before taking a brief hiatus. Jamestown re-entered the league from 1961 to '73 and finally came back for good in 1977.

**FAMOUS ALUMNI**

Marquis Grissom, Delino DeShields, Andres Galarraga, Randy Johnson, Sal Maglie, Nellie Fox and Tony Phillips all played here.

### ◆ BALLPARK EXTRAS

Among the nice additions in 1994 were a tent area with sand volleyball and horseshoe pits for private and public parties.

### ◆ ATTRACTIONS

Chautauqua Institution is a center of learning that features many famous speakers and weekly educational conferences. On Chautauqua Lake about 15 miles from the stadium. The lake is also a big fishing and resort area surrounded by cottages and campgrounds. For information, call (716) 357-6231.

Panama Rocks, a park about 10 miles outside of Jamestown with a unique series of caves, features frequent art and folk festivals. To find out about events, call (716) 782-2845.

For more information about Jamestown, call the Chamber of Commerce at (716) 484-1101.

### ◆ DINING

The Ball Club, about five minutes from the ballpark, calls itself "the other home of the Jammers" and claims to have the best pizza, wings and things in town. 223 W. 3rd Street, Jamestown, (716) 664-9084.

The Italian Fisherman, about 15 minutes away, offers a unique waterfront dining and socializing experience on Chautauqua Lake. A wide menu featuring steaks, seafood and pasta can be eaten indoors or on the deck overlooking the water. Bemus Point, (716) 386-7000.

### ◆ LODGING

Holiday Inn is about five minutes away. 150 W. 4th Street, Jamestown, (716) 664-3400/(800) HOLIDAY.

### ◆ DIRECTIONS

Take Route 60 south into Jamestown, turn left onto Buffalo Street and left onto Falconer Street. The stadium is a ¼ mile down on the left.

---

**COLLEGE STADIUM**
**7 E. 3rd Street**
**Jamestown, NY 14702**
**(716) 664-0915**

---

**Capacity: 3,324**
**LF 335, CF 414, RF 353**

---

### ◆ TICKET AND SCHEDULE INFORMATION

Most games are played at night, starting at 7 P.M. Sunday games begin at 6 P.M.

The Jammers begin their season in mid-June and it ends the first week of September.
Ticket prices: $4.50 box seats; $3.50 grandstand; $2.50 bleachers. Seniors get 50 cents off all tickets.

# NEW JERSEY CARDINALS

## ST. LOUIS CARDINALS

While many minor-league teams claim their ballparks are the real-life versions of Kevin Costner's creation in *Field of Dreams*, they mostly pale in comparison to the Cardinals' home. Just like Costner's movie diamond, Skylands Park was built amid a cornfield. In fact, thousands of corn stalks still surround Skylands. Together with the surrounding lush hills, a pine-tree-covered promontory just beyond the center field wall, trees and a farm or two, Skylands' scenic location is among the minors' most bucolic. The park itself blends well into this setting because its structure, painted a rustlike shade of red, looks like farm buildings. Begun in 1994, Skylands is part of a complex where concerts and wrestling matches are also staged. It was not completed last year, since the company that owns the facility has sought protection from its creditors under Chapter 11 of the U.S. Bankruptcy Code. Team offices, sky boxes and concession stands remained unfinished at the end of the season. This year marks the unveiling of a fully completed Skylands Park.

### LOCAL AND TEAM HISTORY

The New Jersey Cardinals are the first organized-baseball team in this rural corner of northwest New Jersey. Prior to coming to Jersey, this franchise made stops in Erie, Pennsylvania; Hamilton, Ontario; and Glens Falls, New York. In 1994, this community, about an hour from New York City, responded enthusiastically to their first minor-league team. The Cardinals' attendance, 156,447, was an all-time league record. In a fitting end to a memorable inaugural season, the Cardinals also won the New York–Penn League championship. Although this area has no minor-league history, there is an interesting local legend worth investigating. Rumor has it that Babe Ruth, during his New York Yankees career, was a regular visitor to a local tavern.

### BALLPARK EXTRAS

There is a Beer Garden on the concourse behind third base where a variety of brews is sold. The hot dogs, with sauerkraut and onions, and the spicy sausages are among the best concession items. Last year, the fans here, accustomed to watching the big-league Mets and Yankees in New York, took a while to acclimate themselves to minor-league baseball. Eventually, they became fervent supporters, using an assortment of bells, whistles, and sirens to keep the ballpark lively. The team also made a splash with its two celebrity radio announcers, Sparky Lyle, former Yankees ace reliever, and Phil Pepe, longtime sports columnist.

### ATTRACTIONS

Action Park/Great Gorge, a combination summer theme park and winter ski resort, is in nearby Vernon. Admission to Action Park is $26, $18 for those under 4 feet tall. For further information, call (201) 827-2000.

The Delaware Water Gap National Recreation Area, northwest of Skylands, is located on a stretch of the Delaware River along the New Jersey–Pennsylvania state line. Canoeing, camping, hiking, and swimming are available. Admission to the area is free. For further information, call the park headquarters, (717) 588-2435.

For more information about the surrounding area, call the Sussex County Chamber of Commerce, (201) 579-1811.

### DINING

New Yetter's Diner is across Route 206 from Skylands. This popular diner serves a good variety of seafood and Italian dishes. The specialty here is homemade desserts, such as blueberry cheesecake and apple pie. (201) 383-5641.

### LODGING

Best Western Inn at Hunt's Landing is at the intersection of U.S. 6 and U.S. 209 in nearby Matamoras, Pennsylvania, about half an hour northwest of the park. (717) 491-2400/(800) 528-1234.

### DIRECTIONS

From I-80 west, take exit 34B, Route 15 to Sparta. Stay on 15 for about 18 miles until you get to the intersection of 15 and U.S. 206. At the intersection, turn right on County Route 565. The ballpark will be on your left in 1/2 mile. Skylands charges $2 for parking, exorbitant for a Short Season Class A team. There is plenty of parking available.

**SKYLANDS PARK**
P.O. Box 117
Augusta, NJ 07822
(201) 579-7500

Capacity: 4,400
LF 330, CF 400, RF 330

### TICKET AND SCHEDULE INFORMATION

Most games are played at night, starting at 7:30, but several weekday games are scheduled to begin at noon. Weekend games begin at either 1 P.M. or 5 P.M.

The Cardinals' home opener is usually in mid-June,

and the season ends in the first week of September.

Ticket prices: $8 box seats; $5.50 reserved seats; $3 general admission.

# ONEONTA YANKEES

## NEW YORK YANKEES

Baseball has been played on this historic site since 1903. Elm Park Field, Oneonta's first ballyard, opened here in 1906. In 1968, Sam Nader, then mayor of Oneonta and now the O-Yanks' general manager, gave Damaschke Field its current name in honor of the chairman of the local Parks and Recreation Commission. Damaschke Field, one of the oldest operating ballparks in North America, still has basically the same steel grandstand that was erected here in 1939. Underneath its weathered roof, fans sit in long, blue wooden benches. Several mountains, part of the Catskills range and covered with lush trees, are visible beyond the outfield fence. Summer sunsets in the cliffs surrounding Damaschke Field can be particularly vibrant. The ballpark is located next to a recreational facility with basketball courts, a playground and a small lake. A small replica of the Statue of Liberty stands in back of the ballpark, behind the center-field fence.

### ◆ LOCAL AND TEAM HISTORY
Oneonta received its first taste of organized baseball when the Utica Utes of the New York–Penn League moved here in August 1924, only to disband following the season. After a 15-year absence, baseball returned here in 1940 when Oneonta began a nine-year association (1940-42, '46-51) with the Class C Canadian-American League. Oneonta rejoined the New York-Penn League in 1966 and started its current affiliation with the New York Yankees in '67, the longest connection with the same big-league team of any franchise in this league.

The O-Yankees of 1974 and 1986 compiled two of the best records for short-season teams in the history of minor-league baseball, 53-16 and 59-18 respectively. Those squads were piloted by future big-league skippers Mike Ferraro and Buck Showalter.

Dale Long played for the Oneonta Red Sox in 1947. Nine years later, he set a major-league record with the Pittsburgh Pirates by homering in eight straight games.

Coincidentally, Don Mattingly, who tied Long's record in 1987 by homering in seven consecutive games, also began his career in Oneonta. Following his selection in the 19th round of the 1979 draft, an 18-year-old Mattingly was assigned to Oneonta where he batted .349 in 53 games.

Three years after Mattingly broke into pro baseball here, the Yankees sent their highest selection in the 1981 draft to Oneonta. John Elway was debating between a career in baseball or football in 1981 when the New York Yankees made him their top draft pick and paid him a $140,000 bonus in the hope of luring him to a career in Yankee Stadium. As a first step in Elway's pro baseball education, New York sent its potential future outfielder to Oneonta during the summer of 1982. Elway impressed a lot of people during his six-week stay here, batting .318 and driving in 25 runs over 42 games. But despite his success on the diamond, Elway passed up his baseball opportunities and opted for a career on the gridiron.

Buck Showalter's first job as a manager was with the Oneonta Yankees in 1985. His team won the league championship that season with a record of 55-23. The next season, Showalter's squad went into the record books as one of the winningest short-season teams in minor-league history. Two of Showalter's key ballplayers that year were Hal Morris, who hit .378 in 36 games before being promoted to AA Albany/Colonie, and Jim Leyritz, who batted .363 with four home runs in only 23 games. In 1988, when Oneonta won the league title, Pat Kelly hit .329 with 34 runs batted in.

**OTHER FAMOUS ALUMNI**

Frank Malzone; Willie McGee, Jim Deshaies, Roberto Kelly, Pat Tabler, Bob Tewksbury, Bernie Williams, Dave Bergman and Jim Beattie all played here.

### ◆ BALLPARK EXTRAS
Oneonta features good grilled sausages with onions and peppers, plus burgers and fried dough. The hot dogs, made by Tobin's of Albany, rank among the best minor-league red-hots.

### ◆ ATTRACTIONS
The National Soccer Hall of Fame features numerous exhibits and displays relating to this sport. Several soccer-related events occur here each year. Admission is $3, $1.50 for children 6 to 16. For further information, call (607) 432-3351.

For additional information about Oneonta, call the Chamber of Commerce, (607) 432-4500.

### ◆ DINING

The Metropolitan Diner, about five minutes from the ballpark, has wood paneling and a porcelain ceiling. It offers low prices and several good sandwiches. Noteworthy selections are Queens burger, made from sirloin steak; gyro stadium steak sandwich with peppers, onions and cheese; and fish and chips. Try the New York cheesecake and homemade pies. 139 Main Street, (607) 432-2154.

### ◆ LODGING

Holiday Inn is at exit 15 off I-88, about 10 minutes from the ballpark. (607) 433-2250/(800) HOLIDAY.

Christopher's Lodge is at exit 15 off I-88, about 10 minutes from the ballpark. (607) 432-2444.

### ◆ DIRECTIONS

From I-88, take exit 15 and go west. Turn left at the first light and left again at the next light. The ballpark will be visible on the right. Plenty of free parking is available.

**DAMASCHKE FIELD**
**95 River Street**
**Oneonta, NY 13820**
**(607) 432-6326**

**Capacity: 4,500**
**LF 352, CF 406, RF 345**

### ◆ TICKET AND SCHEDULE INFORMATION

Most games are played at night, starting at 7:15 P.M. Sunday games and doubleheaders begin at 6 P.M.

The Yankees' season opens in mid-June and ends in the first week of September

Ticket prices: $3.50 general admission, $2.50 for seniors 65 and over and children 15 and under.

# PITTSFIELD METS

## NEW YORK METS

On a clear day at Wahconah Park, you can expect to hear this unusual call from the umpire—"Game halted on account of the sun!" This ballpark faces west, so the sun sets behind the leftfield wall, right in the batters' eyes. During Wahconah's brief sun delay, both teams return to their dugouts. While waiting for the sun to set, fans may be treated to water fights among the players or a bottle of suntan lotion from the mascot, Mr. Met.

Wahconah's idiosyncratic placement is just part of its charm. Baseball has been played on this site since 1892. Wahconah was built 27 years later, making it one of the oldest operating parks in the minors. The wood grandstand, which has remained basically unchanged since the park's opening, contains long benches, painted New York Met blue and orange, and eight plastic owls hanging from the roof to ward off pigeons. The tree-framed outfield fence is also unusual since right-center field, 430 feet from home, is the deepest part of the ballpark. From the old scoreboard in right center, the wall forms a sharp right angle before leveling off in center field, 374 feet away from the batter. But Wahconah Park, with several seemingly built-in advantages for pitchers, does offer batters one bit of comfort—the foul territory down the lines is relatively small.

**OTHER FAMOUS ALUMNI**

Bill Madlock, Sparky Lyle, Bill "The Spaceman" Lee and Mike Hargrove played here.

### ◆ LOCAL AND TEAM HISTORY

Pittsfield has fielded teams in five organized-baseball leagues since the pro game debuted here in 1905 when the Hillies were a member of the Class C Hudson River League. Both the team and league proved to be short lived. The Hillies folded before the '05 season ended, and the league disbanded two years later. Since then, Pittsfield had 16 years as a AA city in the Eastern

League (1965-76, '85-88). In 1989, Pittsfield began its current affiliation with the New York–Penn.

Carlton Fisk, holder of the major-league record for most games as a catcher, played 97 games here in 1969 before being promoted to the Boston Red Sox later that season. George "Boomer" Scott was the Eastern League MVP in 1965, leading the circuit in virtually every offensive category. Rafael Palmeiro and Mark Grace also won the MVP in '86 and '87, respectively.

### ◆ BALLPARK EXTRAS

Pittsfield sells locally made Wohrle's hot dogs, among the best in the minors. If you are lucky enough to be in Pittsfield for a two-for-one hot-dog game, try a few. Wohrle's also makes the hamburgers that are sold here. Other noteworthy food items are locally made pizza, cheese dogs, and ballpark cooler iced tea. There is also a stand that offers sundaes with chocolate topping and whipped cream. A picnic area and grill are behind first base.

### ◆ ATTRACTIONS

Arrowhead, located on Holmes Road, was the home of author Herman Melville and is where he completed *Moby Dick*. Admission is $4.50, $4 seniors 62 and over, $3 children 6 to 16. For further information, call (413) 442-1793.

Hancock Shaker Village, on U.S. 20 at State Route 41, is a restoration of an 18th-century Shaker village. Admission is $10, $5 for children 6 to 17. For further information, call (413) 443-0188. Tanglewood, in nearby Lenox, is the summer home of the Boston Symphony Orchestra.

The Tanglewood Music Festival takes place from June through September. For further information, call (413) 637-1940 or (617) 266-1492.

For additional information about Pittsfield, contact the Visitors' Bureau, (800) 237-5747.

### ◆ DINING

The Brewery, about 10 minutes from the ballpark, is an attractive brewpub with a bright and airy interior. Several imaginative varieties of pizza and burgers are featured, as well as tuna fajitas and Cajun tuna kebabs. Several home-brewed beers are also available. 34 Depot Street, (413) 442-2072.

### ◆ LODGING

Travellodge is about 15 minutes from the ballpark, about 3½ miles east on State Route 9. 16 Cheshire Road, Pittsfield, (413) 443-5866/(800) 578-7878.

Heart of the Berkshires Motel is about 15 minutes from the ballpark on U.S. 20 west of downtown. 970 W. Housatonic Street, Pittsfield, (413) 443-1255.

### ◆ DIRECTIONS

Take exit 2 from the Massachusetts Turnpike to State

Route 7 north. Stay on Route 7 into downtown Pittsfield. Go around the traffic circle and continue on 7 north for about 1 mile. At the intersection of Routes 7 and 9, there will be a hospital in front of you. Take the left fork, Wahconah Street. The ballpark will be on the left. There is plenty of free parking available.

**WAHCONAH PARK**
**105 Wahconah Street**
**Pittsfield, MA 01201**
**(413) 499-6387**

**Capacity: 4,000**
**LF 334, CF 384, RF 333**

### ◆ TICKET AND SCHEDULE INFORMATION

Most games are played at night, starting at 7 P.M.

The Mets' season opens in mid-June and ends in the first week of September.

Ticket prices: $6 box seats; $3.75 upper grandstand; $2.75 general admission; $1 seniors.

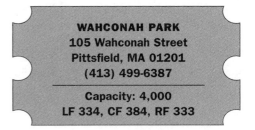

# ST. CATHARINES STOMPERS

**TORONTO BLUE JAYS**

Baseball was first played on this site in the 1930s, in a park referred to simply as the American Ballyard. Community Park today is made of metal, with an uncovered grandstand that is so close to the field—less than 20 feet from home plate—that the team needed a waiver to comply with the ballpark standards set out in the Professional Baseball Agreement. When it first opened in 1986, the home team played before small crowds in the first-base grandstand, which could accommodate only about 500 people. Additional seats were added for the '87 season. Railroad tracks run behind the outfield wall and along the first-base side, and the sounds of passing trains often punctuate the action on Community Park's diamond. Trees and several buildings line the outfield fence, in back of the tracks, including a prominent church spire behind the right-field foul pole. All of these elements make seeing a game here an unusually intimate experience.

## ◆ LOCAL AND TEAM HISTORY

St. Catharines' organized-baseball resume is brief. In 1930, the St. Catharines Brewers played in the ill-fated Class D Ontario League, which folded before the season ended. In 1986, baseball returned when St. Catharines joined the New York–Penn League as a Toronto Blue Jays affiliate.

When General Manager Ellen Harrigan-Charles hired Marilyn Finn as assistant GM in 1991, they became, arguably, the first all-woman management team in Organized Baseball history.

Derek Bell batted .264 with 10 homers and 42 runs batted in for St. Catharines in 1987 after being drafted by Toronto in the second round of the '87 draft. Carlos Delgado, one of Toronto's top prospects, played here in 1989 and '90, batting a combined .252. He led all New York–Penn League catchers in 1990 with 540 total chances and six double plays.

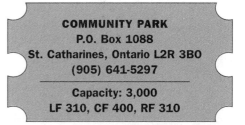

OTHER FAMOUS ALUMNI  OTHER FAMOUS ALUMNI

Rob Butler and Willie Blair also played here.

## ◆ BALLPARK EXTRAS

The Stompers have good grilled burgers and sausage. The soft ice cream is also popular among the fans. There is a pregame performer who stands near the front gate singing songs and playing a musical instrument to entertain the fans.

## ◆ ATTRACTIONS

Tivoli Miniature World has scale-model replicas of many of the most famous building in the world, including the Pyramids and the Kremlin. Admission is about $8, $6 for seniors and children 13 to 18, $4 for children 5 to 12. For further information, call (905) 562-7455.

For additional information about St. Catharines, call the Chamber of Commerce, (905) 685-9455.

## ◆ DINING

The Lancer Restaurant and Tavern, about 10 minutes from the ballpark, is a family-run diner-style restaurant serving various types of Greek fare. The stuffed cabbage, cabbage leaves and genuine mashed potatoes are good, as well as the milk shakes. 45 Geneva Street, (905) 684-8211.

Several fast-food restaurants are located on Merritt Street, about five minutes from the ballpark.

## ◆ LODGING

Parkway Inn is at exit 47 from the Queen Elizabeth Way (QEW), about 15 minutes from the ballpark. (905) 688-2324.

Holiday Inn is near the intersection of the QEW and Lake Street, about 20 minutes from the ballpark. (905) 934-2561/(800) HOLIDAY.

## ◆ DIRECTIONS

From the QEW, take Route 406 south to Glendale Avenue, Route 89. Turn left. Stay on Glendale to the end, about ½ mile, to Merritt. Turn left on Merritt. Turn right on Seymour and cross the railroad tracks. The ballpark will be on the right, less than one mile away. There is plenty of free parking available on the street or behind Merritton High School.

### COMMUNITY PARK
P.O. Box 1088
St. Catharines, Ontario L2R 3B0
(905) 641-5297

Capacity: 3,000
LF 310, CF 400, RF 310

## ◆ TICKET AND SCHEDULE INFORMATION

Most games are played at night, starting at 7 P.M.

The Stompers' season opens in mid June and ends in the first week of September.

Ticket prices: C$5 reserved seats; C$3 general admission. Seniors 65 and over and children 12 and under get C$1 off the price of each ticket.

# UTICA BLUE SOX

### BOSTON RED SOX

Baseball has been played on this site since the 1920s. Donovan Stadium, with a covered grandstand, is located in Murnane Field, a 9-acre recreation complex. A hospital is visible behind the right-field fence, so close to Donovan that one of the Blue Sox who was hospitalized during the 1994 season could watch his teammates play from his bed. The neighborhood next to the third-base side of the stadium is somewhat reminiscent of the Wrigley Field environs. In Utica, like Chicago, when the home team is playing, the balconies of adjacent two- and three-story houses are filled with residents and friends peering into the park. As well as a new facade and entranceway made of old Chicago brick behind first base, there are also attractive, old-fashioned, portico-style ticket booths here that resemble those at Doubleday Field in nearby Cooperstown.

### ◆ LOCAL AND TEAM HISTORY

Pro baseball in Utica goes back to the 1870s when this city fielded a team in the National Association. Utica joined the New York–State League in 1902, beginning a membership that lasted 16 seasons. Subsequently, Utica spent time in three other minor leagues.

This city joined the present New York-Penn League in 1977. Utica began its current affiliation with Boston in 1993.

Richie Ashburn played his first pro seasons, 1945 and '47, here, batting .342 overall (He was in the military in 1946.). In '47, he led the Eastern League with 194 hits and 128 runs scored. One of Ashburn's teammates in 1945 was Wally Schang who spent 19 years in the big leagues, 1913-31, batting .284 for his career. When he suited up for Utica at age 54, he became the oldest player in Eastern League history. Schang continued his career elsewhere for three more years. The 1983 Utica Blue Sox were made semifamous in the best-selling book *Good Enough To Dream* by Roger Kahn, who chronicled his season as president of the then-independent team—a group of castoffs and undrafted free agents who went on to win an unlikely league title. Utica's Don Jacoby, who paced the circuit with 22 home runs and 105 hits, set an all-time league record that season with 185 total bases.

*OTHER FAMOUS ALUMNI*

*Johnny Ruffin, Jesse Barfield and Larry Walker all played here.*

### ◆ BALLPARK EXTRAS

Visit the beer truck with its horseshoe-shaped bar on the first-base side. Here you can sample Matt's Beer, a local microbrew, the only beer sold at the ballpark. You can also try the burgers, pizza and Kunstler's hot dogs, which continue a New York–Penn League tradition of serving some of the best hot dogs in the minor leagues.

### ◆ ATTRACTIONS

About 20 minutes from the ballpark, the Vernon Downs horse track offers nightly harness racing. (315) 829-2201.

The Turning Stone Casino recently opened at the Oneida Indians' reservation, right next to the horse track. (315) 361-7711.

In addition, Cooperstown is just 45 minutes away if you want to visit the Baseball Hall of Fame. (607) 547-7200.

For more information about Utica, call the Chamber of Commerce at (315) 724-3151.

### ◆ DINING

Cavallos, about five minutes from the ballpark, offers good Italian food, and you can find most of the team there after games. 40-A Genesee Street, New Hartford, (315) 735-1578.

Uptown Grill is an old-fashioned sandwich place across the street from the ballpark. 4 Auburn Avenue, Utica, (315) 732-9868.

### ◆ LODGING

Howard Johnson's is about 10 to 15 minutes from the ballpark. 302 N. Genesee Street, Utica (315) 724-4141/(800) 645-2000.

### ◆ DIRECTIONS

From the New York Thruway, take exit 31. Go south about 4 miles on Genesee Street to Shepard Avenue, one block south of Burrstone Road. Turn right on Shepard, which dead-ends at the ballpark, about one block away. Ample parking is available for $1.

---

**DONOVAN STADIUM AT MURNANE FIELD**
**1700 Sunset Avenue**
**Utica, NY 13503**
**(315) 738-0999**

**Capacity: 4,500**
**LF 324, CF 390, RF 324**

---

### ◆ TICKET AND SCHEDULE INFORMATION

Games are at 7 P.M.

Utica's season begins in mid-June and ends the first week of September.

Ticket prices: $6 reserved box seats; $5 field-level seats; $4 general admission.

# VERMONT EXPOS

## MONTREAL EXPOS

Centennial Field is owned by the University of Vermont, and opened in 1906 when it hosted the University of Vermont baseball team against archrival Maine. The stadium has been undergoing a renovation, but this is still one of the oldest parks in the minors and the spirit of its long baseball history remains.

### ◆ LOCAL AND TEAM HISTORY

The Expos are the first organized-baseball team to be based in Winooski, but nearby Burlington has hosted numerous pro squads going back as far as 1887, when this city was a charter member of the Northeastern League. Since the turn of the century, Burlington has fielded teams in three minor leagues: Vermont State (1902), Provincial (1955) and Eastern (1984-88). Vermont's current affiliation with Montreal began in 1994 when pro baseball returned to Vermont. In 1907, Burlington had a difficult time fielding a team for each game, so collegians from the University of Vermont filled in occasionally when the professionals were unavailable. The Vermont Reds had a remarkable run from 1984 to '86, winning three straight Eastern League titles without once finishing the regular season in first place. In 1984, the pitching staff was led by Scott Terry, whose 1.50 ERA was the fourth-best in Eastern League history. Terry also won 14 of 17 decisions that year, while leading the league with six shutouts.

**OTHER FAMOUS ALUMNI**
Ken Griffey Jr., Barry Larkin, Jeff Montgomery, Paul O'Neill, Chris Sabo and Omar Vizquel all played here.

### ◆ BALLPARK EXTRAS

On the beer menu at the ballpark is Catamount Amber, brewed at Vermont's original microbrewery in White River Junction.

### ◆ ATTRACTIONS

The Shelburne Museum in nearby Shelburne offers a look at the history of the region. The Church Street Marketplace in downtown Burlington is a popular spot for shopping and dining. The Stowe ski area, famous nationwide for its slopes, is a close drive. If you have the time, treat yourself to a three-hour cruise on Lake Champlain, enjoying the scenery of the Adirondack Mountains and the Green Mountain range. (802) 864-9804.

For more information about Vermont, call (802) 863-3489.

### ◆ DINING

The Lighthouse is a few minutes from the ballpark and offers steak, seafood, pasta and more. When an Expos player hits a home run, a lucky fan wins dinner for two at the restaurant. Exit 16 on I-89, Burlington, (802) 655-0200.

Pepper's Memphis BBQ is about 20 minutes from the park. It offers great barbecue and gives special deals when you bring in a ticket stub from an Expos home game. Discounts are increased when the Expos win. 1110 Shelburne Road, South Burlington, (802) 864-RIBS.

### ◆ LODGING

Hampton Inn is about 10 minutes away. Exit 16 on I-89, Burlington, (802) 655-6177/(800) 426-7866.

Econo Lodge is between five and 10 minutes from the park. 1076 Williston Road, South Burlington, (802) 863-1125/(800) 446-6900.

### ◆ DIRECTIONS

Take I-89 to exit 14E. Go on Route 2 to East Avenue. Turn right on University Road, and the stadium will be on the right.

---

**CENTENNIAL FIELD**
**4 Champlain Mill**
**Winooski, VT 05404**
**(802) 655-4200**

**Capacity: 4,000**
**LF 335, CF 405 , RF 335**

---

### ◆ TICKET AND SCHEDULE INFORMATION

Most games are played at night starting at 7 P.M. Weekend games begin at 2:05 P.M.

The Expos' season begins in mid-June and ends the first week of September.

Ticket prices: $5 reserved seats; $3 general admission, $2 seniors and $2 children.

# WATERTOWN INDIANS

## CLEVELAND INDIANS

Watertown Indians

Duffy Fairgrounds Park, built in the 1930s, underwent a large-scale renovation in 1994. The grandstand was taken down and then rebuilt to resemble its former self, now with aluminum seats instead of wooden ones. The park boasts two unusual features. First, the press box is behind third base rather than home plate. Second, three rows of *upper* reserved seats are located atop the third-base dugout. The park is in a county fairgrounds, but there are plans to convert the grounds into a sports/recreation complex.

The ballpark, referred to for years as "the Duffy Dome" by a local sportscaster though it's uncovered, is still patronized by its founder and namesake, Alex T. Duffy. Mr. Duffy, now 96 years old, does not need a ticket and can sit wherever he pleases here, so if Alex Duffy is in your seat, introduce yourself and find another place to sit.

### ◆ LOCAL AND TEAM HISTORY

Watertown had pro baseball as far back as 1886, when this city was a charter member of the Central New York League. Since the turn of the century, Watertown has spent time in three leagues: Canadian American (1936), Border (1946-51) and New York–Penn (1983-to date). Watertown began its current affiliation with Cleveland in 1989. In 1984, Jay Buhner was an New York–Penn All-Star after batting .323 and leading the circuit with 58 runs batted in. Six years later Watertown's Bobby Ryan was the league's top pitcher, compiling a 5-3 record and a miniscule 0.73 ERA, third lowest in New York–Penn League history.

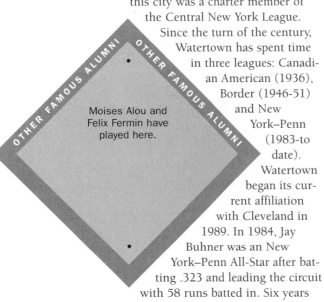

OTHER FAMOUS ALUMNI

Moises Alou and Felix Fermin have played here.

### ◆ BALLPARK EXTRAS

If you're coming to a Watertown game, bring your appetite! Besides your basic burgers and hot dogs on an outdoor grill, there are Italian and Polish sausages, venison burgers, grilled chicken, pizza and nachos.

### ◆ ATTRACTIONS

As cold as it is in Watertown in the winter, that's how beautiful the weather is in the summer. Historic Sacketts Harbor is 15 minutes away, and it is not only famous as a battle site in the War of 1812 but it is also housed in a lovely community.

The heart of the St. Lawrence River, the Thousand Islands and Alexandria Bay is a half-hour north of Watertown. The bay features great night life and excellent golf and fishing.

For more information about Watertown, call the Chamber of Commerce, (315) 788-4400.

### ◆ DINING

Sboro's offers steaks and seafood, about a block from the ballpark. 836 Coffeen Street, (315) 788-1100.

The Fairgrounds Inn, on the fairgrounds with the park, specializes in gourmet sandwiches, pizza and Italian food. 825 Coffeen Street, (315) 782-7335

### ◆ LODGING

Days Inn is three minutes away. 1142 Arsenal Street, Watertown, (315) 782-2700/(800) 325-2525.

### ◆ DIRECTIONS

Take I-81 to exit 46, Coffeen Street. Go down the hill into Watertown. At the foot of the hill, turn left, just past the Cadillac dealer. This road runs into the fairgrounds.

---

**ALEX T. DUFFY FAIRGROUNDS**
**120 Washington Street**
**Watertown, NY 13601**
**(315) 788-8747**

**Capacity: 3,500**
**LF 325, CF 402, RF 325**

---

### ◆ TICKET AND SCHEDULE INFORMATION

Games are 7 P.M., except Sundays at 6 P.M.

The Indians open their schedule in mid-June and close out the first week of September.

Ticket prices: $5 upper and lower reserved seats; $4 grandstand reserved seats; $3 general admission.

# WILLIAMSPORT CUBS

### CHICAGO CUBS

**B**owman Field is an attractive ballpark with an old-fashioned flavor. The outfield wall, and those down the foul lines, are made of large wooden poles resembling Lincoln Logs, and there is a large screen behind the largely covered grandstand with a lattice-type design at the top. The team is also planning to add several historical items along Bowman's concourse.

Pro ball has been played at Bowman Field since it opened in 1926, making it among the minors' oldest stadiums, but if you walk across the street and behind the outfield wall, you will find a stone monument surrounded by trees and flowers that commemorates the other half of Williamsport's historic baseball equation. It was here, on June 6, 1939, that the first Little League game was played. Today, the Little League World Series takes place just minutes away from the site of this first ballgame.

### ◆ LOCAL AND TEAM HISTORY

Organized baseball here dates back to 1907 when Williamsport began a four-season stint in the Class B Tri-State League. Williamsport won that circuit's first two pennants in 1907 and 1908. Following a 12-year absence, pro ball returned in 1923 when Williamsport joined the New York–Penn League (1923-37), which at that time was the predecessor of today's AA Eastern League. After this circuit became the EL in 1938, Williamsport was in the league on and off for more than 50 years (1938-42, '44-56, '58-62, '64-67, '76, 1987-91). The city was without pro baseball until 1994, when the New York–Penn League returned to Bowman Field and the Cubs played their first season in Williamsport. Previously, Williamsport had spent five seasons (1968-72) in the New York–Penn after it had become a Class A league.

One of the strangest events in minor-league history took place at Bowman Field on August 31, 1987. With Rick Lundblade of the Reading Phillies on third, Dave Bresnahan, a reserve catcher for the Williamsport Bills, attempted to pick him off. He took a peeled potato he had hidden in his glove and threw it over third base and into left field. Thinking that the Bills' catcher had thrown away a baseball instead of a spud, Lundblade raced for home, where the bewildered base runner was

tagged out by Bresnahan who was now holding the actual baseball. The umpire ejected Bresnahan from the game for his ploy, and Lundblade was ruled safe at home. The next day, Bresnahan, a .149 hitter and the grandnephew of Hall of Fame catcher Roger Bresnahan, was released. During the '88 season, the Bills invited Bresnahan back to Bowman Field and held a "night" for him. Fans paid $1 plus one potato to get into the ballpark. The team retired the former catcher's number 59 and hung a round blue placard, with Bresnahan's name and number, next to the right-field foul pole. Today, you can see this plaque above the main gate on the concourse.

Rube Vickers was one of the most successful pitchers of his day, winning 240 games, 217 in the minors, over 13 seasons. In 1907, he led the Tri-State League with 25 victories while pitching for the league champion Williamsport Millionaires. Tracey "Kewpie Dick" Barrett's 325 lifetime minor-league wins place him ninth on the all-time list. For the first six seasons (1925-30) of his 29-year career, he played under the name Dick Oliver, including when he won eight games for Williamsport as a 19-year-old rookie in 1925. Bill Mazeroski batted .293 and led Eastern League second baseman with 108 double plays in 1955. Also in '55, Reading's Roger Maris provided Williamsport fans with some excitement during a Sunday doubleheader. While chasing a fly ball, Maris looked back over his shoulder while racing toward the wall and ran right through the outfield fence. Some recall that Maris was the winner in his encounter with Bowman's outfield barrier, as he reportedly took most of the fence along with him.

In 1962, Dick Allen helped Williamsport finish first by leading the circuit with 32 doubles while also batting .329 with 20 home runs and 109 runs batted in. Four years later, Nolan Ryan was the subject of much local attention when he started three games for Williamsport. He lost his only two decisions but struck out 35 in 19 innings pitched. More recently, Tino Martinez led all EL first basemen with 106 double plays and a .995 fielding percentage in 1989. He also topped the loop with 13 intentional walks.

### ◆ BALLPARK EXTRAS

Because this is an old ballpark, concession facilities are limited. Among the best items are Italian sausage with

> **OTHER FAMOUS ALUMNI**
>
> Jim Bunning, Jerry Koosman, Curt Simmons, Ron Swoboda, Jim Rice and Ken Forsch all played here.

onions and peppers and Hatfield hot dogs, which are made in Philadelphia.

### ◆ ATTRACTIONS

The Little League Museum houses several exhibits and interactive displays relating to the history of Little League baseball. Admission is $4, $2 for seniors over 62, $1 for children 5 to 13. For further information, call (717) 326-3607.

Nearby Lamade Stadium is the home of the Little League World Series.

For additional information about Williamsport, call the Chamber of Commerce, (717) 326-1971.

### ◆ DINING

Country House Restaurant, about 15 minutes from the ballpark, offers a view of Lamade Stadium, which is right down the hill. Check out the all-you-can-eat pancake and french toast breakfasts in this attractive restaurant, with several displays relating to the area's 19th-century logging boom. In the City View Inn, (717) 326-2601.

### ◆ LODGING

City View Inn is located on U.S. 15, about 15 minutes from the ballpark. (717) 326-2601.

Quality Inn Williamsport is located on U.S. 15, about 15 minutes from the ballpark. (717) 323-

9801/(800) 4-CHOICE.

### ◆ DIRECTIONS

From U.S. 15 south, take the 4th Street exit. Turn left on 4th. The ballpark will be immediately visible on your left. From U.S. 15 north, take the Maynard Street exit. Turn right on Maynard and stay on this street until it turns into 4th. Turn left on 4th. The ballpark will be about $1\frac{1}{2}$ miles away on your right. There is plenty of free parking.

**HISTORIC BOWMAN FIELD**
P.O. Box 3173
Williamsport, PA 17701
(717) 326-3389

Capacity: 4,400
LF 345, CF 405, RF 350

### ◆ TICKET AND SCHEDULE INFORMATION

Most games are played at night, starting at 7:05 P.M.

The Cubs' season opens in mid-June and ends in the first week of September.

Ticket prices: $4.50 box seats; $3.25 general admission, $2.50 for seniors 60 and over and children 12 and under.

# NORTHWEST LEAGUE

**S**ince Butte won the Pacific National League title in 1902, this circuit has undergone several name changes, classification shuffles and realignments. The league suspended operations from 1922 to '36 and was revived in 1937 as the Western International League, as it remained known until 1955 when it became the Northwest League (the league also suspended play during the war years of 1943-45). The circuit played a full season until 1966, when it switched to short-season play. It now plays a 76-game schedule and is split into North and South divisions. Rosters are limited to 25 players, with no more than two players who are 23 or older and no more than three active players with four or more years of pro experience. Boise is the defending league champion, having won its second consecutive title and its third in four years. League attendance for 1994 was 855,650, up 86,849 from 1993. That marked a single-season league record. Boise (156,950) and Spokane (156,092) each set single-season club records. Eugene (133,860) was the third club in the loop to draw more than 100,000.

• • •

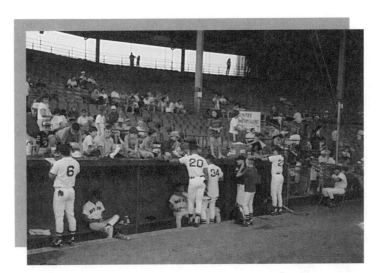

*Young fans get to meet their favorite players at Elmira's Dunn Field.*

# BELLINGHAM GIANTS

## SAN FRANCISCO GIANTS

The location of Joe Martin Stadium, built in 1964, is most fitting when you consider that Washington is nicknamed the Evergreen State. The ballpark is adjacent to a large grove of lush trees located behind the third-base side. Bellingham Bay plus the nearby Cascade and Olympic mountains complete the scenic picture here. A football stadium, used by the University of Western Washington and high school squads, is also in the neighborhood. The covered grandstand here can accommodate more than 2,000 fans, some of whom can sit in wooden seats that date from the opening of the ballpark more than 30 years ago. There is a barbecue pit down the left-field line. Some fans bring blankets to the ballpark and sit in a grassy area with picnic tables near the pit. Yet while this is not the newest stadium around it does have many of the amenities of more modern stadiums, such as VIP box seats, a computer-graphics scoreboard and luxury sky boxes.

### LOCAL AND TEAM HISTORY

Organized baseball first came to this city in 1905, when the Bellingham Yankees spent their only season in the Class B Northwestern League. After being without baseball for 32 years, Bellingham joined the Class B Western International League in 1938. But baseball left town again following the '39 season, not to return until 1973 when Bellingham joined the Northwest League. The group that lured baseball back to town was headed by Joe Martin, known as "Mr. Baseball" in Bellingham, who was honored by having the stadium named for him. This is the first year of affiliation with San Francisco, after Seattle terminated its 18-year relationship with Bellingham following the 1994 season.

**OTHER FAMOUS ALUMNI**

Mark Langston, Mike Scioscia, Pedro Guerrero, Jeffrey Leonard, Bud Black, Chuck Carr, Edgar Martinez, Dave Henderson, David Stewart, Rick Sutcliffe and Omar Vizquel have all played here.

Jimmie Reese, regarded as one of the best fungo hitters in baseball during his coaching career with the California Angels and a former roommate of Babe Ruth, was Bellingham's player-manager in 1939. Reese died in 1994, his 78th season in professional baseball. Ken Griffey Jr. made his pro debut here in 1987, batting .313. This franchise bills itself as the "Fastest-Growing Team in America" because per-game average attendance in Bellingham has gone from 400 in 1988 to almost 2,000. Last season was interesting for this franchise: The entire Bellingham team was featured in a national television commercial, and manager Mike Goff was suspended by the league for removing his pants and mooning an umpire after being ejected from a game in Medford.

### BALLPARK EXTRAS

There are a few sky boxes available to the public for $95 a game, with a maximum occupancy of five people. Among the more popular concession specialties are a half-pound Billy Burger and a half-pound Spyder Dog, which is a mammoth kielbasa sausage.

### ATTRACTIONS

The Whatcom Museum of Art features exhibits of local artists. 121 Prospect Street, Bellingham, (206) 676-6981.

Lake Whatcom is beautiful in the summer, and on a day off fans can also enjoy an orca-watching trip to nearby San Juan Island.

For more information about Bellingham, call the Chamber of Commerce, (206) 734-1330.

### DINING

Billy McHale's is a popular eating and drinking spot about five minutes from the park. 4301 Guide Meridian, Bellingham, (206) 647-7763.

BelPorto features excellent Italian and Mediterranean food, also about five minutes away. 1114 Harris Avenue, (206) 676-1520.

### LODGING

Best Western Lakeway Inn is just a few blocks from the ballpark. 714 Lakeway Drive, Bellingham (206) 671-1011/(800) 528-1234.

### DIRECTIONS

From I-5, take exit 253/Lakeway. Stay on Lakeway and go beneath an underpass, past King and Lincoln streets. Turn left at the softball field, which is located just beyond a school and a pair of flashing lights. This road runs into the ballpark, which will be on the left.

### ◆ TICKET AND SCHEDULE INFORMATION

Games start at 7:05 P.M., Sunday games begin at 6:05 P.M.

The Giants open their season in mid-June and close it out the first week of September.

Ticket prices: $5.50 adult grandstand; $4.50 students and seniors, $3.50 children; $4.50 general admission, $3.50 students and seniors, $2.50 children.

# BOISE HAWKS

### CALIFORNIA ANGELS

There's rarely a dull night at the ballpark when you go to a Boise game, because the Hawks' promotions are among the most original in the league. One emphasis here is fan entertainment. Among the top draws in 1994 were the creation of what was billed as "the world's largest bowl of mashed potatoes," fitting for a team in Idaho. One night the largest crowd in Boise history (5,063) watched the Flying Elvises parachute into the stadium, and another night Morgana the Kissing Bandit bungee-jumped over the outfield fence. The other emphasis here is on success. You most likely will see not only a fun team, but also a winning one—along with a lot of other fans. Boise has led the Northwest League in attendance for four years running and has won the league championship the past two seasons.

Memorial Stadium, built in 1989, is located in the Western Idaho Fairgrounds. Trees, foothills, and the fairgrounds frame the outfield fence. There are bleachers down each line, and the grandstand is uncovered.

### ◆ LOCAL AND TEAM HISTORY

Baseball in Boise goes back to the 1860s when several amateur squads played here. Semipro teams first appeared in the next decade. Since the turn of the century, Boise has belonged to seven minor leagues, beginning with the Pacific National League in 1914. Boise first joined the Northwest League in 1975 and has been in this circuit continuously since 1987.

In 1906, a 19-year-old future Hall of Famer named Walter Johnson left California for a chance to play baseball. He signed with and then was released by a team in Portland, Oregon. Johnson then moved on to Boise, where he played in the semi-pro Idaho State League, which featured teams like the Weiser Kids and the Emmett Prune Pickers. According to local historian Arthur Hart, author of a book about Boise baseball, players in this league, had no contracts. Because they were not bound to any one team, players moved around the league and played for various franchises. Only four players per team were paid. Not surprisingly, Johnson was one of these four. Johnson returned here in 1907 and after pitching 100 consecutive scoreless innings, he was signed by the Washington Senators.

On June 27, 1987, in Boise's Wigle Field, Derrell Thomas of the Boise Hawks and Mel Roberts of the Bend Bucks became the first African-American managers to face each other in a North American organized-baseball game. The Bucks won that day 10-9. From 1990 to '94, Boise has won three league titles (including '94) under the direction of Tom Kotchman, whose championship record and overall 228-152 mark make him the most successful skipper in league history.

**OTHER FAMOUS ALUMNI**

Rickey Henderson, Carl Mays, Bob Uecker, Clay Carroll, Tony Cloninger, Sandy Alomar Sr. and Eduardo Perez played here.

### ◆ BALLPARK EXTRAS

A field-side spa is available for groups of up to six to chill out and watch the game in a hot tub. The price includes a bottle of champagne.

The Hawks have also added an innovative item to their long list of attractions: The Little Gym Boise Hawks Kids Care, where kids aged 4 to 7 can participate in gymnastics, music and fitness skill-building from 7 to 9 P.M. behind right field for only $5 a night. It's perfect if you can't get a baby-sitter but your children are too young to sit through a game.

The Hawks Nest is an attractive outdoor cafe–restaurant open to all ticketholders and located down the right-field line. Complete with televisions and waitress service, the Hawks Nest serves such food as steak, chicken and seafood.

### ◆ ATTRACTIONS

The Discovery Center of Idaho (208-343-9895) is a

hands-on museum, while Boise is also the site of the Idaho Historical Museum (208-368-6080), which includes many Indian relics and a pioneer village.

The Idaho Botanical Gardens feature nine theme gardens. (208) 343-8649.

Summer events include horse racing at Les Bois Park, the Western Idaho Fair in August and National Music Week.

For more information about Boise, call the Chamber of Commerce, (208) 344-5515.

### ◆ DINING
There are several excellent restaurants within a short walk of the stadium. The Dugout Sports Pub and Deli, about five minutes from the ballpark, is right across the street from the stadium. 5811 Glenwood, (208) 375-1330.

Players Pub and Grill is also a popular sports bar. 5504 W. Alworth, (208) 376-6563.

### ◆ LODGING
Ramada Inn is about 20 minutes from the ballpark. 1025 Capitol Boulevard, Boise. (208) 344-7971/(800) 228-2828.

### ◆ DIRECTIONS
From I-84, take the Franklin Street exit. Turn left on Cole Road and stay on Cole for about three miles. After the road takes a slight jog to the left, make your first right onto Glenwood. The ballpark is about 1½ miles away on the right. Parking is severely limited at the ballpark, so you must park on the street.

**MEMORIAL STADIUM**
**5600 Glenwood Street**
**Boise, ID 83714**
**(208) 322-5000**

**Capacity: 4,500**
**LF 330, CF 390, RF 330**

### ◆ TICKET AND SCHEDULE INFORMATION
All games start at 7 P.M.

The Hawks open their season in mid-June and close it the first week of September.

Ticket prices: $7 box seats; $5.50 third-base and home-plate reserved seats; $4.50 first-base reserved bench; $3.50 general admission, $2.50 youth and seniors.

# EUGENE EMERALDS

## ATLANTA BRAVES

The team switches affiliations for 1995 to the Atlanta Braves from the Kansas City Royals, and the Ems will replace the royal blue of the Royals with light navy. The club expects a big seller for 1995 to be the newly revamped baseball caps with a navy-blue crown and Kelly-green details.

The stadium boasts 5,000 seats in the shade, with one-third of them covered, a good move in the great Northwest, where light rains fall so often. Built in 1938 by local lumber barons with help from the WPA, it was completely renovated in 1969 to comply with Pacific Coast League guidelines, but it's still an old-fashioned park made almost completely out of wood.

### ◆ LOCAL AND TEAM HISTORY
Organized baseball came to Eugene in 1904, when the Blues joined the Oregon State League, which folded after its first and only season. Pro ball returned here in 1955, when Eugene began its association with the Northwest League. Eugene played five seasons in the Pacific Coast League (1969-73), winning two division titles, in 1969 and '72, but losing each time in the championship round. Bob Wellman was one of the winningest managers in minor league history, posting 1,663 victories in 25 years, but in May 1970, during his third season as Eugene's skipper, he was fired as his team slid into the PCL Northwest Division's cellar with a 15-28 record. Mike Schmidt batted .291 for Eugene in 1972, while also clubbing 26 homers and 91 runs batted in. The year before, Greg Luzinski led the PCL with 319 total bases, 36 homers, 114 runs batted in and a .312 average.

With 1,670 wins coming into 1995, the Ems lead the Northwest League all-time list in

OTHER FAMOUS ALUMNI — OTHER FAMOUS ALUMNI

Brian McRae, Tom Gordon, Bob Hamelin, Jesus Alou, Kevin Appier, Melido Perez, Larry Bowa and Denny Doyle played here.

that department. The team is named for the local Emerald Valley.

### ◆ BALLPARK EXTRAS

The Ems offer a barbecue pit featuring Polish sausage and chicken breast sandwiches cooked to order. Pregame lines are long, but the wait is worth it. There's also pizza made while you wait, snow cones and one of the more unusual ballpark offerings, but one perfect for the Northwest: espresso.

### ◆ ATTRACTIONS

The University of Oregon, in the heart of the city, is the center of much of the culture that Eugene has to offer. Annual events include the Bach Festival, in which concerts are performed in parks around the city. (503) 346-3111.

Another popular warm-weather feature is the weekly flea markets on Saturdays, when local merchants set up booths around the city. (503) 346-3111.

Other attractions include the Museum of Art (503-346-3027) and the Museum of Natural History (503-346-3024).

If you like road running, this is the place for you. Eugene has been home to such world-class runners as Alberto Salazar and Steve Prefontaine, and there are many roadside tracks set up for running enthusiasts, as well as for bikers and walkers.

For more information about Eugene, call the Chamber of Commerce, (503) 484-1314.

### ◆ DINING

The Steelhead Brewery is a microbrewery and restaurant about five minutes away that features sandwiches, pizza and calzones. The brewing vats are in full view of the patrons, who can buy beer to take home with them. 199 E. 5th, (503) 686-2739.

West Brothers, which is 10 minutes from the park, offers some of the best barbecue in town and also features a microbrewery. 844 Olive Street, (503) 345-8489.

### ◆ LODGING

Eugene Motor Lodge is about 15 minutes from the ballpark. 476 E. Broadway, Eugene, (503) 344-5233.

### ◆ DIRECTIONS

From I-5, take Highway 126 to downtown. From 126, take the 8th Street exit. Turn left on Pearl Street and go south to 20th Street. The ballpark will be on your right. Parking is free but limited at the ballpark. On-street parking is also available.

---

**CIVIC STADIUM**
2077 Willamette
Eugene, OR 97405
(503) 342-5367

Capacity: 7,200
LF 335, CF 400, RF 328

### ◆ TICKET AND SCHEDULE INFORMATION

Game times are Monday through Saturday at 7:05 P.M. and Sundays at either 2 P.M. or 6 P.M.

The Ems open their season in mid-June and it ends the first week of September.

Ticket prices: $5 box seats; $3.50 general admission. Children under 12 and seniors $1 each.

---

# EVERETT AQUASOX

### SEATTLE MARINERS

The team has been so popular that a new stadium is being planned to hold the overflow of fans. It is expected to be ready for 1996 and will expand seating to 4,500 as well as add many new amenities. For now, fortunately, fans who want to see the AquaSox and can't get a seat can still sit on the grass down the lines and enjoy the baseball.

It's hard to find a more beautiful ballpark. Memorial Stadium boasts twin views of the Cascade Mountains on one side and the Olympic mountain range on the other.

### ◆ LOCAL AND TEAM HISTORY

Everett hosted minor-league ball for one year, 1905, in the Northwestern League and was then without pro ball until 1984 when this club joined the Northwest League. If the team itself lacks that patina of baseball history, its owners certainly don't: The club is co-owned by the

OTHER FAMOUS ALUMNI

Matt Williams played here.

husband-and-wife team of Bob and Margaret Bavasi, part of a family that has so many baseball ties in both the majors and minors—niece Aimee is the assistant general manager.

### ◆ BALLPARK EXTRAS

The team's new mascot is a cross between a frog and Brooks Robinson. Expect, judging by recent trends, for it to be a hot seller nationwide as well as in the Puget Sound area. In addition, Everett is well-known for its ballpark food. Homemade soup is served each night (after all, it gets cold in the great Northwest), and yogurt, herbal tea and fruit juices are also among the offerings.

Another highlight is when head groundskeeper Jim Averill (grandson of Hall of Famer Earl Averill) dons a costume and races a fan home from second base.

### ◆ ATTRACTIONS

From July 4 through Labor Day the city operates a ferry to Jetty Island, a man-made island with attractive beaches and nature walks. For further information, call (206) 259-0300. Tours are given twice daily of the Boeing Aircraft factory.  For further information, call (206) 342-4801.

For more information about Everett, call the Chamber of Commerce, (206) 252-5181.

### ◆ DINING

Anthony's Home Port is a few minutes from the ballpark. Everett Marina Village, (206) 252-3333.

Giorgio's Pizza & Spaghetti House is also a short drive away. 9031 Evergreen Way, Everett, (206) 347-1542.

### ◆ LODGING

West Coast Everett Pacific is about five minutes from the ballpark. 3105 Pine Street, Everett, (206) 339-3333.

### ◆ DIRECTIONS

From I-5, take exit 192, which becomes Broadway after you leave the highway. Turn left at the King's Table Restaurant. The ballpark will be on the left. There is plenty of free parking at the ballpark. On-street parking is also available.

---

**EVERETT MEMORIAL STADIUM**
**2118 Broadway**
**Everett, WA 98201**
**(206) 258-3673**

---

**Capacity: 2,300**
**LF 330, CF 395, RF 335**

---

### ◆ TICKET AND SCHEDULE INFORMATION

Games start at 7 P.M. on weeknights and at 6 P.M. on weekends.

The AquaSox open their season in mid-June and finish the first week of September.

Ticket prices: $6.50 adult pavilion seats; $4.50 children's pavilion and adult general admission; $3.50 children's general admission.

# PORTLAND ROCKIES

## COLORADO ROCKIES

**B**ecause Civic Stadium, once known as Multnomah Stadium, is the former home of a AAA team, it should come as no surprise that it is the largest ballpark of any in Rookie, A or AA. The stadium, which opened in the 1930s and hosted greyhound racing more than 50 years ago, is in downtown Portland, with several apartments and stores in the surrounding area. There is a large, roomy concourse here with concession stands. A walkway runs the length of the covered grandstand, which features old wooden benches. While the left-and-center-field fences are about 25 feet tall, their counterpart in right is less than 5 feet high. This ballpark has also become famous for one of the more unusual outfield billboards in the minors, featuring the Jantzen swimwear company's diving girl, which is mounted in play on the left-field side. The team is not sure whether the billboard will be here to open the 1995 season. There are also plans to open a picnic area and to install several hot tubs at the ballpark.

*OTHER FAMOUS ALUMNI*

Darren Daulton, Joe Tinker, Mickey Cochrane, Mickey Lolich, Lee Elia, Johnny Lipon, Luis Tiant and Lou Pinella played or managed here.

### ◆ LOCAL AND TEAM HISTORY

Pro baseball first came to Portland in the 1890s. Since the turn of the century, Portland has been affiliated with six minor leagues, most notably as a charter member of the Pacific Coast League (1904-72, '78-93). In 1928 and 1929, Jim Keesey collected 474 of his 2,966 career minor-league hits for Portland. Bill Thomas, the winningest pitcher in minor-league history with 383 victories, pitched here from 1938 to '40. In that time, Thomas posted 54 victories and led the 1939 PCL in games with 49. Adolph Liska is one of the greatest pitchers in Portland history. In his 14 seasons here, 1936 to '49, Liska won 198 games, including a league-best 24 in 1937. Bernardo Brito captured six minor-league home-run titles, tied for No. 3 all-time, in 13 seasons. In 1990 and 1991, he slugged a total of 52 home runs to win two straight PCL home-run crowns for the Portland Beavers.

When the AAA Beavers relocated to Salt Lake City for the 1994 season, it left the stadium dark until the Colorado franchise took advantage of the site by moving its Short Season Northwest League club over from Bend for 1995.

There have been several memorable moments over the years, ranging from visiting player Willie Stargell's home run to right field, which was estimated at more than 500 feet, to one of the most famous plays in recent minor-league history: the night Vancouver outfielder Rodney McCray chased a fly ball right through the Flav-R-Pac sign in the right-field fence. He broke his nose.

### ◆ BALLPARK EXTRAS
Portland will welcome a new mascot in 1995, one that should be close to the hearts of Beatles fans in particular: Rocky Raccoon. There are also plans for a barbecue grill and a concession stand offering beers from area microbreweries.

### ◆ ATTRACTIONS
The Oregon Sports Hall of Fame honors more than 200 inductees, ranging from Johnny Pesky to Rick Wise. On display are such items as Dale Murphy's Gold Glove and uniforms of the Portland Beavers team. 900 S.W. 5th Street, Portland, (503) 227-7466.

The picturesque Oregon coast is a one-hour drive west on Highway 26. The Columbia and Willamette rivers flow through the city of Portland, making it an especially scenic spot without one's even having to travel. The Cascade Mountains are an hour east.

The Washington Park Zoo, two miles from the Stadium, is also a popular spot. (503) 226-7627.

An hour's drive away in the state of Washington is Mount St. Helen's, the volcano that blew its top in 1980.

For more information about Portland, call the Chamber of Commerce, (503) 228-9411.

### ◆ DINING
There are several good restaurants within a few minutes' walk from Civic Stadium. Red Robin Burger and Spirits Emporium is right next door. S.W. 20th Place and W. Burnside, (503) 222-4602.

Cody's Cafe is about five blocks away. 115 N.W. 22nd, Portland, (503) 248-9311.

### ◆ LODGING
Red Lion Inn/Coliseum is about 10 minutes from the ballpark. 1225 N. Thunderbird Way, Portland, (503) 235-8311/(800) 547-8010.

The Marriott is just ½ block away. 1401 S.W. Front, Portland, (503) 226-7600/(800) 228-9290.

### ◆ DIRECTIONS
Exit freeway I-405 on Everett Street and turn west. Go left on 18th Avenue and then turn right on Morrison Street. Civic Stadium will be on the left.

```
CIVIC STADIUM
P.O. Box 998
Portland, OR 97207
(503) 223-2837

Capacity: 23,000
LF 309, CF 407, RF 348
```

### ◆ TICKET AND SCHEDULE INFORMATION
All home games begin at 7:05 P.M., with the exception of Sunday games from July 23 through August 13, which start at 2:05 P.M.

The Rockies open their home schedule in mid-June and close out in early September.

Ticket prices: $8 VIP box seats; $6 reserved seats; $5 general admission, $4 children under 12.

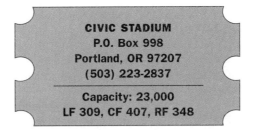

# SOUTHERN OREGON ATHLETICS

**OAKLAND ATHLETICS**

According to reports from the time, baseball was first played on this site in the 1890s. The original field here was built in 1916, only to burn down on July 4, 1951. The remaining home games that season were canceled, forcing the team to embark on an extended road trip with 25 uniforms donated by the Pacific Coast League's San Francisco Seals. Rebuilt in 1961 largely through the efforts of Claude "Shorty" Miles, it was renamed in his honor in 1969. Fans visiting Miles Field today can enjoy a view of Mount McLoughlin, part of the Cascade Mountain chain, from wooden seats in the covered grandstand. Fortunately, since the eight-foot-high outfield wall mostly obscures a nearby shopping mall, the mountain vista offered by Miles Field can be enjoyed without commercial intrusions. The field is currently in the third phase of a four-step renovation plan. By 1996, it is planned to be a state-of-the-art facility thanks to a $3.5 million refurbishing.

### ◆ LOCAL AND TEAM HISTORY

Organized baseball made its Medford debut in 1948 when the Nuggets began a four-year membership in the Class D Far West League. This franchise first joined the Northwest League in 1967 and has been associated with the circuit continuously since 1979. Larry Shepard's 22 wins led the league in '48, when Medford finished in second place, three games out of first, with Shepard at the helm as player-manager. In 13 minor-league seasons, Shepard averaged almost 14 wins per year, finishing with 179 career victories. In 1967, the Medford Giants pummeled the Lewiston Broncos in a four-game series, sweeping the games by a combined score of 61-13. The series included three innings in which the Giants scored at least 10 runs. The 1982 Medford A's won the league championship, posting a 53-17 record and .757 winning percentage, the latter a Northwest League record and one of the 10 best all-time among short-season teams. Rod Beck struggled here in 1986 and 1987, posting a 6-11 record and 5.21 ERA overall.

**OTHER FAMOUS ALUMNI** — Jose Canseco, Kurt Abbott, Frank Lucchesi, Wally Whitehurst, Terry Steinbach and Brent Gates all played or managed here.

### ◆ BALLPARK EXTRAS

One popular recent promotion has been the Lazy Lounge Chair. At every home game, two fans are selected to watch the game from lounge chairs. They are each given a baseball glove as well, and if they catch a foul ball they win $1,000. There is also a carnival booth where fans can win prizes playing such games as ring toss, dart toss and coin toss. Proceeds go toward the stadium's renovation fund. Among the concession offerings are Subway sandwiches, barbecue beef and chicken and gourmet ice cream.

### ◆ ATTRACTIONS

The Britt Festival Concert Series is a popular summer event held at the Medford Center (800-88-BRITT).

Also a big draw is the Oregon Shakespeare Festival. 15 S. Pioneer Road, Ashland, (503) 482-4331.

There is also good golfing and fishing in the area.

For more information about the Medford area, call the Chamber of Commerce, (503) 779-4847.

### ◆ DINING

Adam's Rib is a couple minutes from the ballpark and features ribs, steaks and chicken. 1812 E. Barnett Road, (503) 773-9696.

Digger O'Dells features casual dining and is also just a couple minutes away from the stadium. 333 E. Main Street, (503) 779-6100.

### ◆ LODGING

Horizon Motor Inn is about three minutes away. 1150 E. Barnett Road, Medford, (503) 779-5085.

Red Lion is five to 10 minutes from the park. 200 N. Riverside, Medford, (503) 779-5811/(800) 547-8010.

### ◆ DIRECTIONS

The ballpark is ½ mile south of Barnett Road on South Pacific Highway 99.

**MILES FIELD**
1801 S. Pacific Highway
Medford, OR 97501
(503) 770-5364

Capacity: 2,900
LF 342, CF 384, RF 332

### ◆ TICKET AND SCHEDULE INFORMATION

Game times are at 7 P.M. from Monday through Saturday and at 6 P.M. Sunday.

The A's open their season mid-June and end it the first week of September.

Tickets prices: $7.50 box seats; $6.50 reserved seats; $4.50 general admission.

# SPOKANE INDIANS

## KANSAS CITY ROYALS

Fairgrounds Recreational Park, which was the original name of the current stadium, was built in less than three months back in 1958 as a home for the AAA farm team of the Los Angeles Dodgers. Built for a cost of just over $500,000, the original stadium seated 9,000 and featured a manual scoreboard and a huge black-and-white clock. The batting cage was imported directly from Ebbets Field in Brooklyn. An extensive renovation in 1979 included improved lighting and an electronic scoreboard. When the team was purchased in 1986 by the Brett brothers (Bobby and Ken, later to be joined by future Hall of Famer George), they joined Spokane County in funding more major improvements such as major-league-style sky boxes and new locker rooms.

### ◆ LOCAL AND TEAM HISTORY

Spokane has been home to minor-league ball in several different leagues off and on dating back to 1902, and has hosted baseball uninterrupted since 1958 when it joined the Pacific Coast League. The 1970 team, which featured many future Dodgers stars, went 94-52 and is considered one of the best all-time minor-league teams. That squad was led by Bobby Valentine, who topped the league in several offensive categories. After dropping down to the short-season Northwest League for 1972, Spokane rejoined the PCL from 1973 to '82 before rejoining the Northwest League for good in 1983. In 1946, nine members of the Spokane club were killed when their bus crashed in the Cascade Mountains en route to a game in Bremerton, Wash. Two years later, Fevis Field in Spokane was destroyed by fire. In 1993, when he was managing the San Diego affiliate here, cur-

OTHER FAMOUS ALUMNI
OTHER FAMOUS ALUMNI

Steve Garvey, Bill Buckner, Bobby Valentine, Charlie Hough, Davey Lopes, Tommy Davis, Willie Davis and Sandy Alomar Jr. all played here.

rent Spokane manager Tim Flannery was ejected from a game only to sneak back in dressed as the Indians' mascot Spokane-a-saurus, a blue-and-red dinosaur. He not only danced to *Louie, Louie* but also led the club back from a two-run deficit to win the game.

### ◆ BALLPARK EXTRAS

One unique recent promotion was Fire Prevention Night, which was also a celebration of Smokey the Bear's birthday. The Indians gave away trees.

### ◆ ATTRACTIONS

Spokane's Riverfront Park features the antique Looff Carousel, with its 54 hand-carved horses. It has been part of Spokane history since 1909. For schedule information, call (509) 625-6600.

The Spokane River Centennial Trail, which stretches 22 miles from Riverfront Park downtown to the Washington/Idaho border, is a popular attraction for walkers, joggers and cyclists.

The Bing Crosby Memorabilia Collection is on display at Gonzaga University and features, among other goodies, der Bingle's pipes, gold and platinum records and Oscars. His boyhood home in Spokane is the home of the Gonzaga Alumni Association. 502 E. Boone Avenue, (509) 328-4220.

For more information about Spokane, call the Chamber of Commerce, (509) 624-1393.

### ◆ DINING

Milford's is a Spokane tradition for fresh seafood. It's about 15 minutes from the ballpark. 719 N. Monroe Street, (509) 326-7251.

The Calgary Steak House, about 10 minutes from the ballpark, claims to have Spokane's best steaks. 3040 E. Sprague, (509) 535-7502.

### ◆ LODGING

Value Inns by Cavanaugh is about 15 minutes from the ballpark. 1203 W. 5th Avenue, Spokane, (509) 624-4142.

### ◆ DIRECTIONS

Take I-90 West to Havana exit. Go four blocks north on Havana to signs to fairgrounds. From the west, take I-90 East to Thor/Freya exit. Go west to Havana, then go four blocks north to signs to fairgrounds.

---

**SEAFIRST STADIUM**
**Interfirst Fairgrounds**
**602 N. Havana**
**Spokane, WA 99202**
**(509) 535-2922**

Capacity: 7,101
LF 335, CF 398, RF 335

Monday through Saturday night games begin at 7:05 P.M. with Sunday games starting at 6:05 P.M. Three home games—June 19, July 2 and July 26—have 3:05 P.M. starts.

The Indians' season opens in mid-June and ends the first week of September.

Ticket prices: $5.50 reserved seats; $3.50 general admission, $2.50 children, seniors and the military.

# YAKIMA BEARS

## LOS ANGELES DODGERS

Opened in 1993, Yakima County Stadium is the newest ballpark in the league. The short porches in left and

right fields—293 feet from home plate with 16-foot-walls and the minimal amount of foul territory—make it a hitter's dream. The stadium's asymmetrical design creates some challenging bounces, especially for visiting outfielders unfamiliar with the territory.

If you need something to watch between innings, just look over the right-field fence at the horse-racing track next door and see if you can pick the winner of the third race. The stadium also boasts one of the best scoreboards in the league, a state-of-the-art multicolored gem that combines an old-fashioned look with modern technology.

Yakima is located on the east slope of the Cascade Mountains, and Yakima County boasts the distinction of ranking first among all United States counties in the number of fruit trees. The grape production has helped the local wine industry to boom, as growing conditions are similar to those in Napa Valley.

### ◆ LOCAL AND TEAM HISTORY
Organized baseball first came to Yakima in 1920, when this city began a two-year association with the Class B Pacific Coast International League. The Yakima Pippins, named after the local apple variety, joined the Western International League in 1937, the first of 14 seasons in this circuit. Yakima had notched 12 years in the Northwest League before baseball left town following the 1966 season, not returning until 1990, when Los Angeles began its affiliation. In 1921, Yakima captured the Pacific Coast International pennant behind George

Lafayette, who led all of organized baseball that year with a .428 batting average. Leonard Tucker, the first African-American ballplayer to sign with the St. Louis Cardinals organization, helped the Yakima Bears win the 1960 Northwest League championship by topping the circuit with 48 stolen bases and 126 runs scored. Hub Kittle, now the Cardinals' minor-league pitching instructor, is the most renowned figure in Yakima baseball history, winning 20 games as a pitcher in 1939 and four Northwest League championships as manager.

### ◆ BALLPARK EXTRAS
Concession specialties in Yakima include a foot-long grilled kielbasa smothered in sauerkraut and onions, and a foot-long all-beef hotdog. The family burger from the Bears Barbecue is so huge that many couples share it. It may well be the biggest single food item offered in the minors.

OTHER FAMOUS ALUMNI OTHER FAMOUS ALUMNI

Pedro Astacio played here.

### ◆ ATTRACTIONS
Apart from being able to tour the growing number of wineries (23 offer tasting rooms) the area has to offer, there is much else to do in the Yakima area.

The Yakima Indian Nation Cultural Center offers a look at the past and present of that nation; it includes a museum, restaurant, library and gift shop. For more information, call (509) 452-2502.

Avid golfers may recognize the 17th hole of the local Apple Tree Golf Course, which is an island green shaped like an apple—it has been featured in numerous golf magazines. (509) 966-5877.

For more information about Yakima, call the Chamber of Commerce, (509) 248-2021.

### ◆ DINING
Deli de Pasta offers gourmet Italian cuisine, including homemade pastas. One of Yakima's favorite restaurants, it's about 15 minutes from the ballpark on historic North Front Street, the birthplace of the city. 7 N. Front Street, (509) 453-0571.

Grant's Brewery Pub, like Deli de Pasta, is on North Front Street, about five minutes away. It offers a gourmet pub-food menu to go with the fruits of America's oldest brew pub. 32 N. Front Street, (509) 575-2922.

## ◆ LODGING

The Huntley Inn is five minutes from the park. 12 E. Valley Mall Boulevard, Union Gap, (509) 248-6924.

Holiday Inn of Yakima is also five minutes away. 9 N. 9th Street, Yakima, (509) 452-6511/(800) HOLIDAY.

## ◆ DIRECTIONS

Take I-82 to Nob Hill Boulevard exit. Go west to 10th Street, then north to Pacific.

**YAKIMA COUNTY STADIUM**
**810 West Nob Hill Boulevard**
**Yakima, WA 98902**
**(509) 457-5151**

**Capacity: 4,485**
**LF 293, CF 400, RF 293**

## ◆ TICKET AND SCHEDULE INFORMATION

All home games begin at 7:05 P.M.

The Bears' season opens in mid-June and ends in the first week of September.

Ticket prices: $5.50 box seats, $4.50 bleacher back seats; $3.75 general admission, $2.75 children and seniors.

# MINOR LEAGUE MEMORIES

## ST. CATHARINES

*St. Catharines general manager Ellen Harrigan-Charles, part of what is arguably baseball's first all-woman management team, recalls how her career has developed:*

"I started with the Toronto Blue Jays in 1981 as a secretary in player development. Then I moved up to an administrative assistant and I worked as an administrative assistant for probably five or six years. In 1989, a vacancy occurred down here in St. Catharines. I thought it was an opportunity to see the other side of baseball. I received the job after a couple of interviews. I took over as assistant general manager in 1989. In 1990, I was the interim general manager and in September I was assigned the position of general manager on a full-time basis. That's how I got here."

## GENEVA

*In 1960, Tony Perez was an 18-year-old rookie who had just arrived in upstate New York from Cuba to begin his professional baseball career. He talks about what it's like adjusting to life in a new country:*

"I had to learn a new language. I had to adjust to different places. I had to learn a new culture. My first year, in 1960, I was in Geneva, New York. I can tell you there were six guys from Cuba on the team who came out [of Cuba] for the first time. Only three stayed. The other three got homesick, couldn't take the pressure and went back. They couldn't communicate with people. There were things trying to stop me, trying to get me to go back to my country. I wouldn't do it. I loved the game. I always admired one player in Cuba, Minnie Minoso. I wanted to be a good player like him. I just put that in my mind and did it."

## BELLINGHAM

*Pitcher Lee Guetterman has won 38 games with four big-league teams (Yankees, Mets, Mariners, Cardinals) over his 14-year pro career. He recalls his first season, when he played for Bellingham.*

"In '81—that was my rookie year—we had to push our bus because it wouldn't start. We did that for three or four road trips until it just wouldn't start anymore. The Northwest League is 70 games, 70 hard games because the shortest bus ride was 6 1/2 hours for us and the longest was 12 hours. With 31 players and your coaching staff on a 1957 touring bus, it makes for some interesting occurrences. Everybody had to push the bus. It was [just] too big a bus. The only guy who wouldn't was the guy who was starting that night."

## PORT CHARLOTTE

*Detroit Tigers' catcher Chad Kreuter, who played for five different cities in his minor-league career, ranks Port Charlotte of the Florida State League as his favorite.*

"I was there in 1987. We lived in a place that was on the water. I'd take a little ferry ride out to the beach during the day before the game. I did a lot of fishing. The weather down there is beautiful during the summer on the coastal areas, it doesn't get that hot. I lived in a one-bedroom condo with my wife. We paid $300 a month. I know during the [tourist] season they rent those out for about $1,000 a week. It was very plush, especially for a Single A player."

## WEST PALM BEACH

*Montreal Expos' manager Felipe Alou rates West Palm Beach as his favorite among the five minor-league cities he managed in:*

"We won the pennant in 1981 in Denver [AAA]. That was OK. But winning the pennant in West Palm in 1991 was very special because I live there. I'm known by everybody here, especially the fishermen from all of south Florida."

# APPALACHIAN LEAGUE

**T**he Appalachian League is the oldest operating Rookie League in organized baseball, having begun operations in 1911. In 1963, the Appy League shifted from Class D to its current Rookie status, after previously forming and disbanding four times in its history. Today, there are 10 teams in small towns clustered primarily around the Blue Ridge and Appalachian mountains; they are located in West Virginia, Virginia, Tennessee and North Carolina. Each team plays 68 games, with the regular season beginning June 19 and ending August 28. In 1994, Appalachian League teams attracted 438,070 fans to their ballparks, led by the Danville (Virginia) Braves, who drew 70,862.

• • •

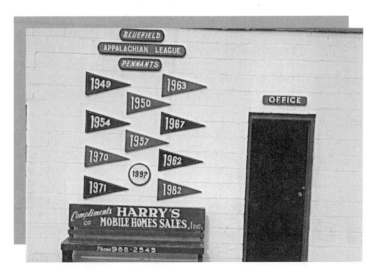

*Bluefield's championship legacy, proudly displayed at Bowen Field.*

# BLUEFIELD ORIOLES

## BALTIMORE ORIOLES

**B**owen Field, built in 1939 and extensively remodeled in 1990, lies in a valley surrounded by green mountains; one particularly prominent peak looms just over the left-field fence. Besides its scenic backdrop, the ballpark is also distinctive due to Bluefield's location astride the Virginia–West Virginia state line. While Bowen Field is in West Virginia, the team's offices are in Virginia. When driving to the park from nearby U.S. 460, you cross back and forth between the two states.

Bowen Field's setting, the nighttime crickets and a lively crowd make this park a lovely spot in which to watch a ballgame. During your visit, amble over to the left-field line, near the visitors' dugout. There, by a green bench with a sign that reads "Railbirds—Reserved Seats," you will find a group of inveterate local fans, engaged in what are likely to be spirited discussions about that night's game, baseball in general or whatever else suits them.

### ◆ LOCAL AND TEAM HISTORY

Bluefield has been affiliated with the Baltimore Orioles since 1958, currently the longest marriage between major- and minor-league teams in baseball. George Fanning, Bluefield's general manager, boasts the longest tenure of any such current minor-league executive, having caught on with this franchise in 1948, two years after Bluefield joined the Appalachian League. Professional baseball had first come here in 1937 when the Bluefield Blue-Grays were a member of the Class D Mountain State League.

The Bluefield of today shares a distinction with Princeton, its Appalachian League neighbor, only 10 miles away. The two towns are the second-closest

**FAMOUS ALUMNI** Don Baylor, Eddie Murray, Doug DeCinces, Cal and Billy Ripken and Mark Belanger played here.

pair of communities in North America to have their own affiliated minor-league baseball teams.

### ◆ BALLPARK EXTRAS

One food item deserves particular mention: chili dogs, the local favorites. Try one with everything—hot dog, tangy chili, onions and mustard. No alcoholic beverages are sold at the park, and none may be brought in by fans.

### ◆ ATTRACTIONS

If you are in Bluefield over Memorial Day weekend, check out the Mountain Festival. Information can be obtained from the Chamber of Commerce, (304) 327-7184.

Pinnacle Rock State Park is about 10 miles northwest of Bluefield on U.S. 52. The park, which offers picturesque views of the surrounding countryside, also features hiking trails and picnic facilities. There is no charge. For information, call (800) CALL-WVA.

### ◆ DINING

Johnston's Restaurant, 10 minutes away, serves well-prepared, country-style Southern food. The glazed ham and browned black beans are particularly good. Don't forget to ask about the dessert specials. Other pluses are low prices and friendly servers who chat freely with the customers. It's next to the Town-n-Country Motel at exit 9 off I-77, in Princeton, (304) 425-7591.

The usual selection of fast-food restaurants can be found in Bluefield along U.S. 52.

### ◆ LODGING

Holiday Inn is 10 minutes from the ballpark, at the junction of U.S. 52 and U.S. 460, west of the Bluefield exit off I-77. (304) 325-6170/(800) HOLIDAY.

Ramada Inn–East River Mountain is five minutes away on U.S. 52, west of I-77. (304) 325-5421/(800) 228-2828.

### ◆ DIRECTIONS

From U.S. 460, take the Westgate Shopping Center exit, which is either the last exit in West Virginia if you are going to Virginia or the first exit in West Virginia if you're coming from the opposite direction. Go to the first traffic light and turn left, re-enter Virginia and take the first right, Route 102. You will see Bowen Field's large parking lot on your left after about 1/2 mile. Parking is plentiful and free.

**BOWEN FIELD**
P.O. Box 356
Bluefield, WV 24701
(703) 326-1326

Capacity: 3,000
LF 335, CF 365, RF 335

### ◆ TICKET AND SCHEDULE INFORMATION

Most games are played at 7 P.M. Doubleheaders start at 6 P.M.

The Orioles' season opens in mid-June and ends in late August. To purchase tickets in advance or for additional information, call the Orioles' offices. Ticket prices: $2.50, $1 for students with identification.

# BRISTOL WHITE SOX

## CHICAGO WHITE SOX

In 1994, De Vault's 25th anniversary, the ballpark underwent a face-lift, resulting in the installation of a new clubhouse, new lights and an improved grandstand area. Named after former Appalachian League president and Bristol resident Chauncey De Vault, it is an attractive ballpark. There is a football stadium used by the local high school right next door, behind the first-base bleachers. A hill rises beyond the tree-lined outfield fence. In 1992, according to team president Boyce Cox, who played for Bristol in the 1940s, one player's home run hit the house perched atop that hill, while over the years, several other homers have landed on the street beside it.

This is Bristol's first year of affiliation with the Chicago White Sox, after the Tigers terminated a 25-year relationship with this town following the 1994 season.

### ◆ LOCAL AND TEAM HISTORY

In 1911, organized baseball made its first appearance in Bristol, a small town evenly divided by the border separating Tennessee and Virginia. Over the years, the team's nicknames, such as the Border Cits and State Liners, have reflected this geographic anomaly. But perhaps Bristol's greatest claim to fame occurred in 1952. On

May 13, "Rocket" Ron Necciai of the Bristol Twins struck out 27 batters in a nine-inning game, the only pitcher in history to do so. Bristol defeated Welch 7-0. Necciai did not stop there. He whiffed 24 batters eight days later before being promoted. He pitched later that year for the Pittsburgh Pirates, posting a 1-6 record in his only big-league season. Arm injuries forced him to retire in 1955. Today, about a mile from De Vault, a dairy occupies the former site of Shaw Stadium where Necciai made what is likely a permanent place for himself in the record books. Also in 1952, Bristol's Bill "Ding Dong" Bell, who would later pitch in five games for Pittsburgh, tossed two consecutive no-hitters, the first minor-league pitcher to accomplish this feat since 1901. He added a third no-hitter later that season.

**FAMOUS ALUMNI**

Bobby Thomson, Alan Trammell, Lou Whitaker, Chris Hoiles, Lance Parrish, Dan Petry, Travis Fryman and Mark "The Bird" Fidrych all played here.

### ◆ BALLPARK EXTRAS

The concession stand, operated by the local high school, offers standard and unremarkable ballpark fare. During the game, check out the sign on the outfield fence with a picture of a cigar and top hat. For several years, an anonymous local resident has paid to have this personal message displayed here. But the person's identity and the sign's meaning remain a mystery.

### ◆ ATTRACTIONS

On U.S. 421 in Tennessee, you will find Bristol Caverns, which features several interesting underground rock formations. Admission is $7, $6 for children 5 to 12 and seniors 62 and over. For further information, call (615) 878-2011. Bristol International Raceway, located on U.S. 11, features NASCAR racing. For information, call (615) 764-1161.

For more information about the Bristol area, call the Chamber of Commerce, (615) 989-4850.

### ◆ DINING

Several fast-food and national chain restaurants are located within the area surrounding the ballpark.

### ◆ LODGING

Holiday Inn is five minutes away, at the intersection of State Route 11W and U.S. 421. (703) 669-7171/(800) HOLIDAY.

Econo Lodge is down the street from the ballpark on

Commonwealth Avenue. Take exit 3 from I-81. (703) 466-2112/(800) 446-6900

### ◆ DIRECTIONS

From I-81, take exit 3, I-381 south to Bristol. Go to the second full traffic light and turn right on Euclid. The ballpark, about 1½ miles from I-81, will be on your right shortly after you make the turn. Plenty of free parking is available.

---

**DE VAULT MEMORIAL STADIUM**
P.O. Box 1434
Bristol, VA 24203
(703) 645-7275
_____
Capacity: 1,500
LF 325, CF 365, RF 335

---

### ◆ TICKET AND SCHEDULE INFORMATION

Most games begin at 7 P.M. Doubleheaders begin at 6 P.M.

The White Sox' home opener is usually in mid-June, and the season concludes at the end of August.

Ticket prices: $3, $2 children. Little League teams are admitted free.

---

# BURLINGTON INDIANS

### CLEVELAND INDIANS

BURLINGTON
INDIANS

Burlington Athletic Stadium may have the most unusual past of any minor-league ballpark. The story begins after the 1958 season, when the Danville Leafs decided to drop out of the Carolina League. The company that owned the land where Danville's League Park was located concluded that a shopping center would suit the property better than a ballpark did. Knowing that Burlington, which had been without organized baseball since the end of the '55 season, needed a ballpark in the hopes of attracting a team back to the city, the company offered it League Park. Burlington purchased the ballpark for $5,000 and then moved League Park south to Burlington. The entire 2,000-seat stadium was dismantled, and each piece was carefully cataloged and numbered as though it were an archaeological find. A convoy of flatbed trucks then transported the disassembled ballpark to Burlington, where it gradually reemerged as its former self.

The Athletic Stadium of today still bears some resemblance to League Park, with the same corrugated-metal roof and concrete foundation, but in 1986, the wooden grandstand seats were replaced with metal ones and a new set of bleachers was installed down the foul lines.

### ◆ LOCAL AND TEAM HISTORY

Organized baseball arrived here in 1942, when the Burlington Bees spent their first and only season in the Class D Bi-State League, which folded following that campaign. Three years later, Burlington began a 26-season association (1945-55, '58-72) with the Carolina League. Baseball left town after the 1972 season and did not return until 1986, when the Indians were admitted to the Appalachian League. That was also the year Burlington began its current affiliation with the Cleveland Indians.

In 1946, Gus Zernial set a Carolina League record by belting 41 home runs for the Bees. During his 11 seasons in the majors, he hit 237 homers, including an American League–best 33 for the Philadelphia A's in 1951. Zernial's Carolina League home-run record was broken in '49 by Leo "Muscle" Shoals, who hit 55 four-baggers to lead all of organized baseball. "Rocket" Ron Necciai pitched about two months for Burlington in 1952 after being promoted from Bristol. In 18 games, Necciai posted a 1.57 ERA and 172 strikeouts in 126 innings. He was the winning pitcher in the Carolina League All-Star game, and in two consecutive relief appearances, Necciai struck out 11 straight batters, a feat since unmatched in this league. Although he did not pitch enough innings to qualify for the league ERA title, Necciai did top all pitchers in strikeouts. By the time August rolled around, Ron Necciai was a Pittsburgh Pirate. Necciai returned here in 1953 after injuring his arm but was unable to duplicate his success of the previous season. In only six games, his ERA was 7.04.

Tommie Agee batted .258 for Burlington in 1962. Seven years later, he was the center fielder for the world champion New York Mets. Luis Tiant played for the Burlington Bees one year after Agee. Tiant won 14 of 23 decisions and compiled a 2.56 ERA. His 207 strikeouts led the league. Tiant became famous in his big-league career for an unorthodox pitching delivery, which saw

**OTHER FAMOUS ALUMNI** **OTHER FAMOUS ALUMNI**
Toby Harrah, Mark Lewis and Jim Thome all played here.

him turn his back to the batter before throwing the ball. El Tiante won 229 games over 19 years in the majors. Manny Ramirez, one of Cleveland's hottest prospects, was the Appy's MVP in 1991. That season, he led the circuit with 19 homers, 63 runs batted in, 146 total bases and a .679 slugging percentage.

### ◆ BALLPARK EXTRAS

The Indians are offering burritos for the first time in 1995. You can also try the chili dogs and barbecue pork sandwich. There are picnic areas down each foul line.

### ◆ ATTRACTIONS

The Alamance Battleground Park memorializes a 1777 Revolutionary War battle. Within the park, you will also find an 18th-century log home, typical of those built in North Carolina at that time. Admission is free. For further information, call (910) 227-4785.

For additional information about Burlington, call the Chamber of Commerce, (910) 228-1338.

### ◆ DINING

Zack's Restaurant, about 15 minutes from the ballpark, has been a Burlington fixture for decades. In 1961, Bees' catcher Duke Sims had a memorable meal here. He set an all-time Zack's record that still stands by downing 22 hot dogs in one sitting. Sims went on from Zack's to spend 11 years in the big leagues. But the season he spent in Burlington, when he batted .304 with 21 home runs and 88 runs batted in, turned out to be the best of his pro career, perhaps thanks to Zack's. 201 W. Davis Street, (910) 226-4746.

### ◆ LODGING

Comfort Inn is at exit 145 from I-85, about 10 minutes from the ballpark. (910) 227-3681/(800) 4-CHOICE.

Hampton Inn is at exit 141 from I-85, about 15 minutes from the ballpark. (910) 584-4447/(800) 426-7866.

### ◆ DIRECTIONS

From I-85, take exit 145, State Route 49 north to Mebane Street. Turn right on Mebane. Stay on Mebane and turn right on Beaumont. Stay on Beaumont and turn left on Graham. The ballpark will be immediately visible. There is plenty of free parking.

**BURLINGTON ATHLETIC STADIUM**
P.O. Box 1143
Burlington, NC 27216
(910) 222-0223
_____
Capacity: 3,500
LF 335, CF 400, RF 335

### ◆ TICKET AND SCHEDULE INFORMATION

Most games are played at night, starting at 7:05 P.M.

The Indians' home opener is usually in mid-June and the season concludes at the end of August.

Ticket prices: $5 box seats, $4 general admission, $3 senior citizens and students with identification.

# DANVILLE BRAVES

### ATLANTA BRAVES

**D**an Daniel Stadium, completed in 1993, is the newest ballpark in the league. Built into a bowl-like depression on the side of a hill overlooking the Dan River, the park is in a very scenic location. In summertime, a variety of trees blooms on the hill lying behind the outfield fence. The stadium is located on the grounds of Dan Daniel Memorial Park, a city-run recreation facility complete with hiking trails and Little League fields.

### ◆ LOCAL AND TEAM HISTORY

After an absence of 35 years, minor-league baseball returned to a very appreciative city in 1993. In the Braves' first two seasons, they have drawn more than 150,000 fans, including an Appalachian League–record 80,539 in '93. Although there was a long gap between teams in Danville, pro baseball here nevertheless dates back to 1905, when Danville captured the Class D Virginia–North Carolina League title.

That season, the team was nicknamed the Tobacconists (changed to the Leafs in 1926), reflecting tobacco's role in Danville's history. Tobacco-processing plants still operate in the surrounding area.

FAMOUS ALUMNI  FAMOUS ALUMNI

Willie McCovey, Leon Wagner and Manny Mota all played here.

### ◆ BALLPARK EXTRAS

You should have no trouble finding something to eat here. Popular items include corn dogs, grilled chicken and burgers. But the nachos supreme, with ground beef, tomatoes, lettuce, onions, sour cream, jalapenos, cheese and salsa, are clearly the local favorite.

### ◆ ATTRACTIONS

Danville is the site of the last capitol of the Confederate States of America. Jefferson Davis wrote his final proclamation as Confederate president in what is today Danville's Museum of Fine Arts, 975 Main Street. Admission is free. For further information, call (804) 793-5644.

Information about driving and walking tours of Danville's historical sites, including those related to the Civil War, can be obtained by calling the Chamber of Commerce, (804) 793-5422.

### ◆ DINING

King of the Sea is near the Dan River, about five minutes from the ballpark. This is a family-style restaurant specializing, not surprisingly, in seafood, as well as steak, barbecue chicken and barbecue pork. 1799 Memorial Drive, Danville, (804) 793-0331.

Several national chains and fast-food restaurants are located on U.S. 58.

### ◆ LODGING

The Innkeeper is 15 minutes away on U.S. 58. 3020 Riverside Drive, Danville, (804) 799-1202.

The Stratford Inn is on U.S. 58, just east of the U.S. 29 bypass, five minutes away. 2500 Riverside Drive, Danville, (804) 793-2500/(800) 326-8455.

### ◆ DIRECTIONS

Take U.S. 86 North to U.S. 58 East. Stay on 58 for about two miles and turn right on River Point Drive. After about one mile, turn right on River Park Drive. The ballpark will be immediately visible. While the Braves do not charge for parking at the stadium, there is a city-imposed $2 fee (unheard-of for a Rookie League facility) to enter Dan Daniel Memorial Park. Parking is readily available at the stadium.

**DAN DANIEL STADIUM**
**P.O. Box 3637**
**Danville, VA 24543**

**Capacity: 3,000**
**LF 330, CF 400, RF 330**

### ◆ TICKET AND SCHEDULE INFORMATION

Most games are played at night, starting at 7:30.

The Braves' home opener is usually in mid-June, and the season concludes at the end of August.

Ticket prices: $4 general admission, $2 children 14 and under and seniors 60 and over. There are also $6 reserved seats, but they are almost exclusively sold to season ticketholders.

# ELIZABETHTON TWINS

**MINNESOTA TWINS**

Once you step into this ballpark, cast your eyes towards the outfield to see Joe O'Brien's most distinctive features. Just behind the right-field wall there is a city-owned pool. The Twins shuffle their batting-practice order so that their left-handed power hitters take their cuts after 5:30 P.M., when the pool is closed. So many baseballs were landing in the pool that the city altered its operating hours and the Twins juggled their practice schedule to minimize the risk to swimmers.

The other odd feature is the wooden center-field wall; at 24 feet high, it's among the minors' tallest. Attached to the wall is a large basketball hoop and net, which is tied at the bottom. Ever since the Twins began their affiliation with Elizabethton in 1974, Appalachian League players have taken aim at this basket in order to win $1,000 for hitting a ball into the net, a daunting task. Finally, in 1989, Tom Hardgrove of the Martinsville Phillies did the improbable, becoming the only player to slam dunk a baseball into Elizabethton's net. The local business that sponsors the $1,000 challenge did pay up.

### ◆ LOCAL AND TEAM HISTORY

With one two-year interruption (1943-44) and another of 23 years (1952-73), organized-baseball teams have played in this small northeast Tennessee city ever since 1937, when Elizabethton first entered the Appalachian League. This team's current association with the Appy began in 1974.

OTHER FAMOUS ALUMNI  OTHER FAMOUS ALUMNI

Kirby Puckett, Kent Hrbek and Mark Portugal all played here.

Elizabethton's Hobe Brummitt is probably the greatest manager in league history. He won five straight pennants here between 1937 and 1941 and captured another while managing Kingsport in 1945. His career managerial record was 522-395. Brummitt was also a pretty good player, batting .397 with 26 home runs and 122 runs batted in in 1928 for Greensboro of the Class C Piedmont League, and .356 for Durham in 1924 to lead the Piedmont. Andy Seminick, a catcher for the 1950 Philadelphia Whiz Kids who spent 15 seasons in the majors, hit 31 homers for Elizabethton in 1941 and '42. In 1950, Doug Clark (who never played in the big leagues) set a seemingly unsurpassable league record for Elizabethton by winning 27 games, tied for third best among all minor-league pitchers that season.

### ◆ BALLPARK EXTRAS

A local youth-soccer organization runs the concessions here. The organization's president, Bill Huntsinger, operates a small outdoor grill at the ballpark and serves up good sausages, burgers and hot dogs. On occasion, he has also been known to sell some homemade cheesecake. After the game, he takes care of the ballplayers, the coaches and the manager by giving them some of his fare. For 1995, the team has installed new aluminum seats for the grandstand. Fans bring their own folding chairs to sit along the first-base foul line. Beer cannot be sold at or brought into the park.

### ◆ ATTRACTIONS

Sycamore Shoals State Historical Park is located on U.S. 321. This site commemorates an 18th-century settlement, thought to be the first permanent American community outside the original 13 colonies. Admission is $3, $2 for children 6 to 12. For further information, call (615) 543-5808.

The Carter Mansion on the Broad Street extension off U.S. 321 is one of the oldest surviving homes in this state, dating to 1780. Admission is free. For further information, call (615) 543-6140.

For additional information about this area, call the Northeast Tennessee Tourism Association, (615) 753-4188 (ext. 25) or from outside Tennessee, (800) 468-6882 (ext. 25).

### ◆ DINING

Ridgewood Restaurant, 15 minutes away, has been serving up good barbecue for almost 50 years, with side orders of homemade coleslaw, beans, fries and plenty of sauce. 900 Elizabethton Highway, U.S. Route 19 E, Bluff City, (615) 538-7543.

Several fast-food restaurants are located along State Highway 67/321.

### ◆ LODGING

Comfort Inn is 10 minutes away on the U.S. 19E bypass. (615) 542-4466/(800) 4-CHOICE.

Sky Inn is two or three minutes away on W. Elk Avenue in Elizabethton. (615) 543-3344.

### ◆ DIRECTIONS

From I-81, take I-181. Exit at State Highway 67/321. Stay on 67/321 and turn left at Holly Lane. Holly Lane

is hard to miss because at the corner is Pal's Hot Dog Stand, which features an enormous hot-dog sign and a flagpole. After turning left, drive right into the ballpark's parking lot. Parking is plentiful and free.

> **JOE O'BRIEN FIELD**
> **136 S. Sycamore**
> **Elizabethton, TN 37643**
> **(615) 543-4395**
>
> **Capacity: 1,500**
> **LF 335, CF 407, RF 320**

### ◆ TICKET AND SCHEDULE INFORMATION

Most games are played at night, starting at 7 P.M.

The Twins' home opener is usually in mid-June, and the season concludes at the end of August.

Ticket prices: $3, $2 children under 12.

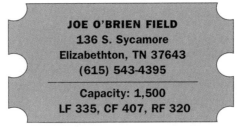

# RIVER CITY RAMPAGE

### INDEPENDENT

This ballpark, originally built in 1910, is reputed to have the oldest existing grandstand of any operating ballpark in organized baseball. Though there's little to substantiate the story, legend has it that earlier this century, the entire wooden grandstand was moved piece by piece from another ballpark in Huntington to its present location. Once you pass through the turnstiles here, find a seat and enjoy St. Cloud's bucolic setting and history. Out beyond the outfield fence, softball fields are surrounded by an abundance of trees.

### ◆ LOCAL AND TEAM HISTORY

Huntington had a brief fling with pro baseball in the 19th century, fielding a team for one season (1894) in the Tri-State League. This city began its 20th-century association with organized baseball in 1910 when St. Cloud Commons opened and Huntington captured the pennant in the Class D Virginia Valley League's only season. The next year, Huntington began an eight-season (1911-12, '37-42) association with the Class D Mountain State League. Huntington also spent time in the Class D Ohio State League (1913-16) and the Class C Middle Atlantic League (1931-36). The Huntington Cubs joined the Appalachian League in 1990 after this city had been without pro baseball for 47 years. Following 1994, the Chicago Cubs terminated their five-year affiliation with this team, which is being operated as a co-op this year, with players from several organizations.

Benny Borgmann was one of Huntington's leading hitters in 1935 and '36. In '35, he led the Middle Atlantic League with 35 stolen bases while batting .307. The next year, Borgmann hit .314 and stole 26 bases. In his 15-year minor-league career, Borgmann swiped 284 bases. But he was more than a basestealer. Before suiting up for the Huntington Red Birds, he was a standout in the American Basketball League, leading all players in scoring for four seasons (1926-27, '28-29, '29-30 and '30-31). Today, he is a member of the Pro Basketball Hall of Fame. Walter Alston, a baseball Hall of Famer, was a 24-year-old teammate of Borgmann's in 1936. That season, Alston was the premier power hitter in the league, topping the circuit with 35 home runs (his career high) while also batting .326 and driving in 114 runs (also a career high). Despite the presence of these two formidable hitters, plus that of pitcher Mike Martynik, who led the league with 226 strikeouts, the Red Birds could finish no better than sixth place, 21 games out of first, with a 60-69 record.

Dave Stevens, who threw the first pitch in Huntington's first Appalachian League game in 1990, became the present franchise's first alumnus to reach the big leagues. In 1994, Stevens was 5-2 in 24 games while posting a 6.80 ERA for the Minnesota Twins.

### ◆ BALLPARK EXTRAS
Huntington has good grilled sausage and barbecue chicken. The Chicago hot dogs, served with tomatoes, onions, peppers and relish, are worth checking out as well.

### ◆ ATTRACTIONS
The Huntington Museum of Art has several 19th- and 20th-century paintings, plus a collection of Ohio Valley glass and a nature center on the museum grounds. Admission is $2, $1 for seniors over 60 and children 12 and older. For further information, call (304) 529-2701.

For additional information about Huntington, call the Chamber of Commerce, (304) 525-5131.

### ◆ DINING
Loredo Steak House, about 10 minutes from the ballpark, offers a good selection of beef, including sirloin, prime rib and filet mignon, plus grilled chicken. 2138 5th Street Road, (304) 697-4810.

### ◆ LODGING
Holiday Inn Gateway is between exits 15 and 20 off I-64, about 15 minutes from the ballpark. (304) 736-8974/(800) HOLIDAY.

Comfort Inn/Barboursville is at exit 20 off I-64, about 20 minutes from the ballpark. (304) 736-9772/(800) 4-CHOICE.

### ◆ DIRECTIONS
From I-64, take exit 6/State Route 52 and turn left at the traffic light on Madison Street. Go about three blocks to 19th Street and turn left. The ballpark will be in front of you and on the right. Plenty of free parking is available.

---

**ST. CLOUD COMMONS**
P.O. Box 7005
Huntington, WV 25775
(304) 429-1700
_____
Capacity: 3,100
LF 332, CF 385, RF 330

---

### ◆ TICKET AND SCHEDULE INFORMATION
Most games are played at night, starting at 7 P.M. Sunday games begin at 6 P.M.

Huntington's home opener is usually in mid-June, and the season concludes at the end of August.

Ticket prices: $5 box seats (lower level grandstand); $5 club seats (behind the dugouts); $4 reserved seats; $3 general admission; $2 seniors 60 and over and children under 12.

# JOHNSON CITY CARDINALS

## ST. LOUIS CARDINALS

Howard Johnson Field underwent a major renovation in 1994. The grandstand now features a new roof and seats, and the new brick gateway entrance to the field effects an old-time ballpark flavor at Howard Johnson, which was built in 1956. An improved scoreboard will be installed for the 1995 season. But despite all the changes to this ballpark, its most memorable feature was thankfully preserved. From the right-field foul line to right-center field, there is a 15-foot-high hill that rises from the warning track up to the wooden outfield fence. Johnson City's hill is the subject of much fascination and attention each season. When the Cardinals arrive here for the first time in the spring, the players practice "playing the hill" for two days. A Cardinals coach stands near first base and hits fungoes to players in rightfield so they can try their hand at running uphill to chase down fly balls. If there is one thing that ballplayers who have spent time in the Appalachian League never forget, it is the hill in Johnson City.

## ◆ LOCAL AND TEAM HISTORY

Organized baseball first came to this northeastern Tennessee community in 1910 when Johnson City fielded a team in the Class D Southeastern League. The next season, this city began its association with the Appy, which has continued since then with only relatively brief interruptions (1914-20, '25-36, '56, '62-63). The team, which has won more games than any other existing Appalachian League franchise, began its current affiliation with St. Louis in 1975.

Leo "Muscle" Shoals, the greatest power hitter in league history, whose 362 career home runs rank him 10th on the all-time minor league list, topped the Appalachian League in 1939 with 16 four-baggers and a .365 batting average for Johnson City. Howie Nunn, who finished his three-year big-league career with a 4-3 record, won 18 games for Johnson City in 1955 while also striking out 23 batters in a 13-inning game. His 249 K's that season led the league. Ron Blomberg, baseball's first official designated hitter, was a 19-year-old rookie when he hit .297 with 10 homers and 55 runs batted in (tops in the league) for Johnson City in 1967. More recently, Danny Cox was virtually unhittable in 1981 as he led the Appy in ERA (2.06), innings pitched (109), strikeouts (87), complete games (10) and shutouts (4). He also hurled an 11-0 no-hitter against Bristol.

*OTHER FAMOUS ALUMNI — OTHER FAMOUS ALUMNI*

*Terry Pendleton, Ray Lankford, Bobby Murcer and Geronimo Pena all played here.*

## ◆ BALLPARK EXTRAS

The concession menu here is rather limited although the Cardinals do serve some good chili dogs and grilled burgers. There is a picnic area in left field.

## ◆ ATTRACTIONS

The Hands On! Regional Museum on Main Street offers a variety of interactive exhibits allowing visitors to experience flying a plane or touching sea creatures. Admission is $4. For further information, call (615) 434-HAND.

Buffalo Mountain Park, located just outside of town, offers hiking trails, scenic overlooks and picnic facilities. For further information, call (615) 283-5815.

For additional information about this area, call the Northeast Tennessee Tourism Association, (615) 753-4188, ext. 25/(800) 468-6882, ext. 25.

## ◆ DINING

House of Ribs, about 15 minutes from the ballpark, serves steaks and seafood, but the specialty is ribs, half and whole rack. The ribs, as well as the chicken and beef barbecue, are served with the House of Ribs' own homemade sauce. For dessert, try some homemade banana pudding. 3100 N. Roan Street, Johnson City, (615) 282-8077.

Several national chain and fast-food restaurants are located on North Roan Street, about 15 minutes from the ballpark.

## ◆ LODGING

Holiday Inn is about 10 minutes from the ballpark, on North Roan Street on U.S. 11 East. (615) 282-2161/(800) HOLIDAY.

Fairfield Inn by Marriott is about 10 minutes from the park, just south of I-181 at the junction of U.S. 11 East and U.S. 19 West. (615) 282-3335/(800) 348-6000.

## ◆ DIRECTIONS

From I-181, take the Main Street exit. Go 1 block and turn left. Turn left at the first traffic light and left again at the second light. The ballpark will be on your left after about 7 blocks. Free parking is available at the ballpark.

**HOWARD JOHNSON FIELD**
P.O. Box 568
Johnson City, TN 37605
(615) 461-4850

Capacity: 3,800
LF 320, CF 410, RF 320

## ◆ TICKET AND SCHEDULE INFORMATION

Most games are played at night, starting at 7 P.M. Doubleheaders begin at 6 P.M.

The Cardinals' home opener is usually in mid-June, and the season concludes at the end of August.

Ticket prices: $3, $2 for seniors, $1 children.

# KINGSPORT METS

## NEW YORK METS

After playing in J. Fred Johnson Stadium since 1956, Kingsport closed the doors on this ballpark for the last time in 1994. In 1995 the Mets' play their first season in their new ballpark, which is only about five miles from Johnson Stadium.

### ◆ LOCAL AND TEAM HISTORY

With the exception of 19 years (1926-37, '55-56, '64-68), organized baseball has been played in this city since Kingsport joined the Appalachian League in 1921. Interspersed with its Appy membership, Kingsport had a two-year (1953-54) association with the Mountain States League. This franchise has been affiliated with the New York Mets since 1980.

Leo Shoals, whose 362 career homers rank him 10th on the minor-league home-run list, is probably the greatest power hitter in the history of this franchise and the Appalachian League. Nicknamed "Muscle" in 1939 after a prodigious hitting display in an exhibition with the St. Louis Cardinals, Shoals was a member of the Kingsport Cherokees for six seasons (1946-47, '51, '53-55) as a player and player-manager. In that time, he led his league in home runs five times, runs batted in twice and batting average twice (the Appy, with a .387 average, and the Mountain States League in 1953, with a .427 average). In 1951, he won the Appalachian League Triple Crown by batting .383 with 30 home runs and 129 runs batted in. But despite his hitting prowess, Shoals never played in the big leagues.

Steve Dalkowski was regarded as one of the hardest-throwing pitchers of his day during his nine-year (1957-65) minor-league career, which began in Kingsport. That season, he gave a preview of the control problems that would bedevil him and, ultimately, prevented him

OTHER FAMOUS ALUMNI OTHER FAMOUS ALUMNI

Darryl Strawberry, Kevin Mitchell, Dwight Gooden and Gregg Jefferies played here.

from reaching the majors. In 1957, he posted an astronomic 8.13 ERA while leading the Appy in walks (129) and earned runs (56) in just 62 innings. He also struck out 121 that season.

In 1971, Steve Blass was the star of the Pittsburgh Pirates pitching staff as he won two World Series games en route to the Bucs' championship. In 1960 he was 4-1 with a 2.57 ERA as an 18-year-old rookie with Kingsport. In 1974, manager Hoyt Wilhelm could not help his team avoid seventh place. The Kingsport Braves finished with a 31-39 record, 21½ games out of first. That was the last time this Hall of Famer managed a professional baseball team.

### ◆ BALLPARK EXTRAS

The Mets feature standard ballpark fare.

### ◆ ATTRACTIONS

Bays Mountain Park is about seven miles outside of town. The park features a nature preserve, an aquarium, hiking trails and a planetarium. Admission is $2, $1.50 more for the planetarium. For further information, call (615) 229-9447.

Gaines-Preston Farm is a restored pioneer homestead dating back to the 1850s. For further information, call (615) 288-6071.

For additional information about this area, call the Northeast Tennessee Tourism Association, (615) 753-4188, ext. 25/(800) 468-6882, ext. 25.

### ◆ DINING

Skoby's is a casual, popular local restaurant 10 minutes from the park that serves steak, seafood and barbecue and features a good-sized salad bar. 1001 Konnarock Road, (615) 247-5629.

### ◆ LODGING

Holiday Inn is 15 minutes away at the intersection of U.S. 11 west and U.S. 36. (615) 247-3133/(800) HOLIDAY.

Ramada Inn is 15 minutes away on U.S. 11 near State Route 93. (615) 245-0271/(800) 228-2828.

### ◆ DIRECTIONS

From I-81, take exit 57 to I-181. From I-181, take the West Stone Drive exit. Turn left onto West Stone and continue for about a mile. Turn right on Granby Road. The ballpark is about one mile away on the right.

**KINGSPORT SPORTS COMPLEX**
433 E. Center Street
P.O. Box 1128
Kingsport, TN 37662
(615) 247-7181

Capacity: 2,000
LF 330, CF 400, RF 330

### ◆ TICKET AND SCHEDULE INFORMATION

Most games are played at night, starting at 7 P.M. Sunday games begin at 7:30 P.M.

The Mets' season opens in mid-June and closes at the end of August.

Ticket prices: $2 for all seats.

# MARTINSVILLE PHILLIES

## PHILADELPHIA PHILLIES

Professional baseball has been played on the site currently occupied by Hooker Field, named for a local furniture company, for more than 60 years. The park was built somewhat below street level so you have to walk slightly downhill from the parking lot and concession area to the diamond. Once inside, you will quickly see that the most popular seating areas are on top of the dugouts and on the hill behind third base. Fans place their own folding chairs here in preparation for an evening of baseball and friendly conversation with neighbors. The dimensions of Hooker Field are also worth noting. In preparation for the '95 season, the center-field wall was pushed back approximately 30 feet from its previous distance of 370 feet from home plate, previously the second-shortest centerfield in the league, behind Bluefield's.

### ◆ LOCAL AND TEAM HISTORY

The Manufacturers, this city's first pro team, took the field in 1934 as a member of the Class D Bi-State League, which Martinsville belonged to through 1941. After a five-year stint in the Carolina League, highlighted by the 1948 championship, Martinsville lost its team following the '49 season. Organized baseball did not return here until 1988, when the current franchise joined the Appalachian League.

### ◆ BALLPARK EXTRAS

Martinsville's concessions all feature a connection to the team's nickname, such as Phillies jumbo hot dogs and the Phill-Up, where beer can be purchased. A good selection of grilled items are sold, including burgers, chicken and Phillies steaks. The home-plate grandstand area is separated from each dugout by a chain-link fence, which enables you to see virtually everything that goes on inside. Throughout the game, fans can be seen standing at the barrier, trying to talk to their favorite players or angling for autographs.

### ◆ ATTRACTIONS

The Virginia Museum of Natural History includes several dinosaur-related exhibits. A token fee is requested for admission. For further information, call (703) 666-8600.

The Martinsville Speedway offers auto racing (such as the Goody's 500 in September) during the spring and fall. For further information, call (703) 956-3151.

For more information about the Martinsville area, call the Chamber of Commerce, (703) 632-6401.

**FAMOUS ALUMNI**  **FAMOUS ALUMNI**

Hall of Famers Enos Slaughter and Heinie Manush both played here.

### ◆ DINING

Mackie's, about 15 minutes from the park, is in an 80-year-old building and is furnished with lots of antiques. It serves country-style Southern food, including fresh beans and greens, homemade biscuits, fresh-cut steaks and a local favorite, the Flowerin' Onion, a large Vidalia onion that opens like a flower after being deep fried. 326 Virginia Avenue, Collinsville, (703) 647-3138.

Several national chains and fast-food restaurants can be found along U.S. 220 North Business near the ballpark.

### ◆ LODGING

Best Western Martinsville Inn is five minutes away on U.S. 220 North Business. (703) 632-5611/(800) 528-1234.

Dutch Inn is 15 minutes away, in nearby Collinsville on U.S. 220 North Business. (703) 647-3721.

### ◆ DIRECTIONS

From U.S. 220 North Business, take Commonwealth Boulevard east about 3 miles to Highway 58 and turn left. Go north on 58 for about 2 blocks, past a high school and car dealership. Hooker Field will be on the right. Parking is plentiful and free.

### ◆ TICKET AND SCHEDULE INFORMATION

Most games are played at night, beginning at 7:15 P.M.

The Phillies' home opener is usually in mid-June, and the season concludes at the end of August.

Ticket prices: $5 gold reserved box seats; $4 general admission, $2 children 14 and under and seniors 60 and over.

# PRINCETON REDS

## CINCINNATI REDS

**H**unnicutt Field is also used by the Princeton High School baseball team, making it a uniquely intimate place to watch Rookie League games. Most of the pros who play at Hunnicutt were high school players themselves before signing their contracts, perhaps just weeks before being assigned to the Appalachian League, so teenagers from Princeton High cheer ballplayers who only recently could have been their classmates. The home crowd generally is fairly lively, especially when the Reds play their local rivals, the Bluefield Orioles. Each year, the two teams compete for the Mercer Cup, named for the county where both cities are located and awarded to the winner of their season series. In 1994, Bluefield won the cup while Princeton captured the Appy League title and set a franchise attendance record (40,209) along the way.

### ◆ LOCAL AND TEAM HISTORY

Princeton is a relative newcomer to minor-league baseball, with the town fielding its first team in 1988. But despite the local franchise's short history, Princeton nevertheless occupies a singular place among minor-league communities. Besides its proximity to Bluefield, Princeton (population of approximately 7,300) is also the smallest town with its own affiliated minor-league team in North America.

### ◆ BALLPARK EXTRAS

The Reds offer rather typical and unremarkable ballpark fare, such as hot dogs, hamburgers and nachos. State law prohibits the sale of beer at Hunnicutt Field. The Reds stage several innovative promotions, most notably, allowing fans to dance on the field with the team mascot, Rosco the Princeton Red Rooster, for various prizes.

### ◆ ATTRACTIONS

Princeton is close to several attractive state parks, including Pipestem Resort, which has facilities for golfing, skiing, canoeing and camping. The park is located on State Route 20, northeast of town. There is no charge. For further information, call (304) 466-1800.

Bluestone Lake, just north of Pipestem on Route 20, features water-skiing. Rafting is available in the Bluestone Scenic River and the nearby New River Gorge National River. There is no charge. For information, call (800) CALL-WVA.

**FAMOUS ALUMNI**
Sam Mejias and Calvin Reese both played or managed here.

To obtain additional information about Princeton, call the chamber of commerce, (304) 487-1502.

### ◆ DINING

Johnston's Restaurant, five minutes away, serves well-prepared, country-style Southern food. The glazed ham and browned black beans are particularly good. Don't forget to ask about the dessert specials. Other pluses are low prices and friendly servers who chat freely with the customers. It's next to the Town-n-Country Motel at exit 9, off I-77, Princeton, (304) 425-7591.

Several fast-food restaurants are located along Route 104.

### ◆ LODGING

Town-n-Country Motel is five minutes away at exit 9 off I-77, or at the Route 104 exit for Route 460. (304) 425-8156.

Days Inn is five minutes away, directly across Route 460 from the Town-n-Country. (304) 425-8100/(800) 325-2525.

## ◆ DIRECTIONS

Exit Route 460 where it intersects Route 104 West and turn left at the traffic light. Turn left at the next light, about a mile distant. Continue for about two miles to Princeton High School on the left. Turn left at the traffic light just after the high school, then left again to reach the field. Parking is free and readily available.

**HUNNICUTT FIELD**
**P.O. BOX 5646**
**Princeton, WV 24740**
**(304) 487-2000**

**Capacity: 1,537**
**LF 330, CF 396, RF 330**

## ◆ TICKET AND SCHEDULE INFORMATION

Most games are played at 7 P.M. Doubleheaders start at 6 P.M.

The Reds' home opener is usually in mid-June, and the season concludes at the end of August. You can bring your own folding chairs to the park and sit directly behind the home-plate screen, beneath the grandstand, which is uncovered.

Ticket prices: $3.25, $2.25 children 7 to 17 and seniors 62 and over. Children under age 6 are free.

# PIONEER LEAGUE

The Pioneer League began play in 1939 and has operated uninterrupted ever since, except for its suspension during the war years of 1943-45. There have been several landmarks of minor-league history in this league. In 1978, Billings outfielder Gary Redus hit .462, which still stands as the highest average in baseball history for a player with more than 200 at-bats. In 1982, a first baseman playing for Kansas City's Butte club set a pair of league records that still stand—28 doubles and 48 extra-base hits. But apparently the Royals weren't very impressed; they dealt Cecil Fielder to the Toronto Blue Jays. In 1987 the independent Salt Lake City Trappers won 29 games in a row, still a minor-league record.

In 1994, the Billings Mustangs won their third consecutive league title. Rosters are limited to 30 players, none of whom may have had more than two years of prior pro experience. This year, the Pioneer League will play two 36-game halves and add an opening round to its playoffs. League attendance for 1994 was 416,985, up 60,432 from 1993. Independent Lethbridge (42,970) set a franchise record, while Billings drew 100,556 to lead the league.

• • •

*As the Helena Brewers score a run, Mt. Helena is visible behind Kindrick Field's outfield fence.*

# BILLINGS MUSTANGS

## CINCINNATI REDS

Cobb Field, built in 1948, is a gem that should not be missed. It benefits from having one of the minors' most spectacular locations, beneath the Billings Rimrocks, 100-foot-tall sandstone cliffs about ½ mile from the ballpark. An airport is located above the cliffs, so it is not unusual to see planes glide over the rimrocks as they approach the runway. Although the wooden seats from the covered grandstand were removed in the early 1980s, you can still see remnants of the original ballpark by looking up at the roof, which is supported by large wood beams. A city-owned swimming pool, where many foul balls have landed over the years, is located behind third base. To avoid injuries to swimmers, the pool is closed during games, unlike its counterpart in Elizabethton. This ballpark is named for Bob Cobb, the owner of the original Brown Derby restaurant in Hollywood, who brought pro baseball to Billings in 1948.

### LOCAL AND TEAM HISTORY

Billings has hosted a pro baseball team since 1948, the year this city became a member of the Pioneer League. At that time, the Mustangs were a farm team of the Pacific Coast League's Hollywood Stars. Several of Bob Cobb's celebrity friends from Tinseltown were team stockholders, including Bing Crosby (who was named honorary chairman of the board), Robert Taylor, Barbara Stanwyck and Cecil B. DeMille. Hall of Fame catcher Mickey Cochrane was a member of the board of directors, while Charlie Root, the pitcher famous for throwing Babe Ruth's called-shot home run in Chicago, was the player-manager. All of these well-known personalities must have been disappointed in Billings' inaugural season, because the Mustangs finished last, with a record of 48-77. Larry Shepard won 20 or more games for Billings three straight times, 1949 to '51, completing a string of four consecutive 20-win seasons that began in Medford in 1948. In 1978, Gary Redus had one of the greatest seasons in baseball history. He batted .462 for Billings, the highest average in the annals of organized baseball. But Redus did not stop there. He also led the circuit with 100 runs scored, 117 hits and 199 total bases, all league records. The Mustangs easily won the Pioneer League title that year, besting second-place Idaho Falls by nine games. Billings began its current affiliation with Cincinnati in 1974, the longest connection with the same big-league parent of any Pioneer League franchise.

### OTHER FAMOUS ALUMNI

George Brett, Gorman Thomas and Kal Daniels played here.

### ◆ BALLPARK EXTRAS

In addition to the usual giveaways, family nights and park buyouts by sponsors, the top promotions include appearances by the Blues Brothers and Billy Bird. The concessions are unremarkable.

### ◆ ATTRACTIONS

Custer's Battlefield is 50 minutes south. (406) 665-2060.

Yellowstone National Park is two hours west on I-90. (307) 844-7381.

There are plenty of outdoor activities such as fishing, camping, biking, hiking, swimming, golf and tennis nearby. For more information about the Billings area, call the Chamber of Commerce, (406) 252-4016.

### ◆ DINING

The Billings Club is about 15 minutes from the park. 2702 1st Avenue N, (406) 245-2262.

Golden Belle is also about 15 minutes away. 1st Avenue and 28th Street, (406) 245-2232.

### ◆ LODGING

The Sheraton is five minutes away. 27 N. 27th Street, Billings, (406) 252-7400/(800) 325-3535.

Radisson Northern Hotel is also five minutes away. 19 N. 28th Street, Billings, (406) 245-5121/(800) 333-3333.

### ◆ DIRECTIONS

From I-90, take the 27th Street exit and proceed north toward the rimrocks and the airport. You will pass through downtown. Cobb Field is at 27th Street and 9th Avenue, next to the large swimming pool.

---

**COBB FIELD**
**901 N. 27th Street**
**Billings, MT 59103**
**(406) 252-1241**

**Capacity: 4,400**
**LF 335, CF 405, RF 325**

---

### ◆ TICKET AND SCHEDULE INFORMATION

All games are at 7 P.M., except July 4 (1 P.M.) and select Sunday games (1 P.M.).

The Mustangs' home opener is usually in mid-June and the season ends in the first week of September.

Ticket prices: $4.50 box seats; $3.50 general admission, $2.50 student and seniors.

# BUTTE COPPER KINGS

## INDEPENDENT

This ballpark, which is on the campus of Montana Tech University, offers fans in the covered grandstand a scenic view of Rocky Mountain foothills beyond the left- and center-field fences. The Montana Tech Orediggers NAIA football team shares the Coliseum with the Copper Kings, who use the left-field football bleachers for large crowds on big promotion nights. These bleachers can accommodate about 2,500 fans. Alumni Coliseum sits atop a hill in an area of the city called Uptown. This name is quite appropriate, since fans can look right into the heart of Butte from their hilltop perch on the right-field side of the ballpark. There is a pavilion-style picnic area in left field.

The Copper Kings' name relates to Butte's mining past. At one time, gold, silver and copper made some in this area quite wealthy, so much so that one of the heights overlooking Butte was called "The Richest Hill in the World." The team's logo, a bearded miner swinging a bat with a crown on his head, is an imaginative tribute to the original copper kings, who made their fortunes from the mineral wealth they took from this area.

### ◆ LOCAL AND TEAM HISTORY

Pro baseball has been played in this city since the 1890s. Since the turn of the century, Butte has been associated with six circuits, including the Pacific Northwest League (1903), Pacific National League (1903-04), Northwestern League (1906-08, 1916-17), Inter-Mountain League (1909), Union Association (1911-14) and Pioneer League (1978-85, 1987-to date). In 1995, the Copper Kings will operate as a co-op, with players from several big-league organizations.

Butte captured the 1903 Pacific National League championship behind the strong pitching of Pete Dowling, who posted a 30-20 record. Dowling's 30 wins in

'03 rank him as one of 84 minor-league pitchers in this century to win at least 30 games in one season. Julio Franco was only 16 years old when he played for Butte in 1978 and batted .305 in 47 games. Four years later, Butte's Cecil Fielder made a strong impression on the league's record book, setting all-time marks for most doubles (28) and extra-base hits (48) in a season while also batting .322 with 20 homers and 68 runs batted in over 69 games. Randy Ready won the first of his two minor-league batting championships in 1980 by pacing the circuit with a .376 average.

**OTHER FAMOUS ALUMNI**

Dion James, Rusty Greer, Robb Nen and Omar Vizquel played here.

### ◆ BALLPARK EXTRAS

The Copper Kings offer a good selection of concession items, including brats, Polish sausage, chicken and burgers. Wine is also available, and the team is considering serving barbecue-beef sandwiches.

### ◆ ATTRACTIONS

The Deer Lodge National Forest has camping and fishing facilities, as well as peaks approaching elevations of 10,000 feet; pine trees; several different types of wild animals; a recreation area designed for handicapped visitors and a 19th-century ghost town. For further information, call (406) 496-3400.

The Copper King Mansion is a restored home of one of Butte's 19th-century mineral barons. Admission is $5, $4.50 for seniors and $3.50 for children 6 to 18. For further information, call (406) 782-7580.

For additional information about Butte, call the Chamber of Commerce, (406) 494-5595.

### ◆ DINING

Uptown Cafe, about five minutes from the ballpark, is a restaurant with many choices. At lunchtime, the Uptown is set up as a cafeteria, with a choice of soups and entrees plus a salad bar. But for dinner, linens are placed on the tables and a varied menu is offered, featuring such imaginative choices as grilled tuna in Oriental mesquite marinade, rack of lamb, fresh pasta and duck. 47 E. Broadway, (406) 723-4735.

### ◆ LODGING

The Capri Motel is at the Montana Street exit off I-15/90, about 10 minutes from the ballpark. (406) 723-4391.

Townhouse Inn is at exit 127 off I-15/90, about 15 minutes from the ballpark. (406) 494-8850/(800) 442-INNS.

### ◆ DIRECTIONS

From I-15/90, take the Montana Street exit and turn right. Stay on Montana for about three miles and head into Butte. Turn left on Park and go uphill for about one mile. The ballpark will be on the left. Parking is free at the ballpark's small lot. Additional parking is available across the street and behind the left-field fence.

---

**ALUMNI COLISEUM**
P.O. Box 186
Butte, MT 59703
(406) 723-8206

Capacity: 5,000
LF 350, CF 410, RF 360

---

### ◆ TICKET AND SCHEDULE INFORMATION

Most games are played at night, starting at 7 P.M.

The Copper Kings' home opener is usually in mid-June, and the season ends in the first week of September. Unlike in most cities, tickets for weekend games here are usually easy to buy because many local residents leave town on Friday to take advantage of the area's many outdoor recreational opportunities.

Ticket prices: $5 reserved seats; $4 general admission, $3 students, seniors and military with identification. Children under 5 are free.

# GREAT FALLS DODGERS

## LOS ANGELES DODGERS

Legion Ballpark is part of Great Falls War Memorial Park, which also includes an 18-hole municipal golf course. The ballpark dates to 1940 and was built by local brewery owner Emil Sick. The park sits above the Missouri River, a few miles northeast of downtown Great Falls. The center-field flagpoles are inside the fence, but a separate chain-link fence protects outfielders from hitting them. The main outfield fence is 16 feet high, preventing any cheap home runs.

### ◆ LOCAL AND TEAM HISTORY

Great Falls' first pro team played the 1892 season in the Montana State League. Eight years later, the Great Falls Indians rejoined the circuit for another campaign. Great Falls next played in the Class D Union Association (1911-13) and the Class B Northwestern League (1916-17). The city joined the Pioneer League in 1948 and has been in the league continuously since 1969. The team was known as the Great Falls Electrics from 1948 to '63 and the Giants from 1969 to '83 before signing with Los Angeles in 1984. Earlier affiliations included the Brooklyn Dodgers, Pittsburgh Pirates and San Francisco Giants. The 1989 Dodgers won the Pioneer League championship with a 53-14 record, a .791 winning percent that is second best in history among Short Season teams.

**FAMOUS ALUMNI** — Joe Tinker, John Roseboro, Jack Clark, John Wetteland, Pedro Martinez, Eric Karros and Raul Mondesi all played here.

### ◆ BALLPARK EXTRAS

The concessions include the Dodger Burger (ham and cheeseburger) and super nachos. Cappuccino will be added in 1995. There is a new barbecue/picnic area sold to groups, but available to the public on Sundays. Vacation Fridays feature trip giveaways to such locales as Memphis, Nashville and Los Angeles. Bands play in the grandstand on Sundays.

### ◆ ATTRACTIONS

Western artist Charles Russell, a Great Falls resident, has works on display in the C.M. Russell Museum, two miles from the stadium. (406) 727-8787.

There is great trout fishing, camping, hunting and hiking in almost any direction. Great Falls is 3 hours north of Yellowstone National Park (307-344-7381) and 3 hours south of Glacier-Waterton International Park (406-888-5441).

For more information about Great Falls, call the Chamber of Commerce, (406) 761-4434.

### ◆ DINING

Bert & Ernie's is downtown, about 15 minutes from the ballpark. 300 1st Avenue S, (406) 453-0601.

Eddie's Supper Club, which features good steaks and burgers, is 10 to 15 minutes from the ballpark. 3725 2nd Avenue N, (406) 453-1616.

### ◆ LODGING

Holiday Inn is about five minutes from the park. 400 10th Avenue S, Great Falls, (406) 727-7200/(800) HOLIDAY.

Heritage Inn is also about five minutes away. 1200 Foxfarm Road, Great Falls, (406) 761-1900.

### ◆ DIRECTIONS

From I-15, take Great Falls/10th Avenue South exit. Proceed four miles to 26th Street South, turn left and go two miles to 8th Avenue North. Turn left and go one block to 25th Street North. Ballpark is 200 yards ahead on the right.

---

**AMERICAN LEGION BALLPARK**
**2600 River Drive North**
**Great Falls, MT 59401**
**(406) 452-5311**

Capacity: 3,700
LF 340, CF 415, RF 340

---

### ◆ TICKET AND SCHEDULE INFORMATION

Games are at 7 P.M. from Monday through Saturday, with 5 P.M. starts on Sunday.

The Dodgers' home opener is usually in mid-June and the season ends in the first week of September.

Tickets are sold downtown at the Downtown Dodgers Office and Souvenir Shop, 11 5th Street North (501 Plaza).

Ticket prices: $5 box seats, $3.75 general admission, $2.50 children. It's $20 for a six-pack of general-admission tickets.

# HELENA BREWERS

### MILWAUKEE BREWERS

The view from the covered grandstand at Kindrick Field, built in 1943, is one of the most spectacular in baseball. A Rocky Mountain range and Mount Helena are about two miles beyond the right- and center-field fences. While the sunsets over the mountains in right can be particularly attractive, they are also somewhat annoying to left-handed batters who face towards the sun when trying to pull the ball. Part of the downtown area, including the spires of the Cathedral of St. Helena and the copper-topped dome of the state capitol, can be seen in left. The grandstand here is one of the few remaining wood structures in the minors. Folding chairs double for box seats in the first several rows behind the plate.

### ◆ LOCAL AND TEAM HISTORY

Pro baseball in Helena dates to the 1890s. Since the turn of the century, this city has been associated with five circuits, beginning with a one-year (1902) stint in the Class B Pacific Northwest League. Subsequently, Helena spent one season each in the Class A Pacific National (1903) and Class D Inter-Mountain (1909) leagues and four seasons in the Class D Union Association (1911-1914). Helena has been a member of the Pioneer League continuously since 1978 and has been affiliated with Milwaukee since 1985.

In 1984, Jack Daugherty was the leading hitter in North American organized baseball when he batted .402 for the Helena Gold Sox, league champions that season. Besides leading the league in hitting, Daugherty's 82 runs batted in, 26 doubles, 179 total bases, 104 hits and 77 runs scored also ranked him at the top of the statistical rolls. That year was the first of four consecutive minor-league seasons in which Daugherty would hit at least .300. The following year, Helena featured another .400 hitter as Todd Brown batted .447. The 1986 Helena Brewers had the league's three leading hitters—Darryl Hamilton (batting champ with a .391 average), Gary Sheffield (runs batted in leader, with 71) and Greg Vaughn (tied for the home-run crown with 16 round-trippers). But despite the presence of these future big leaguers, Helena finished in third place, seven games out of first.

*OTHER FAMOUS ALUMNI* *OTHER FAMOUS ALUMNI*
John Jaha, Jamie Navarro, Bill Spiers, George Bell, Darren Daulton, Dave Nilsson and Ryne Sandberg played here.

### ◆ BALLPARK EXTRAS

You can sample grilled chicken, hot dogs and sausage at the concession stand.

### ◆ ATTRACTIONS

Frontier Town, a replica of a 19th-century pioneer village, is located atop the Continental Divide. Admission is free. For further information, call (406) 442-4560. There is a jazz festival in Helena each June, and the rodeo comes to town in July.

For more information about Helena, call the Chamber of Commerce, (406) 442-4120/(800) 7-HELENA.

### ◆ DINING
Frontier Pies Restaurant and Bakery, about 10 minutes from the ballpark, is decorated in an Old West theme. Burgers, chili, steak and fish-and-chips are on the menu. Pies, including rhubarb, banana cream and pumpkin, are baked daily on the premises. 1231 Prospect Avenue, (406) 442-7437.

### ◆ LODGING
Best Western Colonial Inn is near the intersection of U.S. 12 and I-15, about 15 minutes from the ballpark. (406) 443-2100/(800) 528-1234.

Comfort Inn is at exit 192 off I-15, about 15 minutes from the ballpark. (406) 443-1000/(800) 424-6423.

### ◆ DIRECTIONS
From I-15, take the Cedar Street exit and turn left. Go through two traffic lights and the ballpark will be on your left. Parking is free but very limited at the ballpark. Alternate parking is available on the street.

---

**KINDRICK FIELD**
**P.O. Box 4606**
**Helena, MT 59604**
**(406) 449-7616**

**Capacity: 2,600**
**LF 324, CF 375, RF 314**

---

### ◆ TICKET AND SCHEDULE INFORMATION
Most games are played at night, starting at 7:05 P.M. Sunday games begin at 6:05 P.M.

The Brewers' home opener is usually in mid-June and the season ends in the first week of September.

Ticket prices: $5.75 box seats; $4.75 reserved seats; $3.75 general admission. Seniors 60 and over and children 12 and under receive a $1 discount.

# IDAHO FALLS BRAVES

## SAN DIEGO PADRES

McDermott Field, built in 1976, was constructed on the same site as the 1940s Highland Park, an all-wood structure that burned down. McDermott is located in a municipal park and is surrounded by plenty of trees inside a largely residential area. From the uncovered grandstand, you will see the league's largest scoreboard. Located in left-center field, this scoreboard was purchased from the Salt Lake City Trappers, a AAA Pacific Coast League franchise at the time, who had intended to sell it as scrap metal after tearing down their old ballpark, Derks Field. Now, the Braves have the only AAA scoreboard in the Rookie leagues. The billboards on the outfield fence here have been painted for more than 40 years by the same Idaho Falls resident. Every year, as he finishes his job just days before the season begins, balls hit during preseason batting practice have been known to get lost amid his painting detritus along the outfield fence. There are picnic areas down each foul line.

### ◆ LOCAL AND TEAM HISTORY
Organized baseball made its debut here in 1926, the first of three seasons for Idaho Falls in the Class C Utah-Idaho League, which folded following the '28 season. Idaho Falls joined the Pioneer League in 1940 and has been a member of this circuit continuously since 1946, longer than any other current franchise. This is the first year of affiliation with San Diego.

Future New York Yankees player and manager Billy Martin began his pro career here as a reserve second baseman-third baseman for the 1946 Idaho Falls Russets, named in honor of Idaho's famous potato. Martin batted .254 in 32 games. Stan Wasiak spent about half a season here in 1956, managing his team to a 30-37 record. Less than a week after leaving Idaho Falls, the man who would eventually become the win-

**OTHER FAMOUS ALUMNI**
Devon White, Dick Schofield, Carney Lansford, Tom Brunansky, Brian Harper, Jose Canseco and Mike Hegan played here.

ningest manager in minor-league history was managing the Georgia State League's Hazelhurst-Baxley Cardinals. Larry Himes managed here from 1974 through 1977, winning the '74 Pioneer League championship and twice being named the circuit's Manager of the Year. Although this franchise is no longer affiliated with the Atlanta Braves, Idaho Falls is nevertheless retaining its nickname because this community has grown accustomed to the team's current moniker.

### ◆ BALLPARK EXTRAS

The top-selling concessions are grilled quarter-pound cheeseburgers and hot dogs. The team is adding the Braves Microbrew House, featuring five microbrewed regional ales, in 1995. There is a no-smoking section behind home plate and a community section for charity and non-profit groups.

### ◆ ATTRACTIONS

Many of America's most beautiful natural wonders are near Idaho Falls. Yellowstone National Park (307-344-7381) is 1½ hours away to the northeast; Craters of the Moon National Park (208-527-3257) is an hour west; the Grand Tetons and Jackson Hole, Wy., are two hours northeast and Sun Valley is two hours west.

For more information about Idaho Falls, call the Chamber of Commerce, (208) 523-1010.

### ◆ DINING

There are a number of choices within 10 minutes of the ballpark. Garcia's (2180 E. 17th Street, 208-522-2000) serves Mexican cuisine, and Louie's (340 E. Anderson, 208-524-1010) features Italian.

### ◆ LODGING

Holiday Inn Westbank is about 10 minutes from the park. 475 River Parkway, Idaho Falls, (208) 523-8000/(800) HOLIDAY.

Best Western Stardust is also 10 minutes from the park. 700 Lindsey Boulevard, Idaho Falls, (208) 522-2910/(800) 528-1234

### ◆ DIRECTIONS

From I-15 south, take the West Broadway exit. Turn left onto Memorial Drive and proceed to Mound Avenue. Turn right and proceed ½ mile to stadium.

From I-15 north, take Riverside exit and turn left. Go left on Elva and proceed ¼ mile to stadium.

---

**MCDERMOTT FIELD**
**568 W. Elva**
**Idaho Falls, ID 83403**
**(208) 522-8363**

Capacity: 2,800
LF 350, CF 400, RF 340

---

### ◆ TICKET AND SCHEDULE INFORMATION

Games are at 7:15 P.M. Monday-Saturday and at 5 P.M. Sunday with a 6 P.M. start on July 4.

The Braves' home opener is usually in mid-June and the season ends in the first week of September.

Ticket prices: $5.25 box seats; $3.75 general admission, $2.75 children and seniors.

---

# LETHBRIDGE MOUNTIES

### INDEPENDENT

Henderson Stadium, built in the 1960s, is part of an attractive complex that includes an artificial lake with the same name as the ballpark, tennis courts and a municipal park. There is a city-owned swimming pool across the street from the stadium's first base side, but this pool, unlike the one in Elizabethton, Tenn., is too far away from the ballpark to be a repository for fly balls. The Nikka Yuko Japanese Gardens, renowned locally as one of the most authentic oriental gardens in North America, are located behind the pool. The seating arrangements in Henderson's partially covered grandstand are unusual in that the best seats in the house, in the front row behind the chain-link home-plate backstop, are reserved for handicapped fans. New metal bleachers were installed for 1995, but wooden benches down the lines are still used for overflow crowds.

### ◆ LOCAL AND TEAM HISTORY

The first formal baseball game in Lethbridge took place more than a century ago, on April 25, 1886, when a team of local citizens defeated a squad of Northwest Mounted Police, also known as the Mounties. Amateur matches were a fairly regular occurrence here through the rest of the 19th century. Houk's Lethbridge Savages, a local amateur squad and 1907 Alberta Amateur Champions, played a game here in the middle of winter 1906 against Calgary. According to reports, Lethbridge defeated Calgary 13-1 on January 27 before 800 fans, most of whom did not wear overcoats on a day in which the temperature reached a balmy 53 degrees. Lethbridge made its organized-baseball debut in 1907, the first of three years (1907, 1909-10) in the Class D Western Canada League.

Lethbridge was without pro baseball for 64 years until 1975, when it joined the Pioneer League. It has been a member of this circuit since 1992. Andre Dawson began his career with a bang in 1975, leading the Pioneer League with 13 home runs, 99 hits and 166 total bases while batting .330. In 1977, Michael Zouras' 21 homers set a Pioneer League record that still stands. Five years later, Butte's Cecil Fielder missed tying the mark by one, but unlike Fielder, Zouras never played in the big leagues. The 1980 Lethbridge Dodgers' record of 52-18 is the best in franchise history. That team also set an all-time league record by winning 19 straight games on its way to winning the Pioneer League championship, besting Billings two games to one in the playoffs. Sid Fernandez had a big season here the following year. In his first pro campaign, the 19-year-old Fernandez led the Pioneer League with a 1.54 ERA and 128 strikeouts while compiling a 5-1 record.

**OTHER FAMOUS ALUMNI**

**OTHER FAMOUS ALUMNI**

Mariano Duncan, Walt Hriniak, Steve Sax, Candy Maldonado, Mitch Webster, Jim Lefebvre, Ron Kittleand Greg Brock all played ormanaged here.

### ◆ BALLPARK EXTRAS

The Mounties have a good selection of concessions. Apple slices are served with warm caramel sauce for dipping. This is quite popular with local fans. Veggie plates are also available. Burgers, chicken, hot dogs, smokies (kielbasa) and spicy sausages are served grilled. There is also a Kids Booth, which sells various types of candy and other items oriented toward children. Check out souvenirs with the team's logo, a smiling Canadian Mountie cradling a bat on his shoulder.

### ◆ ATTRACTIONS

The Nikka Yuko Japanese Gardens feature five different gardens complete with tour guides dressed in kimonos. Admission is C$3, C$2 for seniors and students. For further information, call (403) 328-3511.

If you visit in July, you may be here for Lethbridge's Whoop-Up Days, named for Fort Whoop-Up, a local 19th century trading post that was notorious for selling bootleg liquor.

For additional information about Lethbridge, call the Chamber of Commerce, (403) 327-1586.

### ◆ DINING

Treats Eatery, about five minutes from the ballpark, serves steak, ribs, burgers and many different salads, including almond chicken and cold beef. 1104 Mayor Magrath Drive, (403) 380-4880.

### ◆ LODGING

Best Western Heidelberg Inn is on Mayor Magrath Drive, about 15 minutes from the ballpark. (403) 329-0555/(800) 528-1234.

Pepper Tree Inn is on Mayor Magrath Drive, also about 15 minutes from the ballpark. (403) 328-4436.

### ◆ DIRECTIONS

Follow Highway 4 into Lethbridge for about five minutes until it intersects with Mayor Magrath Drive. At Mayor Magrath, turn right and go north. Go through five traffic lights to North Parkside Drive and turn right. The ballpark will be on the left. Plenty of free parking is available.

**HENDERSON STADIUM**
**P.O. Box 1986**
**Lethbridge, Alberta T1J 4K5**
**(403) 327-7975**

**Capacity: 2500**
**LF 330, CF 400, RF 330**

### ◆ TICKET AND SCHEDULE INFORMATION

Most games are played at night, starting at 7 P.M. Sunday games begin at 2 P.M.

The Mounties' home opener is usually in mid-June, and the season concludes at the end of August.

Ticket prices: C$6 box seats; C$4 general admission. Adults 55 and over and children under 12 receive a C$1 discount off the price of each ticket.

# MEDICINE HAT BLUE JAYS

**TORONTO BLUE JAYS**

Athletic Park, built in the 1970s, is bordered by two of Medicine Hat's major landmarks. The South Saskatchewan River flows about 100 yards past the outfield fences while the Arena, home of the Medicine Hat Tigers of the Western Hockey League, borders the stadium's third-base side. A hall for curling, another of Canada's favorite sports, is adjacent to the Arena. A row of houses is directly across the street from the first-base side of this ballpark. While some of these houses have been struck by foul balls over the years, their proximity to the ballpark does have a more tangible benefit, providing a convenient place to watch ballgames for those fans who would rather stay home than cross the street to go to Athletic Park. The grandstand is covered and there is a picnic area down the right-field line.

### ◆ LOCAL AND TEAM HISTORY

Organized baseball made its debut here in 1907, the start of a five-year association (1907, 1909-10, 1913-14) with the Class D Western Canada League. Medicine Hat won the league championship in the circuit's first two seasons, 1907 and 1909. This city's tenure in the Western Canada League started a professional rivalry with Lethbridge, a league rival and neighbor. This competition continued after both cities subsequently joined the Pioneer League. Medicine Hat has been a member of the Pioneer League continuously since 1977 and began its current affiliation with Toronto in 1982. Medicine Hat won the Pioneer League title in '82, with a team featuring Pat Borders, David Wells and Jimmy Key. In 1988, Medicine Hat's 12-58 record was the worst in league history. Over the next four seasons, the team improved slightly, posting records of 23-46, 20-46, 24-45 and 23-52.

**OTHER FAMOUS ALUMNI**

Mark Whiten, Jeff Musselman, Lloyd Moseby, Junior Felix, Mike Timlin, John Cerutti, Mark Eichorn, and Glenallen Hill played here.

### ◆ BALLPARK EXTRAS

The concessions here, including such standard fare as hot dogs and burgers, are unremarkable.

### ◆ ATTRACTIONS

Swimming, fishing and boating opportunities are available in Echo Dale Park. For further information, call (403) 527-2202.

In July, you can attend the three-day Medicine Hat Exhibition and Stampede, featuring rodeo events. For additional information about Medicine Hat, call the Chamber of Commerce, (403) 527-5214.

### ◆ DINING

Beefeater, about 15 minutes from the ballpark, is the place to go for steak. Prime rib is a specialty here but

roast beef seafood, and a 22-item soup and salad bar are also available. 3286 13th Avenue SE, (403) 526-6925.

### ◆ LODGING

Medicine Hat Lodge is on Trans-Canada Highway 1, about 10 minutes from the ballpark. 1051 Ross Glen Drive, Medicine Hat, (403) 529-2222.

Best Western Inn is on Trans-Canada Highway 1, about 15 minutes from the ballpark. 722 Red Cliff Drive, Medicine Hat, (403) 527-3700/(800) 528-1234.

### ◆ DIRECTIONS

From the Trans-Canada Highway, take either the 1st Street or Dumore Road SE exit. The ballpark will be immediately visible. Parking is ample and free.

**ATHLETIC PARK**
**P.O. Box 465**
**Medicine Hat, Alta. T1A 7G2**
**(403) 526-0404**

**Capacity: 1,996**
**LF 350, CF 380, RF 350**

### ◆ TICKET AND SCHEDULE INFORMATION

Most games are played at night, starting at 7 P.M.

The Blue Jays' home opener is usually in mid-June, and the season ends in the first week of September.

Ticket prices: C$6; C$5 seniors and children.

# OGDEN RAPTORS

**INDEPENDENT**

While the Raptors wait for their new ballpark to be finished in 1996, '95 marks their second consecutive season at Serge Simmons Field. Although only a temporary home, Serge Simmons is quite distinctive in its own right. The highlight here is its scenic location at the entrance to Fort Buenaventura State Park. Behind the outfield wall, lush trees and Mount Ogden combine to create an attractive backdrop. The impermanent quality of this ballpark is apparent in its uncovered grandstand. Here, fans watch the games from folding chairs atop metal risers, both of which were borrowed from the Salt Palace, former home of the

NBA's Utah Jazz, in Salt Lake City. Metal bleachers are located down each foul line.

### ◆ LOCAL AND TEAM HISTORY

Organized baseball has been played here since 1905, when Ogden fielded its first and only team in the Class D Pacific National League. Over the next several decades, Ogden spent time in four other minor leagues, including the AAA Pacific Coast League in 1979-80. Ogden was first associated with the Pioneer League in 1939 and rejoined the circuit in 1994 when this franchise moved here from Salt Lake City. Hall of Fame catcher Ernie Lombardi was 19 years old when he batted .398 for Ogden in 1927, but he was ineligible for the Utah-Idaho League batting title because he played in only 50 games.

Pete Hughes may have been the most patient hitter in organized-baseball history. In his 12-year career, he walked 1,666 times, an all-time minor-league record. This includes 10 years with at least 100 walks per season, including two (1947-48) when he drew more than 200 bases on balls. Besides his skill at drawing walks, Hughes could also hit, batting .350 lifetime. In 1939, he topped the Pioneer League with a .409 batting average plus 101 walks while also hitting 41 homers and driving in 131 runs.

This is the second year for the Raptors, the former Trappers franchise which moved to Ogden when Salt Lake City got a AAA team last season. The team's nickname is not as far-fetched as it may seem—one of the largest raptors ever discovered, about 15 feet long, was unearthed in Utah.

**OTHER FAMOUS ALUMNI**

Frank Robinson, Tommy Lasorda, Bill Buckner, Steve Garvey, Rickey Henderson and Mike Morgan all played or managed here.

### ◆ BALLPARK EXTRAS

Raptor Ale is the brew of choice in Ogden, while Raptor Ripple ice cream literally turns teeth, lips and tongues blue. The top-selling souvenirs are caps and logo baseballs. The Raptors feature one of the most extensive food selections in the Short Season leagues. Among the most noteworthy items are stuffed potatoes, burritos, veggie trays and grilled burgers, chicken and spicy sausage.

### ◆ ATTRACTIONS

George S. Eccles Dinosaur Park features more than 50 life-size dino replicas. Naturally, the Utah Raptor (velociraptor for *Jurassic Park* fans) is the featured attraction. (801) 393-3466.

The downtown Antique Car Museum is located at the Union Pacific Railroad Station, a ½ mile from the stadium. (801) 629-8444.

### ◆ DINING

Historic 25th Street, about five minutes south of the stadium, features many bars and eateries, including The City Club (801-392-4447) and Bruski's (801-394-1713).

### ◆ LODGING

Flying J. Motel is 10 minutes from the park. 1206 W. 2100 South, Ogden, (801) 393-8644.

Ogden Park Best Western Hotel is also 10 minutes away. 247 24th Street, Ogden, (801) 627-1190.

### ◆ DIRECTIONS

Heading north on I-15, take Ogden 24th Street exit. Turn right, then right again on A Avenue. Turn left on James Brown Drive and proceed to the stadium.

Heading south on I-15, take Ogden 21st Street exit. Turn left, then right on Lincoln. Take another right at 24th Street, left on A Avenue and left on James Brown Drive to the stadium. All routes to the stadium have Raptor signs guiding the way.

**SERGE B. SIMMONS FIELD**
**2450 A Avenue**
**Ogden, UT 84401**
**(801) 393-2400**

**Capacity: 3,500**
**LF 331, CF 400, RF 331**

### ◆ TICKET AND SCHEDULE INFORMATION

All home games begin at 7 P.M.

The Raptors' home opener is usually in mid-June and the season ends in the first week of September.

Ticket prices: $5 box seats; $4 general admission, children and seniors $2.50.

# MINOR LEAGUE MEMORIES

### BRISTOL

*Ron Necciai recalls the time he made baseball history in 1952 by striking out 27 batters in a nine-inning game:*

"I guess everything went right. It was kind of a fluke, whatever you want to call it. I'm still surprised to this day that it was never done before then or done since. There were four men over the limit of 27. I walked one. I hit one. There was an error and there was a third strike that got by the catcher. When the game was over, someone said, 'Jeez, you struck out 27 guys.' Everybody said, 'So what. What the hell. They've been playing baseball for 100 years. Someone did this before,' and we let it go at that. The next morning, the phone calls started coming. Audrey Frazier, the girl that ran the office, called and said this newspaper's on and that television station's on, and they want to interview you. You find out this has never been done. Then I got branded 'Rocket Ron.' "

### KINGSPORT

*Leo "Muscle" Shoals talks about his hitting style and recalls the years he spent in Kingsport, including what he considers the finest season of his career, 1953, when he hit .427:*

"It seemed they couldn't get me out that year. I could hit just about anywhere—Knoxville, Maryville. You have years like that [when] you're just swinging a good bat. The people in Kingsport were good to me. Fans passed a big jug around when I hit a home run. I'd take a couple of handfuls [of money from the jug] and go to town. I never wrote checks. I spent out of that jug."

### JOHNSON CITY

*Elizabethton Twins manager Ray Smith talks about playing the hill in Johnson City:*

"Every time a ball is hit out there, you hope you're the team hitting the ball, because the outfielder looks like he's been drinking when he's running after the ball. You have to gauge the sun and the ball while running up the bank and it's a steep bank. You can wipe out on that. Every time we go there to play, I spend about 10 to 15 minutes with my team explaining it to them. It's an experience."

### BURLINGTON

*Troy Neel of the Oakland A's played for seven different minor-league teams in six seasons. But he has a soft spot for Burlington, where he played in 1987.*

"My second year of rookie ball, in Burlington, North Carolina, was probably my favorite. The people just really opened up their arms and their families. They let guys live with them. They'd give you their furniture for the summer. You don't see that farther down the road in AAA and stuff. Those are the people that you remember the most, because they're the ones that really helped you out when you weren't making any money."

### LETHBRIDGE

*Joe Citari recalls a game in 1982 in which one of his teammates made a permanent impression on everyone in the ballpark:*

"We got into a fight in rookie ball. We were in Lethbridge, Canada, playing the Lethbridge Dodgers. I was playing for Butte. We had a big first baseman, Cecil Fielder. Me and him switched off playing first and DH'ing. One game, there was a fight on the field. Everybody's up around the pitcher's mound. Cecil was hitting the catcher. I just remember the catcher gettin' up and running away. Cecil's a big guy, and the catcher wasn't. He just got up and ran away."

## NORTHERN LEAGUE

The Northern League played in the National Association, with many of the same teams currently in the six-league circuit, off and on between 1903 and 1971, at which point it finally dropped down to four teams and folded. The league was reborn in 1993 as an independent league under the leadership of founder and league president Miles Wolff, who is also the publisher of the minor-league publication *Baseball America*.

St. Paul featured the league's "big name" player in former Chicago Cubs slugger Leon Durham and won the league title in its inaugural year, beating Rochester in a best-of-five series. Another highlight came when 70-year-old DH Minnie Minoso grounded out in his lone at-bat for St. Paul, an at-bat that let him become the oldest person ever to play professional baseball.

In the league's second year, one team—Rochester, Minn.—folded and moved to Winnipeg, Man. and won the league championship with a victory over Sioux City. The league played an 80-game schedule in 1994 and is not expected to make any changes for 1995.

### Duluth-Superior Dukes
P.O. Box 205
Duluth, Minnesota 55801
(218) 727-4525

### St. Paul Saints
771 Energy Drive
St. Paul, Minnesota 55108
(612) 644-6659

### Sioux City Explorers
3400 Line Drive
Sioux City, Iowa 51106
(712) 277-9467

### Sioux Falls Canaries
P.O. Box 84412
Sioux Falls, South Dakota 57118
(605) 333-0179

### Thunder Bay Whisky Jacks
P.O. Box 864
Thunder Bay, Ontario
Canada P7C 4X7
(807) 344-5225

### Winnipeg Goldeyes
1430 Maroons Road
Winnipeg, Manitoba
Canada R3G 0L5
(204) 982-2273

## TEXAS-LOUISIANA LEAGUE

The Texas-Louisiana League got under way as an eight-team circuit in 1994 after a brief attempt at a 1993 start-up fell short. Once it did get started, however, the league was a rousing success and part of the reason for that might be its unique centralized administration—one office runs all eight teams. In the league championships, the Corpus Christi Sand Crabs beat the Alexandria Aces.

After playing an 88-game schedule in 1994, it will expand to 100 for 1995, stretching from mid-May to Labor Day. The Texas-Louisiana League is expected to expand from eight teams to 10 or possibly 12 for 1995, with Abilene, Texas, appearing to be a lock and other possibilities including Waco and Lubbock, Texas, as well as Pueblo, Colorado.

### Abilene Prairie Dogs
401 Cypress
Suite 420
Abilene, Texas 79601
(915) 673-PDOG

### Alexandria Aces
2 Babe Ruth Drive
Alexandria, Louisiana 71303
(318) 473-ACES

### Amarillo Dillas
817 South Polk
Suite 1
Amarillo, Texas 79101
(806) 342-DILLA

### Beaumont Bullfrogs
902 E. Florida Avenue
Beaumont, Texas 77710
(409) 83-FROGS

### Corpus Christi Barracudas
3062 Oso Drive
Corpus Christi, Texas 78415
(512) 857-CRAB

### Mobile Baysharks
6140 Old Shell Road
Mobile, Alabama 36608
(304) 342-SHARK

### Peublo Big Horns
2200 Bonforte Boulevard
Pueblo, Colorado 81001
(719) 549-2444

### Rio Grande Valley Whitewings
1216 Fair Park Boulevard
Harlingen, Texas 78550
(210) 412-WINGS

### San Antonio Tejanos
One Camino Santa Maria

San Antonio, Texas 78279
(210) 434-JANO

**Tyler Wildcatters**
414 S. Bonner
Tyler, Texas 75702
(903) 597-WILD

## FRONTIER LEAGUE

Originally started as a league for undrafted players between the ages of 17-23, the Frontier League got off to a shaky start in 1993, but after a much more successful 1994 campaign appears to be solidifying its status as a reputable lower-level independent league.

Erie, in its only season in the league, swept through the two rounds of playoffs without losing a game. The city had hosted a team in the New York–Penn League of the National Association but was taking a one-year hiatus from that circuit while a new field was being built. In the interim, the Erie Sailors played at rickety Ainsworth Field before moving to Johnstown for 1995.

Most of the players are acquired through a draft conducted after an annual tryout camp, which has been held the past two seasons in Chillicothe, Ohio.

**Chillicothe Paints**
59 Paint Street
Chillicothe, Ohio 45601
(614) 773-8326

**Evansville Otters**
1701 N. Main Street
Evansville, Indiana 47711
(812) 435-8686

**Johnstown Steal**
211 Main Street
Johnstown, Pennsylvania 15901
(814) 536-8326/(800) 759-8791

**Newark Buffalos**
429 Ohio Street
Newark, Ohio 43055
(614) 349-9866

**Ohio Valley Redcoats**
325 7th Street
Parkersburg, West Virginia 26102
(304) 422-0426

**Portsmouth Explorers**
P. O. Box 950
Portsmouth, Ohio 45662
(614) 353-7647

**Zanesville Greys**
331 Parkway Drive
Zanesville, Ohio 43701
(614) 454-7397

## WESTERN LEAGUE

The eight-team Western Baseball League was scheduled to begin its 90-game schedule in May 1995. Founded by Bruce Engel, who is also the president of the independent Frontier League and was an original owner in the Northern League, the league was surprisingly well organized well before its startup date, with several former major-league stars lining up to get their shots at managerial slots. Engel's Frontier League connection also enabled the league to set up a unique system whereby the Western League clubs could draft the rights to Frontier League players.

Without big-name players on the rosters, teams knew they had to start early with unique promotions. The Palm Springs Suns, whose GM is former Los Angeles Dodgers executive Al Campanis, planned a pre-season barbecue with baseball luminaries and the Salinas Peppers had a "Bobbing for Peppers" contest where they filled a large tub with ice water and different varieties of peppers.

**Bend Bandits**
P.O. Box 1027
Bend, Oregon 97707
(503) 383-1983

**Gray Harbor Gulls**
1017 S. Boone Street
Aberdeen, Washington 98520
(206) 532-4488

**Long Beach Barracuda**
249 E. Ocean Boulevard
Suite 1020
Long Beach, California 90802
(310) 436-1112

**Palm Springs Suns**
1901 E. Baristo Road
Palm Springs, California 92262
(619) 323-7867

**Salinas Peppers**
1398 Northridge Mall
Salinas, California 93906
(408) 449-9100

**Sonoma County Crushers**
6585 Commerce Boulevard
Rohnert Park, California 94928
(707) 588-8300

**Surrey Glaciers**
17702 56th Avenue, Unit 101
Surrey, British Columbia
Canada V3S 1C7
(604) 576-7840

**Tri-City Posse**
P.O. Box 1324
Pasco, Washington 99301
(509) 545-6111

## ARIZONA LEAGUE

Like the Gulf Coast League, the Arizona League is not exactly ready for prime-time exposure. Debuting in 1988, the Arizona League is a Rookie League that plays a short season starting the last week of June and closing at the end of August. They play actual games, but they don't sell tickets, scorecards or food. A fan will not be run off if he ambles into the stands, but he will not be welcomed, either. The smattering of people you see in the stands will most likely be scouts. They will have an idea of who they are watching. You surely will not.

You will be watching very young men making their professional debuts. League rules limit the eight, 30-man teams to a maximum of six players 19 and over. Everyone else must be 18 or younger. No player can have two years or more of professional service.

Only the San Diego Padres and Seattle Mariners, sharing the Peoria Sports Complex, and the Colorado Rockies, using Compadre Stadium, use ballparks used by Major League teams in spring training. The California Angels' team uses the Gene Autry fields in Mesa, the Oakland A's use the Scottsdale Community College fields, the Cardinals use Chandler Regional Park and the Giants use Indian School Park in Scottsdale.

**California Angels**
Gene Autry Park
4125 E. McKollips
Mesa, Arizona 85205
(602) 830-4137

**Colorado Rockies**
4001 S. Alma School Road
Chandler, Arizona 85244
(602) 895-2152

**Milwaukee Brewers**
Chandler Complex
4500 S. Alma School Road
Chandler, Arizona 85248
(602) 895-1412

**Oakland Athletics**
Scottsdale Community College
9000 E. Chaparral Road
Scottsdale, Arizona 85251
(602) 949-5951

**St. Louis Cardinals**
Chandler Complex
4500 S. Alma School Road
Chandler, Arizona 85248
(602) 895-1412

**San Diego Padres**
Peoria Sports Complex
15707 N. 83rd Avenue
Peoria, Arizona 85382
(602) 412-9000

**San Francisco Giants**
Indian School Park
4415 N. Hayden Road
Scottdale, Arizona 85251
(602) 990-0052

**Seattle Mariners**
Peoria Sports Complex
15707 N. 83rd Avenue
Peoria, Arizona 85382
(602) 412-9000

## GULF COAST LEAGUE

You do not go to see a Gulf Coast League game for a true, minor-league experience. You will not pay for a ticket and you can sit anywhere in the stands. Just don't expect to hear hitters or lineup changes announced, to find concession stands or a scorecard. If you are lucky, the scoreboard will keep a running score. The games are open to the public—provided the public is unobtrusive and willing to return a batted ball hit foul—but most of the people in the stands are scouts or development people. The Gulf Coast League is by design not fan friendly. The teams share ballparks with the more advanced Class A Florida State League and the FSL is not interested in losing paying customers.

The GCL has been in operation since 1964, and it is run to expedite player development. League rules limit teams to no more than eight (of 30) players who are 20 or older. No more than two of those eight players can be 21 or older. Consequently, the league is the professional start for many, many ballplayers. Players drafted in June out of college and especially out of high school can expect to start here. It is also particularly well known as an entry league for Latino players, who often find the transition to the U.S. is easiest in Florida.

The season starts around June 20 and ends at the end of August. Most games are day games. On Sundays the fields and ballparks are empty. Teams change from year to year more than most other leagues. This year, for example, the Detroit Tigers will operate from Lakeland, though they were not there last year.

The GCL includes 16 teams divided into three divisions. Every team uses a facility involved in Major League spring training, but not necessarily the one used by the club's major-league affiliate. The Cubs, for instance, conduct spring training in Mesa, Arizona, but field a GCL team in Lee County, Florida. Several of the facilities are used by more than one team. For example, West Palm Beach hosts the Atlanta Braves and Montreal Expos. Sarasota hosts the St. Louis Cardinals and Baltimore Orioles. And the Lee County complex in Fort Myers has the Cubs, Kansas City Royals and Minnesota Twins.

**Atlanta Braves**
Municipal Stadium
715 Hank Aaron Drive
West Palm Beach, Florida 33401
(407) 471-3800

**Baltimore Orioles**
Twin Lakes Park
6700 Clark Road
Sarasota, Florida 34241
(813) 923-1996

**Boston Red Sox**
Red Sox Minor League Complex
4301 Edison Avenue
Fort Myers, Florida 33901
(813) 332-8106

**Chicago Cubs**
Lee County Sports Complex
14200 Six Mile Cypress Parkway
Fort Myers, Florida 33912
(813) 768-4280

**Chicago White Sox**
Ed Smith Stadium
1090 N. Euclid Avenue
Sarasota, Florida 34237
(813) 366-8451

**Florida Marlins**
Carl Barger Baseball Complex
5600 Stadium Parkway
Melbourne, Florida 32940
(407) 633-9200

**Houston Astros**
Osceola County Stadium
1000 Bill Beck Road
Kissimmee, Florida 37444
(407) 833-6500

**Kansas City Royals**
Lee County Sports Complex
14200 Six Mile Cypress Parkway
Fort Myers, Florida 33912
(813) 768-4280

**Minnesota Twins**
Lee County Sports Complex
14200 Six Mile Cypress Parkway
Fort Myers, Florida 33912
(813) 768-4280

**Montreal Expos**
Municipal Stadium
715 Hank Aaron Drive
West Palm Beach, Florida 33401
(407) 471-3800

**New York Mets**
St. Lucie County Sports Complex
525 N.W. Peacock Boulevard
Port St. Lucie, Florida 34986
(407) 871-2100

**New York Yankees**
Tampa Complex
3102 N. Himes Avenue
Tampa, Florida 33607
(813) 875-7753

**Pittsburgh Pirates**
Pirate City
1701 Roberto Clemente Memorial Drive
Bradenton, Florida 34208
(813) 747-3031

**St. Louis Cardinals**
Twin Lakes Park
6700 Clark Road
Sarasota, Florida 34241
(813) 923-1996

**Texas Rangers**
Charlotte County Stadium
2300 El Jobean Road
Port Charlotte, Florida 33948
(813) 625-9500

**Toronto Blue Jays**
Charlotte County Stadium
2300 El Jobean Road
Port Charlotte, Florida 33948
(813) 625-9500

## ATLANTA BRAVES

**AAA:** *Richmond Braves* (80-61, International League champions)
**AA:** *Greenville Braves* (73-63, East Division champions, Southern League)
**A:** *Durham Bulls* (66-70, second, Southern Division, Carolina League)
**A:** *Macon Braves* (73-64, third, Southern Division, South Atlantic League)
**Short Season A:** *Eugene Emeralds* (35-41, third, South Division, Northwest League); last year, affiliated with the Kansas City Royals
**Rookie:** *Danville Braves* (28-39, fourth, North Division, Appalachian League)

### TOP PROSPECTS

*1. Chipper Jones, SS*
Jones was the first player selected in the 1990 draft. He has done nothing to make the Braves doubt that selection. Jones did not play at all in 1994 because he tore up his knee during spring training, just as he was poised to win a spot in left field, but he has fully recovered and should wield a line-drive bat (he hit .325 in AAA in '93) and a fine glove, no matter where he fits in. Jones is a natural shortstop, but the Braves have also contemplated playing him at third base, second base and in left field.

*2. Brad Clontz, RHP*
Clontz was the Rolaids Minor League Reliever of the Year after a season in which he saved 38 games between AA (27) and AAA (11). His final save secured the Turner Cup (International League) championship for Richmond. Clontz had a combined 1.52 ERA. He is a sidearmer who throws harder than most sidearm or submarine pitchers.

*3. Jose Oliva, 3B*
Oliva had a little opportunity last season to show the Braves what he can do. He delivered with a .288 average and six home runs in just 59 at-bats. He hit 24 home runs at Richmond. Oliva is a brawny power hitter who was acquired from the Texas system for Charlie Leibrandt in 1992.

*4. Damon Hollins, OF*
Hollins hit 28 home runs at Durham last year. The Braves consider him an outstanding prospect.

*5. Jermaine Dye, OF*
Dye's skills might be as good as any in the Braves' system. He batted .298 with 15 home runs, 98 runs batted in and 19 steals at Macon last year.

## BALTIMORE ORIOLES

**AAA:** *Rochester Red Wings* (67-74, fourth, East Division, International League)
**AA:** *Bowie BaySox* (84-58, second, Southern Division, Eastern League)
**A:** *Frederick Keys* (76-61, second, Northern Division, Carolina League)
**A:** *High Desert Mavericks* (45-91, fifth, Southern Division, California League); last year, independent
**Rookie:** *Bluefield Orioles* (39-29, second, North Division, Appalachian League)

### TOP PROSPECTS

*1. Armando Benitez, RHP*
Benitez has developed into one of the top closer prospects in the minors. He has a terrific fastball and an imposing presence on the mound that has had him compared to Lee Smith. After a slow start in 1994 at AA Bowie, he turned things around in June and posted a 1.31 ERA over his last 48 innings. He led all Eastern League relievers with a .160 batting average against and 13.31 strikeouts per nine innings, and he fanned 14 in 10 innings with the Orioles.

*2. Curtis Goodwin, OF*
The speedy Goodwin stole 59 bases in 1994 at AA Bowie and was second in the Eastern League with an 85.5% success rate. He led the loop in at-bats (597), hits (171) and sacrifices (13) as well as steals, and has good enough bat control to frequently bunt for hits. He hit .320 when leading off innings and .286 overall.

*3. Jimmy Haynes, RHP*
Haynes solidified his status as one of the pitching jewels in the Orioles system by winning the organizational triple crown—he led the baby O's in wins (14), ERA (3.18) and strikeouts (191), also leading the Eastern League in that category with Double-A Bowie. Haynes throws a fastball in the 90s and has a good curveball as well as excellent control. Opponents have hit just .229 against him since he was drafted in the seventh round in 1991.

*4. Alex Ochoa, OF*
Ochoa is known for a cannon arm that accounted for 22 right-field assists in 1994, best in the Eastern League, but he also has five-tool potential. He hit .301 for AA Bowie, with 25 doubles, 14 homers and 82 runs batted in to go with 28 steals. A third-round pick in 1991 out of high school in Miami, he could be a 20-20 guy in the majors.

*5. Brian Sackinsky, RHP*
Sackinsky was drafted in the second round of 1992 out of Stanford University and was a workhorse for AA Bowie in 1994. He tied for fourth in the league in strikeouts, fanning 145 in 177 innings, but walked just 1.91

per nine innings and held batters to a .190 average with runners in scoring position.

## BOSTON RED SOX

**AAA:** *Pawtucket Red Sox* (78-64, first, East Division, International League)
**AA:** *Trenton Thunder* (55-84, fifth, Southern Division, Eastern League); last year, affiliated with the Detroit Tigers
**A:** *Sarasota Red Sox* (69-64, fifth, West Division, Florida State League)
**A:** *Battle Creek Golden Kazoos* (66-73, fourth, Southern Division, Midwest League); last year known as the Madison Hatters, affiliated with the St. Louis Cardinals
**Short Season A:** *Utica Blue Sox* (35-37, third, Pinckney Division, New York–Penn League)

### TOP PROSPECTS

1. *Cory Bailey, RHP*
The Red Sox' best closer prospect, Bailey dominated for most of the season at AAA Pawtucket before hitting one rough spot in August. He finished the season with seven consecutive scoreless outings, however, posting a 3.23 ERA and collecting 19 saves. Bailey held leadoff batters to a .152 average, and in his five pro seasons, batters have hit just .190 against him as he has posted a 2.65 ERA.

2. *Jose Malave, OF*
Despite playing half of his games at hitter-unfriendly Beehive Park for AA New Britain (now affiliated with the Red Sox), Malave still hit .299 with 24 homers, 92 runs batted in and 37 doubles. The home-run total doubled his career high. He also slugged .563, leading the league in that category, runs batted in, doubles, total bases and extra-base hits. He can hit to all fields and hit breaking pitches as well as he hits fastballs, but may be a DH in the majors.

3. *Trot Nixon, OF*
The Red Sox' first-round pick out of high school in North Carolina in 1993, Nixon has had limited pro experience thus far after signing late in '93 and suffering from back trouble for most of '94. But his upside is tremendous, thanks to exceptional athletic ability, which includes a wonderful swing, a great arm and a hard-nosed attitude.

4. *Frank Rodriguez, RHP*
Drafted in the second round of the 1990 draft, Rodriguez waffled between pitching and playing short-stop and actually was a position player for his first pro year at Short Season Elmira in 1991. Since then, he has been a work in progress on the mound. He possesses one of the best arms in the minors but has taken some time to achieve a pitcher's mentality. He had a terrific

second half to the 1994 season at AAA Pawtucket, however, and may finally be ready to dominate in the majors before long. He finished the season at 8-13 with a 3.92 ERA but led the International League with 160 strike-outs and had six complete games in his last 12 starts.

5. *Jeff Suppan, RHP*
Boston's second pick in 1993 could be a fast riser, thanks to poise and maturity along with talent. At Class A Sarasota in 1994, Suppan was 13-7 with a 3.26 ERA and 173 strikeouts in 174 innings. One of the youngest players in the league at 19, he lost his first five decisions but won 10 of his next 11 and posted a 2.22 ERA from June 1 to the end of the season. He has been compared to a young Greg Maddux.

## CALIFORNIA ANGELS

**AAA:** *Vancouver Canadians* (77-65, Northern Division champions, Pacific Coast League)
**AA:** *Midland Angels* (61-75, third, West Division, Texas League)
**A:** *Lake Elsinore Storm* (65-71, third, South Division, California League)
**A:** *Cedar Rapids Kernels* (77-62, Midwest League champions)
**Short Season A:** *Boise Hawks* (44-32, Northwest League champions)

### TOP PROSPECTS

1. *Garret Anderson, OF*
Anderson strung together a 27-game hitting streak, the longest in pro baseball last season, and hit .321 with 12 homers and 102 runs batted in for the season at AAA Vancouver. He added 42 doubles and set career highs in most categories. The Angels' fourth-round pick in 1990, Anderson is also a good fielder.

2. *George Arias, 3B*
Arias finished third in the Class A California League with 54 extra-base hits and tied for fourth in total bases with 247. Overall, he hit .280 at Lake Elsinore with 23 homers and 80 runs batted in. An outstanding defensive third baseman, he was the Angels' seventh-round pick in 1993 out of the University of Arizona.

3. *Todd Greene, C*
Greene won league MVP awards each of his first two pro seasons after being taken in the 12th round of the 1993 draft out of Georgia Southern. At Class A Lake Elsinore in 1994, he hit .302 and led the loop with 35 homers, while his 124 runs batted in were tops in all of the minor leagues. He also led the league in doubles (39), total bases (306) and slugging (.584). A converted outfielder, his defense is still catching up to his bat.

4. *Andrew Lorraine, LHP*
Lorraine was the Angels' fourth-round pick in the June

1993 draft out of Stanford. After going 4-1 with a 1.29 ERA for Short Season Boise in '93, walking just six in 42 innings, he made the jump to AAA Vancouver in 1994 and went 12-4 with a 3.42 ERA, fourth in the Pacific Coast League. Lorraine throws an average fastball and has a good curve, but his strength is his excellent control and makeup.

### 5. Troy Percival, RHP

The Angels' top closer prospect, Percival was clocked in the high 90s just a year after major elbow surgery. He finished the 1994 season at AAA Vancouver throwing harder than he had before the surgery and collected five saves with a 1.77 ERA in his last 16 outings. He struck out 10.77 batters per nine innings. A sixth-round draft pick in 1990, when he was a light-hitting catcher with a strong arm, Percival was moved to the mound in 1991. He is a prototypical closer with a blistering fastball, a good curve and good control.

## CHICAGO CUBS

**AAA:** *Iowa Cubs* (69-74, fifth, American Association)
**AA:** *Orlando Cubs* (59-78, fifth, East Division, Southern League)
**A:** *Daytona Cubs* (61-73, fourth, East Division, Florida State League)
**A:** *Rockford Cubbies* (89-50, Northern Division champions, Midwest League); last year, affiliated with the Kansas City Royals
**Short-Season A:** *Williamsport Cubs* (26-49, sixth, Pinckney Division, New York–Penn League)

### TOP PROSPECTS

#### 1. Brooks Kieschnick, 1B

The Cubs expect great things from this former college pitching/hitting star, who has progressed quickly in their system. Kieschnick hit .282 with 14 home runs and 55 runs batted in at Orlando last season. He played right field but moved to first base in the Arizona Fall League, where he was voted one of the top big-league prospects.

#### 2. Doug Glanville, OF

Glanville's pro career did not start fast, but he has come on as a very promising leadoff candidate. He has excellent speed and is a standout defender. Glanville hit .263 with 26 steals at Orlando.

#### 3. Matt Franco, 1B

The nephew of film star Kurt Russell, Franco is a slashing hitter who has some power potential. He batted .277 with 11 home runs and 71 RBI at Iowa.

#### 4. Kevin Orie, DH

Orie would have been much closer to the majors, but he missed almost all of last year because of a knee injury. He did manage to bat .412 in six games at Daytona, but

was forced to play as a DH in deference to the injury. When his mobility returns he will again be a big (6-4, 215) shortstop in the Cal Ripken Jr. mode.

### 5. Jessie Hollins, RHP

Another lost-season case, Hollins is actually coming back this season from two lost years. He succumbed to a rotator-cuff problem and missed all of 1993, returning for only four appearances at Daytona in '94. The Cubs think his hard stuff will return this season and he can again be a top relief prospect. Hollins is a former bare-knuckle amateur fighter at San Jacinto Junior College in Houston. His brother, Stacy, is one Oakland's two best pitching prospects.

## CHICAGO WHITE SOX

**AAA:** *Nashville Sounds* (83-61, second, American Association)
**AA:** *Birmingham Barons* (65-74, fifth, West Division, Southern League)
**A:** *Prince William Cannons* (71-65, third, Northern Division, Carolina League)
**A:** *South Bend Silver Hawks* (72-67, fifth, Northern Division, Midwest League)
**A:** *Hickory Crawdads* (86-54, first, Northern Division, South Atlantic League)
**Rookie:** *Bristol White Sox* (27-36, fourth, South Division, Appalachian League); last year, affiliated with the Detroit Tigers

### TOP PROSPECTS

#### 1. James Baldwin, RHP

Baldwin is considered one of the finest pitching prospects in the minors, having posted a 2.84 ERA and fanned 500 in 526 innings the past three seasons. A fourth-round pick in 1990, he is the classic power pitcher—big and strong, with a blazing fastball and a great curveball. He just needs to harness his control a bit more. He was 12-6 with a 3.72 ERA for AAA Nashville in '94, leading the American Association in strikeouts with 156 in 162 innings despite missing a few starts with biceps tendinitis.

#### 2. Scott Christman, LHP

After being selected in the first round of the 1993 draft, Christman jumped to the fast-track Class A Carolina League for 1994, where he was 6-11 with a 3.80 ERA at Prince William. His season was hindered by various injuries, however, affecting the fastball that had been clocked in the 90s while he was at Oregon State. He still managed to strike out 94 in 116 innings.

#### 3. Ray Durham, 2B

The 5-foot-8-inch switch-hitter showed a newfound power potential at AAA Nashville in 1994, when he hit 16 homers after having blasted just three in his first four pro seasons. He added 33 doubles and 12 triples while batting .296 and swiping 34 bases. Durham hit .321 with runners in scoring position for the Sounds and also cut his errors from 30 in 1993 to 19 in '94. He has excellent range in the field and a good glove as well.

**4. Jimmy Hurst, OF**
Hurst emerged as one of the top young outfield prospects around in 1994 when he hit .277 at Class A Prince William, with 21 homers in a pitchers' ballpark to go with 91 runs batted in and 15 steals. He added 31 doubles for the Cannons and led the Carolina League in extra-base hits. At 6-6, Hurst is a power-speed package who has a rifle arm.

**5. Scott Ruffcorn, RHP**
Ruffcorn has never been less than dominating in his minor-league career, and 1994 was no exception, as he went 15-3 with a 2.72 ERA at AAA Nashville with 144 strikeouts in 166 innings. The White Sox were experimenting in the off-season with making the workhorse a reliever. He has posted a 3-to-1 strikeout-to-walk ratio in four years. A first-rounder in 1991, he has been working on developing a good off-speed pitch.

## CINCINNATI REDS

**AAA:** *Indianapolis Indians* (86-57, American Association champions)
**AA:** *Chattanooga Lookouts* (67-73, fourth, West Division, Southern League)
**A:** *Winston-Salem Warthogs* (67-70, Southern Division champions, Carolina League)
**A:** *Charleston Alleycats* (65-75, fifth, Northern Division, South Atlantic League)
**Rookie:** *Billings Mustangs* (50-22, Pioneer League champions)
**Rookie:** *Princeton Reds* (41-25, Appalachian League champions)

### TOP PROSPECTS

**1. Pokey Reese, SS**
An acrobatic fielder, Reese rallied from a slow start last season to bat .269 with 12 home runs at Chattanooga.

**2. Pat Watkins, OF**
Watkins was named organizational player of the year after he batted .290 with 27 home runs, and 83 runs batted in and 31 steals at Winston-Salem. Some Reds scouts say Watkins is the club's best prospect.

**3. Danny Clyburn, OF**
The Reds obtained Clyburn in an off-season trade with Pittsburgh. Clyburn is brawny (6-3, 217) and powerful (22 home runs last year at Class A Winston-Salem).

**4. Kevin Jarvis, RHP**
Jarvis might work in the Reds' rotation this season, not

the minors. He had six appearances with the parent club after going 10-2 with a 3.54 ERA at Indianapolis.

**5. C.J. Nitkowski, LHP**
Nitkowski was drafted out of St. John's last June and appears poised for the majors. He was 6-3, 3.50 at Chattanooga. He has excellent control and a good breaking ball to complement an above-average fastball.

## CLEVELAND INDIANS

**AAA:** *Buffalo Bisons* (55-89, eighth, American Association); last year, affiliated with the Pittsburgh Pirates
**AA:** *Canton/Akron Indians* (68-73, third, Southern Division, Eastern League)
**A:** *Kinston Indians* (60-78, fourth, Southern Division, Carolina League)
**A:** *Columbus RedStixx* (87-51, first, Southern Division, South Atlantic League)
**Short Season A:** *Watertown Indians* (48-26, first, Pinckney Division, NY-Penn League)
**Rookie:** *Burlington Indians* (23-42, fifth, North Division, Appalachian League)

### TOP PROSPECTS

**1. David Bell, 3B**
Like his father, Buddy, Bell is a steady defensive player whose bat has developed with time. After hitting just .244 with 11 homers in his first three pro seasons, he batted .292 in 1993 at AA Canton/Akron and continued to progress in 1994, hitting .293 with 18 homers and 88 runs batted in for AAA Charlotte. He struck out just 54 times in 481 at-bats for the Knights and hit .336 with runners in scoring position. A ninth-round pick in 1990, he can also play second and shortstop.

**2. Brian Giles, OF**
Giles posted his second strong season to move into the echelon of top Indians prospects. At AAA Charlotte (now affiliated with the Cleveland Indians), he hit .313 with 16 homers and 58 runs batted in, stealing eight bases. The 16 homers equaled his career output in five previous seasons. He went hitless in back-to-back games just three times all season. A 16th-round pick in 1989, Giles has posted a .305 career average and has good strike-zone judgment to go with strong defensive skills.

**3. Damian Jackson SS**
Despite a second-half slump, Jackson has the tools to be one of the top position players in the Indians organization. At AA Canton/Akron in 1994, he hit .269 with 37 stolen bases. One of the last players chosen in the 1991 draft, last year Jackson had 29 doubles for the Indians as well.

**4. Julian Taverez, RHP**
Tall and skinny, Tavarez had the best stuff of any of the many prospect starters on the 1994 AAA Charlotte club,

leading the International League in wins by going 15-6 with a 3.48 ERA. He walked just 43 in 176 innings and has an outstanding breaking ball.

**5. Enrique Wilson, SS**
Acquired from the Minnesota Twins for journeyman minor-league reliever Shawn Bryant, Wilson hits for average and power from both sides of the plate. The toughest hitter in the South Atlantic League to fan in 1994 (34 whiffs in 512 at-bats), he hit .279 with 10 homers, 72 runs batted in and 21 steals at Class A Columbus. He is also strong on defense, with good range and a fine arm.

## COLORADO ROCKIES

**AAA:** *Colorado Springs SkySox* (70-69, third, Southern Division, Pacific Coast League)
**AA:** *New Haven Ravens* (77-63, second, Northern Division, Eastern League)
**A:** *Asheville Tourists* (60-73, seventh, Northern Division, South Atlantic League)
**A:** *Salem Avalanche* (64-75, fourth, Southern Division, Carolina League); last year, affiliated with the Pittsburgh Pirates
**Short-Season A:** *Portland Rockies* (29-47, fourth, South Division, Northwest League); last year located in Bend.

### TOP PROSPECTS

**1. Juan Acevedo, RHP**
Acevedo is an out-of-nowhere prospect who came on fast. He throws hard, featuring a sinking fastball and a slider. Acevedo had a sensational season at New Haven: 17-6 with a 2.37 ERA.

**2. Doug Million, LHP**
Million was the 1994 USA TODAY High School Player of the Year. The Floridian was the Rockies' first-round choice last June. He has an above-average fastball and good control. He was 5-3 with a 2.34 at Bend (now Portland) after he signed.

**3. Mark Thompson, RHP**
Thompson was a second-round choice in Colorado's first draft (1992). He was a University of Kentucky teammate of Giants starter William Vanlandingham. Thompson has overcome some arm problems to establish himself in the Rockies' system. He was 8-9 with a 4.49 ERA last year at Colorado Springs.

**4. John Burke, RHP**
Burke suddenly was beset by "Steve Blass' disease" late last year. That refers to an unexplained inability to throw strikes. Burke seemed to rebound in his last three starts and then went to Instructional League to ensure the fix worked. When he is right, he is a quality power

pitcher who keeps the ball down. Burke, taken in 1992, was Colorado's first June draft pick ever.

**5. Derrick Gibson, OF**
Pure power in its raw form. Gibson is very strong. He hit .264 with 12 home runs at Bend (now Portland) last year. Former Rockies instructor Rudy Jaramillo, who once worked with Juan Gonzalez, Dean Palmer and other Rangers sluggers, says Gibson has a chance to be just as powerful as his previous pupils.

## DETROIT TIGERS

**AAA:** *Toledo Mud Hens* (63-79, fifth, West Division, International League)
**AA:** *Jacksonville Suns* (60-77, fourth, East Division, Southern League); last year, affiliated with the Seattle Mariners
**A:** *Lakeland Tigers* (63-68, seventh, West Division, Florida State League)
**A:** *Fayetteville Generals* (62-75, sixth, Northern Division, South Atlantic League)
**Short Season A:** *Jamestown Jammers* (42-32, first, Stedler Division, New York–Penn League)

### TOP PROSPECTS

**1. Sean Bergman, RHP**
Bergman finished third in the International League in strikeouts, fanning 145 in 155 innings at AAA Toledo. He has a fastball in the upper 80s but often uses a change-up effectively as well. He allowed two or fewer runs in half of his starts, and finished at 11-8 with a 3.72 ERA.

**2. Matt Brunson, SS**
The Tigers' first-round pick in 1993 missed all of that season with a broken hand, so 1994 was his pro debut. At age 20, he spent most of the season at Class A Fayetteville and the end of it at Class A Lakeland, combining to steal 53 bases between the two. He finished fourth in the South Atlantic League in walks with 78. The son of former NFL wide receiver Larry Brunson, he has great range and is a switch-hitter.

**3. Tony Clark, 1B**
After the Tigers took him second in the country in 1990, Clark had played in just 88 games over the first four seasons, due to a combination of his playing college basketball and sustaining several injuries. In 1994, though, at AA Trenton (now affiliated with the Boston Red Sox) he made up for lost time, hitting 23 homers and driving in 99 runs to lead all Detroit farmhands. The 6-8, 245-pounder has awesome power and also hit .276 on the season, most of which was spent at Trenton, with a late-season promotion to AAA Toledo. An outfielder in the past, he was moved to first base and was

still adjusting there defensively, but he has a tremendous work ethic and great attitude.

**4. Bob Higginson, OF**

Higginson was taken in the 12th round of the 1992 draft out of Temple University and made great strides in the system in 1994, hitting .275 with 23 homers, 28 doubles and 16 steals at AAA Toledo. The power total was way up; he hit just nine home runs his first two pro seasons.

**5. Jose Lima, RHP**

Lima tossed a no-hitter against Pawtucket late in his AAA Toledo season in 1994, striking out 13 with much of the Detroit brass on hand, and is considered the top upper-level pitcher in the system. He doesn't have an overpowering fastball but uses a circle change as his out pitch and has good control—13 walks in his last nine starts. For the Mud Hens, he was 7-9 with a 3.60 ERA.

## FLORIDA MARLINS

**AAA:** *Charlotte Knights* (77-65, second, West Division, International League); last year, affiliated with the Cleveland Indians
**AA:** *Portland Sea Dogs* (60-81, fourth, Northern Division, Eastern League)
**A:** *Brevard County Manatees* (78-61, East Division champions, Florida State League)
**A:** *Kane County Cougars* (71-68, sixth, Northern Division, Midwest League)
**Short-Season A:** *Elmira Pioneers* (30-43, fourth, Pinckney Division, New York–Penn League)

### TOP PROSPECTS

**1. Charles Johnson, C**

Certainly the best catching prospect in the minors and also one of the best prospects at any position, Johnson is virtually assured of being the Marlins' catcher this season. He was their first pick ever in the June draft (1992). Johnson batted .266 with 28 home runs at Portland in 1994. He is an outstanding player behind the plate as well.

**2. Marc Valdes, RHP**

The Marlins' first pick in the 1993 draft, Valdes is a battler with a good fastball and superior control. He was 8-4 with a 2.55 ERA at Portland.

**3. Josh Booty, SS**

The Marlins lured Booty, the top high school quarterback prospect in the nation, away from Louisiana State and into pro baseball last year. Booty was the 1994 USA TODAY High School Football Player of the Year. He batted .222 between the Gulf Coast League and Elmira before he was sidelined by mononucleosis.

**4. Quilvio Veras, 2B**

The Marlins traded incumbent second baseman Bret Barberie one week after they obtained Veras. Veras provided a great deal of speed with 40 steals at Class AAA Norfolk (now affiliated with the Florida Marlins) last year and more range than Barberie dreamed of.

**5. Nigel Wilson, OF**

The Marlins' first pick in the expansion draft has been a disappointment so far, but Wilson has the combination of speed and power that scouts love. He also has injury problems and nagging difficulties from asthma. Wilson batted .302 at Class AAA Edmonton last year.

## HOUSTON ASTROS

**AAA:** *Tucson Toros* (81-63, second, Southern Division, Pacific Coast League)
**AA:** *Jackson Generals* (74-61, East Division champions, Texas League)
**A:** *Kissimmee Cobras* (46-89, sixth, East Division, Florida State League)
**A:** *Quad City River Bandits* (57-81, fifth, Southern Division, Midwest League)
**Short Season A:** *Auburn Astros* (45-31, second, Pinckney Division, New York–Penn League)

### TOP PROSPECTS

**1. Brian Hunter, OF**

Many people think Hunter is baseball's best rookie prospect for 1995, a dazzling center fielder with great speed who was assured of a starting spot in '95 by the Astros' 12-player Christmas week trade with San Diego. Hunter batted .372 with 49 steals last year at Tucson.

**2. Phil Nevin, 3B**

Nevin was the first pick in the nation in 1992. His progress has been steady but unspectacular. He is an ordinary fielder, but a good run producer. The trade with San Diego created an opening for him, too, although prospect Tom Nevers is also a candidate for the job.

**3. Billy Wagner, LHP**

A small guy (5-11) with a big (97-mph) fastball. Wagner led the minors in strikeouts per nine innings. The Astros cannot decide if he will become a starter or a reliever for them, but assuredly one day he will do one of those tasks well. Wagner was 8-9, 3.29 as a starter at Quad City. He struck out 204 in 153 innings.

**4. Richard Hidalgo, OF**

A tremendous prospect who set a Midwest League record for doubles, led the league in outfield assists and might become a major power hitter. Hidalgo, from Venezuela, hit .294 at Quad City.

**5. Rick Huisman, RHP**

A Giants castoff, Huisman was made into a reliever and became the best in the Texas League, recording 31 saves with a 1.61 ERA for Jackson.

## KANSAS CITY ROYALS

**AAA:** *Omaha Royals* (68-76, sixth, American Association)
**AA:** *Wichita Wranglers* (54-82, fourth, West Division, Texas League); last year, affiliated with the San Diego Padres
**A:** *Wilmington Blue Rocks* (94-44, Carolina League champions)
**A:** *Sultans of Springfield* (69-71, second, Southern Division, Midwest League); last year, affiliated with the San Diego Padres
**Short Season A:** *Spokane Indians* (30-46, fourth, North Division, Northwest League); last year, affiliated with the San Diego Padres

### TOP PROSPECTS

1. *Johnny Damon, OF*
The 1992 supplemental first-round pick is an ideal lead-off hitter thanks to his speed, but he could develop into a three-spot guy as he matures. In his three-year career heading into 1995, Damon has posted a .310 average. He hit .316 in 1994 for Class A Wilmington, helping the Blue Rocks win the Carolina League championship with 44 steals and 75 runs batted in. He fanned just 55 times in 472 at-bats while drawing 62 walks. Defensively he has great range and fielding mechanics.

2. *Bart Evans, RHP*
The Carolina League Pitcher of the Year at Class A Wilmington, Evans was 10-3 with a 2.98 ERA and struck out 145 in as many innings while scattering just 107 hits. He developed an off-speed pitch to complement his 92-mph fastball and won nine games in a row at one point. The 12th-round pick from 1992 allowed three or fewer runs in each of his first 19 starts in 1994.

3. *Jim Pittsley, RHP*
Pittsley, who stands 6-7, is a classic power pitcher with a fastball in the 90s and a sharp curve. A supplemental first-round pick in 1992, he was 11-5 with a 3.17 ERA for Class A Wilmington in 1994, striking out 171 in 162 innings while walking just 42. He led the Carolina League in strikeouts and was fourth in ERA.

4. *Michael Tucker, OF*
The Royals' first-round pick in 1992 out of Longwood College in Virginia, Tucker played for the U.S. Olympic team before making his pro debut in 1993. That year he hit over .300 between Class A Wilmington and AA Memphis (now affiliated with the San Diego Padres), and he batted .276 with 21 homers and 11 steals at AAA Omaha in 1994. He has been moved from shortstop to second base and now to left field, which should be his permanent position.

5. *Joe Vitiello, 1B*
Vitiello strung together a 23-game hitting streak in May en route to winning the American Association batting title in 1994, hitting .344 for AAA Omaha. He added 28 doubles and 10 homers for the Royals, who made him their first-round pick in 1991. Vitiello has been bothered by knee trouble and underwent off-season surgery.

## LOS ANGELES DODGERS

**AAA:** *Albuquerque Dukes* (83-56, Pacific Coast League champions)
**AA:** *San Antonio Missions* (62-74, second, West Division, Texas League)
**A:** *Vero Beach Dodgers* (60-75, fifth, East Division, Florida State League)
**A:** *San Bernardino Spirit* (48-88, fourth, Southern Division, California League); last year independent
**Short Season A:** *Yakima Bears* (49-27, North Division champions, Northwest League)

### TOP PROSPECTS

1. *Billy Ashley, OF*
Ashley was named the 1994 USA TODAY Minor League Player of the Year. He has as much pure power as any player in the game and once hit a batting-practice pitch out of Dodger Stadium. Ashley hit .345 with 37 home runs and 105 runs batted in last year for Albuquerque.

2. *Todd Hollandsworth, OF*
Everyone who sees Hollandsworth remarks on the similarities to a young Kirk Gibson. Hollandsworth batted .285 with 19 home runs and 91 runs batted in last year at Albuquerque.

3. *Roger Cedeno, OF*
The Dodgers center fielder of the future, a speedy lead-off guy who would work well between Ashley and Hollandsworth. Cedeno hit .321 with 30 steals at Albuquerque.

4. *Chan Ho Park, RHP*
Park left South Korea for Dodgers dollars and established himself in spring training last year as a power pitcher to be reckoned with. He was stalled by arm troubles, but returned at San Antonio and finished 5-7 with a 3.55 ERA. Can start or relieve when he reaches Los Angeles.

5. *Antonio Osuna, RHP*
The last great Mexican the Dodgers signed had a pretty good career. No one thinks Osuna can have the same impact as his countryman, Fernando Valenzuela, but he might become a great reliever. Osuna had 19 saves and an 0.98 ERA at San Antonio.

**AAA:** *New Orleans Zephyrs* (78-66, third, American Association)
**AA:** *El Paso Diablos* (88-48, Texas League champions)
**A:** *Stockton Ports* (54-82, fifth, Northern Division, California League)
**A:** *Beloit Snappers* (76-64, second, Northern Division, Midwest League)
**Rookie:** *Helena Brewers* (44-28, South Division champions, Pioneer League)

## TOP PROSPECTS

**1.** *Scott Karl, LHP*
Karl is proof that you don't have to have a great fastball to be a winner. He has gone 30-14 with a 2.69 ERA in his first three pro seasons, including a 10-6 record and a 3.51 ERA between AA El Paso and AAA New Orleans in 1994. He struck out 10 or more in each of his last three starts, and has excellent control as well. A seventh-round pick in 1992, Karl has a great change-up as well as a good curve and he keeps the ball down.

**2.** *Mark Loretta, SS*
Many in the organization have deemed Loretta their shortstop of the future since he was drafted in the 11th round of 1993 out of Northwestern University. That year he combined to hit .358 between rookie-level Helena and Class A Stockton, and in 1994 he batted .282 with 52 runs batted in and 10 steals between AA El Paso and AAA New Orleans. He is an acrobatic fielder.

**3.** *Sid Roberson, LHP*
Roberson stands just 5-9 but has stood tall in the honors department, earning California League Pitcher of the Year in 1993 and Texas League Pitcher of the Year in 1994, when he was 15-8 with a 2.83 ERA for AA El Paso. He led the system in ERA and was second in wins despite missing the last two starts of the regular season to return to school. Roberson has great control and a great curveball to go with it.

**4.** *Duane Singleton, OF*
Singleton possesses both outstanding speed and a rifle arm that has led several leagues in outfield assists. In 1994, he hit .286 with 31 steals at three levels—Class A Stockton, AA El Paso and AAA New Orleans—and had a brief call-up to the majors. He also did well in the Arizona Fall League.

**5.** *Derek Wachter, OF*
Wachter started the 1994 season at AA El Paso and was among the Texas League leaders in hitting (.385) and the minor-league leaders in hits (45) when he was promoted to AAA New Orleans in mid-May. Overall, he hit .320 with 25 doubles and 63 runs batted in. A seventh-round pick in 1991, Wachter is a solid enough outfielder, but it will be his bat that gets him places.

**AAA:** *Salt Lake City Buzz* (74-70, second, Northern Division, Pacific Coast League)
**AA:** *Hardware City Rock Cats* (59-81, fifth, Northern Division, Eastern League); last year, affiliated with the Boston Red Sox
**A:** *Fort Myers Miracle* (71-63, fourth, West Division, Florida State League)
**A:** *Fort Wayne Wizards* (66-73, seventh, Northern Division, Midwest League)
**Rookie:** *Elizabethton Twins* (36-30, third, South Division, Appalachian League)

## TOP PROSPECTS

**1.** *Marc Barcelo, RHP*
Barcelo ranked among the Southern League leaders in 1994 in strikeouts (153), innings (183) and ERA (2.65), going 11-6 for AA Nashville (now affiliated with the Seattle Mariners). A supplemental first-round pick in 1993, he is a polished pitcher with good command who can both throw hard and change speeds well. He already has a good fastball and curveball and is working on a slider and a change-up.

**2.** *Marty Cordova, OF*
Cordova opened eyes in 1992 with Class A Visalia (now independent) when he led the minors with 131 RBI while hitting .341. Though his numbers dropped off in 1993—and it would be hard to imagine how they couldn't have—he still led the Southern League in extra-base hits for AA Nashville. He hit 19 homers and had 77 runs batted in. He got a late start to the 1994 season after breaking his wrist in spring training, but when he did join AAA Salt Lake, he hit .358 with 19 homers and drove in 66 runs in just 385 at-bats. He also stole 17 bases.

**3.** *LaTroy Hawkins, RHP*
Hawkins has developed into the Twins' premier pitching prospect since being a seventh-round pick in 1991 out of high school in Gary, Indiana, where he was teammates on the basketball team with Milwaukee Bucks forward Glenn Robinson. After two lackluster seasons in the bullpen, Hawkins was converted into a starter in May 1993 and has been on a roll since. He led the Class A Midwest League that year in wins, ERA and strikeouts and continued his success among three levels in 1994, going 18-6—sharing the minor-league lead in wins—with a 3.07 ERA at Class A Fort Myers, AA Nashville and AAA Salt Lake.

**4.** *Torii Hunter, OF*
Just 19 years old, the Twins' first-round pick in 1993 hit .293 with 10 homers and eight steals at Class A Fort Wayne, despite being one of the youngest players in the league. He has tremendous potential with power, speed, a strong arm and the ability to be a premier center field-

er. He missed the beginning of the 1994 season with a pulled shoulder muscle, but hit .322 in the second half.

5. *Scott Stahoviak, 3B*
Stahoviak was a supplemental first-round pick in 1991, and he had his best season yet in 1994, hitting .318 with 13 homers and 94 runs batted in at AAA Salt Lake. He added 41 doubles and had a total of 60 extra-base hits. At 6-5, Stahoviak puts on a show at batting practice with tape-measure home runs, but in games he sacrifices power displays to hit for average. He is an adequate fielder at third base but is likely to move to first.

## MONTREAL EXPOS

**AAA:** *Ottawa Lynx* (70-72, third, East Division, International League)
**AA:** *Harrisburg Senators* (88-51, Southern Division champions, Eastern League)
**A:** *West Palm Beach Expos* (71-60, second, East Division, Florida State League)
**A:** *Albany Polecats* (63-74, fourth, Southern Division, South Atlantic League); last year, affiliated with the Baltimore Orioles
**Short Season A:** *Vermont Expos* (42-33, second, McNamara Division, New York–Penn League)

### TOP PROSPECTS

1. *Carlos Perez, RHP*
Another Perez brother is on the way. Carlos has the arm to be as prominent as Pascual and Melido ever were. Carlos was 7-5, 3.33 at Ottawa last year, after starting the season going 7-2, 1.94 at Harrisburg.

2. *Mark Grudzielanek, SS*
Grudzielanek was MVP of the Eastern League last year after he batted .322 with 11 home runs and 66 RBI at Harrisburg. He also starred in the '94 Arizona Fall League.

3. *Ugueth Urbina, RHP*
Urbina struggled at times last season after a family tragedy. He still has a great arm, though, and was 9-3 with a 3.28 ERA at Harrisburg.

4. *Shane Andrews, 3B*
A powerful prospect who has on occasion battled weight problems, Andrews has moved steadily through the Expos system. He hit .254 with 16 home runs last year at Ottawa.

5. *Brad Fullmer, 3B*
The Expos think he was the best high school hitting prospect in the 1994 draft. His signing kept Fullmer from attending Stanford on scholarship, but he was injured before he could play professionally last season.

## NEW YORK METS

**AAA:** *Norfolk Tides* (67-75, fourth, West Division, International League)
**AA:** *Binghamton Mets* (82-59, Eastern League champions)
**A:** *St. Lucie Mets* (71-65, third, East Division, Florida State League)
**A:** *Capital City Bombers* (59-76, fifth, Southern Division, South Atlantic League)
**Short Season A:** *Pittsfield Mets* (37-38, fourth, McNamara Division, New York–Penn League)
**Rookie:** *Kingsport Mets* (36-30, second, South Division, Appalachian League)

### TOP PROSPECTS

1. *Bill Pulsipher, RHP*
This tough power pitcher had the Mets' attention even before he threw a no-hitter last September. He has emerged as the Mets' best pitching prospect, one of the best anywhere. Pulsipher was 14-9 with a 3.22 ERA at Binghamton.

2. *Rey Ordonez, SS*
He is simply the flashiest infielder in the minors, the likely heir to Ozzie Smith's mantle. Ordonez's story is even more compelling because he escaped from the Cuban National Team. He batted .262 for Binghamton last year.

3. *Edgardo Alfonzo, 2B*
The Mets management said last year that Alfonzo might be the best prospect in the system. He has great range and a very lively bat, hitting .293 with 15 home runs and 75 runs batted in last year at Binghamton.

4. *Jason Isringhausen, RHP*
A good, poised power pitcher who was 6-4, 2.23 at St. Lucie.

5. *Paul Wilson, RHP*
How could we name a guy who was 0-5 with a 5.06 ERA at St. Lucie last year? It is simple. Wilson was tired from leading Florida State to the College World Series. Wilson was the first pick overall in the June draft for a good reason.

## NEW YORK YANKEES

**AAA:** *Columbus Clippers* (74-68, third, West Division, International League)
**AA:** *Norwich Navigators* (71-70, third, Northern Division, Eastern League); last year located in Albany/Colonie
**A:** *Tampa Yankees* (80-52, Florida State League champions)

**A:** *Greensboro Bats* (71-69, third, Northern Division, South Atlantic League)
**Short Season A:** *Oneonta Yankees* (30-45, fifth, Pinckney Division, New York–Penn League)

## TOP PROSPECTS

### 1. *Russ Davis, 3B*
Davis has hit 77 doubles and 73 homers over his last three minor-league seasons, including .276 with 30 doubles and 25 homers for AAA Columbus in 1994. He has good bat speed and a strong arm and is a solid defensive third baseman. The 26th-round pick in 1988 has been hounded by nagging injuries for the past two seasons, however, including being hit by a pitch, which put him out of action for the end of 1994.

### 2. *Derek Jeter, SS*
*Baseball Weekly's* Minor League Player of the Year for 1994, Jeter cruised from Class A Tampa to AA Albany to AAA Columbus in 1994 without missing a beat. He combined to hit .344 among the three spots, stealing 50 bases and cutting his error total in half from 1993. The Yankees' first-round pick in 1992 out of high school in Kalamazoo, Michigan, was the Florida State League MVP for 1994 as well as the Eastern League Player of the Month for the short time he was there. He has a tremendous work ethic and maturity.

### 3. *Andy Pettitte, LHP*
Pettitte jumped to the head of the pitching-prospect class in 1994, going 14-4 with a 2.86 ERA between AA Albany and AAA Columbus while walking just 39 in 170 innings. He has a fastball in the 90s and a good curveball. A 22nd-round pick in 1990, he has never walked more than three batters in an outing.

### 4. *Ruben Rivera, OF*
Though Rivera never played baseball until his late teens while growing up in Panama, he has made up for the lost time by developing into a legitimate five-tool prospect. Between Class A Greensboro and Class A Tampa in 1994, he hit .281 with 33 homers, 101 runs batted in and 48 steals. Though he fanned 163 times, he is still learning the game. He has a strong arm—20 outfield assists—and has been compared to many of the greats of the game.

### 5. *Brien Taylor, LHP*
The first player taken in the 1991 draft, Taylor missed all of 1994 after suffering a shoulder injury in a fight during the off-season. When he signed with the Yankees, it was for a then-record $1.55 million bonus thanks to a blazing fastball, and his first two seasons provided impressive if not astounding stats. He underwent surgery on the injured shoulder and by the end of the summer was rehabbing on the mound in Tampa. Though it's believed he will have lost a few miles off his vaunted fastball when he returns, he is still expected to throw in the 90s and he still has his hard-nosed attitude.

## OAKLAND ATHLETICS

**AAA:** *Edmonton Trappers* (67-75, fourth, Northern Division, Pacific Coast League); last year, affiliated with the Florida Marlins
**AA:** *Huntsville Stars* (81-57, Southern League champions)
**A:** *Modesto A's* (96-40, Northern Division champions, California League)
**A:** *West Michigan Whitecaps* (74-65, fourth, Northern Division, Midwest League)
**Short Season A:** *Southern Oregon A's* (38-38, second, South Division, Northwest League)

## TOP PROSPECTS

### 1. *Willie Adams, RHP*
A supplemental first-round pick in 1993 out of Stanford, Adams opened 1994 with Class A Modesto, going 7-1 with a 3.38 ERA to earn a promotion to AA Huntsville, before bone chips in his elbow ended his season in July. A member of the 1992 U.S. Olympic team, Adams is not overpowering but has excellent command.

### 2. *Jose Herrera, OF*
Herrera is a phenomenal athlete and a versatile player who came to the A's from Toronto with Steve Karsay in the 1993 trade for Rickey Henderson. He was named the top prospect in the Class A South Atlantic League in 1993, and hit .286 with 11 homers, 56 runs batted in and 21 steals for Class A Modesto in 1994. Herrera has great range and a cannon arm and can play all three outfield positions, and he should hit for more power as he gets older and stronger.

### 3. *Stacy Hollins, RHP*
Hollins, the brother of Cubs pitcher Jessie Hollins, was Oakland's 43rd-round pick in '92. While he does not have his brother's blazing fastball, he has a good change-up and breaking pitch. He was 13-6 with a 3.39 ERA at Class A Modesto in 1994, winning 10 decisions in a row at one point. Hollins really impressed scouts in the Arizona Fall League, where he was one of the top pitchers, leading the league in wins and ranking second in ERA (7-1, 2.38 ERA).

### 4. *John Wasdin, RHP*
The A's first-round pick in 1993 out of Florida State, Wasdin began the 1994 season at Class A Modesto but was promoted to AA Huntsville after posting a 1.69 ERA in six games in the California League. Between the two stops, Wasdin was 15-4 with a 3.15 ERA, walking just 34 while fanning 138 in 168 innings. He has excellent command of his pitches, throwing them all for strikes: a fastball in the upper 80s, a slider and a change.

### 5. *Ernie Young, OF*
Young put together a pair of tremendous minor-league seasons in 1993-94, hitting 28 homers and driving in 86 runs in 1993 and going on to combine for 20 homers

and 71 runs batted in between AA Huntsville and AAA Tacoma (now affiliated with the Seattle Mariners) in 1994. He is an exciting player, with great power potential and good speed, and has worked on his weak points: For example, he cut his strikeouts from 128 in '93 to 80 in '94 while raising his average 30 points to .308. A 10th-round pick in 1990, Young is a solid outfielder with a strong arm who can play all three outfield positions.

## PHILADELPHIA PHILLIES

**AAA:** *Scranton/Wilkes-Barre Red Barons* (62-80, fifth, East Division, International League)
**AA:** *Reading Phillies* (58-82, fourth, Southern Division, Eastern League)
**A:** *Clearwater Phillies* (72-62, second, West Division, Florida State League)
**A:** *Piedmont Phillies* (67-72, fourth, Northern Division, South Atlantic League); last year, located in Spartanburg, South Carolina
**Short Season A:** *Batavia Clippers* (40-34, second, Stedler Division, New York–Penn League)
**Rookie:** *Martinsville Phillies* (32-36, third, North Division, Appalachian League)

### TOP PROSPECTS

1. *Scott Rolen, 3B*
The Phillies named him their top minor leaguer for 1994. Rolen is 6-4, a former college basketball recruit who has good agility at third base and excellent potential at the plate. He batted .294 with 14 home runs and 72 runs batted in at Spartanburg last year.

2. *Mike Lieberthal, C*
The Phillies will some day move All-Star catcher Darren Daulton to first base to save his knees and maintain his bat. Lieberthal will be ready to step in. He is an excellent defender. Lieberthal must overcome two shortcomings—his bat and his stamina.

3. *Ryan Nye, RHP*
The Phillies are looking to emphasize college pitching prospects. Nye is a collegian who has looked sharp since he signed. He was 7-2 with a 2.64 ERA at Batavia.

4. *Wayne Gomes, RHP*
Gomes was the Phillies' first-round pick in 1993, a big-shouldered hard thrower who reminds some scouts of Lee Smith. Gomes struggled with control last season (102 strikeouts and 82 walks in 104 innings), but he seemed to overcome the problem in Instructional League workouts. He could become a fine power reliever.

5. *Ricky Bottalico, RHP*
Another power reliever. Bottalico has a nasty sinking fastball that handcuffs hitters from either side of the plate. He was 2-2, 2.53 with 22 saves for Reading last year.

## PITTSBURGH PIRATES

**AAA:** *Calgary Cannons* (71-72, third, Northern Division, Pacific Coast, League); last year, affiliated with the Seattle Mariners
**AA:** *Carolina Mudcats* (74-66, Eastern Division champions, Southern League)
**A:** *Lynchburg Hillcats* (52-87, fourth, Northern Division, Carolina League); last year, affiliated with the Boston Red Sox
**A:** *Augusta Greenjackets* (50-86, seventh, Southern Division, South Atlantic League)
**A:** *Erie SeaWolves* (30-44, fourth, Stedler Division, New York–Penn League); last year located in Welland

### TOP PROSPECTS

1. *Trey Beamon, OF*
The jewel of the system, Beamon is a line-drive left-handed hitter who won the Class AA Southern League batting crown (.323) as one of the youngest players in that league. He runs well (24 steals), but has not yet developed much power. The Pirates figure that because he is 6-3, that will come. He was one of the stars of the Arizona Fall League last year until he tired and faded near the end.

2. *Midre Cummings, OF*
Cummings still has rookie status after 86 at-bats with the Pirates (.244). The product of the Virgin Islands was obtained from the Twins in a 1992 deal for John Smiley. There is little question of his offensive ability—it is substantial—but his defense is suspect.

3. *Jason Christiansen, LHP*
The demand for a left-handed reliever could land Christiansen in Pittsburgh fast. He is a power guy (66 strikeouts in 62 innings) who jumped quickly from AA to AAA last year.

4. *Esteban Loaiza, RHP*
The Pirates have a need for good, young pitching. Loiaza could satisfy. He was 10-5, 3.79 last year at Carolina.

5. *Jason Kendall, C*
The son of former major leaguer Fred Kendall has consistently showed maturity and skill behind the plate. He surprised even the Pirates with his bat skills, hitting .318 in Class A before a 13-game promotion to AA.

## ST. LOUIS CARDINALS

**AAA:** *Louisville Redbirds* (74-68, fourth, American Association)
**AA:** *Arkansas Travelers* (68-67, third, East Division, Texas League)
**A:** *St. Petersburg Cardinals* (74-65, third, West Division, Florida State League)
**A:** *Peoria Chiefs* (68-70, third, Southern Division, Midwest League); last year, affiliated with the Chicago Cubs
**A:** *Savannah Cardinals* (82-55, second, Southern Division, South Atlantic League)
**Short Season A:** *New Jersey Cardinals* (43-32, New York–Penn League champions)
**Rookie:** *Johnson City Cardinals* (42-26, South Division champions, Appalachian League)

### TOP PROSPECTS

1. *Alan Benes, RHP*
The not-so-little (6-5, 215) brother of major-league standout Andy Benes might have been the most promising pitcher in the minors last season. Benes started in St. Petersburg (7-1, 1.61), advanced to Arkansas (7-2, 2.98), then on to Louisville (1-0, 2.93). He throws hard and with control, and should be in the Cardinals' 1995 rotation.
2. *Brian Barber, RHP*
Barber, like Benes, is a power pitcher who was a first-round choice by St. Louis. Unlike Benes, he has experienced control problems. Barber was 4-7 with a 5.38 ERA at Louisville last year, but the Cardinals believe he will someday harness his stuff and win in the majors.
3. *Terry Bradshaw, OF*
Bradshaw is like so many Cardinals outfielders of the last 10 to 15 years, very fast and good on the carpet. He batted .280 with 13 steals at Arkansas last year, then .250 in 22 games at Louisville.
4. *John Mabry, OF*
Mabry reminds many Cardinals observers of Andy Van Slyke, who started with St. Louis. Mabry has a great arm, runs well and has shown some power.
5. *Dmitri Young, OF*
Young's problem is his glove. He has been tried at third base, first base, in right field and left. The Cardinals fear he is really a DH prospect for a league that has none. There is no doubt Young will hit someday. He batted .272 at Arkansas last year.

## SAN DIEGO PADRES

**AAA:** *Las Vegas Stars* (56-87, fifth, Southern Division, Pacific Coast League)
**AA:** *Memphis Chicks* (75-82, second, West Division, Southern League); last year, affiliated with the Kansas City Royals
**A:** *Rancho Cucamonga Quakes* (77-59, California League champions)
**A:** *Clinton Lumber Kings* (57-82, sixth, Southern Division, Midwest League); last year, affiliated with the San Francisco Giants
**Rookie:** *Idaho Falls Braves* (30-42, third, South Division, Pioneer League); last year, affiliated with the Atlanta Braves

### TOP PROSPECTS

1. *Dustin Hermanson, RHP*
Hermanson was the third player taken overall in the draft last June, coming off a fine season at Kent State and a stint on the U.S. national team. He has one of the better arms in the game, and it served him well in the Padres system. He jumped from Rancho Cucamonga to Wichita to Las Vegas and is poised to join the parent Padres' 1995 bullpen.
2. *Raul Casanova, C*
The Padres' catcher of the future was a candidate for minor-league player of the year after a season in which he hit .340 with 23 home runs and 120 runs batted in for Rancho Cucamonga.
3. *Derrek Lee, 3B*
With a father and uncle who played in the majors, the talented Lee was a San Diego high school star drafted in the first round in 1993. He batted .267 and drove in 53 runs last year at Rancho.
4. *Glenn Dishman, LHP*
Quality left-handers are always in demand. Dishman matured last season, going 11-8, 2.82 at Wichita and 1-1, 3.46 at Las Vegas.
5. *Mel Nieves, OF*
The Padres would really like Nieves to thrive, if only because he was a key part of the 1993 package from Atlanta for slugger Fred McGriff. Nieves has not clicked as much or as fast as the Padres had hoped. He did hit 25 home runs with 92 runs batted in and a .308 average last year at Las Vegas.

## SAN FRANCISCO GIANTS

**AAA:** *Phoenix Firebirds* (70-72, fourth, Southern Division, Pacific Coast League)
**AA:** *Shreveport Captains* (73-63, second, East Division, Texas League)
**A:** *San Jose Giants* (74-62, second, Northern Division, California League)
**A:** *Burlington Bees* (55-82, seventh, Southern Division, Midwest League); last year, affiliated with the Montreal Expos
**Short Season A:** *Bellingham Giants* (42-34, second,

North Division, Northwest League); last year, affiliated with the Seattle Mariners

## TOP PROSPECTS

**1. *Joe Rosselli, LHP***
He was sidelined for a time by arm problems, but Rosselli is still the Giants' top pitching prospect. He was 7-2, 1.89 last year at Shreveport, earning a promotion to Phoenix, where he was 1-8, 4.94.

**2. *J.R. Phillips, 1B***
He has retained his rookie eligibility despite brief stays with the Giants in 1993 and '94. Phillips has the opportunity to stick this year after he batted .300 with 27 home runs and 79 runs batted in at Phoenix.

**3. *Dante Powell, OF***
The Giants sought speed and a quick bat from first-round choice Calvin Murray in 1993, who has not delivered much yet, even in the minors. They might have secured a better future of the same stuff from Powell. The former Fresno State star batted .309 last year in Class A and stole 27 bases in 41 games.

**4. *Rikkert Faneyte, OF***
From the Netherlands, Faneyte has filled in admirably as a Giants spare outfielder, but not often enough to lose his rookie status. He is a fine fielder and promising hitter who batted .334 at Phoenix.

**5. *Chris Singleton, OF***
The Giants feel they are deep in outfield prospects, and Singelton is one of the better ones. He has speed and a chance to hit for power. He batted .249 with 19 steals at San Jose.

## SEATTLE MARINERS

**AAA:** *Tacoma Rainiers* (61-81, fifth, Northern Division, Pacific Coast League); last year, affiliated with the Oakland Athletics
**AA:** *Wilmington, N.C.* (74-66, third, West Division, Southern League); last year known as the Nashville Xpress and affiliated with the Minnesota Twins
**A:** *Riverside Pilots* (87-49, first, Southern Division, California League)
**A:** *Wisconsin Timber Rattlers* (75-64, third, Northern Division, Midwest League); last year known as the Appleton Foxes
**Short Season A:** *Everett AquaSox* (37-39, third, North Division, Northwest League); last year, affiliated with the San Francisco Giants

## TOP PROSPECTS

**1. *Marc Newfield, OF***
Newfield, a 1990 first-rounder, was slowed by foot problems early in his career, but is back on track as his .349

average, 19 homers and 83 runs batted in for AAA Calgary in 1994 can attest. He led the Pacific Coast League with 44 doubles and tied for the lead with 65 extra-base hits. He also posted an impressive .593 slugging percentage. Newfield has a great swing and doesn't strike out much.

**2. *Desi Relaford, SS***
Relaford opened the 1994 season at AA Jacksonville, but after a slow start went to Class A Riverside, where his bat came alive. He ended up second in the league in on-base percentage (.429) while hitting .310. Relaford employed his speed effectively, stealing 37 bases at an 84% success rate. Relaford is spectacular defensively, with exceptional range and hands and a quick release. He is expected to be moved to second base where he will eventually team with shortstop Alex Rodriguez as the Mariners' middle infield of the future.

**3. *Alex Rodriguez, SS***
The first pick in the 1993 draft, Rodriguez has been called the best prospect to come out of high school since Ken Griffey Jr., and in his first pro season he showed why, hitting a combined .312 with 21 homers and 20 steals between Class A Appleton, AA Jacksonville (now affiliated with the Detroit Tigers) and AAA Calgary (now affiliated with the Pittsburgh Pirates). He is a pure hitter with good power potential and speed. He also has terrific range and an outstanding arm.

**4. *Mac Suzuki, RHP***
The Mariners outbid several other clubs and paid the Japanese free agent Suzuki a $750,000 bonus last winter. In his first pro season here, 1993, he posted a 3.68 ERA and collected 12 saves at Class A San Bernardino, an independent club, to set up the bidding war. In 1994, though, he was hampered by an assortment of elbow and shoulder problems and threw just 12⅔ innings. He has a hard fastball and has worked on a change-up and breaking pitch. He needs to improve his command, but is young and has a great arm.

**5. *Ron Villone, LHP***
After a rough start, Villone was unhittable in the second half for AA Jacksonville, posting seven saves and a 1.18 ERA while holding hitters to a .160 average and striking out 12.32 per nine innings. The Mariners' first-round pick in 1992 out of U Mass split the 1993 campaign between Class A Riverside and AA Jacksonville as a starter. He was switched to the bullpen last May, however, and has thrived as an aggressive closer with a fastball that can reach 95 mph, a good slider and change-up.

## TEXAS RANGERS

**AAA:** *Oklahoma City 89ers* (61-83, seventh, American Association)
**AA:** *Tulsa Drillers* (63-73, fourth, East Division, Texas League)

**A:** *Port Charlotte Rangers* (60-76, eighth, West Division, Florida State League)
**A:** *Charleston River Dogs* (56-81, sixth, Southern Division, South Atlantic League)
**Short Season A:** *Hudson Valley Renegades* (37-37, third, McNamara Division, New York–Penn League)

## TOP PROSPECTS

*1. Mike Bell, 3B*
Another son of Buddy Bell, he was a supplemental first-rounder in 1993 and made his pro debut in the Gulf Coast League that summer. In 1994 at Charleston (South Carolina), he hit .263 with six homers, 58 RBI and 16 steals. He also led South Atlantic League third basemen with 51 errors but has the tools to become a very good defensive player.

*2. Benji Gil, SS*
Gil was the Rangers' first-round pick in 1991, and though he struggled somewhat at AAA Oklahoma City in 1994, his 36 extra-base hits were a career high. He had 20 doubles and 10 homers, and stole 14 bases as well. Defensively, Gil has great range, good hands and a cannon arm, as well as the tools to provide good power for a shortstop.

*3. Luis Ortiz, 3B*
The Rangers acquired Ortiz from the Boston Red Sox in December 1993 along with center fielder Otis Nixon, in a trade for slugger Jose Canseco. Long one of the best pure hitters in the Boston system, Ortiz' rise had been plagued by various nagging injuries. He's a .302 career hitter who batted .312 at AAA Pawtucket in 1994 before his season ended in July due to a wrist injury.

*4. Terrell Lowery, OF*
Lowery has been the Rangers' center fielder and leadoff man of the future since he was drafted in 1991. After skipping the '92 season to try to pursue an NBA career, the former Loyola Marymount point guard dedicated himself to baseball in 1993, hitting .270 with 24 steals between Class A Charlotte and AA Tulsa. Back at Tulsa for 1994, he raised his average to .286 and stole 33 bases along with hitting eight homers and 34 doubles.

*5. Julio Santana, RHP*
A converted shortstop, Santana's first full season on the mound was 1993, when he dominated Gulf Coast League hitters, posting a 1.38 ERA and walking just seven in 39 innings while fanning 50. In '94, he established himself as the system's top pitching prospect by far, combining to go 13-9 with a 2.66 ERA between Class A Charleston and AA Tulsa. Santana has a smooth delivery and changes speeds well, to go with a 90-mph fastball.

## TORONTO BLUE JAYS

**AAA:** *Syracuse Chiefs* (71-77, East Division champions, International League)

**AA:** *Knoxville Smokies* (64-76, third, East Division, Southern League)
**A:** *Dunedin Blue Jays* (65-68, sixth, West Division, Florida State League)
**A:** *Hagerstown Suns* (80-56, Northern Division champions, South Atlantic League)
**Short Season A:** *St. Catharines Stompers* (35-39, third, Stedler Division, New York–Penn League)
**Rookie:** *Medicine Hat Blue Jays* (36-36, second, Northern Division, Pioneer League)

## TOP PROSPECTS

*1. Howard Battle, 3B*
Battle possesses a speed-power package rarely found in a third baseman. The Jays' fifth-round pick in 1990 hit .277 for AAA Syracuse with 14 homers and 26 steals. He has performed consistently every year, and his defense has improved as well. His 93% success rate on the basepaths led the International League.

*2. Alex Gonzalez, SS*
Though he was Toronto's Opening Day shortstop in 1994, it was a big jump for the 20-year-old; he needed another full season at AAA. When he was sent to Syracuse, he adjusted immediately and made the All-Star team, hitting .284 with 12 homers and 23 RBI for the Chiefs. He had a 79% stolen-base success rate and hit .361 with runners on base. A 14th-round pick in 1991, he is considered one of the top shortstop prospects in the game.

*3. Shawn Green, OF*
Toronto's first-round pick in 1991 was named International League Rookie of the Year after hitting .344 at AAA Syracuse to win the batting title. One of the youngest players in the league, the 21-year-old added 13 homers and 19 steals. He posted a 15-game hitting streak at one point in 1994 and struck out just 54 times.

*4. Jose Silva, RHP*
At 6-5, the right-hander came into the 1994 season having scattered just 145 hits over 202 career innings while fanning 239 and limiting the opposition to a .201 average. His 1994 numbers weren't quite as impressive, but he remains one of the top pitching prospects in the system and is highly sought-after by other clubs in trades.

*5. Shannon Stewart, OF*
The Jays' first-round pick in 1992 missed half of the 1994 season after suffering a shoulder injury in a collision at home plate but he had been off to a fine start at Class A Hagerstown, hitting .324 with four homers and 15 steals in 225 at-bats. He posted a 13-game hitting streak in April and increased his slugging percentage from .372 in 1993 to .467 last season.

# About the Authors

While developing the concept for this book, **Bruce Adelson** visited some 80 minor-league ballparks, and drove more than 100,000 miles throughout the USA and Canada. Besides writing *The USA SPORTS Minor League Baseball Book*, Bruce has been a contributing editor for *The USA SPORTS Four Sport Stadium Guide* and a commentator for National Public Radio. He has written about the minors and other baseball topics for *Baseball Weekly*, *The Washington Post*, *Sport*, *Canadian Magazine* and *Baseball America*. He now resides in Alexandria, Va.

**Rod Beaton** was among USA TODAY's original staff, covering hockey from 1982 to '86 before moving to the baseball beat, where he now covers the National League along with writing a baseball column and handling minor-league notes. Before coming to USA TODAY, he covered the Philadelphia Phillies, Baltimore Orioles and Philadelphia Flyers, as well as other assignments, for the Wilmington (Del.) *News Journal*. Having seen minor-league games everywhere from Bowie, Maryland to Bakersfield, California, he's convinced that the minor leagues can't be beat for a pure baseball experience.

**Bill Koenig** has been with *Baseball Weekly* since its inception in 1991, creating and carrying out its trademark minor-league coverage. An award-winning writer, Koenig is a veteran of the minor-league fields, having covered the Rochester Red Wings of the International League since 1979 before joining *Baseball Weekly*.

**Lisa Winston** covers minor-league baseball for USA TODAY *Baseball Weekly*, where she has worked since 1992. Prior to joining *Baseball Weekly*, Winston was a beat writer covering the Prince William (Va.) Cannons and the Class A Carolina League for three years. She also worked for Westchester-Rockland Newspapers in New York for three years, covering high school and college basketball. She is two-time defending champion of her Rotisserie league. Winston lives with her husband Wayne and their four-year-old daughter Dana in suburban Maryland. Dana wants to grow up to be Ron Gant.